The MEASURE *of* CIVILIZATION

The
MEASURE
of
CIVILIZATION

How Social Development Decides the Fate of Nations

IAN MORRIS

PRINCETON UNIVERSITY PRESS

PRINCETON AND OXFORD

Copyright © 2013 by Princeton University Press
Published by Princeton University Press, 41 William Street, Princeton, New Jersey 08540
In the United Kingdom: Princeton University Press, 6 Oxford Street, Woodstock,
    Oxfordshire OX20 1TW

press.princeton.edu

Library of Congress Cataloging-in-Publication Data

Morris, Ian, 1960-
  The measure of civilization : how social development decides the fate of nations / Ian
    Morris.
    p. cm.
  Includes bibliographical references and index.
  ISBN 978-0-691-15568-5 (cloth : alk. paper)   1. Social structure.   2. Social history.
    3. Economic history.   I. Title.
  HM706.M67 2012
  306.09—dc23

                                2012026350

British Library Cataloging-in-Publication Data is available

This book has been composed in Stempel Garamond

Printed on acid-free paper. ∞

Printed in the United States of America

10 9 8 7 6 5 4 3 2 1

For my father

CONTENTS

||||||||||||||||||||||||||||||||||||||||||||||||||

ILLUSTRATIONS

TABLES

ııııııııııııııııııııııııı

PREFACE

IIIIIIIIIIIIIIIIIIIIIIIIIIIIIIIIIIIIIIIIII

THE MEASURE OF CIVILIZATION IS A COMPANION VOLUME to my earlier book *Why the West Rules—For Now*. It is a very different kind of book, though. In *Why the West Rules*, I tried to tell the story of social development across the last fifteen thousand years; here, I describe the evidence and methods I used in constructing the index of social development that lay behind that story.

Like many books, this one has grown out of conversations that have been going for years. I was introduced to the idea of social evolution when I was a graduate student at Cambridge (UK) in the early 1980s, and have been talking and thinking about it, in fits and starts, ever since. Along the way I have incurred debts to many people, and I would particularly like to thank Daron Acemoglu, James Anderson, John Bennet, Francesca Bray, Mat Burrows, Ewen Cameron-Watt, John Cherry, Eric Chinski, David Christian, Jack Davis, Stephan de Spiegeliere, Jared Diamond, Al Dien, Tom Gallant, Peter Garnsey, Banning Garrett, Jack Goldstone, Deborah Gordon, Steve Haber, John Haldon, Paul Halstead, Ian Hodder, Agnes Hsu, Parag Khanna, Karla Kierkegaard, Kristian Kristiansen, David Laitin, Michael Lässig, Mark Lewis, Anthony Ling, Li Liu, Angus Maddison, Alessio Magnavacca, Paolo Malanima, Joe Manning, Michael McCormick, Tom McLellan, Joel Mokyr, Suresh Naidu, Reviel Netz, Doug North, Josh Ober, Isaac Opper, Anne Porter, Michael Puett, Kumar Ramakrishna, Anna Razeto, Colin Renfrew, Jim Robinson, Richard Saller, Walter Scheidel, Glenn Schwartz, Hugo Scott-Gall, Steve Shennan, Dan Smail, Vaclav Smil, Larry Smith, Mike Smith, Anthony Snodgrass, Peter Temin, Nick Thomas, Peter Turchin, Barry Weingast, Todd Whitelaw, James

Whitley, Greg Woolf, and Norm Yoffee. All of them have helped me see things differently. I hope they will think that I have put their advice to good use.

I would never have written *The Measure of Civilization* without the encouragement of Rob Tempio at Princeton University Press and Daniel Crewe at Profile Books, who saw a book where I had seen only a dataset; without the guidance of Sandy Dijkstra and Arabella Stein, who brought everyone together; without the support and patience of Kathy St. John; or without the example of my father, Noel Morris, who taught me early on that it pays to count things.

Singapore
April 2012

The MEASURE *of* CIVILIZATION

CHAPTER 1

||||||||||||||||||||||||||||||||||||||||||||||

INTRODUCTION: QUANTIFYING SOCIAL DEVELOPMENT

THE PROBLEM

A quarter of a millennium ago, intellectuals in Western Europe discovered that they had a problem. As problems went, theirs was not a bad one: they appeared to be taking over the world, but did not know why. The explanations that eighteenth-century theorists came up with varied wildly, although the most popular ideas all held that since time immemorial, something had made the West different from the rest and determined that Europe would one day dominate the world.

In the early twenty-first century, these ideas are still with us, albeit in heavily modified forms. The most influential argument, now as in the eighteenth century, is probably the theory that Europeans are the heirs to a distinctive and superior cultural tradition.[1] The roots of this Western civilization are most often traced back to the ancient Greeks and Romans, although other advocates identify prehistoric Indo-Europeans, ancient Germans, or medieval Europeans as the founders.[2]

A second strand of eighteenth-century thought credited environment and climate with making Europeans more energetic and creative than other people, and this too has plenty of modern champions.[3] Some scholars combine the ecological and cultural ideas, arguing that it was the back-and-forth between the two that sent

1

early modern Europe down a new path.[4] Even the idea that Europeans are biologically superior to other humans has been revamped: some economists claim that since the thirteenth century natural selection has made Europeans thriftier and more industrious than anyone else,[5] while a handful of paleoanthropologists suggest that divergent genetic evolution in the ten thousand years since the origin of farming has made Europeans and their descendants more dynamic and inventive than other populations.[6]

These theories all took shape in the eighteenth century, when the explosion of European wealth and power cried out for explanation; and it was only in the later twentieth century, when East Asia was experiencing a similar explosion, that serious challenges emerged. As Japan, the Asian Tigers, and China developed into major economic powers, more and more scholars concluded that theories explaining West's success through long-term cultural, environmental, or racial causes simply could not be right. The big story in world history, they began suggesting, was not the long-term, inexorable rise of the West; it was the tale of a multipolar world, which the West had only recently, temporarily, and perhaps even accidentally come to dominate.

These new ideas are even more varied than the old long-term lock-in theories. The most extreme versions argue that the eighteenth-century theorists got things exactly back to front. According to the new theories, it was in fact China that had a long-term lock-in on global dominance, and only a bizarre series of accidents briefly tipped things in Europe's favor.[7] Most versions, however, reject long-term explanations altogether, arguing that the complex societies of Asia and Europe developed down roughly parallel tracks until the eighteenth or even the nineteenth century, when small differences in state structure, natural endowments, physical and political geography, or intellectual trends gave Europe the lead.[8]

The argument over the causes and consequences of Western power has attracted enormous interest, but the champions of the different theories often seem to be talking past one another. They regularly define key terms in different ways, use different kinds of evidence, and apply different standards of proof. As a result, the antagonists rarely agree on exactly what they are trying to explain, let alone how to do the explaining.

As I see it, the real question at issue is about what I would call *social development*, by which I mean social groups' abilities to master their physical and intellectual environments and get things done in the world. Defenders of the new versions of the eighteenth-century theories tend to argue that Western social development has been higher than that in other parts of the world for hundreds or even thousands of years; their critics tend to argue that Western development pulled ahead only in the past half dozen generations. It seems to me that if we really want to explain why the West rules, we need to measure social development and compare it across time and space. Only when we have established the basic pattern of the history of social development can we start asking why it takes the form it does.

Quantification does not necessarily make debates more objective, but it does normally make them more explicit, forcing rivals to spell out exactly what they mean by the terms they use and to explain why they assign specific numerical values to these differences. Anyone who disagrees with another scholar's judgments will then be able to focus on the evidence and methods being used to calculate the scores, instead of trading vague, undertheorized generalizations. Under one name or another, numerical indices of concepts similar to social development are well established in anthropology, archaeology, economics, finance, policy making, and sociology, and there is an obvious model for such a yardstick in the United Nations' Human Development Index.[9]

In the 1960s and 1970s, some historians began applying similar methods to the past, addressing big questions by mustering vast amounts of statistical data. The classic case was probably Robert Fogel and Stanley Engerman's *Time on the Cross*, which brought together data from thousands of plantation records to work out just how profitable slavery was in the nineteenth-century American South and just what the physical experience had been like for the slaves themselves.[10]

Time on the Cross provided a successful model for quantitative history. The study appeared two volumes, the first providing a broad overview and set of interpretations aimed as much at a general readership interested in American history as at professional scholars, while the second volume detailed the statistical techniques and sources that Fogel and Engerman had used.

The Measure of Civilization follows this format. It is a companion volume to my earlier book *Why the West Rules—For Now: The Patterns of History, and What They Reveal about the Future*. When I was writing *Why the West Rules—For Now*, my editors and I decided to post supporting materials on a website rather than producing a second print volume in print, but since then it has become clear that there is some interest in having a revised and expanded version of this material available in print.[11]

I have two main goals in *The Measure of Civilization*. First, I want to provide critics of *Why the West Rules—For Now* with the ammunition they need to subject the conclusions I reached in that book to systematic analysis. While I naturally hope that my thesis withstands such attempts at falsification, the next-best outcome would be to see explicit debate over my own analysis lead to improved versions of the social development index and a stronger explanation of the rise of Western power and wealth.

My second goal in setting out a full account of the social development index is to contribute to making comparative history more explicit and quantitative. "The history of science is emphatic," the biologist-turned-historian Peter Turchin has pointed out: "a discipline usually matures only after it has developed mathematical theory."[12] There will never be such a thing as a one-size-fits-all numerical index that answers every question that any comparative social scientist might want to ask, but one of the best ways to turn comparative history into such a mature discipline may be through the design of multiple indices, each crafted to solve a particular problem.

I begin by setting out, very briefly, a formal definition of what I have in mind when I speak of "social development." I follow up this brief definition with an overview of the ideas it draws on and the objections that have been raised to them across the past fifty years. In chapter 2, I try to distill from these criticisms the key challenges facing a social development index, and then explain how I have tried to address these challenges. In the main part of the book (chapters 3–6) I set out the evidence behind the scores in my four traits of energy capture, organization, war making, and information technology. In the final chapter, I consider some of the ways an index of social development might contribute to other debates within the social sciences.

SOCIAL DEVELOPMENT: A DEFINITION

Social development, as I use the expression, is *a measure of communities' abilities to get things done in the world*. I label this property "social development" because it seems to me to have much in common with the central ideas of development economics.[13] The historian Kenneth Pomeranz has suggested that it might be better to call the concept "social power," but I am not convinced, not least because the concept is sufficiently different from previous influential uses of the label social power (particularly the version developed by the sociologist Michael Mann) that this terminology would probably introduce unnecessary confusion.[14]

Social development is an important concept because the major reasons that the West (another key concept in need of definition: see chapter 2, "Units of Analysis") has dominated the world in the past two hundred years are that (a) its social development has reached higher levels than that of any other part of the planet and (b) these levels have risen so high that the West has been able to project its power globally.

"Communities' abilities to get things done in the world" is what we might call a minimal definition of social development. It is handy but imprecise, and, like all minimal definitions, it is framed at such a high level of abstraction that it is difficult to operationalize (that is, it is not obvious what we would need to do on the ground to put such a vague formulation to use).

Consequently, social scientists often follow up a minimal definition with an "ideal-type" definition, one that "aims for a collection of attributes that is maximal—that is, including all (nonidiosyncratic) characteristics that help to define the concept in its purest, most 'ideal' (and perhaps its most extreme) form."[15]

Putting matters more formally, *social development is the bundle of technological, subsistence, organizational, and cultural accomplishments through which people feed, clothe, house, and reproduce themselves, explain the world around them, resolve disputes within their communities, extend their power at the expense of other communities, and defend themselves against others' attempts to extend power.*[16]

Social development is—in principle—something we can measure and compare through time and space. If Western social development has been higher than that in the rest of the world since time immemorial, the answer to the why-the-West-rules question must lie very deep in the past, as the champions of biological or environmental theories of Western supremacy hold. If, however, Western social development surged ahead of that in other regions during the first millennium BCE, we might conclude that advocates of the importance of Greece and Rome in fact got things right. But if it should turn out that Western social development outstripped that of other civilizations only in very modern times, we will be forced to conclude that these old theories are wrong, and must seek explanations elsewhere.

I want to emphasize that social development is a *measure* of communities' abilities to get things done in the world, not an *explanation* of communities' abilities to get things done. Social development shows us the pattern that we need to explain.

Social development is also not a measure of the worth of different societies. For instance, twenty-first-century Japan is a land of air conditioning, computerized factories, and bustling cities. It has cars and planes, libraries and museums, high-tech health care and a literate population. The contemporary Japanese have mastered their physical and intellectual environment far more thoroughly than their ancestors a thousand years ago, who had none of these things. It therefore makes sense to say that modern Japan has higher levels of social development than medieval Japan. Yet this implies nothing about whether the people of modern Japan are smarter, worthier, or luckier (let alone happier) than the Japanese of the Heian era. Nor do social development scores imply anything about the moral, environmental, or other costs of social development. Social development is a value-neutral analytical category.

THE INTELLECTUAL BACKGROUND

Scholars have been interested in ideas similar to social development for a very long time. There are several excellent reviews of this history, so I will not attempt a comprehensive survey here.[17] Instead, I will look only at the ideas that seem to be most relevant to the social development index that I construct in this book, and then at some of the most important criticisms of these approaches.

The most useful starting point is probably the essay "Progress: Its Laws and Cause" that the eccentric English polymath Herbert Spencer published in the *Westminster Review* in 1857.[18] Like many English intellectuals in the mid-nineteenth century, Spencer felt that he was living in an age of previously unimaginable progress and wanted to explain it. "From the remotest past which Science can fathom, up to the novelties of yesterday," he argued, "that in which progress essentially consists, is the transformation of the homogeneous into the heterogeneous." He proposed calling the mechanism through which things that began simply became more complex "evolution":

The advance from the simple to the complex, through a process of successive differentiations, is seen alike in the earliest changes of the Universe to which we can reason our way back, and in the earliest changes which we can inductively establish; it is seen in the geologic and climatic evolution of the Earth; it is seen in the unfolding of every single organism on its surface, and in the multiplication of kinds of organisms; it is seen in the evolution of Humanity, whether contemplated in the civilized individual, or in the aggregate of races; it is seen in the evolution of Society in respect alike of its political, its religious, and its economical organization; and it is seen in the evolution of all those endless concrete and abstract products of human activity which constitute the environment of our daily life.[19]

Spencer spent the next forty years bundling geology, biology, psychology, sociology, politics, and ethics into a single evolutionary theory of everything, explaining how the universe had gone from being simple and undifferentiated to being complex and highly differentiated. In the three volumes of his *Principles of Sociology*, Spencer argued that human societies had evolved through four levels of differentiation, from the simple (wandering bands without leaders) through the compound (stable villages with political leaders) and doubly compound (groups with churches, states, complex divisions of labor, and scholarship) to the trebly compound (great civilizations like Rome, and, of course, Victorian Britain).[20]

Spencer's ideas won an enormous audience, and in recognition of the way they have shaped much of the thinking since the 1850s, I will use the expression "social evolutionism" as a broad label for all the approaches that I discuss in this section. I will also treat "social evolution" (the term most favored in British English) and "cultural evolution" (the term most favored in American English) as synonyms.

By 1870 Spencer was probably the most influential philosopher writing in English; when late-nineteenth-century Japanese and Chinese intellectuals decided they needed to understand Western success, he was the first author they translated. Even Charles Darwin, who did not use the word "evolution" in the first five imprints of his *Origin of the Species*, felt compelled to borrow it from Spencer in the sixth version, published in 1872.

Several other late-nineteenth-century theorists (often lumped together with Spencer as "classical evolutionists") produced their own versions of his typologies. Edward Tylor, for instance, spoke in his book *Primitive Culture* of the shift from savagery through barbarism to civilization, and Lewis Henry Morgan used the same terminology in his *Ancient Society*, a book that massively influenced Friedrich Engels's *Origins of the Family, Private Property and the State*.[21]

There were very few archaeological data available to these theorists, so they relied heavily on the assumption that the colonized peoples of nineteenth-century Africa, Asia, Australia, and South America were living ancestors, illustrating how people who were now at the trebly compound/civilized stage of differentiation must have lived in prehistoric times. However, even this limited ethnographic information was full of problems. Most of it came from missionaries and colonial administrators, who tended to be interested only in very particular aspects of the groups they encountered. As a result, when the first generation of professional anthropologists began doing fieldwork in their own right in the early twentieth century, they quickly discovered that a lot of the evolutionists' supposed facts were simply wrong.

By the 1910s, a serious backlash was under way, and across the twentieth century Spencer's notion that evolution and differentiation should be at the heart of historical inquiry has gone in and out of fashion.[22] The most important critics were initially Franz Boas (a

German scholar who moved to the United States) and Bronislaw Malinowski (a Polish scholar who moved to Britain), who, by the 1920s, had convinced many anthropologists that the field's subject matter consisted of a vast number of discrete "cultures," each of which was a unique, seamless whole that had to be understood as a coherent system.

Functionalism—the theory that ideas, institutions, and values settled into equilibrium within each of these discrete cultures—became increasingly popular, often striking anthropologists as a much sounder basis for the construction of a natural science of society than the speculative leaps of classical evolutionists.[23] One of the costs of adopting a functionalist approach was of course that cross-cultural comparison and explanation of change through time became much more difficult, but social scientists were often willing to pay that price, and Spencerian evolution quickly collapsed as an organizing principle for thinking about societies.

Marxists remained wedded to evolutionary narratives in the 1920s, but in liberal democracies (and, albeit in rather different ways, in fascist regimes) most sociologists and anthropologists concluded that arranging human groups along a simple-to-trebly-compound or savage-to-civilized spectrum was no better than making up just-so stories that were (a) conjectural and (b) pointless.

The 1930s were probably the high point of Boasian particularism, but the pendulum was already swinging back. The career of the archaeologist V. Gordon Childe, yet another academic émigré (this time an Australian who moved to Britain), illustrates this nicely.[24] In the interwar years, stratigraphic excavation (i.e., separating out the layers of deposits on a site and arranging the deposits into sequences that could be dated relative to one another) was becoming the norm in archaeology, and enough evidence was accumulating to make broad syntheses possible.

In his first really successful book, *The Dawn of European Civilisation*,[25] Childe was fairly typical of the times in focusing on a particular region rather than thinking in Spencer's global terms, and in explaining cultural change through diffusion and migration rather than evolution and differentiation. But in the 1930s, Childe—like many social scientists in liberal, democratic countries—turned toward Marxism and began asking very different questions. In *Man*

Makes Himself and *What Happened in History*, he recognized that archaeology's enlarged database now showed beyond reasonable doubt that agriculture and cities had evolved independently in different parts of the world. By 1951 he even felt ready to call a book *Social Evolution*.[26]

In just the same years, many American social scientists were also returning to evolutionary frameworks. Some, like Childe, leaned toward Marxism (the anthropologist Leslie White, for instance, published a string of left-wing political essays under pseudonyms),[27] while others strongly opposed it (the economist Walt Rostow gave his classic book *The Stages of Economic Growth* the subtitle *A Non-Communist Manifesto*).[28] But regardless of their political agendas, Americans tended to prefer Spencer's emphasis on differentiation to Childe's more humanistic evolutionism.

The most influential of these thinkers was probably the sociologist Talcott Parsons. In a series of studies, Parsons proposed not only a new typology of social stages (primitive, intermediate [subdivided into archaic and advanced], and modern) but also a complicated framework for explaining the development from primitive to modern.[29] Parsons argued that social evolution consisted of accumulating six "evolutionary universals," each of which comprised "a complex of structures and associated processes the development of which so increases the long-run adaptive capacity of living systems in a given class that only systems that develop the complex can attain higher levels of general adaptive capacity."[30] First came social stratification and cultural legitimation (i.e., hierarchy and differentiation within societies combined with group identity and differentiation between societies), then bureaucracy and markets, and finally universalistic norms (particularly in law and religion) and democracy.

Parsons's thinking was even more ambitious than Childe's in its intention to subsume everything from human evolution to twentieth-century capitalism within a single framework, but it was also widely criticized for its circularity in identifying differentiation as both the cause and consequence of evolution.[31] As a result, some social scientists who found the general thrust of Parsons's theories interesting nevertheless turned elsewhere to try to explain social evolution.

After Parsons himself, the most widely read evolutionist in these years seems to have been the anthropologist Leslie White, who emphasized energy capture as the motor driving evolution.[32] Like other evolutionists, White divided history into stages (in his case, of primitive, civil, and complex societies), but departed from most of his predecessors in arguing that *"culture develops when the amount of energy harnessed by man per capita per year is increased; or as the efficiency of the technological means of putting this energy to work is increased; or, as both factors are simultaneously increased."*[33] History, White concluded, could be summed up in the equation $C = E \times T$: culture = energy × technology.[34] Societies evolved from primitive to civil when they adopted agriculture and from civil to complex when they industrialized.

This was an important departure from the Spencer/Parsons line, but White hewed more closely to social evolutionary orthodoxy when he turned to the consequences of rising energy use. The most important result of the shift from primitive through civil to complex society, he argued, was increasing differentiation. As he explained it,

Agriculture ... greatly increased the food supply, which in turn increased the population. As human labor became more productive in agriculture, an increasing proportion of society became divorced from the task of food-getting, and was devoted to other occupations. Thus society becomes organized into occupational groups: masons, metal workers, jade carvers, weavers, scribes, priests. This has the effect of accelerating progress in the arts, crafts, and sciences (astronomy, mathematics, etc.), since they are now in the hands of specialists, rather than jacks-of-all-trades. With an increase in manufacturing, added to division of society into occupational groups, comes production for exchange and sale (instead of primarily for use as in tribal society), mediums of exchange, money, merchants, banks, mortgages, debtors, slaves. An accumulation of wealth and competition for favored regions provokes wars of conquest, and produces professional military and ruling classes, slavery and serfdom. Thus agriculture wrought a profound change in the life-and-culture of man as it had existed in the human-energy state of development.[35]

American thinking about social evolution in the twenty or thirty years after World War II is often bundled under the label "neo-evolutionism," to distinguish it from the (predominantly European)

"classical" evolutionism of the nineteenth century, and two big ideas run through much of the neo-evolutionary discussion. One was the return to differentiation as the most important consequence (and, in Parsons's view, cause) of evolution; the other, the desire to quantify evolution to make comparisons more explicit.

Numerical scales for ranking the evolution of societies went back to the late-nineteenth-century heyday of classical evolutionism. The earliest attempt to base such rankings on reliable, cross-cultural data was probably Sebald Steinmetz's long essay "Classification des types sociaux," which looked primarily at subsistence technology.[36] Hans Nieboer elaborated this in his classic study of *Slavery as an Industrial System*, and Leonard Hobhouse and his collaborators expanded the framework further.[37]

By the end of World War II, mountains of new evidence and growing statistical sophistication among American social scientists had made these early efforts look hopelessly inadequate. In a brief discussion in a general textbook, the anthropologist Carleton Coon floated the idea that it should be possible to produce a much better quantitative index by counting the number of specialists, amount of trade, number of corporate groups, and complexity of institutions with a society, but the first really usable index was Raoul Naroll's.[38]

Naroll was a researcher on the Human Relations Area Files (HRAF), an ambitious program established at Yale University in 1949 to create a database for global comparisons of human behavior, society, and culture.[39] Randomly choosing thirty preindustrial societies from around the world (some contemporary, others historical), Naroll scoured the HRAF files to find out how differentiated they were.

Since differentiation has an almost infinite number of possible dimensions, Naroll established a pair of principles for operationalizing the concept. First, he suggested, the only way to proceed was by narrowing the study down to down to the smallest possible number of traits that covered most of the ideas Spencer had in mind when he spoke of differentiation; and second, the selected traits had to meet certain basic criteria. They had to have culture freedom (i.e., be free of ethnocentric bias), logical independence (i.e., not be riddled with spurious correlations), adequate documentation, reliability (i.e., experts could not disagree too wildly over the facts), and convenience (if the data were too difficult to obtain, the scoring system would become impractical).

Naroll came down on three traits: the size of the largest settlement in a society, the specialization of its craft production, and the number of its subgroups. After looking into various definitional and methodological problems, he quantified the three traits and converted the results to a standard format, generating an index of social development on which sixty-three points was the maximum possible score. At the bottom of his league, with twelve points, came the Yahgan of Tierra del Fuego, who had struck Charles Darwin on his visit there in 1832 as "exist[ing] in a lower state of improvement than [people] in any other part of the world";[40] at the top came the fifteenth-century Aztecs, with fifty-eight points.

Within a few years, Robert Carneiro, then on the staff of the American Museum of Natural History, came up with a very different way to build an index.[41] Like Parsons, Carneiro was interested in whether there were evolutionary universals (which Carneiro called "functional prerequisites") that every society had to possess to move from one level of complexity/differentiation to another. Borrowing the technique of scale analysis from social psychologists, he next looked for traits with "the following characteristics: (1) their presence indicates a greater degree of complexity than their absence, and (2) once developed they tend to be retained, if not indefinitely, at least over long periods."[42]

Carneiro selected eight such traits (social stratification, pottery, fermented beverages, state-level government, agriculture, stone architecture, metallurgy, and weaving) and scored them for presence/absence rather than assigning numerical values as Naroll had done. He then picked nine South American societies and arranged them into what he called a scalogram (figure 1.1).

Carneiro argued that the scalogram allowed him not only to rank the complexity of the nine societies, from zero (once again, the nineteenth-century Yahgan) up to nine positives (the fifteenth-century Inca), but also to argue that the eight traits were all functional prerequisites, in that "*x necessarily precedes y*, which is to say that *y* cannot come into existence without the prior existence of *x*."[43] In a later essay, Carneiro tested his index against the historical evidence for the sequence in which traits appeared in the ancient Near

	Yahgan	Sherente	Kuikuru	Tupinambá	Jívaro	Cumaná	Anserma	Chibcha	Inca
stone architecture	−	−	−	−	−	−	−	−	+
political state	−	−	−	−	−	−	−	+	+
smelting of metal ores	−	−	−	−	−	−	+	+	+
social stratification	−	−	−	−	−	+	+	+	+
loom weaving	−	−	−	−	+	+	+	+	+
fermented beverages	−	−	−	+	+	+	+	+	+
pottery	−	−	+	+	+	+	+	+	+
agriculture	−	+	+	+	+	+	+	+	+

Figure 1.1. Carneiro's scalogram showing the presence (+) and absence (−) of eight selected culture traits among nine South American societies.

East and Anglo-Saxon England, and argued that his approach could boast a "coefficient of reproducibility" of greater than .90.[44]

Indices and experiments with different statistical techniques for manipulating the results proliferated across the next decade. Most followed the Naroll-Carneiro model of trying to get a snapshot of entire societies, bundling together traits reflecting a range of different activities,[45] but a few opted for narrowing the focus to a particular kind of evidence held to reflect differentiation more directly, such as burials or settlement patterns.[46] Despite all their differences, though, most of the varied numerical indices produced rather similar results; by Carneiro's calculations, analysts agreed on scores 87–94 percent of the time.[47]

By the late 1970s neo-evolutionism was becoming a fairly coherent research program, thanks in part to the very clear expositions of differentiation-based theories in Elman Service's book *Primitive Social Organization* and Morton Fried's *The Evolution of Political Society*.[48] The former classified societies into bands, tribes, chiefdoms, and states, and the latter (more influenced by Marxism) into egalitarian, ranked, stratified, and state stages. These typologies (particularly Service's) more or less displaced Parsons's and White's terminologies all across the social sciences.

The 1970s were probably the high tide of American neo-evolutionism. But in an uncanny echo of the 1910s, when classical evolutionism had seemed to be on the verge of creating a great new synthesis, the pendulum abruptly swung away from anything resembling Spencerian theory in many of the social sciences. Economic history and political science were partial exceptions, perhaps because the growing influence of institutional analysis encouraged stage-theory approaches to the past, and in the Soviet bloc quantitative evolutionism remained in favor.[49] But in Western Europe and the United States, sociological, anthropological, and archaeological debates over evolutionism took on the same kind of political edge in that they had had in the 1910s. Accusations of partisan bias, bad faith, and worse scholarship disfigured much of the pro- and anti-evolutionism literature in the 1980s and 1990s.

Some anthropologists and archaeologists argued that "the metanarrative of simple to complex is a dominant ideology that organizes the writing of contemporary world prehistory in favour of a modernizing ethos and the primacy of the West,"[50] while others responded that the critics needed to "abandon their fixation on 'alterity,' 'reflexivity,' and the like, and turn instead to an assessment of real and important objective problems, and to the application of some hard thinking and rigorous quantitative methods to their solution."[51] University anthropology departments, where the fights tended to be fiercest, regularly divided into cultural and evolutionary wings that did their own faculty and graduate recruiting (as at Harvard) or even split into two entirely separate departments (as at Stanford).

Since about 2000, though, another swing back toward social evolutionism seems to have begun. During neo-evolutionism's heyday in the 1970s, self-styled Darwinian archaeologists had been among its fiercest critics. According to one of the leading Darwinians, Robert Dunnell, "cultural evolution is neither science, nor theory, nor evolution, if evolution is taken to mean what it does in the sciences. As such, it is inappropriate as an explanatory framework in an archaeology committed to a scientific approach."[52]

The latest upswing in social evolutionism, however, has been driven largely by theorizing about the coevolution of biology and social behavior.[53] Jared Diamond's *Guns, Germs, and Steel: The Fates of Human Societies* has been by far the most influential contribution, gracefully blending biology, archaeology, anthropology, and history into a compelling narrative of the coevolution of plants, animals, and human societies across the past fifteen thousand years.[54]

Diamond had begun his career as a biologist, and taught for many years in the medical school at the University of California, Los Angeles. He is now a member of UCLA's geography department, but with the exception of a brief term as a visitor at Stanford, he has never held an appointment in an anthropology, archaeology, or history department, despite now being the most widely read writer in any of these fields.

Given the polemical tone of academic arguments over evolutionism in the 1990s, it is probably not a coincidence that Diamond's book succeeded in large part because it reached out to nonacademic audiences, having much impact within universities only after it had already sold several million copies outside them. This seems to be typical of the new social evolutionism; and although no one else has quite matched Diamond's success, scholars in political science, economics, the philosophy of religion, psychology, archaeology, anthropology, and history have all written for broader readerships.[55] This trend breaks with the narrowly specialist tone of most neo-evolutionism, and hearkens back to the days of Spencer and Darwin, when serious contributions were expected to speak directly to nonspecialists.

Despite the continuing arguments within the academy, there are good reasons to think that the 2010s might see a new synthesis of biological and social evolutionism, aimed at audiences both inside and outside universities.[56] One of my main hopes in writing *Why the West Rules—For Now* and *The Measure of Civilizations* is of contributing to this. The notion of social development that I present grows out of ideas about social evolution going back to Spencer and builds on the tradition of index building that goes back to Naroll, but it also tries to take seriously the criticisms of these ideas that resurfaced so often during the twentieth century.

In the next section, I summarize some of the most important objections that have been raised against social evolutionism. I concentrate on the past fifty years, and particularly the 1980s criticisms, which seem to me to have identified the most pressing problems of this approach. I close this chapter by drawing out from these debates what I see as the most important challenges that an index of social development must overcome.

DEBATES OVER THE CORE CONCEPTS OF SOCIAL EVOLUTIONISM

Differentiation

I start with differentiation because most theorists since Spencer have seen this as the dimension of a society that increases when that society progresses/evolves/becomes more complex. In practice, however, despite the widespread agreement that differentiation is the core concept, it has had a checkered history.

Archaeologists have probably faced greater difficulties with differentiation than anyone, because they have found it extremely difficult to measure.[57] In the 1970s some social evolutionists in archaeology were attracted to study burials on the hope that death rituals make explicit the social personas into which societies are differentiated,[58] but in the 1980s critics showed that what buriers express in their differentiated treatment of the dead is really a set of conceptions about what the ideal relationships among the living ought to be like, not social personas as a Parsonian sociologist might identify them.[59] As a result, despite the weight that differentiation receives in formal definitions, it rarely has much role in archaeologists' actual judgments about evolution/complexity. In Naroll's 1956 social development index, for example, only one trait (settlement size) might reasonably be seen as a proxy for differentiation; and in the final version of Carneiro's trait list, just one-sixth of the dimensions related directly to differentiation.[60]

Since the 1980s, archaeologists have generally continued drifting away from differentiation as an analytical tool, but sociologists have gone much further. In some ways, they point out, the societies we might think of as the most complex—the great modern nation-states—are actually *less* differentiated than premodern archaic states, with their complicated webs of estates, orders, and ranks.[61] *Dedif-ferentiation*, Charles Tilly argues, has been the hallmark of the rise of homogeneous citizen communities.[62]

Nor is this process unique to modernity: in another well-known case, the homogeneous citizen community of fifth-century BCE Athens was also much less legally differentiated than the city-states of the preceding archaic period. Despite a massive increase in state capacity and prosperity between the sixth and fifth centuries,[63] the complexity of the status structure expressed in Athenian burials declined sharply.[64]

Tilly concluded from this that "we have no warrant for thinking of differentiation in itself as a coherent, general, lawlike social process," and since the 1980s, differentiation has disappeared from sociological debates even more completely than from archaeological ones.[65]

COMPLEXITY

If differentiation is too incoherent to form the basis of a theory of social evolution, complexity—which, in most social scientists' formal definitions, depends entirely on differentiation—must be jettisoned along with it.[66] However, in the past twenty years, a number of social scientists have suggested that complexity can be retained as a central concept if we replace social-scientific ideas based on Spencerian differentiation with theories of complexity drawn from the natural sciences.[67]

Many versions of complexity theory argue that if we look at organizations as complex adaptive systems, we quickly see that pattern and structure at the macroscale emerge from the microscale behavior of agents acting in accordance with completely different ideas, or even no ideas at all.[68] Spencer would probably have appreciated the argument that the emergence and collapse of order and hierarchy are physical processes (often referred to as self-organized criticality, or SOC), equally relevant to the formation of the universe 13.7 billion years ago and the formation of human organizations. Related ideas have been taken up in anthropology, archaeology, management, history, international relations, and political science.[69]

Complexity theorists often draw on neo-evolutionists' categories, particularly when they want to describe premodern human societies. However, they also tend to see neo-evolutionism as imprecise, empiricist, and lacking clear explanations.

EVOLUTION

While complexity theorists have revived Spencer's vision of evolution as a catchall concept covering everything from geology to legal processes, some social scientists have gone in the opposite direction since the 1970s, recoiling from using the same label to describe Darwinian descent with modification in biological organisms and the very different types of change that happen in social organizations.

The most trenchant criticisms are probably those of the sociologist Anthony Giddens, who suggests that for any theory calling itself evolutionary, "there must be at least some presumed conceptual continuity with biological evolution ... [and] social evolutionism must specify something more than just a progression of change in respect of certain designated criteria, that something being a mechanism of change." He argues that social evolution shares little with biological evolution, particularly because it depends on extending Darwin's mechanism of change—adaptation—until it becomes "irremediably amorphous."[70]

Many biologists agree. John Maynard Smith, a pioneering figure in the application of game theory to biological evolution, has been particularly blunt, arguing that the "explanatory power of evolutionary theory rests largely on three assumptions: that mutation is nonadaptive, that acquired characters are not inherited, and that inheritance is Mendelian—that is, it is atomic, and we inherit atoms, or genes, equally from our two parents, and from no one else. In the cultural analogy, none of these things is true."[71]

Some archaeologists have responded to concerns of this kind by thinking of artifacts as extensions of the human phenotype, focusing on how natural selection operates on their differential persistence through time.[72] Summarizing the thinking of self-styled "Darwinian archaeologists," Robert Leonard explained that "[t]o a processualist [i.e., a social evolutionist], an adaptation is any behavior that has a function in an environment. To an evolutionist, it is a phenotypic feature that has been modified over time by natural selection so that it serves an important evolutionary function."[73] Darwinian archaeologists tend to be even more critical of social evolutionism than complexity theorists, typically portraying it as hopelessly confused about the unit of selection and even more so about adaptation.[74]

Progress

Very few social scientists nowadays use the word "progress" as a synonym for social evolution or differentiation. It was, however, one of Spencer's core concepts, and therefore calls for a brief comment.

Spencer, I suspect, would have seen social-scientific concepts such as Parsons's "evolutionary universals" and Carneiro's "functional prerequisites" as representing much the same idea as his notion of progress, no matter how strenuously post-Weberian social scientists struggle to separate facts and values, and many critics of social evolutionism seem to agree. The archaeologists Michael Shanks and Christopher Tilley, for instance, argue that discussions of evolution, differentiation, and related concepts "easily slip into ideologies of self-justification or assert the priorities of the West."[75] If they are correct, it may be that implicit assumptions about progress are inevitably built into any discussion of social evolution.

Stage Theories

Virtually all classical and neo-evolutionists, from Spencer with his typology of simple through trebly compound to Service with his alternative of band, tribe, chiefdom, and state, produced stage theories of social evolution. Such theories have many advantages, not least their potential for predicting variables that cannot be directly observed. If it is true, say, that all bands live in small, mobile groups, with low population densities, minimal technology, weak ranking, and shallow gender hierarchies, then archaeologists who know just

one or two things about a society—say, its subsistence basis and settlement pattern—might be able to reconstruct dimensions that are
undocumented, such as law or kinship.

Arguing from HRAF data, the archaeologist Charles McNett
claimed 50 percent accuracy for such predictions,[76] and in the 1970s
many prehistorians worked hard to clarify the stages' archaeological
correlates and to place specific societies within them.[77] But, as often
happens, this research created its own problems. Case studies found
that some societies did not work the way the stage theories said they
should,[78] and factor analyses of HRAF data failed to demonstrate
clear correlations between variables, because different rotations
produced wildly different loadings.[79]

More careful cross-cultural surveys in the 1980s suggested that
the statistical problem reflected a genuinely messy reality. A survey
of New World societies found "considerable variability . . . for each
examined attribute. This diversity was continuous rather than discrete and no clear societal modes or subtypes were readily apparent.
In addition, relationships of varying strength were found between
the different organizational characteristics."[80]

Worse still, because the sharp lines between stages blur so badly
in the real world, it can be hard to know when empirical data have
actually falsified any specific stage theory. In one case, contributors
to the same conference volume reached diametrically opposed conclusions on whether population density and settlement size correlate positively with political systems.[81]

Some archaeologists tried to clarify matters by splitting Service's
four original stages into subtypes,[82] or suggesting that chiefdoms
and states represent alternative paths of development, not successive
stages. Service himself responded to the messiness by proposing a
simpler "great divide," before which "primitive societies were seg-
mented into kin groups that were egalitarian in their relations to
each other," and after which "some of them became hierarchical,
controlled and directed by a central authoritative power—a power
instituted as a government."[83] Most archaeologists, however, moved
in the opposite direction, increasingly thinking of stages as mere
shorthand descriptions or ideal types superimposed for heuristic
purposes on a reality of continuous change.[84]

Society

Alongside challenges to the coherence of the stages into which theorists had bundled societies came challenges to the coherence of "society" itself.

Sociologists have long insisted that "societies" are groups constituted through practice, not unitary systems. People may define their societies in ethnic, political, religious, cultural, or other terms, and generally belong to several societies at once, choosing between them (or being chosen) depending on context. Michael Mann calls societies "confederal, overlapping, intersecting networks," and Giddens speaks of "social systems which 'stand out' in bas-relief from a background of a range of other systemic relationships in which they are embedded. They stand out because definite structural principles serve to produce a specifiable overall 'clustering of institutions' across time and space."[85]

Anthropologists share these concerns. Criticizing what they call "the stereotypical 'among the so-and-so' mold" of thinking that dominated ethnography through most of the twentieth century, Akhil Gupta and James Ferguson argue that

> whatever associations of place and culture exist must be taken as problems for anthropological research rather than the given ground that one takes as the point of departure; cultural territorializations (like ethnic and national ones) must be understood as complex and contingent results of ongoing historical and political processes. It is these processes, rather than pregiven cultural-territorial entities, that require anthropological study.[86]

The "societies" that sociologists analyze are often very different from the "cultures" that anthropologists study, and neither seems very like the clusters of artifact types that archaeologists commonly call "cultures" (in the classic definition, *polythetic set[s] of specific and comprehensive artefact types which consistently recur together in assemblages within a limited geographic area*").[87]

Naroll recognized the problem and responded by coining a new term, the "cultunit,"[88] which he divided into four types, varying on two chronological scales, but this complicated idea won little support. If the unit of analysis is really so slippery, then the long-term, large-scale comparisons that are the staple of social evolutionism seem doomed to failure.

QUANTIFICATION

Quantification is central to most approaches to social evolution, and half a century ago Naroll and Carneiro were already wrestling with the fundamental problem of how to convert nominal into interval data. By the 1970s, however, the desire to reduce unique humans or historical situations to serial data that could be counted was itself being challenged. As Shanks and Tilley saw it, the "mathematization" of the past was part of the evolutionists' hidden agenda of legitimizing Western domination: the mistaken assumption behind mathematization, they argued, was that when we quantify, "[w]e rediscover our essentially mathematical selves, and in our obsession with immediacy and factuality discover the inevitability of the present being as it is; it becomes objectively necessary."[89]

In a classic essay, the sociologist Mark Granovetter once suggested that social scientists are pulled in two opposite directions. One leads toward "over-socialization" of the social sciences' subject matter, embedding every problem in so much context and allowing so much scope for competing constructions and subversions of meaning that no solution is possible; the other, toward "under-socialization," wrenching details out of the context that gives them meaning and therefore finding only superficial answers.[90]

The challenge, of course, is to find the best possible balance between abstraction and immediacy. Different disciplines tend to favor different points on the spectrum, with anthropology and history perhaps moving furthest toward oversocialization and economics and psychology furthest toward undersocialization. If Peter Turchin (quoted earlier in this chapter) is right that "a discipline usually matures only after it has developed mathematical theory," social evolutionism requires more (and more sophisticated) quantification; if Shanks and Tilley and those who share their views are right, mathematization and social evolutionism are simply extreme versions of undersocialization.

CONCLUSION

This is a formidable set of criticisms. If they are justified, the Spencerian tradition of social evolutionism—and with it, any hope of using a social development index to answer the why-the-West-rules question—would seem to be fatally flawed.

There has been no shortage of evolutionists ready to defend the tradition against its critics.[91] In this book, though, I want to take a different tack. It seems to me that many of the criticisms raised in the past half century are quite justified, and deserve to be taken seriously; but that does not mean that the 1980s to 1990s trend toward abandoning social evolutionism altogether was also justified. In chapter 2, I try to show if we take the criticisms seriously, it is possible to build a more focused and robust kind of index that avoids many of the shortcomings of neo-evolutionist theory and really can provide the tools that show us what we need to explain if we are to know why the West rules—for now.

CHAPTER 2

‖‖‖‖‖‖‖‖‖‖‖‖‖‖‖‖‖‖‖‖‖‖‖‖‖‖‖‖‖‖‖‖‖‖‖‖‖‖

METHODS AND ASSUMPTIONS

IN CHAPTER 1, I SUGGESTED THAT THE BEST WAY TO RE-
solve the two-century-old debate about why the West rules is by
building a social development index, because this will allow us to
compare Western with non-Western development over long periods. Only when we have identified the shape of the history that
needs to be accounted for will we be able to come up with better
explanations for why the West rules.

I then looked at research on social evolution since the 1850s
and the criticisms leveled against the most recent version, neo-
evolutionism, since the 1970s. In this chapter, I describe a social development index that seems to me to respond to the most serious
criticisms of evolutionism without losing sight of the central goal of
being able to measure and compare social development across time
and space.

My approach depends on nine core assumptions. I begin by describing them, and then go on to explain how my social development index works. I close the chapter by explaining why I think this
index improves on twentieth-century neo-evolutionist indices.

CORE ASSUMPTIONS

I make nine basic assumptions, which require varying amounts of
discussion.

1. Quantification

Social development is not a useful concept unless it is quantifiable. Historians have argued for generations over the relative merits of quantitative and qualitative approaches, and I will not rehash these increasingly sterile debates.[1]

I do not assume that quantitative approaches are somehow more objective than qualitative ones; judgment calls and potentially arbitrary distinctions must always be made, whether we count or whether we describe. Chapters 3–6 describe the most important such calls and distinctions I have made.

That said, quantitative approaches should be more explicit than qualitative ones, since the act of quantification forces the analyst to focus on these decisions and to formulate reasons for choosing one option rather than another. If we do not approach social development quantitatively, the debate will continue to be bogged down in a definitional morass. The goal must be a numerical index of social development, allowing direct comparisons between different parts of the world and different periods of history.

2. Parsimony

Although no one has ever managed to trace the quotation back to a primary source, Albert Einstein is supposed to have said that "in science, things should be made as simple as possible, but no simpler." This, I assume, must be the goal in studying social development, but not all humanists share this assumption. (Nor, for that matter, do all scholars who call themselves social scientists.)

Academics often suggest that the goal of scholarship should be to add complexity to our understanding of the world. There are certainly many questions—particularly in cultural studies—that call for methods that complicate our perceptions and add nuance, even at the cost of clarity, but in discussions of why the West rules the main problem has generally been *too much* complexity, obscuring the central issues in masses of detail. Analysis has run into the classic problem of not being able to see the wood for the trees.

3. Traits

Operationalizing a broad concept like social development requires us to break it down into smaller, directly measurable units. Following the model of the United Nations Human Development Index,[2] I have tried to identify the minimum number of concrete traits that cover the full range of criteria in the formal definition of social development. No trait list can ever be perfect, but the challenge is to select the optimal set—that is, a set that would fail Einstein's simplicity test if we were to add more traits, because that would make things unnecessarily complex, or if we were to subtract traits, because the list would then no longer cover the full range of elements in the definition and would *oversimplify* things.

The first Human Development Index, or HDI, was designed in 1990 by the economist Mahbub ul Haq with the aim of shifting development economists' focus from national income accounting toward human well-being.[3] Working with Amartya Sen and a team of United Nations economists, ul Haq crafted the HDI to provide a single score that would tell development officers how well each country was doing in enabling its citizens to fulfill their innate potential.

The HDI uses three traits: life expectancy at birth (e_0), knowledge and education (with adult literacy rates accounting for two-thirds of the score and enrollment in schools and universities for the other one-third), and standards of living (gross domestic product per capita [GDP/cap] measured in U.S. dollars at purchasing power parity [PPP] rates). The UN Human Development Programme constantly revises its calculation methods, and made particularly large changes in 2011. It provides a convenient calculator for generating scores.[4]

The HDI has been criticized for everything from its selection of traits, errors in the underlying data, and the way it weights education and income to its neglect of ecology and morality,[5] but it has nevertheless proved extremely useful and is very widely used.

Human development is different from social development as I defined it in chapter 1 above, but the basic principle of identifying a manageably small number of quantifiable traits is transferable. Great differences of course remain between the HDI and my social development index, most obviously the fact that each published HDI is a synchronic snapshot. It could, up to a point, be used to measure change through time by simply comparing a single country's score in each annual report, but because the maximum possible score is always 1.0, the HDI does better at charting a nation's relative position within the world at a single point in time than at measuring diachronic changes in development levels.

In sum, although the HDI has very different aims from my social development index, the principle underlying it—that a small number of quantifiable traits can act as proxies for a much broader concept—is an excellent starting point.

4. The Criteria for a Useful Trait

There has been much discussion within the social sciences of how to select good traits, and most accounts focus on six criteria:[6]

i.   The trait must be *relevant*: that is, it must tell us something about social development as I defined it in chapter 1.

ii. The trait must be *culture independent*. We might, for example, think that the quality of literature and art are useful measures of social development, but judgments in these matters are notoriously culture bound.

iii. Traits must be *independent of each other*—if, for instance, we use the number of people in a state and the amount of wealth in that state as traits, we should not use per capita wealth as a third trait, because it is a product of the first two traits.

iv. The trait must be *adequately documented*. This is a real problem when we look back thousands of years because the evidence available varies so much. Especially in the distant past, we simply do not know much about some potentially useful traits.

v.   The trait must be *reliable*, meaning that experts more or less agree on what the evidence says.

vi. The trait must be *convenient*. This may be the least important criterion, but the harder it is to get evidence for something or the longer it takes to calculate results, the less useful that trait is.

5. Focusing on East and West Rather Than the Whole World

A genuinely global survey of social development, reviewing in as much detail as possible every region of the world, would be very welcome. It would, however, require an enormous amount of work, and would in fact be rather a blunt tool for explaining why the West rules, failing the parsimony test by adding unnecessary complexity.

The central question in the why-the-West-rules debate is whether Western social development has been higher than development in the rest of the world since the distant past or whether the West has only scored higher in recent times. To answer that, we do not need to examine the social development of every region in equal detail. For reasons discussed in Jared Diamond's *Guns, Germs, and Steel* and in chapter 2 of *Why the West Rules—For Now*,[7] at the end of the most recent ice age, around 13,700 BCE, social development began rising faster in a small group of societies in the "lucky latitudes" (roughly 20–35° north in the Old World and 15° south to 20° north in the New; figure 2.1) than anywhere else on earth.

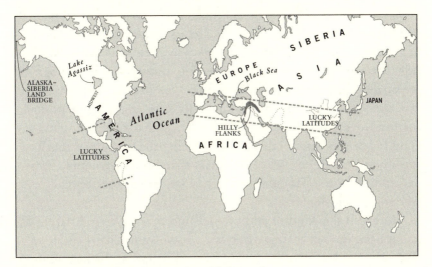

Figure 2.1. The "lucky latitudes." Map by Michele Angel.

The only parts of the world that could plausibly have produced rivals to the West in the past few hundred years are those that developed from cores in the New World, South Asia, and East Asia, which, at the end of the last ice age, had the densest concentrations of potentially domesticable plants and animals; and in reality, the only regions that have scored higher on social development than the West since the end of the last ice age have been in East Asia. Following the principle of parsimony, I therefore focus on East-West comparisons.

6. THE MEANING OF EAST AND WEST

One of the greatest difficulties in explaining why the West rules has been the tendency of different scholars to define "the West" in different ways, reducing the debate to a definitional impasse. The historian Norman Davies has counted no fewer than twelve distinct definitions in the academic literature, united only by what he calls their "elastic geography." The West, Davies concludes, "can be defined by its advocates in almost any way that they think fit," with the result that "Western civilization is essentially an amalgam of intellectual constructs which were designed to further the interests of their authors."[8]

The problem, Davies points out, is that historians have tended to start from some value that they like to associate with Westernness—democracy, say, or Christianity, or science, or freedom—and then identify a group of countries that seem to share this value. They then normally compare this set of countries to a set of "non-Western" countries that they define as lacking this value, and suggest an explanation for the difference. The difficulty is that rival historians can simply identify some other value as being the essence of the West, producing a different set of countries that exemplify it and a different comparison set, coming—naturally—to different but equally self-serving conclusions.

To avoid this kind of ethnocentrism, I make a very different assumption. Rather than starting with some value that I think of as Western and tracing it backward in time, I start at the beginning of the story and look forward. Radically different regional lifestyles

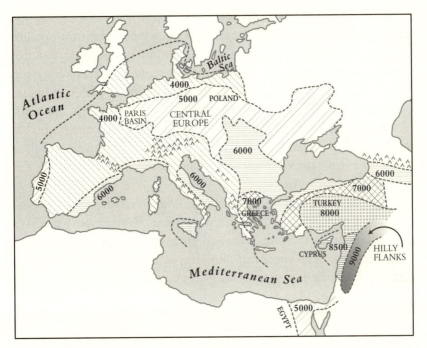

Figure 2.2. The early expansion of the West, 9000–4000 BCE.

only really began to develop after the end of the last ice age, when some groups began domesticating plants and animals while others continued to make their living from foraging.[9] As I explain in chapter 2 of *Why the West Rules—For Now*,[10] I define the "West" as the societies that have developed and spread through a combination of colonization and emulation from the westernmost original core of domestication in Eurasia, in the headwaters of the Euphrates and Tigris Rivers.

Within this area, domestication drove rising population, which simultaneously pushed social development upward and pushed people outward. By 4000 BCE "the West" had grown to include much of continental Europe, what is now Egypt, the western edge of what is now Iran, and some of the oases of Central Asia (figure 2.2). By the first millennium CE it had expanded still more to include the whole of what we now call Europe, and in the second millennium CE Europeans carried it to the Americas, Australasia, and the coasts of Africa.

Similarly, when I refer to the "East" I mean those societies that have developed and spread—again, through a combination of colonization and emulation—from the easternmost original core of domestication in Eurasia, between the Yellow and Yangzi Rivers. As in the West, domestication drove rising population, which simultaneously pushed social development upward and pushed people outward. By 2000 BCE "the East" had grown to include much of what we now call Southeast Asia. By 1500 BCE it included the modern Philippines and Korea (figure 2.3), and in the first millennium CE incorporated Japan too.

This way of defining "East" and "West," as the societies that have developed out of the easternmost and westernmost cores of domestication in Eurasia, seems to me a matter of common sense. It also has the great merits of allowing us to apply consistent concepts to the long run of human history and of avoiding the ideological extremes that dog so much of the debate about why the West rules.

7. CHRONOLOGICAL INTERVALS OF MEASUREMENT

One of the main goals of the social development index is to measure change through time, so the index must have a diachronic dimension. I begin my scoring in 14,000 BCE, near the end of the last ice age, and continue through to 2000 CE, which not only provides a convenient end point but also allows us a few years to see how the trends have continued to play out.

Following the principle of parsimony, I assume that social development scores should be calculated at chronological intervals short enough to illustrate the broad pattern of change but no shorter. In prehistory, dating techniques often involve very broad margins of error, but the rate of social change was often very slow. Even if we had good enough evidence to distinguish between social development in (say) 12,000 BCE and 11,900 BCE, the difference would probably be too small to measure.

I therefore use a sliding interval. From 14,000 through 4000 BCE, I measure social development every thousand years. From 4000 through 2500 BCE the quality of evidence improves and change accelerates, so I measure every 500 years. I reduce this to every 250

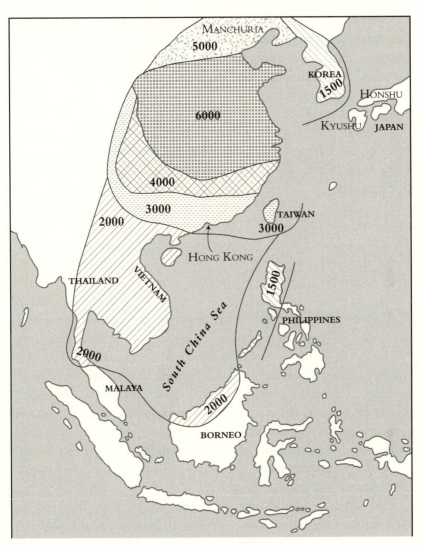

Figure 2.3. The early expansion of the East, 6000–1500 BCE.

years between 2500 BCE and 1500 BCE, and finally measure every century from 1400 BCE through 2000 CE. In the twentieth century CE the quality of data would allow us to trace changes just year-by-year or even (at least in the second half of the century) month-by-month if we wanted to, but this level of precision does little to answer the question of why the West rules while adding enormously to the effort of quantification, violating criterion 6 under assumption 4 above.

One downside of this approach is that prehistoric change is inevitably smoothed out. It does seem to be true that over the long run, development changed much more slowly in the first few thousand years after the end of the ice age than in the past few hundred, but on the rare occasions that prehistoric archaeological remains can be dated very accurately (e.g., among lake villages in the French Alps, dated by dendrochronology within margins of error of just a few years),[11] it is clear that these long waves conceal many shorter cycles. At present, there seems to be no way around this problem.

8. UNITS OF ANALYSIS

In his landmark book *The Great Divergence*, the historian Kenneth Pomeranz points out that historians eager to promote the primacy of Europe often make the elementary error of comparing the most developed parts of early modern Europe, such as Britain and the Netherlands, with the whole of China, and then concluding that Europe was more developed in the eighteenth or even the seventeenth century.[12] Comparing inappropriate regions produces meaningless results (which was why, as mentioned in chapter 1, Naroll proposed replacing archaeologists' and anthropologists' normal units of comparison with his own more abstract "cultunit").[13] It is therefore crucial that we examine social development in comparable and appropriate spatial and temporal units.

One solution would be to take the whole of the Eastern and Western zones as defined above as our analytic units, although that would mean that the Western score for, say, 1900 CE would bundle together industrialized England with Russia's serfs, Mexico's peons, and Australia's ranchers. We would then have to calculate an average development score for the whole Western region, then do it again for the East, and repeat the process for every earlier point in history. This would get so complicated as to become impractical, violating rule 6 in the discussion of criteria for good traits; and it would probably be rather pointless anyway. When it comes to explaining why the West rules, the most important information will normally come from comparing the most highly developed parts of each region, the cores that were tied together by the densest political, economic, so-

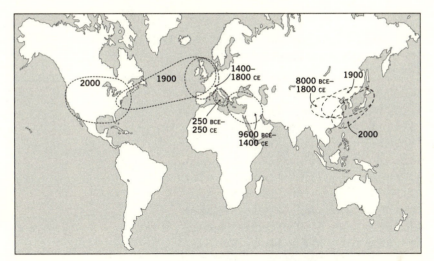

Figure 2.4. The shifting locations of the Eastern and Western cores. Map by Michele Angel.

cial, and cultural interactions. An index of social development needs to measure and compare changes within these cores.

These core areas have shifted and changed considerably across time (figure 2.4). The Western core was geographically very stable from 11,000 BCE until about 1400 CE, remaining firmly at the east end of the Mediterranean Sea except for the five hundred years between about 250 BCE and 250 CE, when the Roman Empire drew it westward to include Italy. Otherwise, it always lay within a triangle between what are now Iraq, Egypt, and Greece. Since 1400 CE it has moved relentlessly north and west, first to northern Italy, then to Spain and France, then broadening to include Britain, the Low Countries, and Germany. By 1900 CE it straddled the Atlantic, and by 2000 CE it was firmly planted in North America.

In the East the core remained in the original Yellow-Yangzi River zone right up until 1850 CE, although its center of gravity shifted northward toward the Yellow River's Central Plain after about 4000 BCE, back south to the Yangzi Valley after 500 CE, and gradually north again after 1400 CE. It expanded to include Japan by 1900 CE and southeast China too by 2000 CE.

There will inevitably be disagreement between specialists over the precise boundaries of the Eastern and Western cores at any given moment in time; I indicate approximately the areas I treat as the cores in table 2.1.

Table 2.1

Western and Eastern core regions, 14,000 BCE–2000 CE

The West	
14,000 BCE	Hilly Flanks (SW Asia)
13,000 BCE	Hilly Flanks (SW Asia)
12,000 BCE	Hilly Flanks (SW Asia)
11,000 BCE	Hilly Flanks (SW Asia)
10,000 BCE	Hilly Flanks (SW Asia)
9000 BCE	Hilly Flanks (SW Asia)
8000 BCE	Hilly Flanks (SW Asia)
7000 BCE	Hilly Flanks (SW Asia)
6000 BCE	Hilly Flanks (SW Asia)
5000 BCE	Hilly Flanks (SW Asia)
4000 BCE	Mesopotamia (SW Asia)
3500 BCE	Mesopotamia (SW Asia)
3000 BCE	Egypt (NE Africa)
2500 BCE	Egypt (NE Africa), Mesopotamia (SW Asia)
2250 BCE	Egypt (NE Africa), Mesopotamia (SW Asia)
2000 BCE	Egypt (NE Africa), Mesopotamia (SW Asia)
1750 BCE	Egypt (NE Africa), Mesopotamia (SW Asia)
1500 BCE	Egypt (NE Africa), Mesopotamia (SW Asia)
1400 BCE	Egypt (NE Africa), Mesopotamia-Anatolia (SW Asia)
1300 BCE	Egypt (NE Africa), Mesopotamia-Anatolia (SW Asia)
1200 BCE	Egypt (NE Africa)
1100 BCE	Egypt (NE Africa)
1000 BCE	Egypt (NE Africa)
900 BCE	Assyria-Mesopotamia (SW Asia)
800 BCE	Assyria-Mesopotamia (SW Asia)
700 BCE	Assyria-Mesopotamia (SW Asia)
600 BCE	Egypt (NE Africa), Mesopotamia (SW Asia)
500 BCE	Persian Empire (SW Asia)
400 BCE	Persian Empire-Aegean (SW Asia–NE Africa–SE Europe)
300 BCE	Hellenistic kingdoms (SW Asia–NE Africa–SE Europe)
200 BCE	Mediterranean basin (SW Asia–NE Africa–SE Europe)
100 BCE	Central Mediterranean (S Europe)
1 BCE/CE	Central Mediterranean (S Europe)
100 CE	Central Mediterranean (S Europe)
200 CE	Central Mediterranean (S Europe)

Table 2.1 (*continued*)

The West (cont.)

300 CE	Eastern Mediterranean (SW Asia–NE Africa–SE Europe)
400 CE	Eastern Mediterranean (SW Asia–NE Africa–SE Europe)
500 CE	Eastern Mediterranean (SW Asia–NE Africa–SE Europe)
600 CE	Eastern Mediterranean (SW Asia–NE Africa–SE Europe)
700 CE	Egypt (NE Africa), Syria-Iraq (SW Asia)
800 CE	Egypt (NE Africa), Syria-Iraq (SW Asia)
900 CE	Egypt (NE Africa), Spain (SW Europe)
1000 CE	Mediterranean basin (SW Asia–N Africa–S Europe)
1100 CE	Mediterranean basin (SW Asia–N Africa–S Europe)
1200 CE	Mediterranean basin (SW Asia–N Africa–S Europe)
1300 CE	Mediterranean basin (SW Asia–N Africa–S Europe)
1400 CE	Mediterranean basin (SW Asia–N Africa–S Europe)
1500 CE	Atlantic littoral (W Europe)
1600 CE	Atlantic littoral (W Europe)
1700 CE	France, Britain, Netherlands (NW Europe)
1800 CE	France, Britain (NW Europe)
1900 CE	Germany, France, Britain, USA (N Europe, N America)
2000 CE	USA (N America)

The East

14,000 BCE	Yellow-Yangzi River Valleys (China)
13,000 BCE	Yellow-Yangzi River Valleys (China)
12,000 BCE	Yellow-Yangzi River Valleys (China)
11,000 BCE	Yellow-Yangzi River Valleys (China)
10,000 BCE	Yellow-Yangzi River Valleys (China)
9000 BCE	Yellow-Yangzi River Valleys (China)
8000 BCE	Yellow-Yangzi River Valleys (China)
7000 BCE	Yellow-Yangzi River Valleys (China)
6000 BCE	Yellow-Yangzi River Valleys (China)
5000 BCE	Yellow-Yangzi River Valleys (China)
4000 BCE	Yellow-Yangzi River Valleys (China)
3500 BCE	Yellow-Yangzi River Valleys (China)
3000 BCE	Yellow-Yangzi River Valleys (China)
2500 BCE	Yellow-Yangzi River Valleys (China)

Table 2.1 (*continued*)

The East (cont.)	
2250 BCE	Yellow-Yangzi River Valleys (China)
2000 BCE	Yellow River Valley (China)
1750 BCE	Yellow River Valley (China)
1500 BCE	Yellow River Valley (China)
1400 BCE	Yellow River Valley (China)
1300 BCE	Yellow River Valley (China)
1200 BCE	Yellow River Valley (China)
1100 BCE	Yellow River Valley (China)
1000 BCE	Yellow River Valley (China)
900 BCE	Yellow River Valley (China)
800 BCE	Yellow River Valley (China)
700 BCE	Yellow River Valley (China)
600 BCE	Yellow River Valley (China)
500 BCE	Yellow-Yangzi River Valleys (China)
400 BCE	Yellow-Yangzi River Valleys (China)
300 BCE	Yellow-Yangzi River Valleys (China)
200 BCE	Yellow-Yangzi River Valleys (China)
100 BCE	Yellow-Yangzi River Valleys (China)
1 BCE/CE	Yellow-Yangzi River Valleys (China)
100 CE	Yellow-Yangzi River Valleys (China)
200 CE	Yellow-Yangzi River Valleys (China)
300 CE	Yangzi River Valley (China)
400 CE	Yangzi River Valley (China)
500 CE	Yangzi River Valley (China)
600 CE	Yellow-Yangzi River Valleys (China)
700 CE	Yellow-Yangzi River Valleys (China)
800 CE	Yellow-Yangzi River Valleys (China)
900 CE	Yangzi River Valley (China)
1000 CE	Yellow-Yangzi River Valleys (China)
1100 CE	Yellow-Yangzi River Valleys (China)
1200 CE	Yellow-Yangzi River Valleys (China)
1300 CE	Yellow-Yangzi River Valleys (China)
1400 CE	Yellow-Yangzi River Valleys (China)
1500 CE	Yellow-Yangzi River Valleys (China)
1600 CE	Yellow-Yangzi River Valleys (China), Japan
1700 CE	Yellow-Yangzi River Valleys (China)
1800 CE	Yellow-Yangzi River Valleys (China)
1900 CE	Japan
2000 CE	Eastern China, Japan

9. Approximation and Falsification

I take it for granted that there is no such thing as an index that is 100 percent accurate, whether we interpret "accurate" in a strong sense, meaning that every single detail is absolutely correct, or a weaker sense, meaning that all experts will make exactly the same estimates, even if they cannot prove that these estimates are correct. In all historical scholarship there is little we can be completely sure about and even less that experts will agree on. There is therefore no point in asking whether the social development scores I calculate are correct. Of course they are not. The only meaningful question is, *how* incorrect are they? Are they so wrong that I have misidentified the basic shape of the history of social development, meaning that my explanation for why the West rules is fatally flawed? Or are the errors in fact relatively trivial?

There are two main ways to address these questions. One is to assume that I have made systematic errors, pervasively overestimating the Western and underestimating the Eastern scores (or vice versa), then to ask (1) how much we would need to change the scores to make the past look so different that the arguments advanced in *Why the West Rules—For Now* would cease to hold good and (2) whether such changes are plausible. I address these questions in chapter 7.

The other way is to assume that the errors are unsystematic, over- or underestimating both the Eastern and Western scores in random, unpredictable ways. The only way to address errors of this kind is to work through the evidence on which I base my individual scores, which I present in detail in chapters 3–6.

METHODS OF CALCULATION: TRAIT SELECTION

The first challenge is to find the minimum number of traits that fulfill the six criteria listed under assumption 4 above. After trying several permutations, I settled on four traits: (a) energy capture per person, (b) social organization, (c) information technology, and (d) war-making capacity.

a. *Energy capture* must be the foundation for any usable measure of social development. Newton's Second Law of Thermodynamics tells us that complex arrangements of matter break down over time without the input of additional energy from their environment. Without capturing energy, humans (like plants and other animals) die. Similarly, unless they take up energy from their environments, the societies humans have created break down. To increase their mastery of their physical and intellectual environments and get things done, groups of people have to increase their energy capture.

However, energy capture alone is not adequate to measure everything that is important to social development. Even the most reductionist definition of culture that I know of, Leslie White's $C = E \times T$ (chapter 1 above; culture = energy × technology), took it for granted that measuring the ways people use the energy they capture is as important as measuring the energy itself. White's category of "technology," however, strikes me as too loose and too difficult to quantify, so I have subdivided it into three further traits.

b. *Social organization* is the first of these. This concept inevitably overlaps to a considerable degree with Spencer's notion of differentiation, but to sidestep the endless debates over definition and measurement that I mentioned in chapter 1, I have borrowed a trick from economists and used the population size of the largest permanent settlement within a society as a rough proxy measure of organizational capacity.[14]

This might seem like an odd strategy. Some of the biggest cities in the world today are dysfunctional nightmares, riddled with crime, squalor, and disease. But that, of course, has been true of most big cities throughout history. Rome had a million residents in the first century BCE; it also had street gangs that regularly brought government to a halt and death rates so high that more than a thousand country folk had to migrate into Rome every month just to maintain its numbers.[15] Yet for all Rome's foulness, the organization needed to keep the city going was vastly beyond anything that any earlier society in the world could have managed—just as running Lagos (population 11 million) or Mumbai (population 19 million), let alone

Tokyo (population 35 million), calls for organization far beyond the Roman Empire's capabilities.

This is why social scientists regularly use urbanism as an approximate measure of organizational capacity. There are several ways to do this. We might calculate the proportion of a society's population that lives in settlements over a certain size (ten thousand people is a popular cut-off point), or we might classify settlements into different ranks, and count how many ranks each society has. The method I have chosen, however, is simply to count the number of people in the largest permanent settlement in the East and the largest settlement in the West. I have chosen this approach (a) because it seems the best suited to the kinds of evidence we have to use if we are going to take the study all the way back to 14,000 BCE and (b) because I know of no studies showing that this method is any less useful than more complicated alternatives.

c. *Information technology* is the next indispensable element in the use of energy. As social development increases, people have to process and communicate prodigious amounts of information. No society can develop very far without systems for writing and counting; to go further still, it needs increasingly sophisticated media for storing and transmitting this information and institutions to impart the skills of literacy and numeracy to more and more people.

d. Finally, *war-making capacity* is a crucial part of social development. Like plants and all other animals, humans must compete as well as cooperate if they are to survive; and, having evolved as a social species, humans (like ants and chimpanzees) regularly direct part of their cooperative activities toward competing violently as groups against other rival groups.[16] Weapons and fortifications are prominent in the archaeological record, and descriptions of wars and battles fill the written sources in most cultures once information technology has reached the stage that this kind of detail can be stored.

These four traits do not add up to a comprehensive picture of social development across the last sixteen thousand years, any more than the United Nations' traits of life expectancy, education, and income tell us everything we might want to know about human development. Their function is more limited: they just need to give us a usable snapshot of social development, revealing the patterns that need to be explained if we are to know why the West rules.

Nor do I claim that these four traits are the only ones that would do the job. I looked at several other possible traits, including population sizes of the largest political units, scientific capacity, and broad measures of technological capacity, but none seemed to me to perform as well on the criteria listed under assumption 4 as energy capture, organization, information technology, and war-making capacity. That said, there does seem to be considerable redundancy among the traits, suggesting that any bundle of traits that relates well to the core concept of social development is likely to produce rather similar sets of scores.

CALCULATING SCORES

The greatest challenge for any index is of course deciding how to assign points to the traits. In order to keep things simple, I decided to make one thousand points the maximum possible score by the year 2000 CE, the endpoint of the index. However, this cap works very differently from the maximum possible score of 1.0 in the United Nations' Human Development Index. In the UN index, 1.0 represents some kind of perfection, meaning that it will never be possible for a society to score higher than 1.0. In my social development index, by contrast, one thousand points is simply the highest score possible in the year 2000 CE. In the dozen years that have passed between the end of the index and writing these words, Western development scores have continued to rise, and have already passed one thousand points. If Eastern and Western development continue to rise at twentieth-century rates, by the end of the twenty-first century both will have reached five thousand points; and if the rate of increase accelerates beyond twentieth-century rates, which seems to be what is happening, both scores will be higher still in 2100.

The economists who designed the United Nations' Human Development Index came up with an elaborate weighting system, normalizing the scores on their three traits and then calculating the geometric mean of the combined scores. By contrast, when Naroll published his original social development index back in 1956, he assigned equal weight to each of his three traits, if only, he explained, "because no obvious reason appeared for giving one [trait] any more weight than another."[17]

There will always be scope to argue over the merits of different weightings,[18] and I return to this question in chapter 7, but Naroll's approach seems more relevant here than the United Nations'. Even if good reasons could be identified to weight one trait more heavily than another, there would be no grounds to assume that the same weightings would hold good across the whole sixteen thousand years under review, or that they would apply equally to East and West throughout.

I therefore divide my one thousand points equally among the four traits. This means that the society that has the highest value on record for that particular trait picks up 250 points for the period in which it attains that level (which, in every case, is the year 2000 CE), with other societies getting proportionately lower numbers of points for lower values. I go into detail about the evidence, the definitional issues, and how I have calculated the scores on each trait in chapters 3–6, but I give a brief concrete example here to illustrate the mechanics of the scoring system. I will take the case of organization, measured through the proxy of the size of the largest settlement (see "Methods of Calculation," section b, above), because it is probably the most straightforward of the traits.

Most geographers classify Tokyo in 2000 CE as the biggest city known from the period 14,000 BCE–2000 CE, with about 26.7 million residents. Tokyo in 2000 CE, then, scores the full 250 points allotted to organization/urbanism, meaning that each 106,800 people (that is, 26.7 million divided by 250) scores 1 point on the index. The biggest city in the Western core in 2000 CE was New York, with 16.7 million people; at 106,800 people per point, New York scores 156.37 points.

The data for 1900 CE are not as good, but all historians agree that cities were much smaller. In the West, London had about 6.6 million residents (scoring 61.80 points) in 1900 CE, while in the East Tokyo was again the greatest city, but with just 1.75 million people, earning 16.39 points.

By the time we get back to 1800 CE, historians have to combine several different kinds of evidence, including records of food supply and tax payments, the physical area covered by cities, the density of housing within them, and anecdotal accounts, but most conclude that Beijing was at this time the world's biggest city, with perhaps 1.1 million souls (10.30 points). The biggest Western city was again London, with about 861,000 people (8.06 points).

The further we push back in time, the broader the margins of error, but for the thousand years leading up to 1700 CE the biggest cities were clearly Chinese (with Japanese ones often close behind). First Chang'an, then Kaifeng, and later Hangzhou came close to or passed a million residents (around 9 points) between 800 and 1200 CE. Western cities, by contrast, were never more than half that size (and the biggest Western cities were usually in the Muslim areas of Southern Europe and Southwest Asia rather than in Christian Northern and Western Europe). A few centuries earlier, this situation was reversed: in the first century BCE Rome's million residents undoubtedly made it the world's metropolis, while Chang'an in China had probably half a million citizens.

As we move back into prehistory the evidence of course becomes fuzzier still and the numbers become much smaller. However, the combination of systematic archaeological surveys and detailed excavation of smaller areas still gives us a reasonable sense of city sizes. This is very much chainsaw art, but while the most commonly accepted estimates might be as much as 10 percent off, they are unlikely to be much wider of the mark than that; and since we are applying the same methods of estimation to Eastern and Western sites, the broad trends should be fairly reliable.

Because it requires 106,800 people to score 1 point for organization, slightly over one thousand people will score 0.01 points, the smallest number I felt was worth entering on the index. The biggest Western villages reached this level around 7500 BCE and the biggest Eastern ones around 3500 BCE. Before these dates, West and East alike score zero (see chapter 4).

The scores for the other three traits are calculated in similar ways: I (a) identify the society with the highest score on this dimension of life (e.g., for energy capture, the United States in 2000 CE, where each citizen on average burned through some 228,000 kcal of energy per day), (b) assign that society the full score of 250 points, (c) calculate the performance needed to earn one point (for energy capture, 228,000 divided by 250 equals 912 kcal per capita per day per point), (d) estimate values on this trait for each society at different dates through history, and (e) divide these estimates by the denominator needed to turn them into scores on the index. After calculating the scores on each trait for the whole period between 14,000 BCE and 2000 CE, I simply add the four traits together for produce a series of social development scores for each region. This allows us to compare social development through time between different parts of the world.

MAJOR OBJECTIONS

Based on the debates over neo-evolutionism reviewed in chapter 1, it seems to me that there are four major charges that might be leveled against my methods. I will say a few words about each, explaining why none of these objections strikes me as being fatal.

1. *Quantifying and comparing social development in different times and places dehumanizes people, and we should therefore not do it.*

This was one of the most influential arguments in the turn against neo-evolutionism in anthropology and sociology in the 1970s and 1980s, and similar ideas won many followers among historians too. However, it is the least impressive of the objections that might be raised because its force largely evaporates as soon as we recognize that different questions require us to work at different levels of abstraction.

By the late 1980s, scholars in many fields had come to feel that the highly abstract categories of neo-evolutionism, neoclassical economics, and cognate approaches left too much unexplained, and they quite reasonably turned to other ways of thinking that seemed to do a better job of answering the questions they found interesting. Many sociologists, for instance, dropped differentiation and utility in favor of *habitus* and structuration as organizing concepts, and even demography and economics, the social sciences most firmly committed to quantification and abstraction, had their own postmodern turns.[19]

I certainly found this to be true in my own research. After drawing on neo-evolutionary and comparative frameworks in the mid-1980s to make sense of social change in Iron Age Greece,[20] the limitations of these approaches became increasingly obvious. Some of the most important dimensions of ancient Greek society, such as its combination of radical male democracy with large-scale chattel slavery, fit awkwardly with schemes like those of Service, Parsons, and Fried, which made democracy a correlate of advanced modern states.[21] Far from explaining where Greek democracy came from, assigning Greece a score on a social development index seemed to make the task harder, by diverting attention away from the Greeks' unique achievements.[22]

But this did not mean that social evolutionism and indices of social development were a waste of time; it meant just that other tools were needed to answer this specific question. A narrower, more particularist approach to ancient Greek society yielded many gains over comparative, evolutionary treatments; but this too had limits, above all its inability to explain the economic, military, and political growth that clearly drove the changes of the first millennium BCE. Trying to make sense of these more material factors drew me back toward broadly evolutionary tools and the need to situate Greece within a global framework.[23]

Asking why the West rules is a different kind of question from asking why some Greek city-states gave the vote to all adult male citizens. It is a grand comparative question, which requires us to range across thousands of years of history, look at millions of square miles of territory, and bring together billions of people. For this task an index of social development is exactly the tool we need.

2. *Quantifying and comparing societies is a reasonable procedure, but social development in the sense I defined it (as societies' abilities to get things done) is the wrong thing to measure.*

This objection can be addressed more briefly. A critic who feels this way would need to show that there are other things we could measure and compare that would be more helpful for explaining why the West rules than social development in the sense I define it. I do not know what these other things might be, so I leave it to the critics to identify them and to show that they yield more useful results.

3. *Social development in the sense I defined it may be a useful way to compare regions through time, but the traits I use to measure it (energy capture, organization/urbanization, information technology, and war-making capacity) are not the best ones.*

As I see it, this objection could come in three forms:

i. We should add more traits to my four traits of energy capture, organization, war-making capacity, and information technology. But while there are certainly many traits we could examine, the principle of parsimony dictates that we should avoid adding more traits to the minimum set that covers the full range of what is meant by social development. A critic would need to show that my four traits in fact fail to cover one or more important aspects of social development, and that covering these aspects would produce results different enough from those of my index to make the extra effort and complication worthwhile.

ii. We should use different traits. Again, there are certainly other variables we could measure, but all the alternatives that I have examined perform poorly on various criteria, generally suffering from serious empirical problems, culture dependence, or mutual overlap. As noted earlier, most traits in any case show high levels of redundancy through most of history, and any plausible combination of alternative traits will tend to produce much the same final result.

iii. We should look at fewer traits. In view of the redundancy among the four traits, we might drop some of them, increasing parsimony. The obvious strategy might be to drop organization, war-making capacity, and information technology and concentrate only on energy capture, on the grounds that organization, war making, and information technology are merely ways of *using* energy.[24] Figure 2.5 shows what an energy-alone index would look like. It is different from figure 2.6, showing the scores produced by the full index, but not hugely so. In the energy-alone graph, just as in the full social development graph, the West still leads the East for 90 percent of the time since the Late Ice Age; the East still overtakes the West between roughly

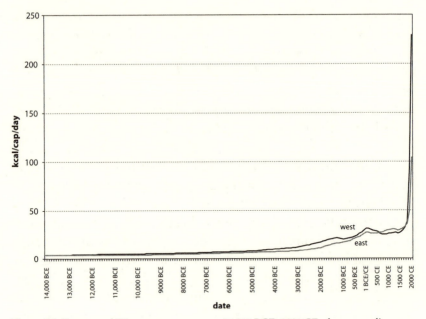

Figure 2.5. Eastern and Western energy capture, 14,000 BCE–2000 CE, shown on a linear-linear scale.

550 and 1750 CE; there is still a hard ceiling that blocks development around 100 and 1100 CE (at just over 30,000 kcal per person per day); post–industrial revolution scores still dwarf those
of earlier ages; and in 2000 CE the West still rules.

Focusing on energy alone certainly has the advantage of increasing parsimony, but it also has one great drawback. The four traits I
use are not *completely* redundant, and since the industrial revolution began around 1800 CE the relationship between energy capture and the other traits has become nonlinear. Increases at the
margins of energy capture have produced vastly greater increases in
energy use in selected fields, because human energy use is highly
elastic relative to energy capture. Thanks to new technologies, city
size quadrupled across the twentieth century, war-making capacity
increased fiftyfold, and information technology surged eightyfold,
while energy capture per person merely doubled. Looking at energy alone fails Einstein's test by being *too* simple, and distorts the
shape of history.

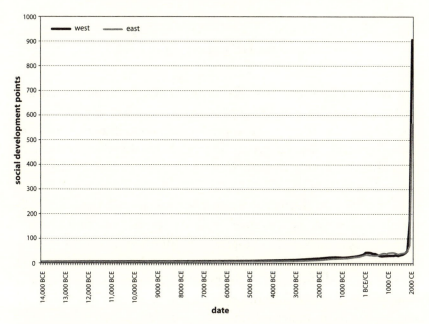

Figure 2.6. Eastern and Western social development scores, 14,000 BCE–2000 CE, shown on a linear-linear scale.

4. *These four traits are a good way to measure social development, but I have made factual errors and got the measurements wrong.*
As noted in the discussion of approximation and falsification (assumption 9), there are two main ways to address this objection. One is to assume that I have made systematic empirical errors, consistently overestimating the Western and underestimating the Eastern scores (or vice versa), then to ask (a) how much we would need to change the scores to make the past look so different that the arguments advanced in *Why the West Rules—For Now* would cease to hold good and (b) whether such changes are plausible. I will argue in chapter 7 that there is good reason to think that think that this is not the case.

The other way to interpret the objection would be to assume that there are persistent but unsystematic empirical errors, over- or understating the Eastern and/or Western scores in random, unpredictable, and serious ways. The only way to address this danger is of course to work through the references provided in chapters 3–6, checking the scores in the index against the evidence.

CONCLUSION: THE ADVANTAGES OF
THE SOCIAL DEVELOPMENT INDEX

The major claim I want to make for my social development index is that it reflects the criticisms of social evolutionism as much as the contributions made by the social evolutionists themselves. Ever since Spencer's original essay,[25] critics of social evolutionism have argued that in trying to explain everything, evolutionists often end up explaining nothing.

The critics are clearly correct that there is no such thing as a one-size-fits-all social development index. Throughout the twentieth century, the sheer variety of topics that index makers wanted to subsume within their frameworks tended to make operationalization impossible, and efforts to fix the problem often just made the situation worse. Carneiro's solution, for instance, was to add more and more traits to his index, which ballooned from 8 categories in 1962 to 618 in 1970, with no obvious end in sight.[26]

Instead of trying to explain everything, the index offered here focuses on the single question of why the societies at the western end of Eurasia came to dominate the world in the nineteenth century, with their overseas colonies in North America displacing them in the twentieth.

This focus has three advantages. It makes it possible to (a) define the core concept of social development with this specific question in mind, (b) choose traits that speak directly to the core concept while remaining reasonably easy to operationalize, and (c) design the index in such a way that it can measure change through time.

These advantages allow me to avoid many of the difficulties that dogged the neo-evolutionist indices. The most significant of these may have been the intractable concept of differentiation, inherited from Spencer, but almost impossible to put into practice. Something along the lines of Spencerian differentiation has to form part of any usable definition of social development or social evolution, and it does appear in my index as part of the broader trait of social organization, measured through the proxy of city size. However, the index offered here has no need to fall into the traps that McGuire identified in neo-evolutionist treatments of differentiation.[27]

The index also avoids being wedded to any specific theory of social evolution (by contrast, say, to Carneiro's scale analysis, which was explicitly tied to unilineal stage theories). It can be used equally well to measure whether all societies do indeed develop along the lines that Carneiro proposed or whether self-organized criticality is consistent with long-term, macroscale social change.

The methods described in this chapter also do something to reduce the unit-of-analysis problem that bedeviled so much twentieth-century social evolutionism. The approach described here allows a lot more flexibility in identifying a "core" area within the East and another within the West, defined by higher levels of social development than the peripheral areas around them.

This works well for the trait of social organization, measured along the proxy variable of city size, although it does not altogether resolve the unit-definition problem for energy capture, information technology, and war-making capacity. On these traits it remains possible to define a core tendentiously, deliberately combining high- and low-scoring areas to produce artificially low overall scores.

In *Why the West Rules—For Now*,[28] I call this the "Pomeranz Problem," after the observation of historian Kenneth Pomeranz (mentioned earlier in this chapter) that historians who believe that Europe was already more developed than China well before the industrial revolution often try to make their point by an inappropriate comparison between a small, developed core in Europe—usually consisting of England and the Low Countries—and the whole of China. A more appropriate comparison, Pomeranz observes, would be between England and the Yangzi Delta, or between the whole of China and the whole of Europe.[29]

The main way my index responds to the Pomeranz Problem is by forcing analysts to be explicit. Table 2.1 spells out exactly which region is being counted as the core in each region at each point in time, allowing critics to challenge the definition and propose alternative cores, showing how they would alter the scores. I believe that this approach, exposing assumptions to challenge and falsification, is a much better basis for index building than attempts to legislate rules that cover every eventuality.

Finally, quantification. The main lesson of the fifty-year-old debate over numerical approaches to social evolution seems to me to be that the debate itself is a red herring. There are some scholars who oppose quantitative approaches on principle and others who oppose qualitative approaches on equally principled grounds, but both groups of scholars are wrong. Some questions can be answered only quantitatively and others qualitatively. If the why-the-West-rules question is really a question about social development, then it is best approached quantitatively, using a social development index that will show us the shape of the history that needs to be explained.

CHAPTER 3

||||||||||||||||||||||||||||||||||||||||||||||

ENERGY CAPTURE

LESLIE WHITE ARGUED SEVENTY YEARS AGO THAT ENERGY capture has to be the foundation of any attempt to understand social development.[1] Complex arrangements of matter persist through time only if they are able to capture free energy from their environment and put it to work, and humans and their societies are no exceptions.[2]

Deprived of oxygen, the complex arrangements of matter that constitute our bodies begin to break down after a few minutes. Deprived of water, we break down after a few days; deprived of food, we break down after a few weeks. To create superorganisms bringing together multiple people, humans have to harvest even more energy, making energy capture the foundation of social development.

By "energy capture," I mean the full range of energy captured by humans, above all

food (whether consumed directly, given to animals that provide labor, or given to animals that are subsequently eaten);
fuel (whether for cooking, heating, cooling, firing kilns and furnaces, or powering machines, and including wind and waterpower as well as wood, coal, oil, gas, and nuclear power);
raw materials (whether for construction, metalwork, pot making, clothing, or any other purpose).

Energy capture defined in this way is related to, but broader than, more commonly used measures of physical well-being such as real wages, gross domestic product per capita (GDP/cap), gross national product per capita (GNP/cap), or national disposable income per capita (NDI/cap). Real wages measure individual incomes (whether earned in cash or kind) corrected for inflation; GDP measures expenditure, value added in production, and income generated within the territory of a country; GNP measures GDP plus or minus net receipts from transfers of property or labor income from the rest of the world; and NDI measures GNP plus or minus net current transfers received in money or in kind from the rest of the world, including taxes and tribute, whether paid in cash or in kind. GDP, GNP, and NDI are converted into per capita figures by simply dividing each by the number of people in the territory under study.

Economists normally focus on real wages, GDP, GNP, and NDI per capita rather than energy capture, largely because these measures are much better documented in the statistics available for modern (i.e., post-1800 CE Western, post-1900 CE Eastern, and post-1950 CE for the rest of the world) economies than is the broader category of energy capture. However, energy capture is a more flexible measure for comparing very large stretches of time, across which the nature of subsistence practices changed dramatically.

THE COOK FRAMEWORK

An enormous literature has grown up on human energy use, with contributions from medical researchers, engineers, natural scientists, social scientists, and humanists. However, relatively few historical syntheses have been attempted,[3] and the task of forming an overall picture is complicated by the way various researchers focus on different dimensions of energy capture (e.g., food consumption, net energy use, material standards of living, total consumption), measure it in different ways (e.g., kcal/cap/day, life expectancy at birth, real wages, stature), or describe changes qualitatively rather than quantifying them. I therefore begin by defining some of my terms more closely.

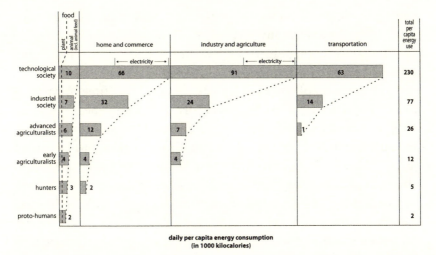

Figure 3.1. Earl Cook's diagram of energy consumption at different stages of social development. *Source*: Cook, "Flow of Energy," 137.

My general framework begins from a widely reprinted diagram (figure 3.1) originally published in *Scientific American* magazine in 1971.[4] In it, the geoscientist Earl Cook of Texas A&M University offered rough estimates of typical per person energy capture among hunter-gatherers, early agriculturalists (by which he meant the farmers of Southwest Asia around 5000 BCE), advanced agriculturalists (those of Northwest Europe around 1400 CE), industrial folk (Western Europeans around 1860), and the "technological" societies of North America and Western Europe in his own day. Cook divided each score into the four categories of food (including animal feed), home and commerce, industry and agriculture, and transportation. This diagram has become a regular point of departure for historians of energy capture.

Cook's food/nonfood energy distinction is fundamental. Human consumption of food energy is tightly constrained: if it falls much below an average of 2,000 kilocalories per person per day (kcal/cap/day) for any length of time, people will become too weak to work. They will lose body functions and die prematurely. If inputs of food energy stay above 4,000 kcal/cap/day for any length of time, however, people will become obese, suffer serious health complications, and again die prematurely. (Nutritionists conventionally use "calories" to describe what physicists would call nutritional kilocalories, and the caloric content listed in "nutrition facts" on food packaging actually refers to kilocalories.)

Consumption of food energy has changed over time in part because people have shifted back and forth between "cheap" calories such as grains and "expensive" calories such as meat (as a rough measure, it takes about ten calories of plants to grow one calorie of meat). Meat-rich twenty-first-century diets typically represent about 10,000 kcal/cap/day. Consumption of energy in nonfood forms, however, has changed much more dramatically. Most hunter-gatherers consume rather few nonfood calories: they need biomass for cooking fuel, clothes, weapons, baskets, and personal ornaments, but typically have only very simple shelters and few substantial material goods. Peasant societies normally have much more substantial homes and a wide range of artifacts, and modern industrial societies of course produce nonfood goods in extraordinary quantities. Total (i.e., food + nonfood) energy capture in the simplest tropical hunter-gatherer societies can be as low as 4,000–5,000 kcal/cap/day; in the contemporary United States it has reached 230,000 kcal/cap/day, and the global average is now around 50,000 kcal/cap/day.

Through most of history per capita nonfood energy capture has tended to rise, but people have had few ways to convert nonfood calories into food. As a result, the difficulty of increasing food calories has been the major brake on both population size and rising living standards. Thomas Malthus already recognized this in his *Essay on the Principle of Population*: "It should be remembered always," he wrote, "that there is an essential difference between food and those wrought commodities, the raw materials of which are in great plenty. A demand for these last will not fail to create them in as great a quantity as they are wanted. The demand for food has by no means the same creative power."[5]

Even in prehistoric times, nonfood energy could slightly loosen the constraints on food supply, for instance by providing manure,[6] improving transport so that food could be moved from places where it was plentiful to those where it was scarce, and providing fuel to process food. Only since the nineteenth century CE, however—ironically, beginning during Malthus's lifetime—have transport, processing, fertilizers, and scientific interventions revolutionized the food supply, relentlessly increasing stature, life expectancy, and health.[7]

Despite its prominence in Malthus's and Cook's work, social scientists interested in long-term economic history regularly ignore the food/nonfood calories distinction and, focusing solely on food, conclude that between the invention of agriculture more than ten thousand years ago and the industrial revolution two hundred years ago not very much happened.[8] In one of the most widely cited recent discussions, the economic historian Gregory Clark explicitly suggested that "the average person in the world of 1800 [CE] was no better off than the average person of 100,000 BC."[9] But this is mistaken. As Malthus recognized, if good weather or advances in technology or organization raised food output, population did tend to expand to consume the surplus, forcing people to consume fewer and cheaper food calories; but despite the downward pressure on per capita food supply, increases in nonfood energy capture have, in the long run, steadily accumulated throughout Holocene times.

Cook suggested that while typical hunter-gatherers captured just 2,000 kcal/cap/day of nonfood energy, early farmers raised this to 8,000 kcal/cap/day, and advanced preindustrial farmers to 20,000 kcal/cap/day. My own reconstruction suggests that in the long run (passing for the moment over several periods of collapse), nonfood energy capture rose slowly but steadily across the thirteen millennia after the end of the ice age around 12,700 BCE, until in Roman Italy—the core of the most advanced ancient agrarian empire—it may have reached 25,000 kcal/cap/day. This seems to have been the ceiling on what was possible in a preindustrial society, corresponding to the boundary between what the economic historian E. A. Wrigley has called advanced organic economies and fossil-fuel economies.[10]

For nearly two thousand years, agrarian empires pressed against this ceiling without breaking it. In the seventeenth and eighteenth centuries, when globalization reached the point that plants and animals could be moved between continents, calories invested in transport began being turned indirectly into food calories. It was only in the nineteenth century, however, after entrepreneurs had learned to convert the energy released by burning coal from heat into motion, that nonfood energy capture increased so much that it could in turn be converted into food calories. This freed humans from the Malthusian trap—for the time being, at least.

Cook's estimates are of course only a starting point, since he offered just six data points (proto-humans, hunters, early agriculturalists, advanced agriculturalists, industrial society, technological society), and made no attempt to distinguish between different parts of the world. He also provided no sources for his estimates. In reconstructing Western and Eastern energy capture, I have therefore proceeded by using Cook's figures as points of departure, establishing an order of magnitude for "normal" consumption in a given energy regime and then using more detailed evidence to estimate how far from these normal figures the actual Eastern and Western cores diverged at each point in time.

UNITS OF MEASUREMENT AND ABBREVIATIONS

I use the following conventional units of measurement and abbreviations:

1 calorie = amount of heat energy needed to raise the temperate
of 1 cm³ of water by 1°C
1 calorie = 4.2 joules
1 joule = 0.238 calories
1 British thermal unit = 1,055 joules
1 ton wheat equivalent = 3,300,000 kilocalories
1 ton oil equivalent = 10,038,000 kilocalories
1 liter of wheat = 0.78 kilograms = 2,574 kilocalories
1 megajoule = 239,999 kilocalories
1 watt = 1 joule per second
1 horsepower = 750 watts
Basic adult physiological food requirement = approx. 2,000–
2,700 kilocalories per capita per day (= 8–11 megajoules = approx. 90 watts)[11]

BTU	British thermal unit	kcal	kilocalorie (1,000
bya	billion years ago		calories)
C	centigrade	kya	thousand years ago
cal	calorie	MJ	megajoule (1 billion
cap	capita		joules)
cm	centimeter	mya	million years ago
GJ	gigajoule (1 billion	toe	tons oil equivalent
	joules)	twe	tons wheat equivalent
hp	horsepower	W	watt
J	joule	yr	year

THE NATURE OF THE EVIDENCE

Reliable statistics on energy capture go back only part way into the twentieth century in the Eastern core and to the early nineteenth century in the West, and even these data generally omit the large quantities of biomass used for fuel and construction in peasant societies.[12] Patchier statistics go back to the nineteenth century in parts of China and Japan and to at least the seventeenth century in Western Europe. Before then there are textual records and occasional quantitative documents from both regions, stretching back to 1200 BCE in China and 3000 BCE in Mesopotamia and Egypt, but these cannot yield anything like the detail available for modern periods.

The further we go back in time, the more we must rely on archaeological and comparative evidence. The former sometimes give us quite a clear picture of the crops grown and technologies used, and a vaguer but still important sense of levels of trade and standards of living. In combination with comparative evidence for the energy yields of similar crops, technologies, trade, and lifestyles in well-documented modern contexts, we can get at least some idea of energy capture, and we can occasionally cross-check the results against entirely independent classes of evidence, such as records of pollution from ice cores and peat bogs.

Combining such diverse data is of course a challenge and calls for constant guesswork. On the one hand, this makes that it unlikely that experts will ever agree precisely on scores before 1900 CE in the East and 1700 CE in the West; but on the other hand, the evidence does establish parameters for energy capture in the past that no expert would question. No one, for instance, would suggest that energy capture in the cores of the West (roughly Iraq-Egypt) or East (the Yellow River) in 1000 CE was as high as it would be in the United States or Japan a thousand years later or, for that matter, as high as it would be in the cores in 1900, 1800, or even 1700 CE. Similarly, few experts would argue that Western energy capture in 1000 CE was as high as it had been under the Roman Empire a thousand years earlier, but almost all would agree that it was higher than during the Mediterranean "dark age" around 1000 BCE. In the East, most Chinese economic historians would probably agree that Eastern capture was higher under the Song dynasty in 1000 CE than it had been under the Han in 1 CE, and much higher than under the Western Zhou a millennium before that. Any conclusions that violate these expectations will call for close scrutiny.

Within certain limits we can certainly establish rough, ballpark figures for energy consumption; the important question is whether we can constrain the margins of error sufficiently to produce estimates that allow us to tell whether the best explanation for why the West rules is a long-term lock-in theory, a short-term accident theory, or some other kind of theory altogether.

ESTIMATES OF WESTERN ENERGY CAPTURE

Table 3.1, figure 3.2, and figure 3.3 show my estimates for Western energy capture since 14,000 BCE.

The best way to calculate energy capture in different periods is to proceed from the best to the least well known, so rather than starting in 14,000 BCE and moving continuously forward until 2000 CE I will begin my discussion in the present and work back to 1700 CE, then make two jumps backward, before filling in the gaps between

Table 3.1
Western energy capture, 14,000 BCE–2000 CE

Date	kcal/cap/day	Points	Date	kcal/cap/day	Points
14,000 BCE	4,000	4.36	500 BCE	23,000	25.06
13,000 BCE	4,000	4.36	400 BCE	24,000	26.15
12,000 BCE	4,500	4.90	300 BCE	26,000	28.33
11,000 BCE	5,000	5.45	200 BCE	27,000	29.42
10,000 BCE	5,000	5.45	100 BCE	29,000	31.06
9000 BCE	5,500	5.99	1 BCE/CE	31,000	33.78
8000 BCE	6,000	6.54	100 CE	31,000	33.78
7000 BCE	6,500	7.08	200 CE	30,000	32.69
6000 BCE	7,000	7.63	300 CE	29,000	31.60
5000 BCE	8,000	8.72	400 CE	28,500	31.06
4000 BCE	10,000	10.90	500 CE	28,000	30.51
3500 BCE	11,000	11.99	600 CE	26,000	28.33
3000 BCE	12,000	13.08	700 CE	25,000	27.24
2500 BCE	14,000	15.26	800 CE	25,000	27.24
2250 BCE	16,000	17.44	900 CE	25,000	27.24
2000 BCE	17,000	18.52	1000 CE	26,000	28.33
1750 BCE	19,000	20.65	1100 CE	26,000	28.33
1500 BCE	20,500	22.34	1200 CE	26,500	28.88
1400 BCE	21,000	22.88	1300 CE	27,000	29.42
1300 BCE	21,500	23.43	1400 CE	26,000	28.33
1200 BCE	21,000	22.88	1500 CE	27,000	29.42
1100 BCE	20,500	22.34	1600 CE	29,000	31.06
1000 BCE	20,000	21.79	1700 CE	32,000	34.87
900 BCE	20,500	22.34	1800 CE	38,000	41.41
800 BCE	21,000	22.88	1900 CE	92,000	100.00
700 BCE	21,500	23.43	2000 CE	230,000	250.00
600 BCE	22,000	23.97			

the three periods. The first jump is back to the classical Mediterranean world of roughly 500 BCE–200 CE, for which several economic historians have recently generated figures for consumption levels, and the second is back to the beginning of our story around 14,000 BCE, at which point (surprising as it may sound to nonarchaeologists) we can make fairly confident estimates about Late Ice Age hunter-gatherer consumption.

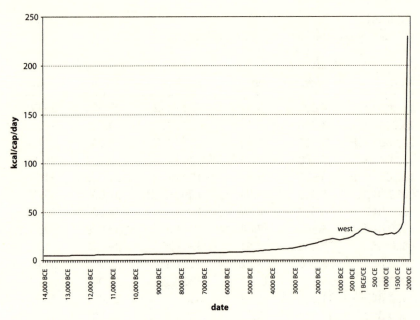

Figure 3.2. Western energy capture, 14,000 BCE–2000 CE, seen on a linear-linear scale.

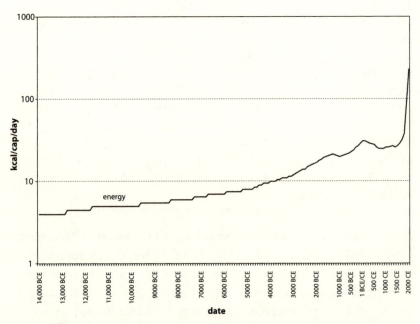

Figure 3.3. Western energy capture, 14,000 BCE–2000 CE, seen on a log-linear scale.

The Recent Past, 1700–2000 CE

High-quality statistics are available for 2000 CE, putting total food + nonfood per capita energy capture in the Western core (the United States) at about 230,000 kcal/cap/day.[13] Following the methods described in chapter 2, 230,000 kcal/cap/day—which is the highest level of energy capture known in history—gets the full complement of 250 points, meaning that each 920 kcal/cap/day scores 1 point on the index.

Our data are reasonably good for at least some aspects of the most advanced Western economies (around the northern shores of the Atlantic) in 1900 and even 1800. There are relatively rich data on industrial output in some parts of Europe going back to 1700,[14] but the major challenge is how to combine this information with the use of biomass for fuel, housing, clothing, and so on. The peasants who relied most heavily on biomass tended not to leave extensive textual records, which forces us to turn to estimates based on comparative evidence, cross-checked against qualitative evidence from literature and art. The qualitative evidence is often very rich,[15] but the need to bring these different sources together inevitably increases margins of error.

Combining figures for fossil and biomass fuels and population data from Maddison suggests that typical energy capture in the Western core was somewhere around 92,000 kcal/cap/day in 1900 and 38,000 kcal/cap/day in 1800.[16] By my rough estimate, the 92,000 kcal/cap/day in 1900 can be broken down into about 41,000 from fossil fuels, 8,000 as food/animal feed, and 43,000 from nonfood biomass, and the 38,000 kcal/cap/day in 1800 can be broken down into about 7,000 from fossil fuel, 6,000 as food/animal feed, and 25,000 from nonfood biomass. The figures of 92,000 kcal/cap/day in 1900 and 38,000 kcal/cap/day in 1800 neatly bracket Cook's estimate of 77,000 kcal/cap/day for advanced Western economies in 1860 and, insofar as such data can be made commensurate, seem consistent with the evidence of probate records and industrial archaeology for the increase in household goods.[17] The figures for 1800 and 1900 involve wider margins of error than the figure for

2000 but are consistent with the impressionistic historical literature on energy use and with Robert Allen's reconstructions of trends in real wages.[18]

My estimate of a 242 percent increase in per capita energy capture in the Western core between 1800 and 1900 is smaller than the well-established statistics for the growth of industrial output in the developed Euro-American core.[19] That is because estimates of industrial output normally leave biomass and muscle power out of the calculus completely, producing a misleading picture of overall energy capture. A significant slice of the nineteenth century's industrial output went toward replacing biomass and muscle, rather than simply adding to them, in the process allowing much higher population densities in the industrial core without producing environmental catastrophe.

When we look back before 1800 CE the uncertainties of course multiply, but strong constraints continue to apply to our estimates. Western energy capture clearly grew more slowly in the eighteenth century than in the nineteenth, but faster than in the seventeenth or sixteenth; and if Cook was correct that the advanced agriculturalists of the late Middle Ages were already capturing 26,000 kcal/cap/day, early modern Northwest Europeans around 1700 CE must have been consuming somewhere between 30,000 and 35,000 kcal/cap/day.

I base this guess of a roughly 5:4 ratio between energy capture in the Western core in 1700 and 1400 CE on the plentiful textual and archaeological evidence across the entire social spectrum for the improvement in the quality of housing, the increasing quality and variety of household goods, rising real wages in Northwest Europe, rising consumption of expensive calories, and the longer hours being worked.[20]

Angus Maddison estimated that Western European GDP/cap increased from $798 (expressed in Geary-Khamis dollars, a hypothetical unit with the same purchasing power as US$1 in 1990) to $1,032 between 1500 and 1700.[21] Several economists have argued that Maddison's numbers are underestimates,[22] but the general trend seems unmistakable—so long as we bear in mind that nearly all the gains seem to have been in nonfood calories. Adult stature, a robust indicator of levels of childhood nutrition,[23] was much the same in 1700 as in 1400 CE.[24]

My figure of 32,000 kcal/cap/day for 1700 CE is necessarily a guess, but I suspect that it is no more than 10 percent wide of the mark, for the following reasons:

1. If Northwest European consumption was already above 35,000 kcal/cap/day in 1700 CE but rose to only 38,000 in 1800, it is hard to explain where all the extra energy being consumed in industry and transport was coming from (as the economist Robert Allen has shown, real wages probably declined between 1750 and 1800 and then grew only slowly until 1830, thanks to massive profit taking and reinvestment by the new economic elites).[25]

2. If, on the other hand, Northwest European consumption remained below 30,000 kcal/cap/day in 1700 despite already having reached 26,000 by 1400, it would be hard to explain how trade, industry, agriculture, and forestry could have expanded as vigorously as we know they did across the fifteenth, sixteenth, and seventeenth centuries while energy capture grew so slowly.

3. If, to make room for Western consumption to have been below 30,000 kcal/cap/day in 1700 despite having risen sharply since 1400, we push the figure for 1400 down from 26,000 toward 20,000 kcal/cap/day, we would have to argue either (a) that the (by premodern standards) quite productive European societies of around 1400 CE were no more successful at energy capture than those of the southeast Mediterranean Bronze Age some three thousand years earlier, which seems unlikely, or (b) that energy capture around 1600 BCE was lower still, perhaps somewhere around 15,000 kcal/cap/day; which, in turn, would require us to depress earlier figures still further. Since we can fix a floor of at least 4,000 kcal/cap/day under post–Ice Age energy capture, pushing second-millennium BCE energy levels down to 15,000 kcal/cap/day makes it hard to explain the enormous differences in living standards between the substantial homes at sites like Ur around 1500 BCE and the very simple ones at sites like 'Ain Mallaha in Israel around 12,000 BCE.[26]

Figure 3.4 shows my estimates for modern times.

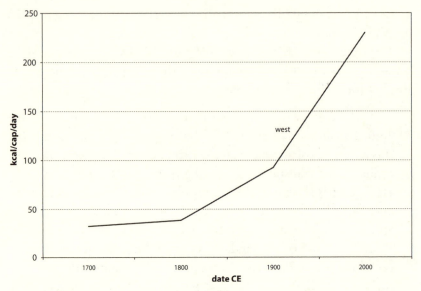

Figure 3.4. Western energy capture, 1700–2000 CE.

CLASSICAL ANTIQUITY (500 BCE–200 CE)

In the past few years several historians and economists have tried to quantify real wages and GDP/cap in the classical Mediterranean. These are not the same things as total energy capture as defined here, but the calculations are a very helpful step forward.

REAL WAGES

We have spotty but useful information on both wages and the prices of food in the ancient Mediterranean, and for a handful of times and places we can calculate how much wheat certain categories of people could afford to buy each day. In an important recent article, Walter Scheidel follows the example of the early modern historian Jan van Zanden in converting ancient wage data into a "wheat wage," representing the number of liters of wheat a worker could buy with one day's income.[27] Armed with that information and the fact that a liter of wheat (0.78 kg) contains 2,574 kcal of energy, we can calculate the energy capture represented by wage levels.

Scheidel shows that shortly before 400 BCE the real wages of an adult Athenian man bought more than 22,400 kcal/day, and by the 320s BCE the real wage had risen to the equivalent of somewhere between 33,500 and 40,000 kcal/day. These are extremely high figures, coming close to those for the eighteenth- or even early-nineteenth-century Western core.

Scheidel's figures for Roman Italy in the first few centuries CE vary much more, with wages in the city of Rome ranging from the equivalent of 15,500 kcal/day to more than 43,000 kcal/day, and those from Pompeii ranging from 12,000 kcal/day through 30,000 kcal/day. The average of these data points is about 25,000 kcal/day, but—as Scheidel points out—it is hard to put much confidence in this number, given the amount of variance.

These numbers represent a great step forward, but there are nevertheless two drawbacks to the real-wage approach to energy capture. First, as Scheidel himself stresses, the data points are so scattered that we rarely know how typical they are. There is only one case in ancient Western Eurasia, in Babylon between 385 and 61 BCE, where we have a really detailed series of price points for a range of commodities, and here prices fluctuated wildly.[28] Since we normally have to deal with single price points separated by centuries of silence, we could well be misunderstanding our sparse information.

Second, it is far from obvious exactly how the wage levels relate to total food + nonfood energy capture. We have wage information for only a few professions, and many people probably worked partly or largely outside the monetized economy, spending their lives in family farms or firms. In classical Athens, the wage data are dominated by state employment such as military pay and pay for holding public offices.[29] In these sectors the state acted as a monopsonist, making it is hard to say how pay levels related to the private sector.

The Roman data are not so badly skewed toward state pay,[30] but they too have their problems. We do not know how the undocumented professions compared to documented ones, what sources of income families normally had to supplement the wages that are mentioned in our texts, or how much of the typical family's energy capture came from biomass that lay completely outside the monetized economy.

GDP/CAP

A second approach is to calculate an ancient society's GDP and divide this by the size of its population, and several historians and economists have provided estimates for the Roman Empire in the first two centuries CE (table 3.2). This approach avoids some of the problems of real wages but adds new challenges of its own, most obviously that the calculations depend on a string of assumptions.[31] Scheidel and Friesen go so far as to concede that "[s]tudents of the Roman world who are unfamiliar with our approach might be tempted to dismiss this project as a tangled web of conjecture."[32]

The most important assumptions are estimates of minimum food needs, a "step up" to represent nonfood consumption, another to represent government spending, and guesses at the typical number

Table 3.2

Estimates of Roman GDP/capita

	kg wheat equivalent/ cap/yr	kcal/cap/ yr	kcal/cap/ day
Hopkins	491	1,620,000	4,438
Goldsmith, Maddison	843	2,780,000	7,616
			Italy only: 12,712
Temin	614	2,030,000	5,561
Goldsmith and Maddison as adjusted by Scheidel and Friesen	620	2,050,000	5,616 Italy only: 9,370
Egypt "bare bones," Scheidel and Friesen	390	1,290,000	3,534
Egypt "respectable," Scheidel and Friesen	940	3,100,000	8,493
Scheidel and Friesen	714	2,360,000	10,710
Diocletian's Price Edict of 301 CE, after Allen	204	670,000	1,836

Sources: Hopkins, "Taxes and Trade in the Roman Empire"; Goldsmith, "Estimate of the Size and Structure"; Maddison, *Contours of the World Economy*; Temin, "Estimating GDP"; Scheidel and Friesen, "Size of the Economy"; Allen, "How Prosperous Were the Romans?"

of workdays per year. Opinions differ on each of these numbers, with the result that estimates of GDP/cap in the first to second century CE range from the equivalent of 7,364 kcal/cap/workday suggested by the ancient historian Keith Hopkins, to the 12,636 kcal/cap/workday suggested by the economists Raymond Goldsmith and Angus Maddison.[33] Scheidel and Friesen themselves stress the need to operate with a range of estimates, but do offer 10,710 kcal/cap/workday as a summary figure (total output of 50 million twe/70 million people/220 workdays). Combining the estimation approach with data from Roman Egypt, they suggest the actual figure must lie between 5,864 and 14,091 kcal/cap/workday, and that several different approaches all converge on this same range.

These energy capture scores are considerably lower than those derived from real wages. There appear to be two reasons for this. First, the GDP/cap estimates apply to the whole Roman Empire, rather than the core region in Italy. This raises once again the "Pomeranz Problem" (see chapter 2 above) of unit selection. We need to focus on the most developed core within the West, in this case Italy. Maddison recognized this, suggesting that tax and tribute flows into Italy raised its NDI/cap two-thirds higher than that of the rest of the empire, which would push Maddison's estimate of Italian energy consumption to 12,712 kcal/cap/workday (or, following the adjustments that Scheidel and Friesen suggest to his scores, 9,370 kcal/cap/workday).[34]

This Italian score, however, is still lower than even the bottom end of the range of energy capture implied by Scheidel's real wages from Rome and Pompeii, and close to Cook's calculation for early agriculturalists (by which he meant Southwest Asian farmers around 5000 BCE). The explanation for this is that the "step up" used in all the proposed GDP figures underestimates very seriously the quantities of biomass used for fuel and construction, wind and waterpower, and raw materials in the Roman economy. Hopkins allowed just a 33 percent step up to cover seed and wastage, and even the highest estimate, by Goldsmith (shared by Maddison and Scheidel and Friesen), is only 75 percent. Comparative data on energy capture suggest that the true level must have been much higher.[35]

In his masterly studies of biomass energy, Vaclav Smil divides biomass fuels into two categories by energy density (table 3.3).[36] His

Table 3.3

Energy densities

Foodstuffs and fuels		Energy densities (MJ/kg)
Foodstuffs		
Very low	Vegetables, fruits	0.8–2.5
Low	Tubers, milk	2.5–5.0
Medium	Meats	5.0–12.0
High	Cereal and legume grains	12.0–15.0
Very high	Oils, animal fats	25.0–35.0
Fuels		
Very low	Peats, green wood, grasses	5.0–10.0
Low	Crop residues, air-dried wood	12.0–15.0
Medium	Bituminous coals	18.0–25.0
High	Charcoal, anthracites	28.0–32.0
Very high	Crude oils	40.0–44.0

Source: Derived from Smil, *General Energetics*.

"very low density" class (peats, green wood, grasses), yielding 5–10 MJ/kg (= 1,200–2,400 kcal/kg), and "low density" class (crop residues, air-dried wood), yielding 12–15 MJ/kg (= 2,880–3,600 kcal/kg), seem most relevant to ancient Rome. Coal use was not completely trivial in the Roman Empire, particularly in the northern provinces, but fossil fuels did remain marginal fuel sources.[37]

We of course have no statistics on biomass fuel use in the Roman Empire, but we do have some suggestive comparative evidence. Twentieth-century CE tropical hunter-gatherer groups often got by with less than 500 kg/cap/yr of biomass fuel, most of which presumably consisted of very-low-density types, representing perhaps something like 1,300–2,600 kcal/cap/day. Farming societies in colder climates often used as much biomass fuel as 2.5 tons/cap/yr, presumably mixing the low and very low categories; a 50/50 low/very low mix would generate 12,329–22,191 kcal/cap/day. The advanced organic economies of eighteenth-century Northwest Europe and North America used 3–6 tons/cap/yr. If we again assume a 50/50 split between low- and very-low-density fuels, that would be something like 21,699–43,397 kcal/cap/day.[38]

These data for biomass fuel use in other societies are consistent with Cook's nonfood estimate of 20,000 kcal/cap/day for advanced agriculturalists in late medieval Western Europe. The most important question is where the economies of the ancient Mediterranean fit within this range, and to answer that we must turn to archaeology.

ARCHAEOLOGICAL EVIDENCE

The archaeological approach involves starting from the actual material remains left by ancient attempts to capture energy, in the form of human and animal bones, carbonized seeds, pollen, houses, artifacts, and chemical traces of pollution. This ground-up approach is much messier than the more stylized real-wage and GDP/cap approaches, but it is also more empirical. Most important, it produces finer-grained pictures than the very abstract GDP/capita approach and suggests that both the real wage and the GDP/capita methods seriously underestimate energy capture in premodern societies.

The archaeological evidence confirms the impression of the real wage numbers that fourth-century BCE Greeks enjoyed high energy capture by premodern standards.[39] Their diet was relatively good, with a generally rather low meat content, although this varied significantly from site to site.[40] Olives, wine, fruit, garlic, and fish made quite large contributions, although fish consumption varied as much from one site to another as did meat consumption.[41] Food consumption was not enough to push average adult male stature much above 168 cm,[42] but given the quantities of "expensive" calories, typical Greek intake of food energy must have been relatively high by premodern Mediterranean standards, perhaps reaching 4,000–5,000 kcal/cap/day.

The good classical Greek diet (and population growth) might be partly explained by a decline in solar activity, driving the shift from a Sub-Boreal to the Sub-Atlantic climate regime after 800 BCE, and bringing cooler, wetter weather to the Mediterranean, to the benefit of dry-grain farmers reliant on winter rainfall. The most recent synthesis of eighty studies from the east Mediterranean, however, reveals extraordinary levels of regional variation and only a mild pattern of change between about 800 and 200 BCE.[43]

Whatever the role of climate, behavioral changes in Greece do also seem to have played a part. Since the 1980s, survey archaeologists have realized that older models of Greek agriculture, seeing it as inefficient and risk averse, simply could not be correct, because an agricultural system of this kind could not have generated enough food to support the population densities known from the classical Greek world.[44]

The evidence of settlement patterns and excavated farmsteads may indicate a shift between 500 and 200 BCE toward intensively worked blocks of contiguous land, making heavy use of manure and often producing for the market, obtaining yields from dry-grain farming that would not be matched again until at least the nineteenth century.[45] Pollen data support this, with peaks for cereal and olive production in the period circa 500–200 BCE not only in Greece but also all across the east Mediterranean and as far into Asia as western Iran.[46]

Classical Greek houses were large and comfortable, typically having 240–320 m² of roofed space. The evidence for house prices is disputed,[47] but an average house probably cost 1,500–3,000 drachmas at a time when a 5,000 kcal daily diet cost about half a drachma — meaning that an average house represented 15–30 million kcal. Amortized out over a thirty-year lifespan, that represented close to 1,375–2,750 kcal/day. (There is no way to know what Greek expectations about the lifetime of a house were, but thirty years seems roughly consistent with the rate of rebuilding observed on archaeological sites.)

It is harder to quantify the per capita energy consumption represented by the kilns, furnaces, workshops, and so on that produced all the artifacts we find in Greek houses, or by the temples, fortifications, arms and armor, warships, public buildings, private monuments, roads, harbors, artworks, and countless other categories of objects archaeologists have recovered, or by the transport costs of bringing much of the food Greeks ate from farms as far away as Ukraine and Egypt. However, comparing the quality of housing and sheer abundance of artifacts on classical Greek settlements (e.g., Olynthus, destroyed in 348 BCE and published in great detail) with those in medieval or early modern Northern European settlements in Northern Europe (e.g., Wharram Percy in England) and, *a forti-*

ori, those in medieval and early modern Greece gives a good sense of the high material standard of life enjoyed by classical Greeks.[48]

It is also striking that classical Greece supported not just relatively high levels of nonfood consumption but also high population densities around the Aegean Sea in the fourth century BCE. In several parts of Greece, the densities of the fourth century BCE would not be equaled until the twentieth century CE, and the simple fact that so many Greeks lived in towns or small cities, rather than hamlets or farms, must mean that their energy capture reached unusual heights.[49] In an important paper, Geof Kron has used the housing evidence to suggest that in many respects, the typical Greek actually lived better than the typical eighteenth-century Briton.[50]

The Greek archaeological data point clearly toward high (by premodern standards) energy capture; I suggest a figure somewhere between 20,000 and 25,000 kcal/cap/day in the fourth century BCE (most likely closer to the upper than to the lower figure), having risen sharply from a "dark age" level closer to 16,000 kcal/cap/day between 1000 and 800 BCE.[51]

The copious Roman evidence suggests that energy capture in first- to second-century CE Italy was even higher than that in fourth-century BCE Greece. The level of agricultural yields remains disputed, although output in irrigated Egyptian agriculture seems to have been extremely high by premodern standards.[52] Quantitative studies of consumption—including everything from animal bones in settlements to numbers of shipwrecks, levels of lead and tin pollution generated by industrial activity, the scale of deforestation, frequencies of public inscriptions on stone, numbers of coins in circulation, and quantities of archaeological finds along the German frontier—also point the same way: per capita energy capture in the Mediterranean world increased strongly during the first millennium BCE, peaked somewhere between 100 BCE and 200 CE, then fell again in the mid-first millennium CE.[53] Figure 3.5 illustrates the tight fit between the rise and fall of shipwrecks (normally taken as a proxy for the scale of maritime trade) and levels of lead pollution in the well-dated deposits at Penidho Velho in Spain.

Each category of material has its own difficulties,[54] but no single argument can explain away the striking increase in evidence for nonfood consumption across the first millennium BCE and the peak in

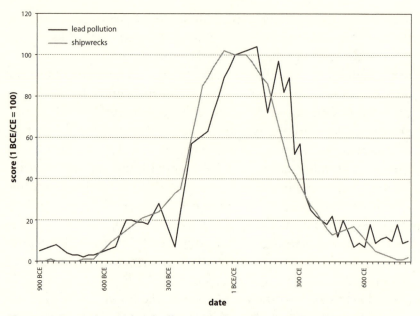

Figure 3.5. Economic growth and collapse in the first millennia BCE and CE, as documented by shipwrecks and lead pollution. *Sources*: Parker, *Ancient Shipwrecks*; Kylander et al., "Refining the Preindustrial."

the first two centuries CE. The shipwreck data and the vast garbage dumps of transport pottery surrounding the city of Rome (a single one of which, at Monte Testaccio, contains the remains of 25 million pots, used to ship 200 million gallons of olive oil)[55] also attest to the use of nonfood energy to increase food supply and the extraordinary level of consumption of "expensive" food calories. Some scholars also identify an increase in stature in the first to second century CE, although others are more pessimistic, suggesting that adult male Romans in early imperial Italy were typically under 165 cm tall, which would make them shorter than Iron Age or medieval Italians.[56] More evidence—and more consistent application of statistical techniques—should resolve the question, and we must look forward to the appearance of Geertje Klein-Goldewijk's database of Roman skeletons.

As in Greece, the housing evidence may be the most informative, and Robert Stephan and Geof Kron are now collecting and analyzing this material.[57] Data from Egypt and Italy already suggest that by the first centuries CE typical Roman houses were even bigger than classical Greek houses had been, and that sophisticated (by premodern standards) plumbing, drainage, roofs, and foundations spread far down the social ladder.[58]

The explosion of material goods on Roman sites is even more striking. Mass production of wheel-made, well-fired pottery, amphoras for wine and olive oil, and base-metal ornaments and tools reached unprecedented levels in the first few centuries CE.[59] Similarly, distribution maps show that by 200 CE trade networks were more extensive and denser than they would be again until at least the seventeenth century.[60] The scale of trade with India, far outside the empire's formal boundaries, is particularly impressive.[61]

The archaeological data suggest that the real-wage and particularly the GDP/cap approaches to the Roman economy underestimate energy use in the Roman core. All of the GDP/cap calculations to date have begun with human physiological requirements for food calories and added an arbitrary "step up" for nonfood consumption, taking neither the comparative evidence for biomass energy nor the archaeological evidence for the extraordinary surge in nonfood consumption into consideration. As noted in the "GDP/cap" section above, the largest step up that has been proposed has been 75 percent, but the comparative evidence suggests that even this is too low for a complex agrarian economy.

Cook concluded that even in a "normal" advanced agricultural economy the step up should be well over 300 percent,[62] and the archaeological evidence makes it clear that Roman Italy between about 200 BCE and 200 CE was anything but a "normal" advanced agricultural economy. There is no way at present to be very precise about the step up, but the archaeological evidence suggests to me that it was considerably larger than in classical Greece. I suspect that it was more like 400 percent, suggesting total energy capture of about 31,000 kcal/cap/day in the Roman core by the first century CE.

This estimate puts energy capture in the Roman core around 100 CE just slightly behind that in the Northwest European core in 1700 CE. This is a more optimistic assessment of the Roman economy than the GDP/cap estimates imply, but would resolve some inconsistencies between the different ways of looking at the Roman economy. Maddison's figures suggest that the Roman Empire in the first few centuries CE compares best with Northwest Europe around

1500 CE, although he then goes on to point out that Roman urbanization levels are in fact much closer to West European levels around 1700 CE than those around 1500. Similarly, while Scheidel and Friesen conclude that the empire-wide Roman economy in the second century CE lacked the sophistication of the Dutch economy around 1580–1600 CE or the English around 1680–1700, they do note that performance may have been better in the Italian core. The economist Paolo Malanima reaches similar conclusions.[63]

I know of only two other attempts to calculate total Roman energy capture in the terms I am using here. The first is Vaclav Smil's analysis in his book *Why America Is Not a New Rome*.[64] This book aimed to highlight the differences between the contemporary United States and ancient Rome, one of which, Smil quite rightly emphasizes, is an enormous gap in energy capture. However, in trying to demonstrate this very valid point, Smil offers what seem to me implausibly low estimates of Roman energy use. He suggests that contemporary American energy use is thirty to fifty times higher than Roman, which would set Roman total energy capture somewhere between 4,600 and 7,700 kcal/cap/day; if we assume that roughly 2,000 kcal/cap/day of this was food (which means ignoring the archaeological evidence for relatively high levels of expensive calories from meat, oil, and wine), that leaves just 2,600–5,700 kcal/cap/day to cover all other energy consumption. To justify this estimate, Smil suggests that Roman fuel use was just 180–200 kg of wood equivalent per capita per year, or roughly 1,750–2,000 kcal/cap/day.

It is impossible to reconcile these numbers with the archaeological evidence for Roman consumption or the levels of Roman-era lead pollution in bogs, ice cores, and lakebeds. Smil's numbers are also incompatible with his own data on premodern biomass use in his book *Energy in World History*.[65] Smil's estimates for Rome would group its energy capture with some of the simplest agricultural societies on record. My own estimates and Lo Cascio and Malanima's calculations place peak Roman energy capture (ca. 100 CE) alongside Northwest Europe's in 1700 CE, while Maddison's and Scheidel and Friesen's place it closer to sixteenth-century Northwest Europe's.[66] However, Smil's suggestion in *Why America Is Not a New Rome* that Roman nonfood energy capture was just 2,600–5,700 kcal/cap/day would set the Roman level at barely one-eighth of Smil's own estimate for eighteenth-century Northwest European energy capture (21,700–43,400 kcal/cap/day) in *Energy in World History*, and closer to hunter-gatherers than to early-modern farmers. All the other classes of evidence make this seem much too low.

The second discussion is Paolo Malanima's in his paper "Energy Consumption and Energy Crisis in the Roman World," delivered at a conference at the American Academy in Rome in 2011.[67] An appendix to this paper directly responds to my arguments in *Why the West Rules—For Now*, arguing that Roman energy capture peaked between 6,000 and 11,000 kcal/cap/day. This is roughly twice as high as Smil's estimate, but less than one-third as high as mine.

Some of the differences between our calculations are definitional. As noted above, different kinds of food energy have different costs; it typically takes about 10 kcal of feed to produce 1 kcal of meat, which means that periods that see shifts toward meat consumption also see an increase in per capita energy consumption. Someone living off bread and water may put the same number of kilocalories of food energy into his or her mouth as someone living off steak and champagne, but the steak/champagne diet represents a much higher overall level of energy consumption. The archaeological evidence shows that Roman times saw a great increase in the costs of most people's diets. This was most spectacular at Rome itself, where the explosion in consumption of wine and olive oil produced Monte Testaccio; but even the humblest village sites produce striking evidence of the shift toward more expensive food calories, which involved tens of millions of people. While ordinary Romans did not have steak-and-champagne diets, they did at least get olive oil and imported wine.

Malanima also excludes the energy content of the materials used in construction, industry, and transport. Through most of the pre-Roman era, this definitional difference would not have a huge impact on the calculations, since construction, industry, and transport remained very simple; but the archaeological evidence once again shows unambiguously that one of the greatest contrasts between Roman and pre-Roman times was the expansion of activity in all these areas.

Malanima's definitional decisions consistently produce lower energy capture scores than mine, and the difference is increased further by his preference for low estimates when—as is very often the case—there seems to be a range of plausible guesses (for instance, on the numbers of draft animals and therefore the amount of feed consumed by them per person in the Roman Empire, or on the amount of wood consumed per person). These disagreements combine to yield a big difference in the size of the "step up" each of us would add to the food energy being consumed.

If the argument were purely definitional, it would not be very significant: since both Malanima and I have done our best to be explicit, readers could choose which index to use, depending on the question they wanted to answer. However, Malanima also suggests that the figures I reach for the Roman Empire must be exaggerated. He suggests that my figures would mean that Romans had access to more energy than did many nineteenth-century Europeans, and also that energy intensity (the ratio between energy consumption and GDP, or basically the dollars earned per kcal expended) would have been twice as high in the early Roman Empire as in Western Europe in 1800 CE.

Malanima reaches this conclusion by comparing my 31,000 kcal/cap/day estimate of energy consumption in the Roman heartland to his own estimate that Europeans were capturing only about 15,000 kcal/cap/day in 1800 CE. This is much lower than the figure of 38,000 kcal/cap/day for the Western European core around 1800 CE that I derive from Cook, Smil, and Maddison's calculations because throughout the period up to the nineteenth century, Malanima defines energy capture more narrowly than Cook or I have done. As a result, Malanima's pre-1900 CE scores are consistently about half of those in my calculations or Earl Cook's,[68] and comparing my energy capture figure for 100 CE to his own for 1800 CE produces nonsensical results. Our pictures certainly do differ—by Malanima's calculations, the average person in the Western core was consuming roughly 75 percent more energy in 1800 than in 100 CE;[69] by mine, that person was consuming 25 percent more energy—but the absurd outcome that Malanima ascribes to my scores, with energy being cheaper in the Roman Empire than in the British, is simply the result of his insistence on directly comparing results derived from indices that define the terms differently.

I see two ways to interpret the differences between my energy calculations and Malanima's. First, we might just treat the definitional disagreements as being two different ways to think about the data, with Malanima's definitions leading to low results and mine to high ones. The interesting thing about our results would then be how similar the general pictures are. Malanima and I agree that the old picture of steadily rising energy use in Europe between the Middle Ages and the industrial revolution is mistaken; energy capture fell along the with Roman Empire, and as late as 1700 CE Europeans were still only just catching up with Roman levels. Even when we come to the twentieth century, our pictures are rather similar. In the Western core, as I define it, consumption jumped from 92,000 kcal/cap/day in 1900 CE to 230,000 in 2000 (a factor of 2.5); in Western Europe, as Malanima defines it, consumption jumped from 41,500 kcal/cap/day in 1900 CE to 100,000 in 2000 (a factor of 2.4).

However, this way of comparing Malanima's calculations and mine would overlook the big contrast between them. As I suggested in the previous paragraph, when we look only at the past two thousand years, the two approaches produce rather similar pictures. However, when we look at the whole run of history going back to the end of the last ice age, the pictures differ much more. Malanima's figures imply that per capita energy capture must have roughly doubled (from about 4,000 kcal/cap/day, the lowest level needed to maintain viable populations, to about 8,500 kcal/cap/day) between the age of Lascaux and that of Monte Testaccio, while mine suggest that it grew seven- or eightfold, to 31,000 kcal/cap/day.

Malanima does not go as far as Gregory Clark, who, as mentioned above, argues that "the average person in the world of 1800 [CE] was no better off than the average person of 100,000 BC." However, Malanima's numbers imply that the rate of increase in energy capture averaged just 0.005 percent per annum in the past fourteen millennia BCE. The growth rate implied by my figures, of 0.02 percent per annum, is hardly meteoric, but it provides a very different—and, I would say, more realistic—perspective on premodern economic growth.

Earlier in this chapter I observed that economists interested in the Roman world usually try to reconstruct either real wages or

GDP/cap, and only rarely concern themselves with the messy details of the archaeological record. One consequence of this is that they often seem not to have a very clear sense of the gulf that separated the Roman world from prehistoric societies. The assumptions Malanima makes about what to measure and how to measure it fail to capture the contrasts between life in imperial Rome, life in a ten-thousand-year-old agricultural town like Jericho, and life in a hundred-thousand-year-old site like Pinnacle Point in South Africa. Looking at the history of energy over the very long run requires a fuller confrontation with the archaeological record and methods like those pioneered by Earl Cook, which are far more sensitive than Malanima's to the kinds of energy flows that mattered most in prehistoric and ancient societies.

Conclusion

Per capita energy capture increased across the first millennium BCE, peaking somewhere around 30,000 kcal/cap/day in the first century CE. By premodern standards this was an extremely high level, close to that of the Western core around 1700 CE, although by modern standards it remained very low, probably never reaching even 15 percent of contemporary American levels. Figure 3.6 shows my estimates for the ancient (500 BCE–200 CE) and modern (1700–2000 CE) periods.

Between Ancient and Modern (200–1700 CE)

The next challenge is to bridge the long gap between ancient Mediterranean and early modern European data. I divide the fifteen-hundred-year period into three phases: (a) 200–700, (b) 700–1300, and (c) 1300–1700.

200–700 CE

Figure 3.5 indicates a profound, centuries-long decline in industrial and commercial activity in this first phase, suggesting that energy capture also fell.

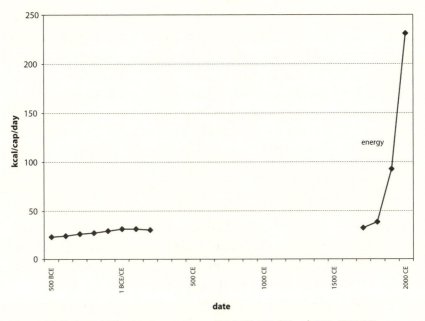

Figure 3.6. Estimated Western energy capture, 500 BCE–200 CE and 1700–2000 CE.

In principle, a famous edict on prices and wages set up by the Roman emperor Diocletian in 301 CE ought to provide a starting point by allowing us to reconstruct real wages at the start of the fourth century, but in practice there are serious difficulties. Scheidel calculated that the real wage for unskilled workers implied by the edict was just 9,376 kcal/cap/day, down from roughly 25,000 kcal/day (but with a very wide variance of ± 12,000 kcal/day) in first-to-second century CE Italy. Robert Allen's calculations, however, suggest a real wage worth just 1,439 kcal/cap/day, as low as the most depressed regions in eighteenth-century Europe, which would be hard to sustain for any length of time even if 100 percent of the wages were spent on food. The edict certainly seems to suggest that real wages fell between 150 and 301 CE, but Scheidel and Friesen are probably right to urge that we treat its figures as wishful thinking, diverging significantly from real-world prices.[70]

Several recent surveys of the archaeological evidence reinforce the impression of falling energy capture between 200 and 700 CE, although they also show that the details and pace of change varied wildly from region to region.[71] Some new forms of energy capture, such as moldboard plows and water mills, became more common after 200, especially on the Roman core's otherwise rather backward northern fringe; but the general trend ran strongly in the other direction.

Until specialists in late Roman archaeology quantify the evidence more precisely, it will be difficult to make accurate estimates, but between 200 and 700 the general picture is of large houses of stone and brick being replaced by smaller structures of wood and clay; paved streets being replaced by mud paths; sewers and aqueducts stopping working; life expectancy, stature, and population size falling, and the surviving people moving from cities to villages; long-distance trade declining; plain, handmade pottery replacing slipped, wheel-made wares; wood and bone tools being used more often, and metal ones less; factories going out of business and village craftsmen or household producers taking their places.[72]

I suggest in *Why the West Rules—For Now* that energy capture began declining in the Western core in the 160s CE when population movements across the steppes merged microbes from previously distinct Eastern and Western Eurasian disease pools.[73] Figure 3.5 suggests that the disruptions set off by this so-called Antonine Plague had already begun driving energy capture down before 200 CE.[74] The third century certainly saw decline, especially in the western parts of the Roman Empire, as the climate began deteriorating;[75] but a second wave of collapse beginning in the fifth century had much more profound results. As early as 450 CE a steep decline in material well-being can be seen in Britain in the far northwest. By 500 it is also clear in Gaul; by 600 in Italy and Spain; and by 700 it had engulfed North Africa and the Byzantine heartland around the Aegean.

The wave of collapse that rolled from northwest to southeast between 400 and 700 often generated complicated patterns, as witnessed by the recent archaeobotanical study of a sixth-century latrine complex at Sagalassos in western Anatolia, which revealed an apparently contradictory combination of more intensive agriculture and the breakdown of the urban fabric.[76] Over its three-century course, however, the overall effects are unmistakable. The Western core contracted geographically, and as it shrank onto Egypt, Syria, and Iraq, its smaller scale corresponded to lower per capita levels of energy capture.

That said, we should recognize that the decline in energy capture in the Western core between 200 and 700 was not catastrophic. Irrigation systems, cities, and rudimentary states remained intact in Egypt and Iraq, and the Arab conquests may have stimulated increases in agricultural productivity.[77] Elsewhere, even in the darkest days (such as the sixth century in Italy or the seventh in Anatolia) people went on gathering wood, cooking dinner, and doing most of the same things that they had done in the heyday of the Roman Empire. However, their overall energy capture definitely declined. Recent stable isotope analyses from England, for example, show that very simple, monotonous cereal diets replaced the more varied Roman-era diets in the seventh century.[78]

In the present state of the evidence, we can only bandy around impressionistic guesses based on the pictures created by specific excavation reports. My own impressionistic guess is that energy capture perhaps fell about 10 percent between 200 and 500 CE (from about 31,000 kcal/cap/day in the core to about 28,000 kcal/cap/day) and then a further 10 percent, to about 25,000 kcal/cap/day, between 500 and 700. Egyptian and Iraqi per capita energy levels probably fell little, if at all, between 200 and 700,[79] but the collapse of Italy, North Africa, and southern Gaul resulted in energy capture in the West's most developed core area being 20 percent lower in 700 than it had been in 200 CE.

This is a much less dramatic collapse than figure 3.5 would seem to indicate (the reason being that figure 3.5 probably reflects chiefly those nonfood and expensive food kilocalories that changed most), but it might still seem like an excessive suggestion to some Roman historians. Through the nineteenth century and much of the twentieth century, historians had tended to agree that Edward Gibbon had got the main outlines of the story of late antiquity correct, but in the 1960s critics reacted against this view. According to the most important revisionist, Peter Brown, "It is too easy to write about the Late Antique world [of 200–700] as if it were merely a melancholy tale of 'Decline and Fall.'" Instead of Gibbon's gloomy picture, Brown claimed, "we are increasingly aware of the astounding new beginnings associated with this period . . . we have become extremely sensitive to the 'contemporary' quality of . . . so much that a sensitive European has come to regard as most 'modern' and valuable in his own culture."[80]

Brown's goal was to remind historians that the decline-and-fall narrative should not obscure the complex and fascinating reality of late antique cultural change, but after three decades of reminders, many historians have now gone to the other extreme. "There is now a widespread conviction," Andrea Giardina has observed, "that . . . concepts such as 'decline' or 'decadence' are ideologically charged and consequently misleading."[81] Brown was quite right that we should see the period 200–700 as the time of the transformation of classical into early medieval culture, but too many historians have allowed this new perspective to blind them to the fact that this was also an era of political and economic collapse. The strategist Edward Luttwak has recently observed that "the newly fashionable vision of an almost peaceful immigration and a gradual transformation into a benign late antiquity is contradicted by the detailed evidence of violence, destruction, and the catastrophic loss of material amenities and educational attainments that would not be recovered for a thousand years, if then."[82] I find little to disagree with in this conclusion.[83]

The best antidote to the gradualist model that has become popular since the 1960s is simply to compare site reports and survey data for virtually any part of the Roman Empire in the second century CE with those for the same region in the seventh century CE.[84] Every site (even in Egypt, which weathered the storm better than any other part of the Roman Empire) reveals falling material standards of living and energy capture.

700–1300 CE

While there can be little doubt that there was a general slow upward trend in energy capture in the Western core across these six hundred years, the details are difficult to pin down, largely because historians and archaeologists of the medieval Muslim world have paid less attention to energy capture than those of classical antiquity.[85]

By 700 the Western core had contracted to the Egypt-Syria-Iraq region. There is some evidence that energy capture was falling in Syria by the eighth or ninth century and in Iraq by the ninth or tenth century,[86] and across the whole of Southwest Asia by the time of the eleventh-century Seljuk invasions, but it seems to have remained high in Egypt throughout the period 700–1300 and to have risen in Spain. Christian Europe definitely saw a vigorous economic revival after 900, and by 1300 the richest area, Italy, was catching up with the Islamic core in Egypt.

The Byzantine Empire also saw rapid economic recovery in the tenth century, and in a valuable paper, the economist Branko Milanovic has used the relatively rich sources to calculate that the average real wage of unskilled workers in the Byzantine heartland around 1000 CE was roughly $680 per year (PPP in 1990 Geary-Khamis international dollars).[87] Like the Roman GDP/cap calculations, this figure considers little except food calories, and Milanovic allows a particularly small "step up" for nonfood income.[88] He does, however, observe that the figure he reaches for Byzantine GDP/cap is roughly 20 percent lower than most estimates for GDP/cap in the early Roman Empire and 20–25 percent higher than Jan Luiten van Zanden's calculation for English incomes in 1086 and Gregory Clark's for English builders in the early thirteenth century.[89] All these GDP/cap studies use similar methods, suggesting that even if the absolute numbers understate levels of energy capture, the relative shifts over time may accurately reflect the realities.

Extrapolating from these comparisons by making a bigger "step up" for nonfood calories, I suggest that if energy capture in the first-century CE Roman core was about 31,000 kcal/cap/day, in Byzantium around 1000 CE it was about 26,000 kcal/cap/day; and if Milanovic is correct in following Robert Lopez's suggestion that Byzantine and Abbasid energy levels were rather similar around 1000 CE, the score for the Western core as a whole should also be 26,000 kcal/cap/day, with energy capture on the distant periphery in early-second-millennium England around 21,000 kcal/cap/day.[90] If anything, the comparison between Roman and Byzantine GDP/cap and real wages might slightly underestimate the overall decline in energy capture between 100 and 1000 CE because the decline probably affected nonfood calories much more than food calories, and the Goldsmith/Maddison/Milanovic estimates largely ignore these nonfood calories.

If this chain of inferences is justified, we must conclude that energy capture in the Western core increased only very slightly, from 25,000 to 26,000 kcal/cap/day, between 700 and 1000 CE. The weakness of the archaeological evidence makes it difficult to test this, al-

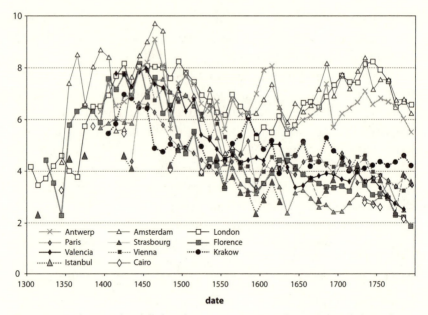

Figure 3.7. Real wages of unskilled workers, 1300–1800 CE. After Pamuk, "Black Death," 297, fig. 2.

though the numbers certainly seem consistent with finds from Greece.[91] I suggest that energy capture in the core remained fairly flat at about 25,000 kcal/cap/day between 700 and 900, and then started rising in the tenth century, to 26,000 kcal/cap/day in 1000, before reaching perhaps 27,000 kcal/cap/day by 1300. The archaeological evidence from Europe seems consistent with this, with clear signs of increasing household inventories, more substantial homes, more trade, and much more state spending.[92] Even on the distant Polish periphery, diets were much richer and more varied by the eleventh and twelfth centuries than previously,[93] but Italy seems to have remained the richest part of Europe.

The impossibility of making direct archaeological comparisons between thirteenth-century Italy and Egypt is frustrating, but the real wage data collected by the economic historian Sevket Pamuk suggest that by 1300 wages (and presumably energy capture as a whole) in northern Italy were probably catching up with those in Egypt and were ahead of those in Byzantium; and by 1400 Italy had pulled ahead of Egypt too (figure 3.7).[94]

1300–1700 CE

If these estimates for energy capture in the Middle Ages and modern times are roughly correct, then the period 1300–1700 must have seen an increase of roughly 23 percent in the Western core, from about 26,000 kcal/cap/day to about 32,000 kcal/cap/day. This would be faster than in any other period of the same length except for 400–1 BCE, which saw a 29 percent increase (24,000 kcal/cap/day to 31,000 kcal/cap/day). The similarities between the rates of increase and overall scores in ancient and early modern times suggest that the fondness of historians for drawing analogies between these periods may not be misplaced.

Quite detailed series of real wages are now available for many European cities since the later Middle Ages.[95] These suggest a general decline in wages for unskilled labor across the thirteenth and early fourteenth centuries followed by a great surge after 1350, when the Black Death increased land:labor ratios. As population grew in the later fifteenth and sixteenth centuries real wages generally fell, but by 1600 a gap was opening between wages in Northwest Europe, which were trending back up, and those in Southern and Eastern Europe, which continued to decline. By 1700 real wages for the unskilled in Amsterdam were 30 percent higher than they had been in 1350 and those in London were 80 percent higher. Both these increases are larger than those for energy capture mentioned in the previous paragraph.

Angus Maddison's estimates of GDP/cap give a rather different picture for the period 1500–1700.[96] Maddison calculated that productivity continued to increase everywhere in Western Europe except Italy across the sixteenth century; as he saw it, Holland and Britain took the lead by 1700 not because their growth revived in the seventeenth century while other regions went backward but because they grew even faster than other European economies. He identified a 29 percent increase in Western European productivity between 1500 and 1700.

The difference between these pictures of real wages and GDP/cap, like those between these measures in ancient times, is largely to be explained by the fact that they are measuring rather different things.[97] The inability of Western European lords to reassert their authority after the Black Death caused a major shift in resources toward the poor, driving real wages up much faster than productivity; and as population rose in the sixteenth century, power shifted back toward the aristocracy and real wages declined even though GDP/cap continued to rise.[98]

The century-long surge in real wages after 1350 also obscures the evidence for a broader fourteenth-century depression,[99] afflicting many dimensions of trade and industry. Research in the 1990s showed that this was not as severe as some earlier historians had believed,[100] but the calamities and uncertainties of the fourteenth century nonetheless do seem to have driven energy capture down. I suggest a small decline from 27,000 kcal/cap/day in 1300 to 26,000 in 1400, but in the absence of quantified archaeological evidence from settlements, this can only be a guess.

The archaeological evidence for rising energy capture between 1300 and 1700 is very clear, and seems consistent with the 23 percent increase suggested above, although it is not detailed enough to allow a test of my suggestion that levels fell 1,000 kcal/cap/day during the fourteenth century. The evidence for rising agricultural yields in Northwest Europe is strong,[101] as is textual and material documentation of the enormous increase in fishing catches and the expansion into new fishing grounds in the thirteenth and fourteenth centuries under pressure from growing urban populations.[102]

The increase in food calories was still not enough to affect adult stature noticeably, but in nonfood calories the changes were more striking, especially after 1500.[103] Details in wills and legal suits as well as excavated remains all suggest that in town and country alike, Western Europeans had bigger, more sophisticated houses and a wider range of material goods in 1700 than they had had in 1300.[104] Industrial production was rising, people were working longer hours, and fossil fuels such as peat and coal were beginning to contribute enormous amounts of energy.[105] While precise comparisons necessarily remain speculative, Northwest European energy capture per capita probably overtook the Roman peak (ca. 100 CE) during the seventeenth century.

Figure 3.8 shows the complete sequence of estimates from 500 BCE through 2000 CE.

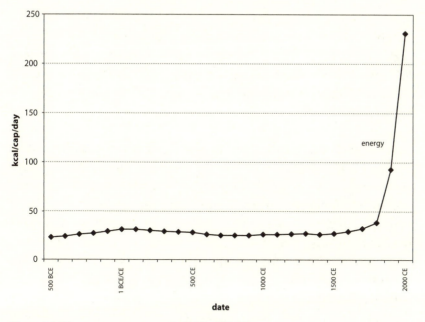

Figure 3.8. Western energy capture, 500 BCE–2000 CE.

Late Ice Age Hunter-Gatherers (ca. 14,000 BCE)

Surprising as it may seem, we are on a sounder footing with estimates of energy capture at the end of the Ice Age than in any subsequent era until the eighteenth century. Although thousands of years have passed since farmers drove the last foragers out of the initial Western core in the Hilly Flanks, and although the climate and ecology of the region have changed dramatically, comparative studies fix the parameters of possible energy capture fairly precisely.

The well-established fields of bioenergetics and primate ecology provide a good picture of energy use among the great apes,[106] our nearest evolutionary neighbors, and economic anthropologists have measured energy capture among contemporary foragers everywhere from hot African environments to cold Siberian ones.[107]

The earliest known species of *Homo* living in East Africa between 2.5 and 1.8 mya had energy needs similar to those of chimpanzees, but the evidence is fairly good that *Homo habilis* ate meat more often than chimpanzees do,[108] and they may even have become active hunters rather than scavengers. It typically takes about 10 kcal of chemical energy, photosynthesized by plants from solar energy, to produce 1 kcal of kinetic energy in an animal, so *Homo habilis* was already substituting expensive calories for cheap ones. Even so, with their small bodies and brains and simple material culture, *Homo habilis* probably required on average only something like 1,500 kcal/cap/day.

Energy capture probably increased significantly with the evolution of *Homo erectus/ergaster* in East Africa around 1.8 mya. Brain size increased by roughly 40 percent (from 610 to 870 cc), body weight by 75 percent (from 35 to 62 kg), and stature by nearly 50 percent (from 1.15 to 1.7 m).[109] *Homo erectus/ergaster* may have been able to make fire at will, greatly increasing their nonfood energy capture and transforming their food in ways that allowed them to absorb more of its calories.[110] Because the archaeological record before about 50 kya is so flimsy, the evidence is disputed, but recent finds at Gesher Benot Ya'aqov in Israel strongly suggest that *Homo erectus/ergaster* had mastered fire by 790 kya.[111] If cooking food by releasing energy from wood had become a commonplace strategy, total energy capture among *Homo erectus/ergaster* may have risen as high as 2,000 kcal/cap/day.

As proto-humans moved north of the line 40° N, they would have been forced to increase energy capture to deal with the colder climate. There is good evidence for regular fire making 400 kya at Beeches Pit in Britain and Schöningen in Germany.[112] Stable isotope analysis suggests that Neanderthals got a tremendous amount of their food energy in the form of expensive meat calories,[113] particularly in colder regions/periods,[114] and bioenergeticists have estimated that they typically consumed at least 3,000 and probably closer to 5,500 kcal/cap/day.[115]

Modern humans in the Late Ice Age needed rather fewer calories for food and therefore for fuel,[116] but other categories of nonfood energy capture increased dramatically. Genetic analyses of lice suggest that humans started wearing fitted clothes at least 50 kya and possibly 150 kya,[117] and anatomical studies of fossil foot bones show that shoes were in regular use by at least 40 kya.[118] *Homo sapiens* also began using small amounts of energy for personal decoration around 50 kya and much larger amounts for building shelters. Archaeologists have as yet found no convincing evidence for proto-humans building houses,[119] but since at least 50 kya modern humans began investing energy in buildings. From the very earliest times, these buildings required the capture of thousands of kilocalories of nonfood energy, but repaid the effort by trapping heat from fireplaces as well as providing shelter when caves were not available.[120]

Toward the end of the Ice Age, around 14,000 BCE, total human energy capture (food + nonfood) at sites like Ohalo in the Western core in Southwest Asia must have been around 4,000 kcal/cap/day.[121] I make this suggestion because (a) food energy cannot have fallen much below 2,000 kcal/cap/day for long periods, (b) if nonfood energy capture had fallen much below an additional 2,000 kcal/cap/day Natufian material culture would have been much poorer than the archaeological record shows it to have been, and (c) if nonfood energy capture had risen much above an additional 2,000 kcal/cap/day the archaeological record would be much richer than it in fact is.

From Foragers to Imperialists (14,000–500 BCE)

As figure 3.9 makes clear, there is a very wide gap to fill between the reasonably secure estimate of energy capture for Late Ice Age hunter-gatherers in the Western core (4,000 kcal/cap/day in 14,000 BCE) to the next reasonably secure estimate, of 23,000 kcal/cap/day for the city dwellers of the east Mediterranean in 500 BCE. We could simply assume a steady growth rate, either arithmetic or geometric, across these 13.6 millennia, but in fact the combination of the actual archaeological and textual data, comparanda from economic anthropology, and comparisons with the scores after 500 BCE allow us to be more precise (figure 3.10).

I divide the period into six phases, first briefly describing some of the developments in each phase in general terms and then trying to quantify what these changes meant for energy capture.

Affluent Foragers, 14,000–10,800 BCE

The archaeological evidence seems quite clear that as the weather became warmer and more stable at the end of the Ice Age in Southwest Asia, diets grew richer, huts became bigger and more elaborate, and material culture expanded.[122] Finds from Abu Hureyra in Syria

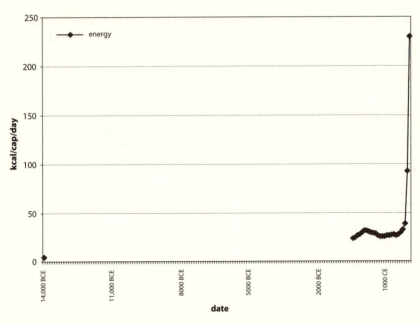

Figure 3.9. Western energy capture, 14,000 BCE and 500 BCE–2000 CE.

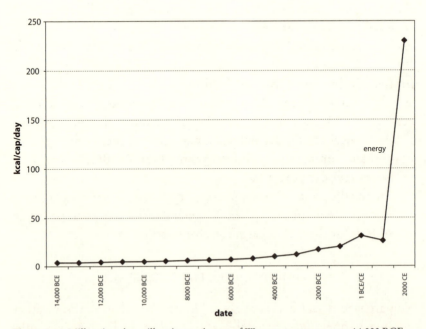

Figure 3.10. Millennium-by-millennium estimates of Western energy capture, 14,000 BCE– 2000 CE.

suggest that cultivation of rye had selected for bigger seeds by 11,000 BCE.[123] People in Southwest Asia remained foragers (and increasingly sedentary ones), and in 11,000 BCE their energy capture was still much closer to the 4,000 kcal/cap/day of the Late Ice Age than to the 12,000 kcal/cap/day that Cook ascribed to early agriculturalists, but we must assume a substantial increase in percentage terms (if not, by the standards of later times, in the absolute number of kilocalories) across these three millennia.

The Younger Dryas Mini–Ice Age, 10,800–9600 BCE

What the twelve-hundred-year mini–ice age known as the Younger Dryas (10,800–9600 BCE) meant for energy capture is debated.[124] On the one hand, many permanent villages seem to have been abandoned by 10,000 BCE, their residents returning to more mobile strategies and investing less energy in construction and material culture; on the other, the first monuments appear at sites like Qermez Dere, Jerf al-Ahmar, and Mureybet,[125] implying an increase in energy capture. It seems to me that the safest procedure, at least until our evidence improves significantly, is to assume that energy capture remained basically flat between 10,800 and 9600 BCE. This involves a major departure from the steady arithmetic growth and the geometric growth models, both of which predict that energy capture increased by 17 percent between 10,800 and 9600 BCE (from 9,000 to 10,500 kcal/cap/day in the arithmetic model and from 6,000 to 7,000 kcal/cap/day in the geometric model).

The Agricultural and Secondary Products Revolutions, 9600–3500 BCE

As the weather warmed up and settled down after 9600 BCE, we see two contrasting trends. First, cultivation resumed relatively rapidly. Unnaturally large seeds of wheat and barley appear at multiple sites in the Jordan, Euphrates, and Tigris Valley by 9000 BCE and become normal by 8500 BCE, by which time the first fully domesticated wheat and barley (with tough rachis and hulls that do not shatter) is seen at a handful of sites. By 8000 BCE about half the carbonized cereal seeds from the "Hilly Flanks" region along the borderlands of modern Iran, Turkey, Syria, Lebanon, Israel, and Jordan are domesticated; by 7500 BCE, virtually all are.[126]

Domestication raised energy capture per hectare under cultivation and, in the short run at least, raised energy capture per capita too. However, one of the main uses of excess energy was to produce more babies, which set off a second trend. Villages were caught in Malthusian traps: geometric population growth outpaced arithmetic growth in the food supply, driving the per capita food supply back down toward bare subsistence. Together, the two trends generated the paradoxical result that while nonfood energy capture clearly rose substantially between 9600 and 3500 BCE, overall food supply was at best stagnant. Cheap domesticated cereal calories increasingly replaced more varied diets based on hunted and gathered wild foods, and the skeletal record suggests that on the whole early farming populations were less healthy than preagricultural hunter-gatherer groups.[127]

Excavations across the past thirty years have also revealed that the rate of change in energy capture after the Younger Dryas was much slower than was previously thought.[128] Rather than a single "agricultural revolution," we should probably think of a drawn-out transition from full-time foraging, through a combination of foraging and cultivation, to the gradual replacement of most wild and cultivated food by domesticated plants and animals. The most recent studies suggest that this took about two thousand years, from roughly 9600 through 7500 BCE, in the Hilly Flanks.

Furthermore, this was only the first stage; the shift toward domesticated plants and animals was followed by the even longer "secondary products revolution" in food energy,[129] in which farmers gradually intensified practices and discovered new applications of domesticated plants and animals. It took many centuries for people to learn to alternate cereals with beans to replenish the soil; to process cereals more effectively, removing impurities; to bake bread effectively; to harness animals for milk and/or traction rather than eating them all while still young; and to build efficient plows and wheeled carts. Storage facilities increased in sophistication, and wells provided water for places streams did not reach.[130]

The "full package" of ancient dry-grain agriculture in Southwest Asia was not in place until at least 4000 BCE. By then weeding, rotating, and manuring crops were all standard practice, significantly

Figure 3.11. House remains from Abu Hureyra, Syria. At the bottom are postholes from huts of around 12,000 BCE; at the top, remains of a mud-brick house, ca. 8000 BCE. *Village on the Euphrates: From Foraging to Farming at Abu Hureyra* by A.M.T. Moore, A. J. Legge, and G. C. Hillman (2000); figure 5.4, p. 107. By Permission of Oxford University Press, Inc. www.oup.com.

increasing energy capture per hectare,[131] even if most or all of the energy surplus was converted into extra people rather than into higher food-energy capture per capita.

The increase in nonfood energy capture was just as slow but is much more visible. As when trying to calculate energy capture in the post-Roman period, the best method is simply to compare settlement sites of different dates. A famous photograph from Abu Hureyra (figure 3.11) illustrates the point nicely: at the top is part of a small but sturdy house built around 8000 BCE, and below are the remains of much flimsier huts dating back to 12,000 BCE. If we continue moving through time, we find more substantial houses still by 6500 BCE (with Çatalhöyük providing the best-known examples), and by 4500 BCE the Ubaid phase houses of Mesopotamia were still more impressive. Michael Roaf describes a fairly typical but particularly well-preserved example, covering 170 m², from Tell Madhhur in Iraq. By that time houses were solidly built from mud bricks, usually organized around a shady courtyard, with waterproof roofs, a well, and large storage facilities.[132]

Typical household goods increased similarly. Pottery came into use around 7000 BCE, with specialist producers using the potter's wheels soon after that. Weaving seems to have steadily increased in sophistication, and copper ornaments, tools, and weapons came into use by 3500 BCE. So far as I know no archaeologist has systematically quantified and compared household goods from Southwest Asia over time, but the contrast between the contents of the houses from Abu Hureyra (ca. 12,000 and 8000 BCE) and Tell Madhhur (ca. 4500 BCE) is striking.

The energy consumed on public monuments of various types also increased sharply. Jericho had some kind of fortification tower as early as 9000 BCE, but this pales in comparison with the elaborate temple at Eridu or the enormous earth platform heaped up at Susa by 3500 BCE. Figure 3.12, a reconstruction drawing of the sequence of temples at Eridu from 5000 through 3500 BCE, makes the point about increasing nonfood energy capture as effectively as the photograph of the Abu Hureyra houses.[133]

Energy captured for transport also increased. The first unambiguous evidence for linking animal power to wheeled vehicles is Sumerian representations of ox-drawn carts from around 4000 BCE, and by 3000 BCE actual carts were being included in tombs.[134] Wind and waterpower were also harnessed; canoes were being used for fishing by 5000 BCE, and models from Eridu show that proper boats were in use by 4000.

The increase in nonfood energy capture between 9600 and 3500 BCE is very clear.[135] As in the case of the affluent foragers of 14,000–11,000 BCE, though, we should remember that while the increase in energy capture between 9600 and 3500 must have been very large in percentage terms, in terms of absolute kilocalories it was nevertheless small by modern standards. Even at the end of this long period,

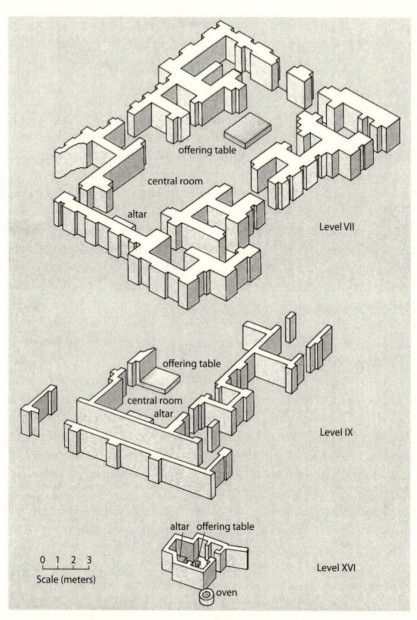

offering table

central room

altar

Level VII

offering table

central room
altar

Level IX

altar offering table

Level XVI

0 1 2 3
Scale (meters)

oven

Figure 3.12. Temple remains from Eridu, Iraq. At the bottom is the temple built around 5000 BCE; at the top, the version built around 3000 BCE. From *Cultural Atlas of Ancient Mesopotamia and the Near East* by Michael Roaf (1990); p. 52. New York: Facts on File.

people in the Western core were still villagers, their energy capture somewhere around Cook's "early agriculturalists" stage in figure 3.1.

Archaic States, 3500–1200 BCE

The rate of increase in energy capture accelerated after 3500 BCE with the development and spread of states with centralized governments in the Western core. Once again the lack of a systematic collection of data on skeletal stature hampers discussion, as does the scarcity of stable isotopic and other anthropological analyses of paleodiet, but the general impression created by the scattered data is that there was relatively little overall change in food calorie intake.

We can sketch very generalized pictures of diet and nutrition in different parts of the Western core,[136] but more detailed studies reveal enormous local variation.[137] There probably was a long-term trend toward higher yield: seed ratios across the third and second millennia (reaching perhaps 30:1 in irrigated Mesopotamian barley farming by 2000 BCE),[138] but population seems to have increased just as quickly, consuming the gains.

As in earlier periods, however, we also see a large increase in per capita capture of nonfood calories. The most striking aspect is the spread of metal use, which gives the period its standard name, the Bronze Age. Royal bureaucratic records document enormous bronze foundries at palaces, and excavators have found plenty of examples of private foundries.[139] Stone tools largely disappeared from the Western core by 1200 BCE.

The famous pyramids, ziggurats, palaces, and temples of the Bronze Age of course consumed massive amounts of energy.[140] The Great Pyramid at Giza (ca. 2600 BCE) is still the world's heaviest building, weighing around a million tons. The scale of long-distance trade also increased sharply, especially after 1600 BCE, and is vividly illustrated by shipwrecks found off the coast of Turkey.[141] Most important of all, though, is the increase in energy consumed by the much larger populations of the third and second millennia BCE. In every part of the core, standards of housing and the quantity and craftsmanship of household goods rose between 3500 and 1200 BCE.[142]

As in other periods, there is strong regional variation as well as local episodes of collapse. In the Aegean, for instance, the Neopalatial period (ca. 1800–1600 BCE) on Crete was a time of apparent wealth, with very large houses (median size of floor plan 130 m²)[143] and rich material culture. After 1600 BCE, however, nonfood wealth seems to have declined on Crete, while continuing to increase in mainland Greece.

The biggest episodes of collapse in this period seem to have been in Mesopotamia after 3100 BCE, when Uruk was burned and its large material culture zone broke up, and across the whole area from Mesopotamia through Syria and the Levant to Egypt (and with echoes across much of the Mediterranean) between 2200 and 2000 BCE. However, while both these episodes left clear archaeological traces, it is less obvious that they had much impact on energy capture.

There seem to be several reasons for this. A large part of the explanation is that both collapses were in fact very spotty, with some sites destroyed and abandoned while others flourished (e.g., in Syria, Tell Leilan and Sweyhat were abandoned around 2200 BCE, while Tell Brak and Mozan grew even larger). Archaeologists disagree over the underlying causes, and some even debate whether "collapse" is an appropriate term.[144]

A second factor is the emergence of a new core area in Egypt by 3100 BCE. The Nile Valley was unaffected by the 3100 BCE collapse, and while the disasters after 2200 BCE did have a major impact on Egypt, they did so on a different schedule than in Mesopotamia. By 2100 Egypt's Old Kingdom and Mesopotamia's Akkadian Empire had both unraveled, but the strong new Ur III state had reunited much of Mesopotamia. By 2000 Ur had also collapsed, but the Middle Kingdom had reunited Egypt. Despite the obvious traumas of the 2200–2000 BCE period, energy capture seems to have kept growing in the Western core. The same is true of the new round of upheavals between 1800 and 1550 BCE.

Finally, the way I have measured energy capture may understate the impact of the crises. In this stretch of early history I calculate scores every half millennium until 2500 BCE and every quarter millennium between 2500 and 1500 BCE. The 3500 BCE score measures energy capture before the Uruk collapse, and while Mesopotamian energy capture may still have been lower in 3000 BCE than it had been before 3100 (the evidence is not very clear), Egyptian energy capture was definitely higher by 3000 BCE than Mesopotamian had been in 3500. Similarly, the 2250 BCE calculation shows energy capture before the great collapse began, and although Mesopotamia was still in chaos in 2000 BCE, order had by then been restored in Egypt. As I noted in chapter 2, the inevitable result of taking measurements at widely separated points is to smooth the realities of change.

So long as we set the threshold for urbanism low (at around five thousand people), we can say that by 1250 BCE many people in the Western core had become city dwellers, and the majority of the population in Western Eurasia lived in archaic states with functioning centralized governments. They had moved far beyond the 12,000 kcal/cap/day energy capture of the early agriculturalist stage in Cook's diagram (figure 3.1), although comparison of even the richest Late Bronze Age settlements such as Ugarit (destroyed ca. 1200 BCE) with classical Greek settlements such as Olynthus (destroyed in 348 BCE) suggests that Bronze Age societies had not matched the classical Greek level of roughly 25,000 kcal/cap/day.[145]

The End of the Bronze Age, 1200–1000 BCE

The collapse that spread over the entire Western core between 1200 and 1000 BCE provides the first indisputable evidence of falling energy capture.[146] In the worst affected regions (modern Greece and Turkey), cities and elaborate elite monuments disappeared altogether, and even in the least affected area (Egypt), there was a sharp decline in elite activity.

There is not much evidence so far for changes in ordinary people's lives in Egypt, but in Syria, Israel, and the Aegean, standards of housing, the quantity and quality of material goods, and the scale of exchange networks all fell sharply.[147] Again the lack of large-scale systematic skeletal comparisons is a problem, but in the Aegean, at least, adult age at death declined and there is some evidence for increased morbidity, and a downward trend in adult stature is unmistakable.[148]

The Early Iron Age, 1000–500 BCE

Energy capture must have risen quite sharply to get from the post–Bronze Age trough around 1000 BCE to the figure of around 25,000 kcal/cap/day calculated for 500 BCE, the beginning of the classical period of Mediterranean antiquity.

Most of the available data belong to the same categories used for earlier periods. As usual, elite monuments are the most obvious evidence: the sixth-century BCE Persian palaces at Persepolis and the temples and palaces of Babylon dwarf anything from the previous few centuries, as do temples like that of Artemis at Ephesus or Capitoline Jupiter in Rome, on the fringes of the expanding core.

The housing evidence is less straightforward in the core itself, where multiroom rectilinear houses typically covering 50–100 m² had been normal for centuries, but in Israel substantial, two-floored "pillared houses" became more common, larger, and more lavish between 1000 and 500 BCE. Farther west in the Mediterranean, multiroom rectilinear houses steadily displaced smaller, curvilinear, single-room ones. The process had begun in Greece by 750 BCE and was largely complete by 500; in southern Italy and Sicily it began by 600 and had run its course by 400; and in southern France it began around 400 and was nearly complete by 200 BCE.[149]

In Greece, the evidence for stature is somewhat mixed, but average adult ages at death definitely rose between 1000 and 500 BCE, and morbidity probably declined, suggesting that underlying energy capture also increased. The direct evidence for diet remains unclear, however, because at present intersite variability in food remains generally swamps diachronic trends.[150]

Another very striking change was the spread of iron, which greatly multiplied the effectiveness of muscle power. The metal had been in occasional use since quite early in the second millennium BCE, but soon after 1100 BCE smiths on Cyprus turned to it more systematically. This was probably a response to the difficulty of obtaining tin for bronze when trade routes collapsed after 1200 BCE, but by the time trade revived on a large scale after 800 the advantages of iron (especially its abundance and cheapness) had become clear, and iron remained the normal material for tools and weapons.[151] By 1000 BCE nearly all weapons in Greece were made from iron, and around 700 the first iron tools appear in Greece. By then iron weapons were also normal in Italy, southern France, and eastern Spain.[152]

The incorporation of the central and western Mediterranean between 800 and 500 BCE was the most rapid expansion the Western core had yet seen. While economic activity certainly increased in the old Southwest Asian core, it did so much faster in Greece, Italy, Spain, southern France, and what is now Tunisia.[153] The most easily quantifiable evidence comes from the shipwrecks and pollution records (figure 3.5).

Estimates are once again hampered by the lack of systematic collections of skeletal, housing, and other forms of evidence outside Greece, but the overall picture seems clear: energy capture rose in the Western core—as fast, probably, as it had ever done before—between 1000 and 500 BCE. It rose particularly quickly in the central and western Mediterranean basin.

Calculating the Scores

One way to fill the 13,500-year gap between the energy capture score of 4,000 kcal/cap/day in 14,000 BCE and that of 23,000 kcal/cap/day in 500 BCE would be by simply assuming constant growth rates, either arithmetic or geometric (figure 3.13). However, the evidence discussed in this section suggests that that would lose significant amounts of information.

The archaeological evidence shows very clearly that energy capture increased much faster in the last few millennia BCE than it did in the Late Ice Age and immediate post–Ice Age period, meaning that the arithmetic growth curve must be very misleading. A constant geometric increase (of 0.013 percent per annum) would approximate better to the facts, but even that would leave out significant details, such as the Younger Dryas interruption of 10,800–9600 BCE, the apparent acceleration after about 3500 BCE, and the decline in energy capture after 1200 BCE. The best estimated curve seems certain to lie beneath the geometric curve as well as the arithmetic curve; its growth rate will be exponential, but the exponent will generally increase over time.

Other than these basic observations, however, we have no fixed points, and the only way we can proceed is by making estimates and

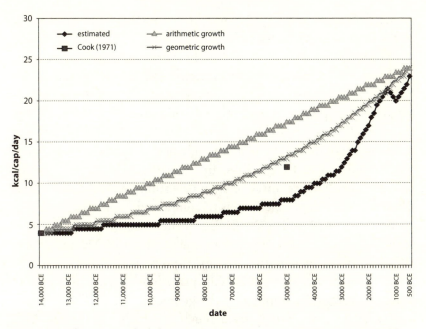

Figure 3.13. Alternative methods for estimating Western energy capture, 14,000–500 BCE.

comparing these estimates with the actual archaeological evidence, the comparative evidence, and the scores we have already estimated for the period 500 BCE–2000 CE.

Between 14,000 and 10,800 BCE, energy capture increased, but extremely slowly. Settlements such as pre–Younger Dryas Abu Hureyra reveal people capturing more energy than Late Ice Age sites such as Ohalo. I would guess that the increase was something like 1,000 kcal/cap/day, from 4,000 to 5,000 kcal/cap/day (i.e., a 25 percent increase across 3,200 years, or 0.007 percent per annum). I have no firm basis for this proposal. Possibly the increase in the size and sophistication of houses, the complexity of food preparation, and the expansion of material culture represented just a 500 kcal/cap/day increase (i.e., 12.5 percent); perhaps it represented a 2,000 kcal/cap/day increase (i.e., 50 percent). Both those numbers seem extreme to me, but even if one of them is closer to the truth than my 1,000 kcal/cap/day estimate, the amount of change between 14,000 and 10,800 BCE was still very small, and assuming that energy capture in 10,800 BCE was 4,500 kcal/cap/day or 6,000 kcal/cap/day rather than 5,000 kcal/cap/day would make only a minor difference to the calculations that follow.

As mentioned in section above, there are conflicting signs in the evidence for the Younger Dryas period (10,800–9600 BCE), so I have decided simply to treat energy capture as flat across this twelve-hundred-year period. Again, this may be a mistake; perhaps energy capture fell back (though not all the way to 14,000 BCE levels) or perhaps it continued to rise (though not as quickly as between 14,000 and 10,800 BCE). As with the earlier period, though, the amounts involved are tiny, and errors in estimation are in any case as likely to cancel each other out as to compound each other.

Between 9600 and 3500 BCE, the increase in energy capture seems to have been far larger than that between 14,000 and 10,800 BCE. Cook estimated that energy capture had already risen to 12,000 kcal/cap/day by 5000 BCE, just slightly below the level of 13,000 kcal/cap/day implied by the geometric curve. The evidence now available makes that seem much too high. Cook may have assumed—as archaeologists sometimes did in the mid-twentieth century—that the agricultural revolution was a single, fairly rapid transformation, whereas we now know that cultivation and domestication were processes spread across about four thousand years and were merely the first stages of an ongoing secondary products revolution that lasted in Southwest Asia until about 4000 BCE.[154] I suggest that total energy capture roughly doubled between 9600 and 3500 BCE, from about 5,500 kcal/cap/day to 11,000 kcal/cap/day (a rate of 0.013 percent per annum, almost double that of the period 14,000–10,800 BCE), rather than more than doubling by 5000 BCE, as Cook suggested. His estimate gives a growth rate of 0.017 percent per annum between 10,800 and 5000 BCE; if that were extended out to 3500 BCE it would produce a score of 15,500 kcal/cap/day in that year. If, as I suggest below, energy capture almost doubled again between 3500 and 1200 BCE, Late Bronze Age energy capture would have reached 30,000 kcal/cap/day—almost the same as the score at the height of the Roman Empire in the first century CE, Song dynasty China in the twelfth century CE, or the West European and Chinese cores around 1600 CE.

That seems very improbable. If Cook's estimate of 12,000 kcal/cap/day in 5000 BCE were correct, the only way to preserve a plausible relationship with later figures would be by assuming a drastic slowdown in the growth rate after 5000 BCE. If growth fell to just 0.015 percent per annum (lower, that is, than Cook's estimate of 0.017 percent for the period 9600–5000 BCE), that would bring the score for 1200 BCE down to 21,000 kcal/cap/day, as in my estimate. However, the archaeological evidence is hard to reconcile with slower growth after 5000 BCE than before. It seems to me that Cook's energy capture estimate for the Western core around 5000 BCE of 12,000 kcal/cap/day must be too high. If energy capture increased roughly 50 percent between 10,800 and 5000 BCE, from 5,500 to about 8,000 kcal/cap/day (rather than more than doubling, from 5,500 to 12,000 kcal/cap/day, as Cook suggested), and then increased by roughly another one-third (from 8,000 to 11,000 kcal/cap/day) between 5000 and 3500 BCE, we get a much more plausible picture of Neolithic energy use and its relationship to the Bronze Age. I suggest that energy capture increased to 8,000 kcal/cap/day in 5000 BCE and then to 11,000 kcal/cap/day in 3500 BCE.

Between 3500 and 1300 BCE—roughly from the age of Uruk to the age of Ramses the Great—I suggest that energy capture roughly doubled again, from 11,000 to 21,500 kcal/cap/day (a rate of increase of 0.029 per cent per annum, just over twice as fast as between 9600 and 3500 BCE, and four times as fast as between 14,000 and 10,800 BCE). If this is correct, my estimated growth curve caught up with the geometric curve (figure 3.13) in the thirteenth century BCE. The figure in 1300 BCE could, of course, be somewhat higher or lower, but any really big changes (say, down to 18,000 or up to 25,000 kcal/cap/day) would mean assuming either strangely slow or strangely fast rates of change in the early first millennium BCE.

The scale of decline in energy capture between 1300 and 1000 BCE is hard to estimate. I have suggested that the figure fell slightly during the thirteenth century, from 21,500 to 21,000 kcal/cap/day, then faster, from 21,000 to 20,000 kcal/cap/day, between 1200 and 1000 BCE (a rate of change of –0.025 percent per annum between 1200 and 1000 BCE). The bottom of the trough may have been a little deeper, in which case growth in the early first millennium BCE must have been slightly faster to reach 23,000 kcal/cap/day by 500 BCE, or slightly shallower, in which case subsequent growth must have been a little slower. However, the claim made by some archaeologists in the 1990s that there was really little or no post-1200 BCE collapse seem to me misguided, rather like the suggestions that there was no post-Roman collapse.[155]

If these numbers are roughly correct, energy capture must have risen by about 15 percent between 1000 and 500 BCE, from approximately 20,000 to 23,000 kcal/cap/day (a growth rate of 0.029 percent per annum, slightly faster than the rate estimated for 3500 through 1200 BCE). By my estimates, energy capture rose a further 35 percent between 500 and 1 BCE (from 23,000 to 31,000 kcal/cap/day).

In figure 3.5, showing shipwrecks and lead pollution as proxies for long-distance trade and metalworking, 15 percent of the first-millennium BCE increase comes before 500 BCE and the other 85 percent after 500 BCE. This may mean that my estimates for 1000 BCE (and, by implication, for 1300 BCE) are too low; or it may just reflect the fact that the bulk of the large population increase in the first-millennium BCE Mediterranean (Scheidel estimates that the population roughly quadrupled between 1200 BCE and 150 CE)[156] came after 500 BCE, meaning that while the aggregate increase in trade and industry seems to be heavily weighted toward the late first millennium, the per capita increase was less heavily weighted.

Western Energy Capture: Discussion

Figures 3.2 and 3.3 show the scores I have calculated for Western energy capture for the whole period between 14,000 BCE and 2000 CE. By their very nature, such graphs involve a lot of approximation. It is hard to imagine that every number could possibly be correct, which means (as noted in chapter 2) that the appropriate question to ask is not whether all the numbers are right—we can be sure they are not—but whether they are so wrong that they seriously misrepresent the shape of the history of Western energy capture.

To this question, I think the answer must be no. The scores are certainly within the right order of magnitude, and, for reasons I discuss in *Why the West Rules—For Now*,[157] the range of systematic errors is probably less than ± 20 percent. The most serious concern,

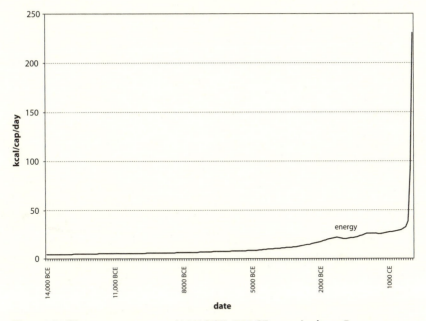

Figure 3.14. Western energy capture, 14,000 BCE–2000 CE, assuming lower Roman rates and higher early modern rates.

however, must be how much the *un*systematic errors distort the shape of the graph.

Figure 3.14 shows what the energy curve would look like if, for example, the increase in energy capture across the first millennium BCE was in reality just half what I have estimated (i.e., growing from 20,000 kcal/cap/day in 1000 BCE to 25,500 kcal/cap/day, rather than 31,000 kcal/cap/day, in 1 BCE/CE) while the increase between 700 and 1500 CE was twice as large as I estimated (i.e., from 25,000 to 29,000 kcal/cap/day rather than from 25,000 to 27,000 kcal/cap/day). These are rather drastic revisions, which strike me as difficult to justify from the surviving evidence; yet they make very little difference to figure 3.14. The increase in energy capture between 1000 BCE and 2000 CE becomes smoother (this is easier to see in figure 3.15, which presents both the actual estimates and these revised estimates and covers just the period 1500 BCE–2000 CE), but the basic pattern remains much the same.

We can experiment with any number of hypothetical modifications, but the main value of such thought experiments is to show

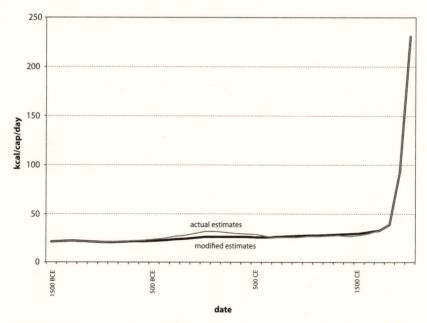

Figure 3.15. Comparison of the actual estimates of Western energy capture, 1500 BCE–2000 CE, with the assumption of lower Roman and higher early modern scores.

just how radically we would need to change the scores to have a serious impact on the fundamental shape of the history of Western energy capture. The basic pattern—a very long period of extremely slow growth from the end of the Ice Age to the rise of the state (i.e., from about 14,000 to about 3000 BCE), accelerating but still very slow growth in the age of early states and empires (roughly 3000–1 BCE), fluctuations pressing against an agrarian ceiling slightly above 30,000 kcal/cap/day (roughly 1–1600 CE), a brief period when the agrarian ceiling was pushed upward (1600–1800 CE), and finally a (so far) brief period of explosive growth (1800 to present)—is very clear.

Economists regularly assume that nothing important changed until the industrial revolution. Gregory Clark's claim (cited earlier in this chapter) that "the average person in the world of 1800 [CE] was no better off than the average person of 100,000 BC" and his accompanying graph (figure 3.16), representing premodern living standards as a random walk around a Malthusian ceiling, are unusual only in being so explicit; but they are mistaken all the same.

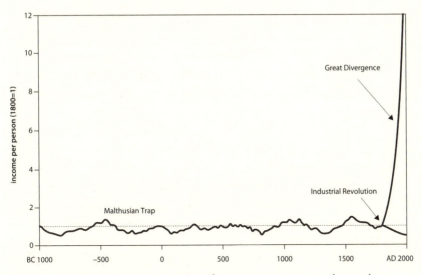

Figure 3.16. Gregory Clark's reconstruction of income per person across the past three thousand years. *Source*: Clark, *Farewell to Alms*, 2, fig. 1.

There were enormous increases in energy capture between the end of the Ice Age and 1800 CE. As Malthus himself recognized (see "The Cook Framework," above), however, these must be divided into food and nonfood calories. Increases in food calories per unit of land were quickly consumed when people converted the energy windfall into more babies, but increases in nonfood energy capture were not canceled out, and the archaeological record attests a striking accumulation across the past sixteen millennia. The upward trend in figures 3.2 and 3.3 was interrupted by various collapses, most strikingly after 1200 BCE, 200 CE, and 1300 CE, but each of these wiped out only part of the preceding increase and proved temporary.

ESTIMATES OF EASTERN ENERGY CAPTURE

Much less research has been done on Eastern energy capture than on Western, and there is a particular dearth of quantitative estimates. Yet while much remains to be done, the main outlines are reasonably clear. At the end of the last Ice Age, around 14,000 BCE, per capita energy capture in the most favored regions of the East was rather similar to that in the West, at around 4,000 kcal/cap/day. For geographical reasons (in this case, ecological differences that had led to the evolution of more potentially domesticable species of plants and anials in Western Eurasia than in Eastern), Eastern scores initially rose more slowly than those in the West, with the first clear signs of cultivation and domestication of plants running about two thousand years behind those in the Western core. The increase in Eastern scores began accelerating by 3000 BCE. As in the West, there was a serious collapse in the early first millennium CE. Eastern energy capture quickly recovered, and was moving upward again by 400 CE, but did not reach the agrarian ceiling of roughly 30,000 kcal/cap/day until after 1000 CE. After another serious collapse between 1200 and 1400 CE the Eastern score returned to the agrarian ceiling by 1600, passed it by 1700, and then grew rapidly (relative to earlier periods) across the eighteenth, nineteenth, and twentieth centuries. Table 3.4, figure 3.17, and figure 3.18 show my estimates for Eastern energy capture since 14,000 BCE.

In comparative terms, the scores for the Eastern core seem to have been lower than those for the Western core throughout prehistory and antiquity and again in the nineteenth and twentieth centuries CE, but were higher in what Western historians call the Middle Ages and early modern times, from roughly the mid-first through the mid-second millennium CE. Refining the comparisons, though, is more difficult.

In this section I begin with the most recent period, since 1800 CE. Next, as I did in my analysis of Western energy capture, I jump back in time to better-known periods (first the Song dynasty of 960–1279 CE and then the Han dynasty of 206 BCE–220 CE) before filling in the gaps. Finally I will turn to the prehistoric East.

The Recent Past, 1800–2000 CE

As in the Western core, high-quality statistics are available for energy capture in 2000 CE, putting total food + nonfood per capita energy capture in the Eastern core (in Japan) at about 104,000 kcal/

Table 3.4
Eastern energy capture, 14,000 BCE–2000 CE

Date	kcal/cap/day	Points	Date	kcal/cap/day	Points
14,000 BCE	4,000	4.36	500 BCE	21,000	22.88
13,000 BCE	4,000	4.36	400 BCE	22,000	23.97
12,000 BCE	4,000	4.36	300 BCE	22,500	24.52
11,000 BCE	4,000	4.36	200 BCE	24,000	26.15
10,000 BCE	4,000	4.36	100 BCE	25,500	27.79
9000 BCE	4,500	4.90	1 BCE/CE	27,000	29.42
8000 BCE	5,000	5.45	100 CE	27,000	29.42
7000 BCE	5,500	5.99	200 CE	26,000	28.33
6000 BCE	6,000	6.54	300 CE	26,000	28.33
5000 BCE	6,500	7.08	400 CE	26,000	28.33
4000 BCE	7,000	7.63	500 CE	26,000	28.33
3500 BCE	7,500	8.17	600 CE	27,000	29.42
3000 BCE	8,000	8.72	700 CE	27,000	29.42
2500 BCE	9,500	10.35	800 CE	28,000	30.51
2250 BCE	10,500	11.44	900 CE	29,000	31.06
2000 BCE	11,000	11.99	1000 CE	29,500	32.15
1750 BCE	13,000	14.17	1100 CE	30,000	32.69
1500 BCE	15,000	16.35	1200 CE	30,500	33.24
1400 BCE	15,500	16.89	1300 CE	30,000	32.69
1300 BCE	16,000	17.44	1400 CE	29,000	31.06
1200 BCE	16,000	17.44	1500 CE	30,000	32.69
1100 BCE	16,500	17.98	1600 CE	31,000	33.78
1000 BCE	17,000	18.52	1700 CE	33,000	35.96
900 BCE	17,500	19.07	1800 CE	36,000	39.23
800 BCE	18,000	19.61	1900 CE	49,000	53.40
700 BCE	18,500	20.16	2000 CE	104,000	113.33
600 BCE	20,000	21.79			

cap/day[158]—less than half the 230,000 kcal/cap/day consumed in the United States, but much higher than in any earlier period of Eastern (or Western) history.

Reliable government statistics do not go back very far in the East, and (as in the West) the problems are compounded by the scarcity of quantitative data on biomass used for fuel, housing, clothing, and so

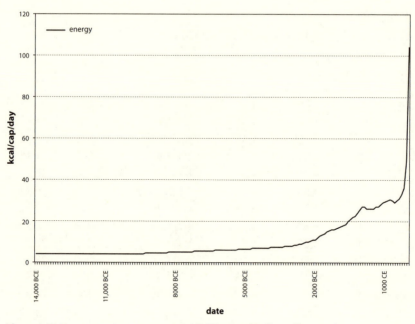

Figure 3.17. Eastern energy capture, 14,000 BCE–2000 CE, linear-linear scale.

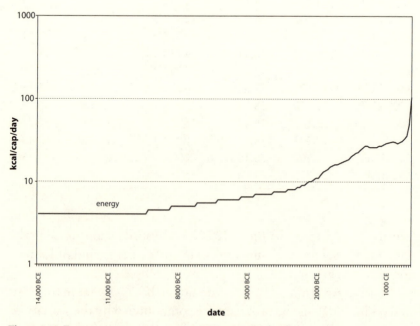

Figure 3.18. Eastern energy capture, 14,000 BCE–2000 CE, log-linear scale.

on in peasant households.[159] In 1900 Japan burned three million tons of coal (roughly 500 kg of coal per person per year, or a little over 500 kcal/cap/day, as compared to 181 million tons = 4.36 tons/cap/year = roughly 40,000 kcal/cap/day in Britain in 1903) and only a tiny amount of oil.[160] Biomass use, however, became efficient as well as intensive as population pressure increased across the eighteenth and nineteenth centuries and the resource base was steadily degraded,[161] probably rivaling that in the advanced organic economies of eighteenth-/nineteenth-century Northwest Europe. Put together, these various sources suggest energy capture just under 50,000 kcal/cap/day in the Eastern core in Japan in 1900 CE.

Early-twentieth-century peasant life in northern China is relatively well documented.[162] Coal and bean curd fertilizer were widely used in the nineteenth century. By 1900 living standards were typically lower than in Japan and in some places were actually falling, but energy capture must have been well over 40,000 kcal/cap/day.

Standards of living in the nineteenth-century East (and particularly China) have been intensely debated since the 1990s, to the point that they have become the major battleground between long-term lock-in and short-term accident theories of Western rule.[163] For most of the twentieth century, the dominant theory among historians was that the Chinese economy had stagnated between 1400 and 1900. Angus Maddison, for instance, estimated that Chinese GDP/cap rose from $450 to $600 (PPP, 1990 Geary-Khamis international dollars) between 1000 and 1500 CE, then stayed at $600 for the entire period between 1500 and 1820. Similarly, Dwight Perkins suggested that after vigorous growth and innovation during the Middle Ages, agriculture reached its limits in Yuan dynasty times (1279–1368 CE), and thereafter the best practices spread across China from the agrarian core in southern China but few important new techniques were added. Mark Elvin made a broader argument that after coming close to an industrial takeoff in Song dynasty times (960–1279 CE), China entered what he called a "high-level equilibrium trap," in which traditional muscle- and water-powered technologies had become as efficient as they could get, but there were insufficient incentives to make the leap to fossil-fuel technologies. Implicitly or explicitly, views of this kind suggested that per capita energy capture in the Eastern core barely changed between the establishment of the Ming dynasty in 1368 and the intrusion of Europeans in the 1840s.[164]

These theories came under serious attack in the 1990s, in part because the People's Republic had opened many of its Ming-Qing archives to scholars in the 1980s.[165] Historians found abundant evidence for economic change, especially in Qing times (1644–1911), and Kenneth Pomeranz in particular argued that the trajectory in the eighteenth- to nineteenth-century Yangzi Delta, the most economically advanced part of China, had far more similarities with than differences from the trajectory in Western Europe. The forms of its proto-industrialization were similar, he argued, as was its industrious revolution. Pomeranz also suggested that living standards were rising in Qing China despite rapid population growth, calculating that nineteenth-century Chinese adult males typically consumed between 2,386 and 2,651 food calories per day, roughly the same as those in Britain. Chinese consumption of sugar, tobacco, candles, furniture, and meat also seems to have risen, and cotton clothing spread throughout the population.[166]

The older, more pessimistic picture of agricultural involution in the East between 1400 and 1900 still has defenders, but as long-term data on Eastern real wages and agricultural yields improve, it increasingly looks as if some compromise between the two theories makes most sense.[167] As the pessimists argue, output per agricultural worker did decline between 1600 and 1800 (figure 3.19). It remained very high, though, and as late as 1700, farm laborers in the Yangzi Delta were probably more productive than those anywhere in Europe.

By contrast, as the optimists suggest, real wages did increase slightly in Beijing between 1738 and 1900 (figure 3.20), but they remained very low, having far more in common with wages in backward Southern Europe than those in dynamic Northwest Europe. In 1738, real wages in Beijing, Shanghai, Suzhou, and Tokyo bought less than half as much as wages in London or Amsterdam, but were roughly comparable with those in Southern (Milan) or Central (Leipzig) Europe. Eastern wages in fact remained very similar to those in Southern European until 1918, but by 1820 Central European wages had pulled away and were gaining on those in Britain.

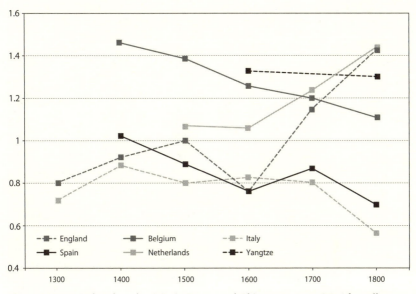

Figure 3.19. Agricultural productivity in Europe and China, 1300–1800 CE. After Allen, "Agricultural Productivity and Rural Incomes."

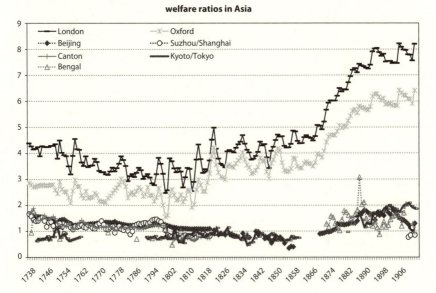

Figure 3.20. Real wages in Europe and Asia, 1738–1918 CE. After Allen et al., "Wages, Prices, and Living Standards."

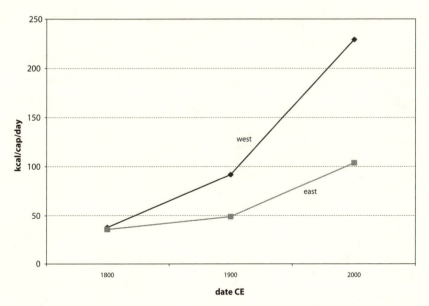

Figure 3.21. Eastern and Western energy capture, 1800–2000 CE.

We can conclude that in 1800 energy capture in the Eastern core was lower than in the Western core, but not *much* lower. By my calculations, Western energy capture was around 38,000 kcal/cap/day at that point. In the Eastern core agricultural output was high and a great deal of coal was being used for heating and cooking, but there was no steam power, and the real wage data suggest that overall living standards were lower than in Northwest Europe. I suggest that typical Eastern energy capture in the core (northern and coastal China plus Japan) was around 36,000 kcal/cap/day. It could not have been much above this level without catching up with Western energy levels, nor could it have fallen much below 36,000 kcal/cap/day without sinking to the level of the Roman Empire, which seems unlikely.

These figures suggest that energy capture in the Eastern core began the modern period (for these purposes, around 1800 CE) only slightly behind the West (figure 3.21). Contrary to the traditional/pessimistic view, the nineteenth century did see rising energy capture in the East, but the increase was much smaller than in the West. Rather than an Eastern decline, the redistribution of global power in the nineteenth-century West's favor was driven by the Western takeoff. Likewise, the East's growing global stature in the twentieth century was driven not by a Western decline but by the East learning to exploit fossil energy sources that had been pioneered by Westerners.

SONG DYNASTY CHINA (960–1279 CE)

The Song dynasty probably saw the peak of premodern energy capture in China. Population grew very rapidly, from around 50 million in the early tenth century to over 120 million by 1200, but all the signs suggest that living standards and energy capture rose even faster.

The clearest textual evidence comes from metallurgy, with its vast demands for fuel. Fifty years ago the economic historian Robert Hartwell reanalyzed Song tax receipts and argued that eleventh-century iron production had been twenty to forty times greater than historians had previously recognized. He calculated that in 1078 total taxed output was 75,000 to 150,000 tons, a twelvefold increase over Chinese production in 850 CE. Moreover, Hartwell pointed out, Chinese output in 1078 was roughly 2.5 times higher than that of England and Wales in 1640, more than half as much as was produced in the whole of Europe in 1700, and about the same as was produced in China each year between 1930 and 1934.[168]

Hartwell's analysis of the texts has been challenged, and in his volume of *Science and Civilisation in China*, Peter Golas suggested that his iron output figures were off by an entire order of magnitude.[169] More recently, however, Donald Wagner has concluded in his own volume of *Science and Civilisation in China* that while Hartwell's readings of these difficult texts are flawed, his numbers must be roughly right.[170] The Chinese historian Qi Xia has independently concluded that the enormous expansion of iron tools in farming meant that the needs of eleventh-century peasant households must have accounted for seventy thousand tons of metal per year;[171] and the state's demand for iron coins and weapons may have been even larger. Copper production was equally extraordinary, increasing fivefold from 2,420 tons in 997 to 12,982 tons in 1070—more than the entire world would be producing in 1800 CE.[172] In the eleventh and twelfth centuries the by-products of Chinese metalworking for the first time left traces in the Greenland and Antarctic ice caps, just as Roman silver processing had done a thousand years before.[173]

Hartwell consistently likened the expansion of Song dynasty metallurgy to that in England between 1540 and 1640, and suggested that—like the English example—one consequence was the increasing substitution of fossil fuels for charcoal in iron smelting. If Chinese ironmasters had powered their foundries solely with charcoal, in 1080 they would have needed to burn 22,000 mature trees, far beyond what was available around Kaifeng. Instead, they learned to smelt iron with coke and turned to large-scale coal mining. By 1050 so much coal was being mined that it was 30–50 percent cheaper than wood for household cooking and heating. By 1075 Kaifeng had special markets that dealt in nothing but coal, and government documents from 1096 discuss the coal supply without even referring to wood as a heat source.[174] Confirmation of this shift comes from recent analyses of iron and steel artifacts found in Mongolia, on the edge of the Song Empire, which show that coal replaced charcoal for smelting in the tenth, eleventh, and twelfth centuries.[175]

Unfortunately there are as yet no statistics from excavated shipwrecks, animal bones, and so on to parallel those from the Western core between 900 BCE and 800 CE (see figure 3.5), but the qualitative evidence from literature, art, and standing remains testifies to the huge expansion of trade, commerce, and manufacturing and the widespread use of spinning machines and water mills.[176] The numerous Song dynasty shipwrecks that have been looted off the Guangdong coast since the 1980s suggest that ships were becoming bigger and cargoes richer, and in 2007 the properly excavated Nanhai 1 ship confirmed this.[177]

Houses may also have become more substantial, and in twelfth-century Hangzhou two-story buildings were the norm, in striking contrast to older Chinese cities. Most people, however, probably still lived in one- and two-room wooden huts.[178] There is some evidence for the growth of mass markets for ceramics and other household goods, but I am not aware of any statistical studies of domestic assemblages.

The eleventh and twelfth centuries certainly saw high (by premodern standards) levels of energy capture, but it is difficult to fix them in absolute terms. The scale of iron production and the pres-

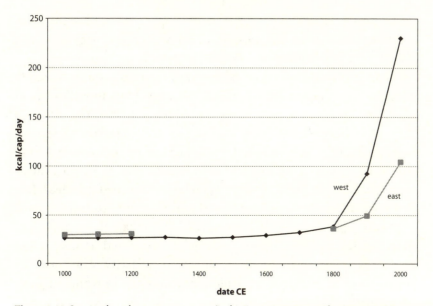

Figure 3.22. Song and modern energy capture in the East, 1000–1200 and 1800–2000 CE, plotted against Western energy capture.

ence of Chinese pollution in the ice cores suggests that energy capture was somewhere around the level attained by the Roman Empire a thousand years earlier (31,000 kcal/cap/day) or that reached in Western Europe around 1700 CE (32,000 kcal/cap/day); the absence of anything we might call an industrial revolution, however, suggests that it did not approach what we see in Western Europe by 1800 (38,000 kcal/cap/day). I tentatively suggest that Song-era energy capture remained very slightly below Roman levels, hitting 30,000 kcal/cap/day in 1100 and perhaps nudging just slightly over that figure by 1200 (figure 3.22). A figure slightly above Roman levels, perhaps even matching the European score of 32,000 kcal/cap/day in 1700 CE, seems equally plausible, but much higher or much lower figures—reaching, say, 35,000 kcal/cap/day or sinking below 25,000 kcal/cap/day—seem very unlikely.

EARLY MODERN CHINA (1300–1700 CE)

In the 1960s and 1970s, economic historians regularly argued that after significant increases in productivity and living standards in the medieval period, Chinese agriculture and industry stagnated between 1400 and 1800, and then actually went backward in the nineteenth century, under the impact of civil wars, mismanagement, and Western imperialism.

There are several versions of this thesis. In his pioneering study of agricultural output between 1368 and 1968, Dwight Perkins built on John Buck's interwar research to suggest that the fifteenth through nineteenth centuries saw best farming practices spreading from the Yangzi Valley to northern China and then, thanks to Qing-era colonization, to Shaanxi and even farther west.[179] Perkins calculated that rice output in the Yangzi Delta had reached very high levels by 1300;[180] at 3.5 tons/hectare (t/ha) it was more than double the level of English output by area in 1800 (1.7 t/ha), albeit only one-third the level of England in 1800 when measured as output per worker (0.3 t/ha vs. 0.92 t/ha). Chinese productivity also compared extremely well to that of irrigated wheat farming in Roman Egypt, which probably managed about 1.67 t/ha and 0.6 t/cap.[181] The spread of best practices across China after 1400, Perkins suggested, enormously increased aggregate output and even raised output per capita by replacing worse practices with better, but the best farmers in the nineteenth century were no more productive than the best farmers of the fourteenth century.

Mark Elvin made a broader argument that after extraordinary increases in energy capture in Tang-Song times, China entered a "high-equilibrium trap" (figure 3.23) in the fourteenth century, in which farming, industry, finance, and transport had reached the highest levels possible with traditional means.[182] The only way to raise productivity, Elvin argued, was by leaping to a fossil-fuel economy; but because traditional techniques had reached such a peak of perfection, there were no incentives in the East for people to make the kind of innovations that led toward an industrial revolution in the West. In the short term, such innovations would actually have decreased output, which therefore ruled them out.

Both these approaches suggested that the Chinese economy stagnated for roughly four hundred years, which matched with conventional mid-twentieth-century Western theories of a timeless, static China.[183] In the same spirit, Angus Maddison suggested that between 1500 and 1820 Chinese GDP/cap was stable at around $600, just half the level in Britain in the year 1700, and, as noted above, Robert

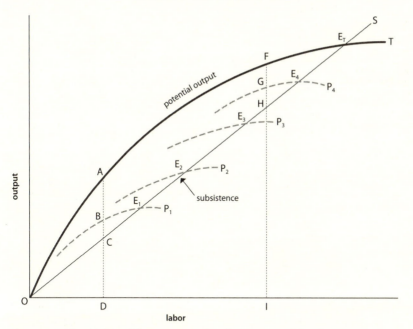

Figure 3.23. The "high-equilibrium trap." After Elvin, *Pattern of the Chinese Past.*

Allen suggested that wages for Chinese urban unskilled workers were relatively stable between 1738 and 1900 and that Yangzi Delta agricultural output declined slightly between 1600 and 1800.[184]

Since the 1990s challenges from Kenneth Pomeranz and others have reopened the debate. My own calculations suggest that in 1200 Song dynasty energy capture was quite similar to that in the Roman Empire (I suggested just over 30,000 kcal/cap/day) while in 1800 it was just slightly lower than contemporary Western scores (I suggested 36,000 kcal/cap/day). That would mean that energy capture per person increased by 15–20 percent between 1200 and 1700. Since so few historians have quantified their suggestions of rising living standards in early modern periods, it is hard to know whether this is closer to the Perkins/Elvin/Maddison/Allen view or the Pomeranz/Wong view.

However, it also seems unlikely that the increase between 1200 and 1700 was smooth. Recent studies of the Yangzi Delta suggest that some areas did experience great stability across these five hundred years,[185] but generally the thirteenth and fourteenth centuries and (to perhaps a lesser degree) the seventeenth century were very

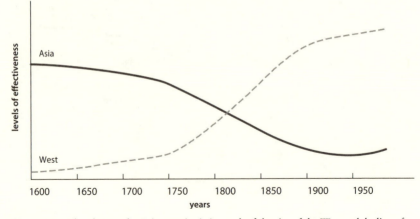

Figure 3.24. Rhoads Murphey's impressionistic graph of the rise of the West and decline of the East, 1600–2000 CE. After Rhoads Murphey, *The Outsiders.*

traumatic. The thirteenth and fourteenth centuries in particular saw massive population decline, destruction of cities, and collapse of trade. I do not know of detailed studies of specific sectors of the economy, but as a very approximate guess I suggest that after peaking just over 30,000 kcal/cap/day around 1200, energy capture fell by perhaps 5 percent (to, say, 30,000 kcal/cap/day in 1300 and 29,000 kcal/cap/day in 1400). That would lead to a rather faster period of recovery between 1400 and 1800 than in the traditional model, adding 20 percent to per capita energy capture across three centuries.

Future research may smooth out these guesstimates, but the overall picture seems plausible: Eastern energy capture grew steadily—indeed, quickly by premodern standards—between 1200 and 1800; but Western energy capture grew much faster. If this is correct, then claims by historians such as Andre Gunder Frank and Rhoads Murphey that an early-modern "decline of the East" was at least as important as an early-modern "rise of the West" in shaping nineteenth-century Western rule must be mistaken, unless we find evidence that before 1400 Eastern energy capture had risen to levels equivalent to those of the nineteenth-century West, and then fell—which is, in fact, exactly what Murphey's graph (which has no numbers on the y-axis) seems to show.[186]

Figure 3.25 shows my estimates for Eastern energy capture in the second millennium CE.

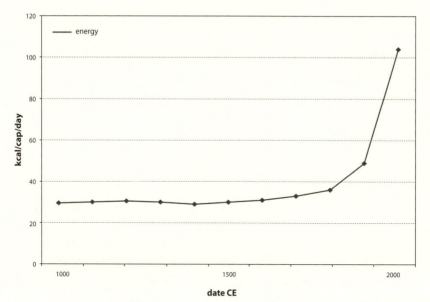

Figure 3.25. Eastern energy capture in the second millennium CE.

Ancient China (200 BCE–200 CE)

Ancient China under the Han dynasty (206 BCE–220 CE, conventionally divided into the Western/Former Han period [206 BCE–9 CE], the Wang Mang interregnum [9–23 CE, also known as the Xin dynasty], and the Eastern/Later Han period [23–22 CE]) was a huge, complex agrarian empire, broadly comparable to the contemporary Roman Empire.[187] The first systematic comparisons of the Roman and Han Empires have appeared only recently, however,[188] and we currently badly need thorough comparisons of the archaeological data, preferably in quantitative form. Until such comparisons become available, the estimates in this section necessarily remain very impressionistic.

The most accessible surveys of the Han economy provide few statistics,[189] but textual sources and qualitative accounts of Han archaeology do allow for some tentative calculations. The most advanced Han agriculture was in northern China, particularly the Central Plain, but it sounds distinctly less advanced than the most productive Roman agriculture. Texts and finds both suggest that even though the most sophisticated Chinese ironworking outstripped anything in the Roman Empire by the first century BCE, iron tools spread only slowly in first-millennium BCE Chinese farming.[190] In 200 BCE bronze, wood, and even bone and shell tools may still have been more common than iron. The evidence for plows is debated, but metal-tipped plows seem to have become common only in Eastern Han times. Extensive use of plow oxen and brick-lined wells for irrigation also seem to be Eastern rather than Western Han features.[191] The literary sources also describe a series of improvements in farming instituted in Han times,[192] beginning with Zhao Guo's "alternating fields method" around 100 BCE, but it is hard to know how widely they were implemented. Many of the most productive techniques and machines may have been restricted to Eastern Han elite estates.

The impression—and it can be no more than that—is that Han farming was less productive than Roman, and particularly less productive than the advanced irrigation farming of the Nile Valley. Productivity certainly rose between 200 BCE and 100 CE, and Jia Sixie's *Essential Methods for the Common People*, written in the 530s CE, shows that techniques (especially in rice farming) continued improving thereafter, even if organization and infrastructure broke down.[193] The texts collected by Hsu suggest that agriculture in Han times was highly sophisticated but nevertheless less developed than Chinese farming would be in Jia's age, and probably also less developed than Roman farming.[194] Systematic comparisons of Han and Roman skeletal evidence on stature and stable isotope analysis of nutrition would be extremely useful.

I know of no comprehensive finds catalogues that would let us directly compare the richness of material goods on settlement sites in the Roman and Han Empires. Full publication of the recent excavations at Sanyangzhuang, a village flooded by the Yellow River in 11 CE, will be particularly valuable. Immediately dubbed "the Asian Pompeii," the village demonstrates a level of preservation that is so extraordinary that archaeologists have recovered the imprints of the villagers' feet as they fled across their muddy fields. Less dramatically, but more valuably, the brief reports available so far describe the brick houses with clay roofs that were like slightly smaller versions of contemporary Roman houses. The villagers were well supplied with tools, many of them made from iron.[195] Han houses in the cities could certainly be quite sophisticated, judging from the clay models that survive and other evidence for layout, but generally the archaeological record points to somewhat simpler and poorer structures in Chinese cities than in Roman.[196]

Literary records describe large-scale iron production, and a recent excavation in Korea has uncovered impressive smelting facilities constructed in the second century CE.[197] Scheidel suggests that the Roman monetary supply was roughly twice the size of that in the Han Empire and that the largest Roman fortunes were also twice as big as the largest Han.[198] These statistics probably correlate only loosely with per capita energy capture, but reinforce the impression that energy capture was higher in the ancient West than in the ancient East. Han energy capture also seems to have been lower than that in Song times; at least there is no suggestion in the published Han evidence of anything to compare with Song levels of coal and iron use, road building, technological invention, financial instruments, or long-distance trade. Trade with steppe nomads and Southeast Asia did increase sharply in Han times,[199] and, as mentioned in *Why the West Rules—For Now*, by the second century CE direct trade contacts probably existed between the Han and Roman Empires.[200]

In the present state of the evidence, any actual numbers for Han energy capture must be speculative. I have suggested that the figure must be lower than the Western peak in Roman times (31,000 kcal/cap/day) and the Eastern peak in Song times (estimated at 30,500 kcal/cap/day). The archaeological and textual records also suggest that Han energy capture was higher than the West's would be at the trough of its post-Roman decline (25,000 kcal/cap/day in the eighth century CE), and much higher than it had been at its Late Bronze Age peak (21,500 kcal/cap/day around 1300 BCE). I have therefore estimated a Han dynasty peak of 27,000 kcal/cap/day in the first century CE, with a slight decline (to 26,000 kcal/cap/day) by 200 CE as organization and infrastructure broke down. The increase during Western Han times seems to have been substantial; I suggest that energy capture rose more than 10 percent across that period, from 24,000 kcal/cap/day in 200 BCE to 25,500 kcal/cap/day in 100 BCE to the peak level of 27,000 kcal/cap/day in 1 BCE/CE and

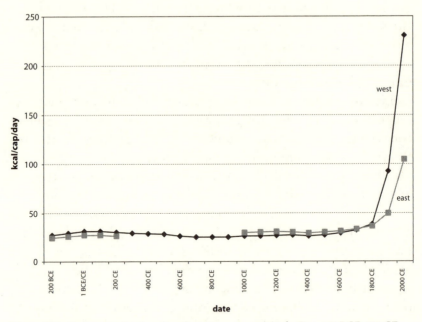

Figure 3.26. Ancient, medieval, and modern energy capture in the East, 200 BCE–200 CE and 1000–2000 CE, plotted against Western energy capture.

100 CE. As noted above, these figures remain speculative and should be corrected when better comparative archaeological data become available; however, the Han peak seems unlikely to have been below 25,000 kcal/cap/day or above 29,000 kcal/cap/day.

Figure 3.26 shows the estimates for Eastern energy capture in the periods 200 BCE–200 CE and 1000–2000 CE and compares the curve with the Western scores for the past 2,200 years, showing the Western core's slight lead in antiquity and the Eastern core's slight lead in medieval and early-modern times, before the West's industrial takeoff.

BETWEEN ANCIENT AND MEDIEVAL (200–1000 CE)

The history of energy capture in the "Period of Disunion" (220–589 CE) is even more obscure than that of Han times. Mark Lewis has recently published an invaluable survey of the period, and Al Dien has collected an equally helpful summary of the archaeological data, but there have been very few quantitative studies.[201]

As in the West, basic economic infrastructures broke down after 200 CE, even though agricultural technology probably improved.[202] Jia's *Essential Methods* displays more detailed knowledge of dry-grain farming than any Han text, and also reveals deep knowledge of rice agriculture being practiced in southern China. It seems that best practices in rice farming steadily spread south of the Yangzi from the third century CE onward, raising yields very significantly by the end of the first millennium CE.[203]

Economic infrastructure also improved, with paddleboats appearing on the Yangzi in the fifth century, water mills at Buddhist monasteries being used by many households, and regional specialties like tea being traded widely. The state intervened drastically in land ownership, most famously in the Equal Field System, but this seems to have helped keep farmers on the land despite the upheavals of the fourth to sixth centuries.[204] Before the reunification of China in 589 and the opening of the Grand Canal in the seventh century, the post-Han economic recovery was largely restricted to the new rice frontier in the south,[205] while commerce declined in the north to the point that coinage largely disappeared; but by 650 CE an empire-wide economic revival was under way. Irrigation came into much wider use, and enormous public markets are documented at Chang'an and other large cities.[206] The collapse of state power after An Lushan's revolt in 755 weakened the Tang dynasty's control over the economy, but any losses involved seem to have been outweighed (particularly in the south) by the gains merchants made from being freed from bureaucratic interference.[207]

Most historians seem to agree that China saw rapid (by premodern standards) economic growth between 600 and 1000 and was economically more advanced than the West in this period.[208] Elite houses in Tang times were at least as impressive as those of the Han era, and Buddhist and court art flourished.[209] However, Chinese medieval archaeologists have so far concentrated rather heavily on art history and architecture, and we have little evidence from which to quantify what these changes meant for energy capture at the individual level. If my estimates of energy capture at 26,000 kcal/cap/

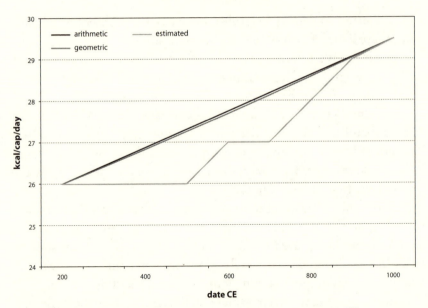

Figure 3.27. Three methods of estimating Eastern energy capture, 200–1000 CE.

day in 200 CE and just under 30,000 kcal/cap/day in 1000 CE are roughly correct, then the seven centuries in between saw a roughly 15 percent increase. The impression created by the sources cited above is that most of this increase came between 700 and 900; I have consequently estimated that energy capture remained fairly flat at 26,000 kcal/cap/day between 200 and 500 CE, then rose to 27,000 kcal/cap/day in 600, rose again to 28,000 kcal/cap/day in 800 and to 29,000 kcal/cap/day in 900. Figure 3.27 shows these estimated scores and the scores if energy capture actually increased steadily across the period 200–1000 (either arithmetically or geometrically). The differences are very small.

Figure 3.28 shows my estimates for East and West for the entire period since 200 BCE. According to these calculations, Eastern energy capture overtook Western for the first time in history in 563 CE; otherwise, though, the history of energy capture was rather uneventful in the two millennia before 1800 CE. At both the Eastern and the Western ends of Eurasia, large empires pressed against the upper limits of what was possible in an organic economy,[210] but could not break through. This is the reality that that underlay the common perception in Eurasian cultures in these years that history

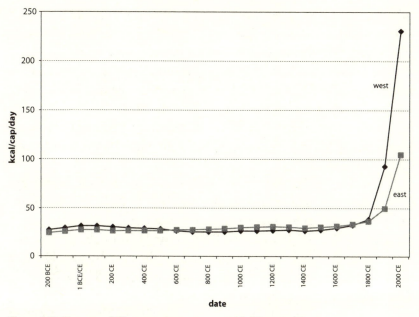

Figure 3.28. Eastern and Western energy capture, 200 BCE–2000 CE.

was cyclical; up to a point, Eurasian elites were correct in thinking that nothing changed very much.

LATE- AND POST–ICE AGE HUNTER-GATHERERS (CA. 14,000 BCE–9500 BCE)

My estimates of Late Ice Age and post–Ice Age energy capture in the East depend heavily on the same research in primate energetics and human evolution as the estimates for the West. *Homo sapiens* in East Asia must have been capturing somewhere around 4,000 kcal/cap/day in 14,000 BCE, otherwise they would have died out; and if they had captured significantly more—even 5,000 kcal/cap/day— we would be able to see it in the archaeological record, in the form of more elaborate buildings, material culture, or expensive food calories. As it is, we see remarkably little change in the archaeological record for nearly five thousand years.

In the Western core, energy capture was already increasing before the Ice Age ended, but in the East structural remains are completely lacking from sites before 9000 BCE.[211] There is some evidence for increasing exploitation of animal carcasses around 25 kya, and crude, handmade, and low-fired pottery—the world's earliest, dating around 16,000 BCE—has been found at Yuchanyan Cave in south China.[212] By 14,000 BCE pottery was also being made in north China and the Russian Far East.[213] The invention of pottery probably means that new kinds of food, requiring boiling, were being eaten, and wild rice (in the south) and wild millet (in the north) seem likely candidates.

However, unlike the situation in the Western core, where rye seeds become plumper at Abu Hureyra by 11,000 BCE, there is little good evidence for increasing per capita capture of food calories between 14,000 BCE and 9500 BCE.[214] At Diaotonghuan wild rice was being gathered and brought back to the cave by 12,000 BCE, well before the Younger Dryas cold period of 10,800–9600 BCE, but seems to have disappeared during this mini–ice age, returning only after 9600. There is as yet no evidence for cultivation of rice or any other plant before the Younger Dryas. There must have been other changes across these millennia, of course, but they seem to have been cyclical and on a scale too small to measure. I therefore estimate energy capture at 4,000 kcal/cap/day for the entire period 14,000–9400 BCE.

From Foragers to Imperialists (9500–200 BCE)

As figure 3.29 makes clear, there is a wide gap to fill between the reasonably secure estimate of energy capture for post–Ice Age hunter-gatherers (4,000 kcal/cap/day) in 14,000–9500 BCE and the next estimate, of 24,000 kcal/cap/day under the Western Han dynasty in 200 BCE. We could simply assume a steady growth rate, either arithmetic or geometric, across these 7,300 years, but the combination of the actual archaeological and textual data, comparanda from economic anthropology, and comparisons with the scores after 200 BCE allows us to be more precise (figure 3.30).

I divide the period into three phases, first briefly describing some of the developments in each phase in general terms and then trying to quantify what these changes meant for energy capture.

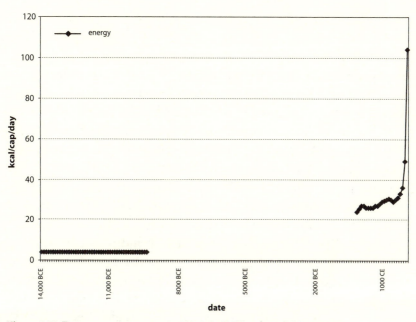

Figure 3.29. Eastern energy capture, 14,000–9500 BCE and 200 BCE–2000 CE.

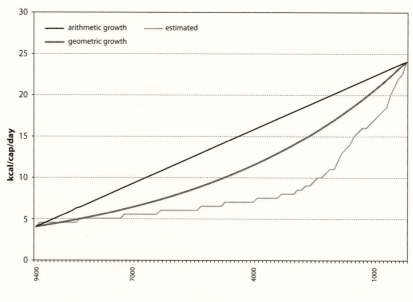

Figure 3.30. Three ways of estimating Eastern energy capture, 9500–200 BCE.

FORAGERS AND FARMERS, 9500–2500 BCE

Archaeologists working in East Asia have often been eager to push the dates of the origins of agricultural as far back into the past as possible. The stone grinders and rollers found at north Chinese sites such as Nanzhuangtou and Hutouling in Hebei as early as 9000/8500 BCE, for instance, have sometimes been treated as evidence of domestication of millet, and in a recent article, Jia-Fu Zhang et al. have even suggested that 25,000-year-old grinding stones from Longwangcan in the Yellow River Valley push the origins of Chinese agriculture back deep into the Ice Age.[215] Analysis of starch residues on Ice Age grinders dating back to 23,000 BCE in Europe, however, has shown that these tools were used to grind wild plants into a paste, to make a kind of preagricultural porridge or bread,[216] and the same is probably true in China. Starches from ninth-millennium BCE ground stone tools excavated recently at Donghulin suggest that these too were used for wild plants, particularly acorns.[217] As late as 6000 BCE acorns still predominated among the starches on ground stone tools from Baiyinchanghan in Manchuria, and wild foods continued to be important in diets in the Wei Valley long after domestication had begun.[218]

The direct physical evidence for domesticated plants in East Asia has become the subject of intense debate.[219] Since the 1980s it had been a commonplace in Chinese archaeology that the rice husks used as temper in pottery at Pengtoushan in the Yangzi Valley around 7000 BCE must have been domesticated, and more recently Jiang and Liu suggested that husk impressions and phytoliths from Shangshan in the Yangzi Delta and Jiahu in the Huai Valley confirmed the domestication of rice by 7000 BCE.[220]

Comparing the evidence and arguments in China with debates over the beginnings of agriculture in Southwest Asia, however, Fuller et al. suggested that there must have been a long period of cultivation of rice before fully domesticated forms evolved.[221] They argued that Jiang and Liu had been misled by the presence of immature spikelets, which would be very common among gathered wild rice, and that the finds from Shangshan and Jiahu are wild. Fuller et al. concluded that cultivation of rice got seriously under way only around 5000 BCE, perhaps in response to a decline in oak cover and with it shortages of the previously important acorns. Fully domesticated rice, they suggested, evolved only around 4000 BCE. They suggested that the domestication of millet in northern China actually preceded that of rice in the south, with clear evidence for cultivated millet by 5500 BCE and domesticated plants by 4500.

Heated exchanges have followed.[222] As so often is the case, there seem to be valid points on both sides of the debate: if the cultivation and domestication of rice began as late as Fuller insists, some of the features of its dispersal across China would be hard to explain; yet if cultivation and domestication began as early as Liu insists, the continuing absence of large, unambiguous samples would be equally hard to explain. Further work will certainly resolve the point, and I suspect it will confirm Fuller's model of a long, drawn-out period of cultivation, while probably also vindicating the traditional view that much of the rice found at the waterlogged fifth-millennium site of Hemudu was domesticated, and that cultivated rice was already present at Jiahu, Diaotonghuan, and Pengtoushan in the seventh millennium.

Our picture of the agricultural revolution in the Eastern core in China is coming to look increasingly like that of the same phenomenon in the Western core in Southwest Asia, but beginning approximately two thousand years later. Just as in the West, it seems that the decisive steps happened not in the great river valleys but in "hilly flanks" surrounding them, that the dispersal took millennia and combined emulation and migration, and that it was accompanied by an equally lengthy "secondary products revolution."[223]

This can best be seen in China in the evolution of agricultural tools. At sixth-millennium Banpo, for instance, harvesting knives made up less than one-third of the total tool assemblage, while at fifth-millennium Miaodigou they had risen to more than half. At Banpo, ineffective pottery blades outnumbered stone blades more than 2:1; at Miaodigou, stone blades outnumbered pottery. At Banpo, axes (necessary for felling trees in slash-and-burn agriculture) outnumbered shovels (necessary for turning the soil in already-cleared fields) more than 5:1; at Miaodigou, spades outnumbered axes more than 4:1. The blades of Miaodigou spades were also typically 50 percent longer (30 cm vs. 20 cm) than those from Banpo, suggesting that fifth-millennium farmers were turning soil more deeply, improving aeration, than those of the sixth millennium.[224]

Other categories of evidence support this picture of a drawn-out secondary products revolution, such as new stable isotopic analyses from north China showing that millet became a major food source only after 5000 BCE, and evidence for the slow domestication of animals in the Yangzi Valley.[225]

The great difference between East and West, however, is that cultivation and domestication seem to have begun in the Western core some two thousand years earlier than in the Eastern core. Even if we pass over the cultivated rye seeds from Abu Hureyra dating around 11,000–10,500 BCE (which apparently precede the Younger Dryas), by 9500 BCE, immediately after the end of the Younger Dryas, cultivated barley and wheat are unmistakable in the Western core. On the present state of the evidence, it is hard to see cultivated rice or millet in the East before about 7500 BCE (and even later than this in Fuller is correct). Fully domesticated wheat and barley were firmly established in the West's Hilly Flanks by 7500 BCE, while domesticated millet was not the norm in the East until 5500 and rice not until 4500 (or 4000, according to Fuller). The secondary products revolution, largely complete in the West by 4000 BCE, was still unfolding in the East in the third millennium BCE. Not until 2500 BCE, for instance, do we find really convincing Eastern evidence of classic agrarian gender structures, with men associated with outdoor activities and women with those indoor.[226]

As in the West, the Eastern increase in aggregate capture of food calories went along with great population growth and a slow but impressive increase in the per capita capture of nonfood calories. The earliest houses known date around 8000 BCE, at Shangshan in the Yangzi Delta; earlier sites have produced only hearths. House sizes steadily increased, from the round, semi-subterranean huts averaging just 4–6 m² at seventh-millennium Jiahu to the square, above-ground buildings covering 30–40 m² at fourth-millennium Dahecun. The largest structure at seventh-millennium Jiahu covered 10 m², while fourth-millennium Dadiwan had "palaces" covering 150 m² and 290 m², counting just the roofed space. The contents of houses also increased, slowly until the third millennium, but then jumping sharply.[227]

Archaic States (ca. 2500–800 BCE)

The rate of increase in energy capture accelerated after 2500 BCE, and particularly after 2000, with the emergence of more complex societies. As in the West, there are no large-scale systematic collections or comparisons of skeletal data to document directly the impact of archaic states on the human body, but there are other indications of change.

One is the spread of rice agriculture in northern China, particularly after about 2300 BCE;[228] another, the huge increase in animal bones from settlements in the late third and second millennia. By 2000 BCE domesticated pigs regularly make up two-thirds of the domestic faunal assemblages.[229] The textual record also speaks of various reforms in the organization of first-millennium BCE agriculture, which may reflect genuine changes. *Mencius* 3/1 (a philosophical text composed around 300 BCE) speaks of the Well Field System, supposedly instituted under the Western Zhou dynasty in the early first millennium BCE, although Mencius's account must be an idealized version of a much messier reality.[230] Historians often describe this land-tenure regime as a kind of feudalism, although this does not seem entirely appropriate.[231]

Overall, Eastern agriculture seems to have remained much less productive (per unit of labor or land) than contemporary Western practices. A few copper objects (mostly ornaments) are known from third-millennium sites, but there are very few examples of metal agricultural tools before 800 BCE. Wood, stone, bone, and shell remained overwhelmingly the most important materials in agriculture down to 800 BCE, and until better evidence appears, we have to conclude that agricultural output in the Eastern archaic states rose more slowly than that in the irrigated farming systems of the Western archaic states in Mesopotamia and Egypt.

Nonfood energy capture, however, does seem to have increased strongly between 2500 and 800 BCE. Our picture is limited by archaeologists' surprising lack of interest in post-Neolithic settlements in China (caused by an archaeological focus on elite tombs and monuments rather than by scarcity of actual remains). The few finds do show that by 800 BCE the size and quality of houses had improved. Pit houses continued to be built, but more people lived above ground, sometimes in substantial, rectangular houses with trenched foundations, rammed earth or mud-brick walls, and lime-plastered floors and wall skirting. Some houses had painted decoration, while others were organized around spacious courtyards. Finds of waterlogged carpentry in tombs also show that joinery techniques improved drastically. The chronology of these developments remains unclear, but in broad terms we can be confident that housing standards rose significantly between the late third and early first millennium BCE.[232]

The quantity and quality of household goods also rose. Potters were regularly using fast wheels in the second millennium, and silk, lacquer, and jade became more common. The first copper objects appear around 3000 BCE, almost certainly stimulated by knowledge of Western metallurgy brought over the steppes.[233] Metal seems to have been very rare indeed until the early second millennium BCE, when gigantic foundries appeared at Erlitou, Zhengzhou, and Anyang, casting weapons, some craft tools, and above all ritual vessels. Well-preserved mines at Tongling attest to the scale of Chinese metallurgy as early as 1600 BCE.[234]

The lack of good household archaeology means that we know rather little about the everyday use of metals, though grave goods and hoards seem to imply that bronze vessels did spread some way down the social scale by 800 BCE. At the elite level, metal use was enormous; the largest known ritual vessel, the twelfth-century BCE Simu Wu square *ding* (probably looted from a royal tomb at Anyang), used nearly one ton of bronze.[235] After the Shang/Zhou transition in 1046 BCE the number of inscribed bronze vessels explodes, probably testifying the to the emergence of a very wealthy aristocracy.[236] Archaeologists have also identified a "ritual revolution" in the elite use of funerary bronzes in the ninth century, which seems to have coincided with great advances in bronze working, including use of the lost-wax method and welding.[237]

Elite monuments also expanded enormously after 2500 BCE. The largest sites of the late third millennium (sometimes covering

200–300 ha) began to have stamped earth platforms that were often more than two meters thick. The grandest of all these sites, at Taosi, had a palatial enclosure covering five hectares as early as 2600 BCE; by 2300 it was protected by fortification walls nine meters thick and boasted a great circular monument and a palace with painted walls.[238]

Beginning around 1900 BCE much bigger palaces were constructed at the probable Xia-Shang dynastic capitals of Erlitou and Zhengzhou, and the thirteenth- through eleventh-century Shang royal tombs at Anyang, although looted, are impressive by any standards.[239] The Western Zhou palaces excavated to date are not quite as grand as their Shang predecessors, although the remains from the capital at Feng are still very substantial.[240] Wealthy burials also proliferated after 1046 BCE.[241] The scale of elite ostentation and energy capture may have leveled off between 1000 and 800 BCE, but was nevertheless far higher than in 2500 BCE.

As in the West, the era of archaic states saw the first unambiguous evidence for regional collapses, most obviously with the fall of Taosi and the breakdown of the Shandong complex societies around 2300 BCE. Like the 2200 BCE and 1750 BCE collapses in the West, though, the Taosi/Shandong decline had no obvious impact on energy capture, at least when measured on the coarse grain used here.

The Spring and Autumn/Warring States Period (800–200 BCE)

The East experienced nothing like the catastrophic 1200 BCE collapse in the West, which dragged the core's energy capture down for centuries. Eastern energy capture, by contrast, rose faster and faster. As in the era of archaic states we are handicapped by the lack of syntheses of skeletal data and the scarcity of household excavations, but again the evidence is adequate to establish a general picture.

The literary sources attest further changes in land tenure, particularly a shift toward private landholdings in the possession of legally free peasants, taxed by the state, replacing the dependent peasantry working land for their lords. The first clear sign of this is a tax on yields in the state of Lu in 594 BCE, and by the third century BCE the shift to freehold was probably complete.[242] This change in property rights probably encouraged more investment by the farmers themselves; if so, higher yields may well have been the outcome.

It also went along with the development of a sophisticated literature on the theory and methods of farming, beginning with Li Kui in the state of Wei around 440 BCE.[243]

Textual evidence for multicropping seems to go along with the new property regime. By 200 BCE it was apparently normal to rotate two crops (wheat and millet in northern China, millet and rice in the South), with occasional planting of legumes, potentially producing three crops every two years. Some historians also argue from the spread of names based on "ox" that draft animals also became important (at least among the elite) in the mid-first millennium BCE.[244] We are on more certain ground, however, with the textual evidence for massive state involvement in irrigation projects beginning with the magistrate Ximen Bao in the state of Wei in the 430s. All the Warring States invested heavily in canals to improve agricultural output, culminating in Li Bing's massive project for the state of Qin in newly conquered Sichuan around 300 BCE.[245]

Metal tools probably first began to be used on significant scales only after 800 BCE. Li Xueqin and Donald Wagner have suggested that bronze tools became more and more important in the lower Yangzi area between 800 and 500 BCE, but some archaeologists remain skeptical.[246] By 500 BCE, however, iron was in use in China (probably, like bronze technology, ironworking was initially transmitted from the West across the steppes). Chinese smiths made rapid progress, producing true steel in the sixth century and cast iron in the fifth (European smiths would not master this technology until the fourteenth century CE). By 200 BCE iron weapons had begun to replace bronze and iron tools were definitely becoming more common. Bronze industries continued to flourish, though, with a sixth-century mine at Tonglüshan displaying extraordinarily sophisticated construction in its timber-lined shafts and a huge, equally impressive foundry at Houma.[247]

Commerce also accelerated in this period. Beginning with Zang Wenzhong of the state of Lu in 625 BCE, ministers moved to abolish customs posts within their states. Vassal states had to give guarantees not to interfere with traders, and water transport became increasingly easy. Independent of developments in the West, Chinese traders began minting and using bronze coins in the fifth century. By 200 BCE, millions were in circulation.[248] Archaeologists in China have not yet quantified shipwrecks, animal bones, inscriptions, and lead pollution in the same way as has been done in the West, but a great increase in trade between 800 and 200 BCE nonetheless seems very clear.

CALCULATING THE SCORES

Figure 3.30 shows three different ways of filling the gap in energy capture estimates between 9500 and 200 BCE, by simply assuming steady increases at arithmetic or geometric scales versus making estimates based on the actual evidence. Arithmetic increases seem highly unlikely: the upper line in figure 3.30 would mean that the increase in energy capture between the foundation of Jiahu around 7000 BCE and that of Hemudu around 5000 BCE was as large as that between the destruction of Taosi around 2300 BCE and the Qin irrigation of Sichuan around 300 BCE. That cannot be correct. We should probably assume that the rise in energy capture was exponential, with the exponent increasing through time.

All the challenges that applied to converting archaeological data into consumption levels in the West also apply in the East, but comparing the Eastern and Western finds suggests that the East in fact followed a trajectory very similar to that of the West. The major difference was that the East started down the path of cultivation and domestication about two thousand years behind the West, and its energy capture consequently ran behind the West's. Initially, in the foraging-to-farming era discussed in the "Foragers and Farmers, 9500–2500 BCE" section above, the gap seems to have stayed at about two millennia. I suggest that Eastern energy capture increased by roughly 50 percent, from 4,000 to 6,000 kcal/cap/day, between 9500 and 6000 BCE, and by 2500 BCE had risen by another 50 percent, to 9,000 kcal/cap/day, as the secondary products revolution ran its course. Eastern energy capture at this point, the age when Egyptians were building the great pyramids, seems to have been comparable to levels in the Western core around 4500 BCE, the age when the West's first large towns, like Tell Brak and Susa, were appearing (figure 3.31).

After 2500 BCE, though, Eastern energy capture grew much faster. With such poor Eastern data we can speak only in terms of

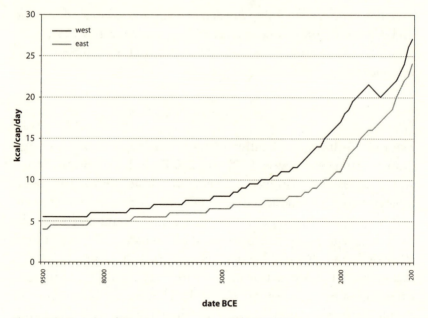

Figure 3.31. Eastern and Western energy capture, 9500–200 BCE.

general impressions, but it seems to me that by 2000 BCE, on the eve of Erlitou's takeoff, Eastern energy capture must have been roughly comparable with where the Western core had been around 3500 BCE, in the age of Susa and on the eve of Uruk's expansion (i.e., 11,000 kcal/cap/day). In 1500 BCE, when the Shang were building Zhengzhou, Eastern energy capture seems to me comparable with the Western level around 2400 BCE, in the era of the Royal Cemetery of Ur and Egypt's great pyramids (14,000 kcal/cap/day). By 1000 BCE, when the Zhou displaced the Shang, Eastern energy capture strikes me as being comparable with that of the Western core just one thousand years before, in the postcrisis recovery that replaced Egypt's Old Kingdom with the Middle Kingdom and Mesopotamia's Ur III Empire with the Akkadian city-states (17,000 kcal/cap/day). By 500 BCE, though, the West's collapse around 1200 BCE and slow recovery had narrowed the gap even further. I would suggest that by 500 BCE, Eastern energy capture was comparable to the West's around 800 BCE, as the Assyrian Empire was approaching the great crisis that drove it to shift toward high-end institutions (i.e., 21,000 kcal/cap/day)—which was also, of course, the level that the West had reached around 1400 BCE, half a century before Akhenaten and Nefertiti began their bizarre religious and political experiment at Amarna.

These estimates will of course need to be tested against better evidence (Western as well as Eastern) and for now can be nothing more than conjectures. If they are in approximately the right range, however, they mean that after roughly doubling in six thousand years between about 9500 and 3500 BCE, Eastern energy capture doubled again in the two thousand years between 3300 and 1300 BCE, and then rose another 50 percent in the eleven hundred years between 1300 and 200 BCE.

The Western collapse around 1200 BCE was the main factor in shrinking the East-West gap to three hundred years by 200 BCE, but the convergence had already begun long before then. In the thousand years between 2200 and 1200 BCE, in fact, Western energy capture increased by just 31 percent, but the East's rose by 52 percent. Why this happened is not entirely clear, although it does now seem likely that the East learned bronze technology from the West and obtained domesticated wheat from the same sources via the agency of travelers over the steppes.[249] Whether this alone explains the East's catch-up, or whether the Central Asian travelers so well preserved as the Tarim Basin mummies transferred more technologies from West to East,[250] or whether as yet unidentified factors caused Eastern society to evolve faster than Western in the archaic states phase remains to be established.

ENERGY CAPTURE: DISCUSSION

Figure 2.5, showing the shape of energy capture across the past sixteen thousand years, shows the backbone of my argument in *Why the West Rules—For Now*. The other dimensions of the social development index—organization (measured through the proxy of city size), war-making capacity, and information technology—are, after all, simply ways of *using* energy; and although measuring energy capture alone would not cover the full spectrum of ideas encapsulated in social development,[251] energy must be the central plank in any index. I have therefore discussed the evidence for energy capture in more detail than that for the other three traits.

Clearly, much work remains to be done. Although energy capture is the backbone of history, our evidence for it is patchy and imprecise. There are generally more data to work with in Western history than in Eastern, and where quantifiable evidence does exist, as in much of prehistoric archaeology, scholars working on the West have usually produced more syntheses of the results than those working on the East. In particular, scholars of the West have done more household archaeology and more research on real wages.

As the evidence base improves, new findings will resolve some of the questions raised here. For instance, in time we may be able to say with more confidence whether the Roman peak in Western energy capture came in the first century BCE or the first or second century CE, and whether it really was higher than the Song peak in the East (and whether that really came in the twelfth century). We should also be able to document whether there really was a decline in energy capture in East and West alike in the early to mid-first millennium CE, whether the Western crisis around 1200 BCE really did drive down energy capture (as I suggest it did), and whether the Western crisis around 2200 BCE and the Eastern one around 2300 BCE also drove down energy capture (as I suggest they did not). Better evidence will inevitably strengthen some of the conclusions I have reached and weaken others.

The overall pattern, though, seems to me to be grounded fairly firmly in evidence, even if there is room to dispute any specific score. Energy capture at the end of the last Ice Age was very low, not much above 4,000 kcal/cap/day, and rose extremely slowly. There were gains in food calories, but, as Malthus saw two centuries ago, these were normally converted into extra bodies, which consumed the gains and kept most people's food consumption below 2,000 kcal/cap/day. But as Malthus also saw, there were more substantial gains in nonfood calories, and these accumulated over time. Total (food + nonfood) energy capture consequently grew exponentially rather than arithmetically, and the exponent increased over time.

In both East and West, we see knees in the curve around the time of the beginnings of cultivation (ca. 9500 BCE in the West and 7500

BCE in the East), the beginnings of domestication (ca. 7500 BCE in the West and 5500 BCE in the East), the rise of archaic states (ca. 3500 BCE in the West and 2000 BCE in the East), the creation of empires (ca. 750 BCE in the West and 300 BCE in the East), and above all the rise of fossil-fuel industries (ca. 1800 CE in the West and 1900 CE in the East). For roughly two thousand years, between the zenith of the great ancient empires and the industrial revolution, energy capture was trapped under what I have called a "hard ceiling," a little over 30,000 kcal/cap/day. This, I suggested, marks the limits of what is possible in agrarian societies. It also largely explains the pervasive sense in the elite writings that survive from ancient and medieval times that humanity had reached its peak, that history was cyclical, and that the best times lay in the past—just as the explosive growth in Western energy capture since 1700 CE largely explains the optimism of so many European thinkers in the eighteenth and nineteenth centuries and Americans in the twentieth and twenty-first.

CHAPTER 4

|||||||||||||||||||||||||||||||||||||||||

SOCIAL ORGANIZATION

METHODS, ASSUMPTIONS, AND SOURCES

A long tradition of research in the social sciences, and particularly in archaeology, anthropology, economics, and urban studies, has demonstrated the strong relationships between the size of the largest settlements within a society and the complexity of its social organization.[1] The correlation is far from perfect, but it works well enough at the coarse-grained level of an index of social development spanning sixteen thousand years.

City size also has the great advantage of being, in principle, conceptually simple. All we need to do is (a) establish the size of the largest settlements in East and West at each point in the past for which an index score is being calculated, (b) establish the size of the world's largest city in 2000 CE, (c) divide the population of the largest city in 2000 CE by 250 (the full complement of social development points to be awarded on this trait), and then (d) divide the populations of past cities by that number.

Opinions do vary among demographers on the size of the world's largest city in 2000 CE, depending on definitions of urban boundaries and the reliability of census data; to establish a fairly uncontroversial baseline, I simply took the estimate of the *Economist Pocket World in Figures* that Tokyo topped the league, with a population of 26.4 million, and that New York was the biggest city in the Western core, with 16.7 million people.[2] There are plenty of other estimates I could have used, but no reliable figures seem to depart very far from these numbers.

This starting point means that the East scores the full 250 points for organization in 2000 CE, and that that a population of 106,800 scores 1 point. New York's 16.7 million residents consequently score 156.37 points for the West in 2000 CE. The smallest score I considered worth recording, 0.01 points, required just over 1,000 people, which means that—unlike the energy capture scores—organization scores *do* fall to zero, becoming too small to measure before 4000 BCE in the East and 7500 BCE in the West.

The main challenges for calculating organization this way are empirical. For early settlements we have to rely on archaeology and ethnographic/historical analogies. Estimates depend heavily on measurements of settlement area and extrapolation from documented densities. The anthropologist Roland Fletcher shows how much densities vary,[3] although they do seem to follow general rules. In some cases, such as classical Greece, estimates are probably reliable within quite narrow margins of error; in others, like third and second millennium BCE Mesopotamia, they may be less so.[4] On the whole, well-documented premodern cities rarely have densities over 200/hectare (ha), and numbers closer to 100/ha are more common. Occasionally, premodern towns might go as high as 500/ha, but such densities are exceptional and need very clear evidence. Very small villages and select areas within twentieth- and twenty-first-century CE supercities, however, sometimes have densities well over 500/ha.

Beginning in ancient times, we get some contemporary literary observations on city size, but these are often unreliable since the inhabitants of ancient cities often did not themselves know how many people lived around them. This means that archaeology and analogy remain very important until the modern era—although since there are no contemporary cities quite like premodern urban giants such as Rome and Chang'an, analogies are more problematic for much of the past three thousand years than for prehistory. In more recent times, data on food imports sometimes survive, which give another way to control population size; and in the most modern periods we can draw on fairly accurate government statistics.

Several writers have offered overviews of urban history with precise figures. Tertius Chandler's *Four Thousand Years of Urban*

Growth is an invaluable reference and is probably the most widely cited work, although it provides few sources (an earlier version, *Three Thousand Years of Urban Growth*, is better documented).[5] There is room for debate over all estimates of premodern city size, and in my opinion some of Chandler and Fox's estimates are not supported well by the data. Their figures for medieval Islamic cities are particularly high, and, like many historians, they greatly exaggerate the size of ancient Greek cities, suggesting for example that Athens had 155,000 residents in 430 BCE, rather than the 30,000–40,000 that probably lived there.[6] Their estimates for medieval and early modern China, however, do avoid the inflated numbers that historians often propose.

While there would be some advantages to taking a single source like Chandler and Fox's *Three Thousand Years of Urban Growth* and then relying on it consistently, the drawbacks seem to outweigh them. The main advantage of relying on a single source is normally that it makes errors more consistent and hence easier to compensate for; however, in this case the errors seem to be rather randomly distributed. I decided instead to rely on what seemed to be the best experts for each time and place, cross-checking their scores to reduce idiosyncrasies. I summarize these results for Western and Eastern cities, in each case providing my sources, any particular problems involved in the estimate, and, if the estimate is my own, my reasons for choosing that figure, collecting my estimates for the West in table 4.1 and for the East in table 4.2. Among archaeologists working on periods before 3000 BCE in the West and before 2000 BCE and among historians working on the second millennium CE, it is conventional to offer estimates for city sizes, even if they vary widely, but unfortunately historians and archaeologists working on periods between 3000/2000 BCE and 1000 CE are much more hesitant to hazard concrete estimates.

ESTIMATES OF WESTERN CITY SIZES

For each date (every century back to 1400 BCE; every 250 years, 1500–2500 BCE; every 500 years, 2500–4000 BCE; every thousand

Table 4.1

Western maximum settlement sizes, 8000 BCE–2000 CE

Date	Settlement	Size	Points
8000 BCE	Mureybet	perhaps 500	
7000 BCE	Beidha, Basta, Çatalhöyük	1,000	0.01
6000 BCE	Çatalhöyük	3,000	0.03
5000 BCE	Tell Brak	4,000	0.04
4000 BCE	Uruk, Tell Brak	5,000	0.05
3500 BCE	Uruk, Susa, Tell Brak	8,000	0.09
3000 BCE	Uruk	45,000	0.42
2500 BCE	Uruk	50,000	0.47
2250 BCE	Akkad, Memphis	35,000	0.33
2000 BCE	Memphis, Ur	60,000	0.56
1750 BCE	Babylon	65,000	0.61
1500 BCE	Uruk, Thebes	75,000	0.7
1400 BCE	Thebes	80,000	0.75
1300 BCE	Thebes	80,000	0.75
1200 BCE	Babylon, Thebes	80,000	0.75
1100 BCE	Memphis, Thebes, Tanis	50,000	0.47
1000 BCE	Thebes	50,000	0.47
900 BCE	Thebes	50,000	0.47
800 BCE	Nimrud/Kalhu	75,000	0.7
700 BCE	Nineveh	100,000	0.94
600 BCE	Babylon	125,000	1.17
500 BCE	Babylon	150,000	1.4
400 BCE	Babylon	150,000	1.4
300 BCE	Babylon, Alexandria	150,000	1.4
200 BCE	Alexandria	300,000	2.81
100 BCE	Alexandria, perhaps Rome	400,000	3.75
1 BCE/CE	Rome	1,000,000	9.36
100 CE	Rome	1,000,000	9.36
200 CE	Rome	1,000,000	9.36
300 CE	Rome	800,000	7.49
400 CE	Rome	800,000	7.49
500 CE	Constantinople	450,000	4.23
600 CE	Constantinople	150,000	1.41
700 CE	Constantinople	125,000	1.17
800 CE	Baghdad	175,000	1.64
900 CE	Cordoba	175,000	1.64

Table 4.1 (*continued*)

Date	Settlement	Size	Points
1000 CE	Cordoba	200,000	1.87
1100 CE	Constantinople	250,000	2.34
1200 CE	Baghdad, Cairo, Constantinople	250,000	2.34
1300 CE	Cairo	400,000	3.75
1400 CE	Cairo	125,000	1.17
1500 CE	Cairo	400,000	3.75
1600 CE	Constantinople	400,000	3.75
1700 CE	London and Constantinople	600,000	5.62
1800 CE	London	900,000	8.43
1900 CE	London	6,600,000	61.8
2000 CE	New York	16,700,000	156.37

years before 5000 BCE),[7] I provide first my identification of the largest city and estimate for its population, then my main source and the number of points the city scores on the social development index, then brief comments on conflicting estimates and the nature of the evidence.

2000 CE: New York, 16,700,000;[8] 156.37 points. The *Economist Pocket World in Figures* estimated the population of Mexico City in 2000 CE at 18,100,000 and that of São Paolo at 18,000,000, but New York remains the largest city in the Western core (i.e., the United States, the borderlands of Canada, and Northwest and Central Europe).

1900 CE: London, 6,600,000;[9] 61.8 points. Chandler estimates London at 6,480,000,[10] and there seems to be general agreement among urban historians on a figure around 6.5 million, based on multiple kinds of official statistics.

1800 CE: London, 900,000;[11] 8.43 points. There is a little more debate about populations in 1800 CE than those for 1900, and some sources put London a little lower.[12] The evidence consists of a combination of government statistics and eyewitness comments. The next-largest Western city was probably Constantinople, which Chandler puts at 570,000.

1700 CE: London and Constantinople, 600,000;[13] 5.62 points. Chandler estimates Constantinople at 700,000 and London at 550,000; Bairoch suggests that Constantinople was the biggest city in the world, with 650,000–1,000,000 people. John Haldon, codirector of the International Medieval Logistics Project, suggests that Constantinople may have been closer to 700,000 people. The arguments combine tax registers, records of food imports, records of births and deaths, and the area covered by the cities.[14]

1600 CE: Constantinople, 400,000;[15] 3.75 points. Eric Jones suggests that Constantinople was 600,000; Chandler says 700,000; and Bairoch says 650,000–1,000,000.[16] The evidence still consists mostly of tax registers, records of food imports, records of births and deaths, and the area covered by the cities, but its quality declines sharply by 1600 CE.

1500 CE: Cairo, 400,000;[17] 3.75 points. Frank says that Bairoch estimated Cairo at 450,000, and Bairoch also suggests that Constantinople had 300,000–500,000 residents, but John Haldon thinks that so soon after the 1453 sack its population was just 100,000. The evidence is still of the same types as for 1600 and 1700, but between roughly 500 and 1500 CE there is much more debate on how to interpret it. Historians of Europe and those of the Middle East also sometimes use very different methods, often leading to unrealistically high estimates for Islamic cities, implying densities of 500–1,000/ha. Historians of Muslim cities also tend to be more cautious than European historians in hazarding estimates. Cairo seems to be particularly problematic. The evidence consists mostly of military registers, contemporary impressions, and the areas covered by the cities, but there are many challenges involved in interpreting it.[18]

1400 CE: Cairo, 125,000; 1.17 points. This is my own estimate, based on comparison with the extremely high mortality rates in European cities during the Black Death. Chandler suggested Cairo still had 360,000 residents in 1400, but that would imply that the population had fallen just 20 percent from its preplague peak of 450,000, which seems inconsistent with the accounts offered by Abu-Lughod and Dols. For the nature of the evidence, see under 1500 CE.[19]

1300 CE: Cairo, 400,000;[20] 3.75 points. On the sources and difficulties, see under 1500 CE.

1200 CE: Baghdad, Cairo, Constantinople, 250,000;[21] 2.34 points. There is some disagreement over the populations of these cities, but general consensus that all had populations between 200,000 and 300,000. Some estimates, however (particularly for Baghdad), go much higher (see under 1000 CE).

1100 CE: Constantinople, 250,000;[22] 2.34 points. Wickham also suggests that Cairo reached 250,000 in the eleventh century.[23]

1000 CE: Cordoba, 200,000; 1.87 points. This is my own estimate. Several estimates put Cordoba at 400,000–500,000. Chandler also thinks that Constantinople's population was 300,000 and Baghdad's 125,000. These estimates, however, all seem very high. Haldon puts Constantinople at 150,000, and the settled area of Baghdad (550–860 ha) seems too small for a population above 100,000. Cordoba covered roughly twice as large an area, and I therefore suggest that its population peaked around 200,000 in the eleventh century.[24]

900 CE: Cordoba, 175,000; 1.64 points. This is my own estimate. Chandler estimates Baghdad at 900,000, Constantinople at 300,000, and Cordoba at 200,000. Several other scholars also put the population of Baghdad quite high, though nowhere near as high as Chandler. Ira Lapidus, for instance, suggests 300,000–500,000, which would require a population density of 350–900/ha. Chandler's estimate would call for a density of 1,050–1,600. Both these figure seem extraordinarily high; other large preindustrial cities rarely managed 200/ha.[25]

800 CE: Baghdad, 175,000; 1.64 points. Again this is my own estimate. Baghdad clearly grew very quickly after its foundation in 762, and its population may have peaked before the sieges of 812–813 and 865. Chandler estimates 700,000 for Baghdad, 250,000 for Constantinople, and 160,000 for Cordoba. Again, these numbers seem very high given the physical size of the cities and the generally small populations in the Western core at this point, after centuries of plagues. Haldon sets the population of Constantinople in 750 CE at just 40,000–50,000.[26]

700 CE: Constantinople, 125,000; 1.17 points. My estimate, extrapolated from Haldon's figures for 500 and 750 CE. Constantinople's population clearly fell very steeply between 550 and 750 CE, beginning with the Justinianic plague and accelerating after the Persian Wars in the 610s and the breakdown of the Constantinople-

Egypt grain trade in the 640s. Haldon estimates Constantinople's population at 40,000–50,000 in 750 CE, but the evidence does not allow us to be sure how much of the fall came before 700 and how much after. I assume that the most severe period of decline came after 700, with the population falling just 15–20 percent in the seventh century then a further 65 percent in the eighth century.[27]

600 CE: Constantinople, 150,000; 1.41 points. See discussion under 700 CE.

500 CE: Constantinople, 450,000;[28] 4.23 points. Cameron and Wickham suggest 500,000, and Chandler says 400,000. The arguments depend heavily on our sources for the grain supply. Rome's population fell very quickly after the loss of North Africa in 439, probably shrinking to just 20,000–40,000 by about 600 CE. Wickham calls seventh-century Rome an "urban village."[29]

400 CE: Rome, 800,000;[30] 7.49 points. The population of Rome probably fell during the third century CE, but it is hard to say just how much. It was clearly by far the biggest city in the Mediterranean in the fourth century, though, and may have still had three quarters of a million residents as late as the Vandal conquest of North Africa in 439. After that, the population fell very sharply. Wickham suggests a lower figure, of 500,000 in the early fifth century.[31]

300 CE: Rome, 800,000; 7.49 points. See under 400 CE. The number of urban districts was lower in 300 CE than in 400, which may mean that the population fell more sharply in the third century than I have allowed for and then grew again during the fourth century, but there is no way to be sure.

200 CE: Rome, 1,000,000; 9.36 points. Most scholars think that Rome had a million residents by the late first century BCE, and that the population stayed somewhere around that level until at least 200 CE, then declined significantly in the third century and dramatically in the fifth.[32] We probably cannot be more precise than that, though. Some scholars suggest that Rome was much smaller, perhaps never exceeding 500,000.[33] That is very much a minority view, however, and 500,000 is probably the minimum possible number.[34] The arguments depend partly on a separate set of heated debates over the population of Italy as a whole (either 4–5 million or 12+ million)[35] and partly on the density of population within the city itself.

100 CE: Rome, 1,000,000; 9.36 points. This is the generally accepted figure for the first two centuries CE (see under 200 CE). It is perfectly possible that the population kept growing until about 200 CE, but it probably never greatly exceeded a million.[36]

1 BCE/CE. Rome, 1,000,000; 9.36 points. See under 200 CE.

100 BCE: Alexandria, perhaps Rome, 400,000;[37] 3.75 points. The grain trade statistics are again important.[38]

200 BCE: Alexandria, 300,000;[39] 2.81 points.

300 BCE: Babylon, Alexandria, 150,000;[40] 1.4 points. Scheidel suggests that Alexandria grew very rapidly after its foundation in 331 BCE and then slowed down in the third and second centuries BCE.

400 BCE: Babylon, 150,000;[41] 1.4 points. Estimates depend on city size, densities, and interpretation of contemporary comments by Herodotus and Aristotle. Some estimates for Babylon are lower; Gates suggests 80,000, which seems reasonable to me for second-millennium BCE Babylon, but may be too low for the mid-first millennium BCE.[42]

500 BCE: Babylon, 150,000; 1.4 points. See under 400 BCE.

600 BCE: Babylon, 125,000; 1.17 points. My estimate, extrapolated from estimates for 400 BCE and 500 BCE.

700 BCE: Nineveh, 100,000;[43] 0.94 points. Estimates once again depend largely on guesses at densities and interpretation of contemporary comments such as Jonah (3:3, 4:11). Consequently, they vary wildly; Åkerman, for instance, suggests 300,000 at Nineveh, which would mean a density of 630/ha.[44]

800 BCE: Nimrud (also known as Kalhu), 75,000; 0.7 points. See under 700 BCE.

900 BCE: Thebes, 50,000;[45] 0.47 points. Egyptian written sources during the Third Intermediate Period (ca. 1100–650 BCE) are particularly poor,[46] and archaeologists have rarely made settlement excavations of sites of this period a priority, so our estimates are particularly speculative.

1000 BCE: Thebes, 50,000;[47] 0.47 points.

1100 BCE: Memphis, Thebes, Tanis, 50,000;[48] 0.47 points.

1200 BCE: Babylon, Thebes, 80,000;[49] 0.75 points. The residential areas of the New Kingdom city at Thebes and Bronze Age Babylon lie largely beneath the water table, which makes serious study difficult. However, Thebes was clearly much larger than the Middle Kingdom city, which covered only about 50 ha and was probably the world's largest city between 1500 and 1200 BCE. Most of our scanty information about Babylon comes from the early German excavations in the Merkes neighborhood.[50]

1300 BCE: Thebes, 80,000;[51] 0.75 points.

1400 BCE: Thebes, 80,000;[52] 0.75 points.

1500 BCE: Uruk, Thebes, 75,000;[53] 0.7 points. Some estimates are much higher; Christian, for instance, suggests that Babylon reached 200,000 people.[54]

1750 BCE: Babylon, 65,000; 0.61 points. My estimate. We remain ignorant about the size and density of population in Hammurabi's Babylon (reigned 1792–1750 BCE on the "long chronology"), which not only lies under the water table but also is buried under first-millennium BCE Babylon. It was probably the biggest city in the world, commanding an extensive empire.[55] The remains of other eighteenth-century BCE Babylonian cities suggest quite high densities, and a guess of around 65,000 will be in the right range, although we lack information for a proper estimate.[56]

2000 BCE: Memphis, Ur, 60,000;[57] 0.56 points. There is so much disagreement over population densities in third-millennium BCE cities (particularly in Mesopotamia)[58] that most archaeologists avoid offering numbers, and Chandler's estimates have largely stood unchallenged. That said, we can be fairly confident that no city had 100,000 people in the third or even the second millennium BCE, and that the biggest cities were in the 50,000 ± 15,000 range (i.e., 0.33–0.61 points). The figures for Uruk, based on R. M. Adams's survey,[59] are probably more reliable than those for Memphis and Ur, and particularly than the guess for Akkad, which has not even been located.

2250 BCE: Akkad, Memphis, 35,000;[60] 0.33 points. See under 2000 BCE.

2500 BCE: Uruk, 50,000;[61] 0.47 points. See under 2000 BCE.

3000 BCE: Uruk, 45,000;[62] 0.42 points. See under 2000 BCE.

3500 BCE: Uruk, Susa, Tell Brak, 8,000; 0.09 points. The numbers for Uruk and Susa are pure guesses, rather than proper estimates. Uruk seems to have grown very rapidly between 3500 and 3000 BCE. It was clearly the largest settlement in Sumer in 3500,[63] but with the evidence currently available we cannot be very precise about its population. The remains at Susa also show that it was a substantial town, but given the poor quality of the nineteenth-century excavations we are unable to put a precise population figure on it. The recent excavations at Tell Brak suggest that it reached 10,000 people by 3000 BCE and had been very big—perhaps even the largest settlement in the world—across much of the previous two thousand years. However, no good estimates yet exist.[64]

4000 BCE: Uruk, Tell Brak, 5,000; 0.05 points. See under 3500 BCE.

5000 BCE: Tell Brak, 4,000; 0.04 points. See under 3500 BCE.

6000 BCE: Çatalhöyük, 3,000;[65] 0.03 points.

7000 BCE: Beidha, Basta, Çatalhöyük, 1,000;[66] 0.01 points. Jericho may have been roughly the same size, and there may also have been some earlier settlements of roughly this scale; Maisels suggests that Mureybet had 500–1,000 residents around 8000 BCE.[67]

8000 BCE: Probably no site in the Western core had as many as 500 people before 7500 BCE at the earliest, which means that none reaches 0.01 points on the index, the smallest score I record.

ESTIMATES OF EASTERN CITY SIZES

2000 CE: Tokyo, 26,400,000;[68] 250 points. The largest city in China was Shanghai (12,900,000; 120.79 points).

1900 CE: Tokyo, 1,750,000;[69] 16.39 points. Some urban historians make slightly lower estimates,[70] but there seems to be general agreement on a figure in this area, based on multiple kinds of official statistics from censuses, tax returns, food supplies, and military personnel. In China, the largest city was Beijing, with around 1,100,000 residents (10.3 points).

1800 CE: Beijing, 1,100,000;[71] 10.3 points. Estimates for Qing-era Beijing are based heavily on statistics for food imports, and vary wildly. At different points, Braudel suggested 3 million or 2–3 million. Chandler's estimate seems more in line with social historians' accounts of Qing Beijing.[72]

Table 4.2
Eastern maximum settlement sizes, 4000 BCE–2000 CE

Date	Settlement	Size	Points
4000 BCE	Jiangzhai, Jiahu	300	0
3500 BCE	Xipo	2,000	0.02
3000 BCE	Dadiwan	5,000	0.05
2500 BCE	Taosi, Liangchengzhen, Yaowangcheng	10,000	0.09
2250 BCE	Taosi, Liangchengzhen, Yaowangcheng	14,000	0.13
2000 BCE	Fengcheng-Nanshui	11,000	0.1
1750 BCE	Erlitou	24,000	0.22
1500 BCE	Zhengzhou	35,000	0.33
1400 BCE	Zhengzhou	35,000	0.33
1300 BCE	Zhengzhou	35,000	0.33
1200 BCE	Anyang	50,000	0.47
1100 BCE	Anyang	50,000	0.47
1000 BCE	Luoyi, Feng	35,000	0.33
900 BCE	Luoyi, Feng	40,000	0.37
800 BCE	Luoyi, Feng	45,000	0.42
700 BCE	Linzi, Luoyi	55,000	0.51
600 BCE	Linzi, Luoyi	65,000	0.61
500 BCE	Linzi	80,000	0.75
400 BCE	Linzi, Qufu, Luoyi, Xinzheng, Wuyang	100,000	0.94
300 BCE	Linzi, Qufu, Luoyi, Xinzheng, Wuyang	125,000	1.17
200 BCE	Chang'an	250,000	2.81
100 BCE	Chang'an	375,000	3.75
1 BCE/CE	Chang'an	500,000	4.68
100 CE	Luoyang	420,000	3.93
200 CE	Chang'an	120,000	1.12
300 CE	Pingyang, Chang'an, Luoyang, Xuchang, Ye	140,000	1.31
400 CE	Pingcheng	200,000	1.87
500 CE	Luoyang	200,000	1.87
600 CE	Daxingcheng/Chang'an	600,000	5.63
700 CE	Chang'an	1,000,000	9.36
800 CE	Chang'an	1,000,000	9.36

Table 4.2 (*continued*)

Date	Settlement	Size	Points
900 CE	Chang'an	750,000	7
1000 CE	Kaifeng	1,000,000	9.36
1100 CE	Kaifeng	1,000,000	9.36
1200 CE	Hangzhou	1,000,000	9.36
1300 CE	Hangzhou	800,000	7.5
1400 CE	Nanjing	500,000	4.68
1500 CE	Beijing	678,000	6.35
1600 CE	Beijing	700,000	6.55
1700 CE	Beijing	650,000	6.09
1800 CE	Beijing	1,100,000	10.3
1900 CE	Tokyo	1,750,000	16.39
2000 CE	Tokyo	26,400,000	250

1700 CE: Beijing, 650,000;[73] 6.09 points. Beijing's population fell sharply after the terrible sack of 1644, and in 1700 had probably not yet returned to its 1600 level. Some historians, however, suggest much higher figures.[74]

1600 CE: Beijing, 700,000;[75] 6.55 points. Some historians suggest higher figures,[76] but rarely provide evidence to support them.

1500 CE: Beijing, 678,000;[77] 6.35 points. Mote estimated the population of Nanjing and Beijing at about 1 million each through the sixteenth and seventeenth centuries, but this seems unlikely, both because it is very high (Beijing probably did not reach 1 million until late in the eighteenth century) and because Nanjing is generally believed to have seen a roughly 50 percent population decline Beijing replaced it as the capital in 1421, as Mote himself recognizes elsewhere. Bairoch agreed with a lower estimate, thinking that Beijing had at least 600,000 people in 1600.[78]

1400 CE: Nanjing, 500,000;[79] 4.68 points. Mote says that he thinks Nanjing's population was about 1 million, but his own rough calculation actually produces a figure of 400,000–500,000.[80]

1300 CE: Hangzhou, 800,000;[81] 7.5 points. Bairoch suggests that four other Chinese cities around 1300 had populations in the 200,000–500,000 range while Hangzhou was "perhaps considerably larger." His calculations from the figures for rice consumption, however, point more precisely to 800,000, while Elvin calculates 600,000–700,000 from the rice figures. Rozman also thought twelfth-century and thirteenth-century Hangzhou's population was over 500,000, and could have been as high as 1 million. Kuhn and Christian also lean toward 1 million, and Skinner, 1.2 million.[82] I take the higher figure of roughly 1 million for 1200 CE, and the lower figure of 800,000 for 1300 CE, by which time population was falling across China as a whole. The city was certainly the biggest in the world when Marco Polo visited in the late thirteenth century,[83] but the figure implied by Marco's comments—5–7 million—must be far too high. There was probably no way Marco could have known Hangzhou's population, beyond the simple fact that it was enormous compared to European and Muslim cities of his day.

1200 CE: Hangzhou, 1,000,000; 9.36 points. See under 1300 CE.

1100 CE: Kaifeng, 1,000,000;[84] 9.36 points. Chandler and Bairoch think Kaifeng was smaller (suggesting 400,000 and 400,000–450,000, respectively), but this seems at odds with contemporary descriptions of the city.[85] Much of the uncertainty seems to revolve around the question of which wards to count as "urban." The New City was built in 955 with a 27 km fortification wall (extended by 3.3 km in 962), adding seventy-five new wards to the Old City's forty-six, but well before 1000 CE the population was spilling out beyond the walls. By 1021 fourteen large new extramural wards had been recognized. Official statistics say that 890,000 people lived in Kaifeng prefecture around 980 CE, increasing to 1.3 million in 1103, with some parts of the city achieving densities of 500/ha.[86] If we count only the people within the fortification walls, Chandler's and Bairoch's estimates are probably reasonable; if we count the whole population, Mote's, Skinner's, and Kuhn's preference for the official figures seems sensible. I lean toward the latter, but given the ambiguities in the data I simply make an approximate estimate of 1 million people. According to the official figures, Hangzhou probably also had 800,000 to 1 million residents by 1100.[87]

1000 CE: Kaifeng, 1,000,000; 9.36 points. See under 1100 CE.

900 CE: Chang'an, 750,000; 7 points. My estimate. Chinese historians rarely express opinions on Chang'an's population around 900 CE. The bandit Huang Chao sacked the city repeatedly in the late 870s, burning it to the ground completely in 880 and 883 and,

not surprisingly, causing its population to go into sharp decline. Prior to the late 870s Chang'an was certainly the world's biggest city. Benn suggests that its population reached 2 million, and Kuhn suggests "more than one million people," but it is hard to see how even after the construction of the Grand Canal enough grain could have been shipped to Chang'an to feed a population of the size proposed by Benn.[88] Skinner's suggestion that Chang'an probably had around a million residents in middle Tang times seems more plausible, and I use that number for 800 and 700 CE.[89] The city walls, enclosing just over thirty square miles, could certainly have contained a million people, but Benn's 2 million would call for improbably high densities. It is much less clear, though, how sudden the collapse in population was from the 870s onward. Primary sources say that the city was completely ruined when Emperor Xizong returned there in 885,[90] but that is clearly an overstatement because the dynasty remained there for another twenty years, until the warlord Zhu Wen ordered all the remaining buildings pulled down in 904. I have assumed that Chang'an remained a major population center until that point. If that is wrong, however, the East's organization/city size score in 900 CE must still have been high, since Luoyang probably had 500,000–750,000 residents at that time. Wu Zetian is supposed to have transferred 100,000 families to Luoyang when she made it her home in the late seventh century, and Benn put the population as high as 1 million. Rozman, however, suggested 500,000 for Luoyang.[91]

800 CE: Chang'an, 1,000,000;[92] 9.36 points. See under 900 CE.

700 CE: Chang'an, 1,000,000;[93] 9.36 points. See under 900 CE.

600 CE: Daxingcheng (renamed Chang'an by the Tang dynasty in the seventh century), 600,000; 5.63 points. My estimate. The Sui dynasty built Daxingcheng as their new capital with a walled area of more than thirty square miles to accommodate the population of about 1 million that it would have in the seventh century. When the emperor took up official residence in 583, though, the city was still a construction site, with many wards unoccupied. The population must already have been very large in 600 CE, since many tens of thousands of laborers would have been needed for the project, plus families, not to mention plenty of officials and workers (plus families), and thousands of monks and nuns at more than a hundred tem-

ples and monasteries. Furthermore, when the Sui overwhelmed southern China's Chen dynasty in 589, enormous numbers of people from the south were deported to Daxingcheng.[94]

500 CE: Luoyang, 200,000;[95] 1.87 points. Emperor Xiaowen of Northern Wei relocated his capital from Pingcheng to Luoyang in 493, and according to the texts moved 150,000 warriors there by 495, granting them farmlands around Luoyang. The city grew much more during the sixth century, perhaps reaching 600,000 people, like Daxingcheng.[96]

400 CE: Pingcheng, 200,000 (my estimate); 1.87 points. There were several large cities in northern China around 400 CE, but Pingcheng (renamed Datong in 1048) was probably the biggest. The texts say that in 398 CE, 100,000 Xianbei were forcibly relocated to Pingcheng, and in 399, another 100,000 peasants from Henan and 2,000 wealthy ethnic Chinese families were taken there too. With the partial exception of Ye, the archaeological evidence for cities in the period 200–400 CE is particularly poor.[97]

300 CE: Pingyang, Chang'an, Luoyang, Xuchang, Ye, 140,000 (my estimate); 1.31 points. It is difficult to define what exactly counted as a city in the fourth and fifth centuries CE; North Chinese cities were like giant encampments, with the major wars of the period basically being slave raids in which warlords rounded up tens of thousands of families and concentrated them in and around their own fortress to work the abundantly available land.[98] Pingyang, Chang'an, Luoyang, Xuchang, and Ye all became large cities in the years around 300 CE, probably somewhat bigger than the largest cities had been around 200 CE and somewhat smaller than the largest cities would be in 400 CE.

200 CE: Chang'an, 120,000 (my estimate); 1.12 points. In 190 the warlord Dong Zhuo pillaged and destroyed Luoyang, moving its population to Chang'an, and in 196 Cao Cao relocated the imperial court to Chang'an (only for the court to move back to Luoyang as soon as Cao Cao died). These cities were clearly much smaller than Luoyang had been in 100 CE, let alone Chang'an in 1 CE.

100 CE: Luoyang, 420,000;[99] 3.93 points. Archaeologists and historians have described the layout of the major Han cities in some detail,[100] but rarely offer population estimates. The accounts of the excavated areas and surviving city plans make it sound like Chang'an

and Luoyang (capitals for most of the periods 206 BCE–32 CE and 32–220 CE, respectively) had populations running into several hundred thousands. The literary sources say that the Qin First Emperor forcibly resettled 120,000 families in his capital of Xianyang in the 220s BCE and moved more people there to tend his tomb site in the 210s.[101] These figures may well be exaggerated, but Xianyang probably did have 200,000+ residents at the time of his death on 210 BCE, and the Han dynasty's new capital at Chang'an was at least as large. By the first century BCE Chang'an's two main markets covered 50 and 25 ha, which similarly suggest a very large population. The city covered an enormous area of 44.5 km², but the density of occupation within the excavated areas combined with Chang'an's notorious food supply difficulties suggests that it was never as populous as contemporary Rome. I estimate that it probably peaked toward the end of the Western Han dynasty (i.e., ca. 1 BCE/CE) around 500,000 people, though the margin of error in this guess could easily be 20 percent.

Estimates are complicated by the fact that the city also had satellite cities around it, particularly those that grew up around the imperial tombs, scattered for 30 km along the Zheng Guo canal and 20 km along the Ba and Chan Rivers. If we combine Chang'an itself with these satellites, their total population may have surpassed Rome, but since they appear to have been independent cities in every way, I have not done that. There is also some evidence that Chang'an's growth slowed after 100 BCE, and that there was little new state construction after Emperor Wudi's death in 87 BCE.

Luoyang was smaller than Chang'an, but was apparently more densely populated. I therefore make a slightly lower estimate for Luoyang at its peak, of 420,000 people in 100 CE. Again, a margin of error of ± 20 percent seems plausible.

1 BCE/CE: Chang'an, 500,000 (my estimate); 4.68 points. See under 100 CE.

100 BCE: Chang'an, 375,000 (my estimate); 3.75 points. See under 100 CE.

200 BCE: Chang'an, 250,000 (my estimate); 2.81 points. See under 100 CE.

300 BCE: Linzi, Qufu, Luoyi, Xinzheng, Wuyang, 125,000 (my estimate); 1.17 points. The cities of the Spring and Autumn and War-

ring States periods remain poorly known archaeologically, but it seems clear that they increased steadily in size across the second half of the first millennium BCE.[102] The walls of the largest cities (Wuyang [state of Yan], covering 27 km; Xinzheng [Zheng/Hann], 16 km; Linzi [Qi], 15 km; Qufu [Lu], 14 km; Luoyi, later renamed Luoyang [Zhou], 12 km) typically encompassed areas of 9–15 km², suggesting populations in the 100,000–200,000 range. However, some of the cities clearly had large ceremonial and industrial areas, and (at least at first) large areas were probably incorporated within the walls in anticipation of future growth. The estimates that follow are my own. The errors involved are probably larger than for Han cities, and may run as high as ± 50 percent.

The ancient literary sources are not very helpful; the *Shi ji* says that Linzi in Qi had 70,000 households and boasted 210,000 adult males.[103] The city was so crowded, Sima Qian commented, that "when [people] shake off sweat, it feels like rain." His numbers imply a total population of perhaps 350,000–750,000, which would make Linzi's population much bigger than contemporary Babylon's. This seems impossibly high, though, given the physical size of the city; it would also mean that the populations of the largest Chinese cities in fact did not grow between about 500 and 1 BCE, even though the evidence suggests unequivocally that they at least doubled and probably quadrupled in size across this period.

Bairoch suggested that four to six cities had populations over 100,000 during the Warring States period (480–221 BCE), which is broadly in line with the estimates I make here.[104]

400 BCE: Linzi, Qufu, Luoyi, Xinzheng, Wuyang, 100,000 (my estimate); 0.94 points. See under 300 BCE.

500 BCE: Linzi, 80,000 (my estimate); 0.75 points. See under 300 BCE.

600 BCE: Linzi, Luoyi, 65,000 (my estimate); 0.61 points. The evidence is even poorer for the first half of the first millennium BCE than it is for the second half (or, for that matter, for the later second millennium BCE). We can be certain that the biggest cities around 1000 BCE were smaller than those of those around 500 BCE, but we cannot be sure how much smaller. I guess that the populations of the earlier cities were roughly half the size of those of the later ones, but everything depends on estimates of settlement size and density.

The data from the biggest cities (the Western Zhou capitals at Feng and Hao in the Wei Valley, and the Eastern Zhou capital of Luoyi [later renamed Luoyang]) are poor, restricted largely to elite tombs and hoards of bronzes.[105] The finds at Feng are scattered over roughly 12.5 km² and those at Hao across some 6 km², but only small parts of these areas would have been built up. At Luoyi we do not even know if the chance finds come from the city of Luoyi itself or represent both Luoyi and Zhengzhou.

Von Falkenhausen suggests that "the Western Zhou capital in the Plain of Zhou [i.e., the area of Feng and Hao] consisted of a fairly haphazard agglomeration of major religious-cum-residential compounds scattered over an area of perhaps 200 square kilometers, with spacious tracts of agricultural land in between."[106] If this is correct, it implies not only that the population was relatively small, but also that the settlement pattern may have been so dispersed that it is misleading to talk of "cities" at all in early-first-millennium BCE China. This issue also applies to the "cities" of the late second millennium BCE.

That said, there clearly are differences in the density of finds across this 200 km², and it seems reasonable to think (as first-millennium BCE Chinese authors did) of Feng, Hao, and Luoyi as distinct nuclei, even if they were not exactly "urban" in the sense of having dense, continuous areas of housing.[107] I guess at 35,000 residents at Luoyi and Feng around 1000 BCE and perhaps half that many at Hao. I think it is unlikely that Luoyi and Feng had as many as 50,000 residents in 1000 BCE,[108] given the amount of growth that seems to have gone on in the first half of the first millennium BCE, and that they had fewer than 20,000 residents. I therefore project the biggest Eastern cities growing at a fairly smooth rate, slightly more than doubling in population from about 35,000 people in 1000 BCE to about 80,000 in 500 CE.

700 BCE: Linzi, Luoyi, 55,000 (my estimate); 0.51 points. See under 600 BCE.

800 BCE: Luoyi, Feng, 45,000 (my estimate); 0.42 points. See under 600 BCE.

900 BCE: Luoyi, Feng, 40,000 (my estimate); 0.37 points. See under 600 BCE.

1000 BCE: Luoyi, Feng, 35,000 (my estimate); 0.33 points. See under 600 BCE. Chandler suggests 50,000 people for Luoyi.[109]

1100 BCE: Anyang, 50,000 (my estimate); 0.47 points. Anyang, the final Shang dynasty capital, has been extensively excavated since 1928, although the walled city at Huanbei was located only in 1997. Huanbei's walls enclose 470 ha, and a population of 20,000–25,000 seems plausible, but other remains at Anyang sprawl across some 30 km². [110] As in the early first millennium BCE (see under 600 BCE), it becomes hard to define where the boundaries of a "city" are in such a dispersed settlement system. My suggestion of 50,000 is therefore somewhat arbitrary; defining the city very narrowly as just the walled area could cut this estimate by 50 percent, while defining it very loosely to include the suburbs could perhaps raise the total to 100,000 or more. A population of 50,000 would make Anyang as large as Memphis in 1100 BCE; 100,000 would make it the biggest city in the world in the thirteenth through eleventh centuries BCE. I offer the figure of 50,000 as a middle ground between the very narrow and very loose definitions of the city.

Anyang was founded around 1300 BCE and by 1200 had clearly become a major settlement (however defined). Given the uncertainties of the estimate for 1100 BCE, there seems little point in compounding the difficulties by offering a different estimate for 1200, so I simply propose 50,000 for both dates.

1200 BCE: Anyang, 50,000 (my estimate); 0.47 points. See under 1100 BCE. The walled settlement at Sanxingdui may cover as much as 350 ha,[111] and might have been a rival to Anyang for population, but it remains poorly known.

1300 BCE: Zhengzhou, 35,000 (my estimate); 0.33 points. The site of Erligang at Zhengzhou was founded around 1600 BCE and is usually assumed to be an early Shang dynasty capital.[112] The walled settlement covers 300 ha, but a larger peripheral wall encloses a total of 1,300 ha. As with Anyang (see under 1100 BCE), there are two challenges—first, to define what we mean by "city" in such a case and, second, to calculate the density of occupation within the city. Once again, my figure represents a middle ground between a minimalist definition, which might lead to a figure of no more than 15,000 people within the walled core, and a very broad definition, which might come to a number more like 50,000. Zhengzhou seems to have been significantly smaller than thirteenth- through eleventh-century Anyang; my estimate of 35,000 would make it about half the size of contemporary Babylon or Thebes.

1400 BCE: Zhengzhou, 35,000 (my estimate); 0.33 points. See under 1300 BCE. In the absence of detailed evidence, I propose the same figure for Zhengzhou from the sixteenth through the fourteenth centuries BCE.

1500 BCE: Zhengzhou, 35,000 (my estimate); 0.33 points. See under 1400 and 1300 BCE.

1750 BCE: Erlitou, 24,000;[113] 0.22 points. Erlitou is much better explored than the sites of 1500–500 BCE, and in phase III covered roughly 300 ha. This estimate—even though Liu prefers to offer it as merely the midpoint of a range of estimates, from 18,000–30,000—is probably the most reliable prehistoric demographic statistic in the East. The figure of 24,000 represents about 80 people/ha, a low density by the standards of contemporary Western cities like Babylon, but high relative to other prehistoric Chinese settlements.

2000 BCE: Fengcheng-Nanshui, 11,000 (my estimate); 0.1 points. The settlement seems to cover 230 ha,[114] but remains poorly excavated. I assume a low density of 50/ha.

2250 BCE: Taosi, Liangchengzhen, Yaowangcheng, 14,000 (my estimate); 0.13 points. At its height, Taosi covered about 280 ha;[115] I assume a density of 50/ha. Liu also comments that the largest chiefdoms of the Longshan period had perhaps 10,000+ members, which might imply that we should use a lower density figure for Taosi (where the remains are, indeed, extremely dispersed, even by the standards of prehistoric Chinese settlements).[116] Recent studies suggest that Liangchengzhen and Yaowangcheng may have been even bigger than Taosi in the second half of the third millennium, reaching 272.5 and 367.5 ha, respectively.[117]

2500 BCE: Taosi, Liangchengzhen, Yaowangcheng, 10,000;[118] 0.09 points. Taosi was clearly smaller in 2500 BCE than its later peak, but I am not aware of any good estimates of the difference. See under 2250 BCE.

3000 BCE: Dadiwan, 5,000 (my estimate); 0.05 points. The settlement covers roughly 100 ha, and I assume a density of about 50/ha.[119]

3500 BCE: Xipo, 2,000 (my estimate); 0.02 points. The settlement covers roughly 40 ha,[120] and I assume a density of about 50/ha.

4000 BCE: no settlement seems to have covered a large enough area to have had a population of 1,000, the minimum number to register on the index (0.01 points). In 4000 BCE Jiangzhai covered 5 ha, but Liu calculates a density of 44–63/ha, meaning just 220–315 people. Peterson and Shelach develop an interesting dynamic model of the site's population, which produces slightly higher numbers, but still not much above 400 people.[121] Jiahu also covered around 5 ha as early as 6000 BCE, but here too the density was very low. No other site of the seventh through fifth millennia BCE seems to cover more than 2 ha.

CITY SIZE: DISCUSSION

City Size as a Proxy Measure for Social Organization

At every point for which we have textual data (beginning in the third millennium BCE in the West and the late second millennium BCE in the East) until the twentieth century CE, the largest city in the world was always an administrative center. At the beginning of the textually documented period, Memphis was the capital of Egypt and Anyang was the capital of a Shang dynasty state; in the nineteenth century CE London was the capital of the British Empire and Beijing the capital of the Qing Empire. And if we press back in time beyond Memphis and Anyang, there is a certain amount of evidence that Uruk in the West and Zhengzhou (and probably Erlitou too) were also the capitals of early states.[122]

This observation seems to validate the choice of city size as a proxy for social organization: through most of history, the size of the largest city in a region has been a function of the scale of political organization. In a previously published essay I suggested that this was the case in the Greek world of the first millennium BCE,[123] and I would now extend this argument to premodern history as a whole. Only in the twentieth century CE did economic sources of power trump political sources[124] to such an extent that Washington, D.C., the capital of the world's most powerful state, did not rank among the world's thirty biggest cities in 2000 CE, and Beijing, capital of the most powerful state in the East, ranked only twenty-fourth.[125] Throughout all previous history, city size has been a fairly direct reflection of political organizational capacity.

City Size/Organizational Capacity as a Function of Energy Capture

In very general terms, the shapes of the history of energy capture (figure 2.5) and city size/organizational capacity (figure 4.1) have a certain amount in common. Both increased very slowly after the end of the Ice Age, accelerating in the last few millennia BCE, and then exploded in the nineteenth and twentieth centuries CE. In both graphs, the Western score is higher than the Eastern for most of the last ten thousand years. However, the differences between the two graphs are just as interesting as the similarities.

Figures 4.2 and 4.3, respectively, plot Western and Eastern energy capture and city size (expressed in terms of points on the index of social development) against each other on a log-linear scale (figures 4.4 and 4.5 show the same data on a linear-linear scale; the same patterns are visible, though not as sharply as on the logarithmic scale). The most striking contrasts between the energy capture and city size curves seem to be (a) that city size starts rising much later than energy capture and (b) that city size is much more volatile than energy capture. Both these contrasts can be explained very easily: city size is a function of energy capture. Only when a certain level of energy is being captured—somewhere around 7,000–8,000 kcal/cap/day—does the size of the largest settlements start to grow noticeably; but once a community has passed this threshold, relatively small changes at the margin of the energy capture budget have massive consequences for the amount of energy available to organize larger communities.

Consequently, both East and West went through similar episodes of initial urbanization when energy capture reached roughly 11,000–12,000 kcal/cap/day (around 3500–3000 BCE in the West and 2000–1500 BCE in the East; figure 4.6). Both saw settlement size slump at

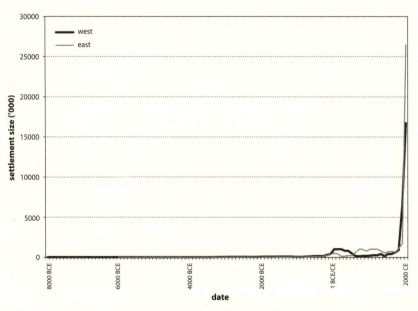

Figure 4.1. Eastern and Western largest city sizes, 8000 BCE–2000 CE.

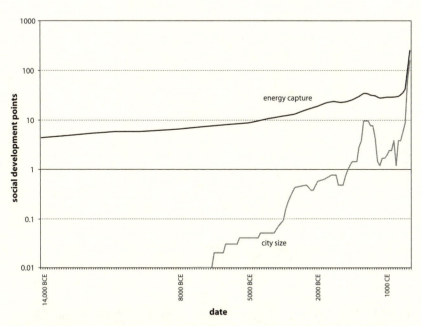

Figure 4.2. Western energy capture plotted against city size on a log-linear scale, 14,000 BCE–2000 CE, measured in social development points.

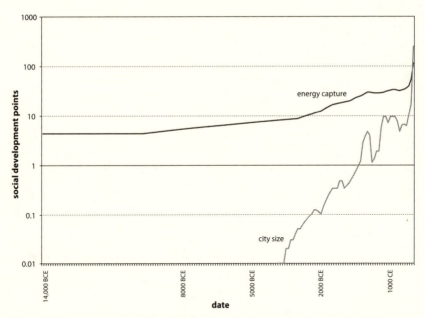

Figure 4.3. Eastern energy capture plotted against city size on a log-linear scale, 14,000 BCE–2000 CE, measured in social development points.

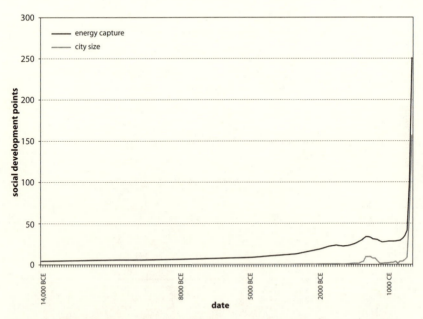

Figure 4.4. Western energy capture plotted against city size on a linear-linear scale, 14,000 BCE–2000 CE, measured in social development points.

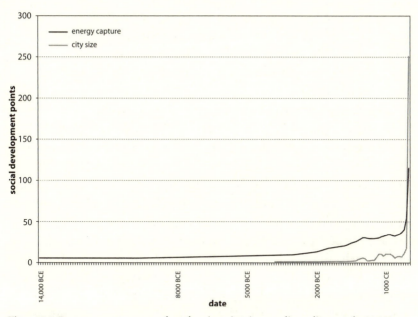

Figure 4.5. Eastern energy capture plotted against city size on a linear-linear scale, 14,000 BCE–2000 CE, measured in social development points.

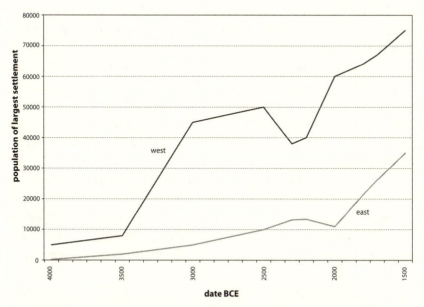

Figure 4.6. The size of the largest Eastern and Western settlements, 4000–1500 BCE.

the end of the third millennium BCE, in the crises associated with the fall of Akkad, Ur, and the Egyptian Old Kingdom in the West and Taosi and the early cities of Shandong in the East,[126] even though the crises of these years had only a tiny impact on energy capture in the West or the East.

The changes in the last three thousand years have been even more spectacular (figure 4.7). In both East and West, the rate of increase in energy capture accelerated in the first millennium BCE, but city sizes grew even faster. Once again, there seems to have been a threshold in energy capture, this time a little over 20,000 kcal/cap/day, above which societies created cities of 100,000+ residents, and another threshold, around 27,000 kcal/cap/day, above which supercities of 500,000 to 1 million people became possible. The great crises of the early first millennium CE reduced energy capture in both East and West much more sharply than any previous crisis (by nearly 20 percent between 100 and 700 CE in the West and by nearly 4 percent between 100 and 300 CE in the East), but their impact on city sizes was much greater—Western cities shrank by more than 85 percent between 200 and 700 CE and Eastern cities by more than 75 percent between 1 and 200 CE).

The East then saw a surge in city size in the mid- and late first millennium CE to rival that of Rome in the late first millennium BCE when it had passed through the same 27,000 kcal/cap/day threshold: Eastern energy capture increased by 13 percent between 500 and 1000 CE (from 26,000 to 29,500 kcal/cap/day), but the biggest Eastern cities grew by 400 percent across the same half millennium (from 200,000 to 1 million residents). The wars that brought down China's Tang dynasty in the late first millennium CE barely touched energy capture but did cause a short-term 25 percent dip in city size.

The energy capture–city size relationship continued operating through the second millennium CE. The Second Old World Exchange of 1200–1400 CE drove energy capture down by 5 percent in the East but halved the population of the largest city;[127] in the West it left energy capture untouched but cities shrank by almost two-thirds.

The surge in energy capture since 1500 CE (and especially since 1800) had a predictably dramatic effect on city size. There seems to have been another threshold somewhere around 45,000 kcal/cap/

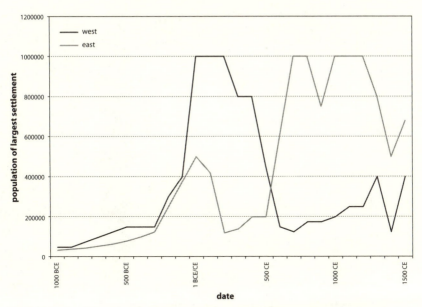

Figure 4.7. The size of the largest Eastern and Western settlements, 1000 BCE–1500 CE.

day, which made multimillion-resident cities possible. The great wars of the twentieth century devastated the East's biggest cities, but such is the volatility of city size that Tokyo and Beijing were bigger than ever by the 1960s, while the West's biggest cities (in the Americas) remained entirely untouched by the wars.

MAGNITUDES OF CITY SIZE

The city-size data also suggest that different levels of social development impose fairly firm orders of magnitude on settlement size. Pr-estate agrarian societies (as found in the Western core before 3500 BCE and in the Eastern before 2000 BCE) do not seem to be able to support settlements of more than roughly ten thousand people; agrarian states (which dominated the Western core between the fourth and early first millennia BCE and the Eastern core between the early second and mid-first millennia BCE) do not seem to be able to support settlements of more than roughly a hundred thousand people; and agrarian empires (which dominated the Western core between the mid-first millennium BCE and late second millen-

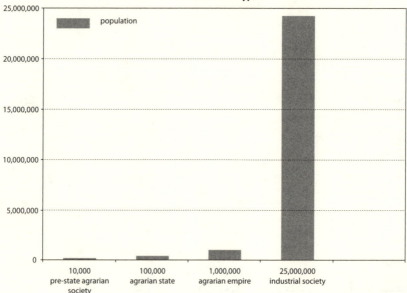

Figure 4.8. Largest known settlements and levels of community organization since the Ice Age.

nium CE and the Eastern core between the late first millennium BCE and late second millennium CE) do not seem to be able to support settlements of more than roughly a million people. Industrial societies, however, can support cities of more than 25 million (figure 4.8).

The neatness of the premodern orders of magnitude of course depends in part on the roughness of the quantitative estimates (the flat tops on the lines in figure 4.7 illustrate neatly the vagueness of our knowledge; Rome, Chang'an, Kaifeng, and Hangzhou could just as easily have had 800,000 or 1.2 million residents as the 1 million that the graph ascribes to them). However, the consistency of the results does suggest a hypothesis that would be worth testing against data from other parts of the world—that without the energy windfall provided by fossil fuels, and the associated organizational and technological gains, no one would be living in cities that grew much beyond a million residents. We have yet to see what limits our current level of development imposes on settlement size and whether we will transcend those limits.[128]

CHAPTER 5

||||||||||||||||||||||||||||||||||||||||||||||||

WAR-MAKING CAPACITY

MEASURING WAR-MAKING CAPACITY

Nothing made Western domination of the world quite so clear as the First Opium War of 1840–42 CE, when a small British fleet shot its way into China, threatened to close the Grand Canal that brought food to Beijing, and extracted humiliating concessions from the Qing government. According to Lord Robert Jocelyn, who accompanied the fleet, "The ships opened their broadsides upon the town [of Tinghai], and the crashing of timber, falling houses, and groans of men resounded from the shore. The firing lasted form our side for nine minutes. . . . We landed on a deserted beach, a few dead bodies, bows and arrows, broken spears and guns remaining the sole occupants of the field."[1]

The Chinese learned the lesson well. "Every communist must grasp this truth," Mao Zedong would say a century later: "political power grows out of the barrel of a gun."[2] It was ever thus, and the capacity to make war has always been a crucial part of social development.[3]

Fortunately for the index, a combination of factors—historians' obsession with recording wars, compulsive military record keeping, artistic patrons' fondness for being portrayed as warriors, the widespread practice of burying dead men with arms and armor, the archaeological visibility of fortifications—means that we are relatively well informed about some aspects of war in many historical contexts. Our problems with quantifying war-making capacity come more from conceptual challenges than from lack of data.

Attempts to measure war-making capacity are as old as war itself. Nearly all decisions to go to war involve some kind of assessment of societies' relative military power (even if aggressors regularly over-estimate their own strength while defenders regularly underestimate theirs), and in the twentieth century a string of military profession-als and outsiders have tried to develop algorithms allowing generals to predict the outcome of conflicts.

The first, and in some ways most influential, of these quantifiers was the polymath Frederick William Lanchester. In addition to being one of Britain's most important automotive engineers, Lan-chester wrote a pioneering book on air warfare,[4] proposing a series of differential equations to predict the outcomes of dogfights. Since then, Lanchester equations have been developed into a general quan-titative approach to attrition in battle.[5]

The Lanchester equations have been criticized repeatedly for their unrealistic assumptions. In the 1970s and 1980s, retired U.S. Army colonel Trevor Nevitt Dupuy developed a much more com-plex Quantified Judgment Model, employing no fewer than seventy-three variables; but in the last decade, much simpler—and much more convincing—alternatives have been developed.[6]

All these approaches have been designed to quantify potential fu-ture conflicts, and have been tested against data from actual histori-cal conflicts.[7] Comparing war-making capacity between societies in different historical periods or so widely separated by geography that they never come into contact, which is what the social develop-ment index needs to do, presents much greater problems. Military professionals often use the "rock-paper-scissors" children's game to describe how fighting systems work: system A (say, infantry with muskets) might be superior to system B (say, cavalry with sabers), and system B superior to system C (smoothbore artillery); but sys-tem C can simultaneously be superior to system A. Because military capacity is always context dependent (i.e., armed forces are created to fight specific kinds of enemies, under particular geographic and political conditions, and armed forces that do well against one kind of enemy may do much less well against other kinds of enemies), comparisons ranging widely across time and space are necessarily much more abstract than similarly broad comparisons of energy capture or city size.

Comparisons of war-making capacity must come down to measuring the destructive power available to societies. By "destructive power" I mean the number of fighters they can field, modified by the range and force of their weapons, the mass and speed with which they can deploy them, their defensive power, and their logistical capabilities. Moreover, these basic facts—which are reasonably well documented for many times and places—must be combined with estimates of less well documented but equally important factors, such as morale, leadership, command and control, clear understanding of strategic, operational, and tactical principles, and organizational learning ability, as well as the broader parameters of the economy, logistics, ideology, and politics.

The technical problems are daunting, but since the late nineteenth century war gamers (both military professionals and amateurs) have been struggling to find ways to reduce the bewildering complexity of reality to numerical values that can be compared.[8] On the whole, the military historian Philip Sabin is probably correct that commercial war games generally try to reproduce too much detail, but, much like the social development index, the great contribution of the games is that they make assumptions explicit.

Some game systems come in multiple versions, simulating fighting in different times and places, providing an excellent starting point for thinking about war-making capacity across time and space. The GMT Games series Great Battles of History, for example, includes variants for second-millennium BCE chariot battles in Southwest Asia, the Roman Republic's wars in the third and second centuries BCE, battles in India in the same period, and thirteenth-century CE Mongol battles.[9] At the tactical level, at least, it allows thought-provoking comparisons—although, like any such system of rules, its greatest value may lie in the questions it raises when the system seems not to work well.

In principle, the transhistorical comparisons required by the social development index should be no different from comparison of actual historical contexts, but in practice the sheer scale of change over time—and the fact that so-called revolutions in military affairs are often designed explicitly to produce war-making systems that are simply incomparable with earlier systems—vastly complicates matters. The most famous example is HMS *Dreadnought*, the massively armed and armored battleship introduced by Britain in 1906 with the aim of rendering all previous warships obsolete—only for naval tactics to evolve to fit this new weapon into a system in which older kinds of warships remained important.[10]

The same is true even of the deadliest modern weapons of all, nuclear arms. Nuclear weapons are far more destructive than nonnuclear weapons, but they are not *incomparably* more destructive. The very fact that the force of nuclear weapons is measured in kilotons and megatons—thousands/millions of tons of TNT equivalent—illustrates this.

The destructive power of nuclear-armed states dwarfs anything in earlier history. In three years of bombing, 1942–45, the U.S. Eighth Air Force dropped 700,000 tons of TNT on Germany; on Halloween 1961, the Soviet Union tested a single bomb (the so-called "Tsar Bomba") with a yield equivalent to 50–57 million tons of TNT. By 1966 a single Soviet SS-9 Model 2 missile could carry a warhead equivalent to 25 million tons of TNT, more than thirty times the destructive power of all the bombs the United States dropped on Germany in World War II; and by the 1970s the Soviet Union had deployed 255 of these ICBMs.[11]

Nevertheless, the destructive force of nuclear weapons does remain measurable on the same scales as conventional weapons, just as the poisoning effects of radioactive fallout can be measured in rads and compared with the smaller poisoning effects of chemical and biological weapons.[12] And like the dreadnought-class battleships built after 1906, nuclear weapons have been fitted into broader warmaking systems that continue to rely on weapon types (albeit in much more effective forms) that were in use before 1945. Nuclear war is unimaginable but not unmeasurable.[13]

The biggest difficulty that the index of social development has in measuring war-making capacity is in quantifying the relationship between the armed forces of 2000 CE and those of earlier periods. The leap in capacity between 1900 and 2000 was so enormous that it is difficult to measure, and similar difficulties, though on a less enormous scale, also apply to the leap between 1800 and 1900.

On the one hand, this means that if we assign the maximum 250 points on the scoring system to the West in 2000, there will be a wide margin of error in percentage terms in estimates of war-making capacity in 1900, let alone in 1800 or any earlier period. On the other hand, because the gulf between modern destructive power and that in earlier periods is so enormous, the pre-1800 CE scores will be tiny, meaning that in terms of actual points on the social development index the margins of error will also be tiny. As we will see, the answers that I offer to these questions mean that no war-making system before 1600 CE merits even 0.2 points (i.e., less than one one-thousandth of the contemporary score), and very few before 1500 CE even reached 0.1 points. War-making capacity, like city size/social organization, is a function of energy capture, surging upward with relatively small changes on the margin once energy capture reached 100,000 kcal/cap/day. The main contribution that measuring war-making capacity makes to the social development index is to underline the vast gulf separating industrialized twentieth- and twenty-first-century societies from all previous societies.

WESTERN WAR-MAKING CAPACITY

The Twentieth-Century Transformation

There are many assessments of modern Western military power. I rely mainly on the annual *Military Balance* volumes of the Institute for International Strategic Studies, which provide data on national spending, force strengths, quality, and logistics.[14]

Even before the post–September 11 buildup began, U.S. military power dwarfed all rivals, and in 2000 CE it earned the West the full complement of 250 points. Plenty of other nations had more men and women under arms than the United States, and Russia's nuclear arsenal was roughly twice as large as the United States',[15] but American advantages in every other dimension of war making hugely outweighed these imbalances. American troops were far better equipped and supplied than those of any other nation, and were better trained and led than those of most nations. They were also vastly more mobile, with America's eleven carrier battle groups completely dominating the world's oceans and the U.S. Air Force doing the same in the skies. U.S. nuclear warheads and launch vehicles were also more reliable and generally more powerful than their Russian counterparts.

The greatest difficulty in quantifying war-making capacity comes as soon as we move back from 2000 to 1900 CE. Data on Western European armed forces in 1900 are good, and easily available, but calculating a score for the West 1900 relative to the West in 2000 is very difficult because the gap between the military systems is so enormous.[16]

Armies were bigger in 2000 than in 1900, although not dramatically so (the biggest standing army in 2000, China's People's Liberation Army, had about 2.25 million active troops and 1.2 million reservists; the biggest in 1900, Russia's, had 1.16 million of all classes). In some respects the basic weapons were also similar—the British Lee-Enfield rifle, introduced in 1895, had an accurate range of about 500 meters and a muzzle velocity of 733 meters/second (m/s), while the M16 rifle (introduced in the U.S. Army in 1963 but still, in modified forms, the normal weapon in 2000) is accurate at 550–800 meters and has a muzzle velocity of 948 m/s. However, the similarities are dwarfed by the differences: the M16 can discharge 700–950 rounds per minute, while the Lee-Enfield normally managed 20–30 (the record, under test conditions, was 38 rounds/minute). An ordinary M16 or Kalashnikov AK-47 shoots faster than the best heavy machine guns of 1900 (the Maxim gun managed just 450–600 rounds/minute).[17] The first weapon vaguely equivalent to an M16 or AK-47—the German MP18 submachine gun—was not introduced until 1918.

Military historians normally date the advent of modern artillery to the "French 75," introduced in 1897. This was a 75 mm rifled cannon with a long recoil mechanism, which meant that the gunners did not have to relay their weapon after each shot. The gun could fire at the astonishing rate of fifteen shells per minute, with a range of 7.5 km. More complex modern artillery fires much more slowly, and the U.S. Army's newest howitzer—the 155 mm M777, introduced in 2005—manages only 2–5 rounds/min; however, the titanium gun is so light it can be airlifted, has a range of 24–30 km, and, when used with Excalibur GPS ammunition, has a circular error probable at 24 km of just 5 m (i.e., 50 percent of the shells will land within 5 m of the target). The revolution in guided weapons since the 1980s has made each modern cannon worth dozens of 1900-era guns, and advances in mechanization of transport, communications, and electronic warfare have been equally spectacular.[18]

On the seas, the greatest weapons in 1900 were new steel-armored steam-powered battleships (the word "battleship" was first used in 1892), typically displacing 15,000–17,000 tons, sailing at 30 km/h (16 knots), and carrying four 12 in. guns that could hurl a 400 kg shell nearly 23 km. After 1906 the dreadnoughts not only added heavier armor and six more 12 in. guns but also raised speeds to 21 knots, and after 1911 navies shifted from coal to oil. Each of these changes had revolutionary consequences; but even so, the disparity between any of these ships and contemporary American *Nimitz*-class nuclear-powered aircraft carriers (displacing 100,000 tons, with a top speed of 56 km/h [30 knots], able to go 20 years without refueling and carrying 90 aircraft with a strike range of more than 700 km) dwarf all the differences between successive types of early-twentieth-century warships.

The most astonishing part of the twentieth-century revolution in warfare has surely been what has happened in the skies. The first military use of a plane was in 1911, when Italy used bombers and reconnaissance flights against Turkey. The gulf between these early efforts and the most sophisticated military planes in 2000 (e.g., the B-2 stealth bomber, introduced in 1989, with a range of 11,000 km and a cruising speed around 900 km/h, virtually undetectable, able to penetrate almost any antiaircraft defense and to deliver GPS guided munitions or more than 10 MT of nuclear weapons) is breathtaking.

We can easily compare the amount of firepower, speed and range of maneuver, and countless other dimensions of the armed forces of each period. It is commonly suggested, for instance, that the power of artillery increased twentyfold between 1900 and 2000 and that of antitank fire sixtyfold between 1918 and 2000; but putting a concrete score on the full range of changes across the twentieth century is much more difficult.

Table 5.1

War-making capacity since 4000 BCE (in social development points)

	West	East		West	East
4000 BCE	0	0	1 BCE/CE	0.12	0.08
3000 BCE	0.01	0	100 CE	0.12	0.08
2500 BCE	0.01	0	200 CE	0.11	0.07
2250 BCE	0.01	0	300 CE	0.10	0.07
2000 BCE	0.01	0	400 CE	0.09	0.07
1750 BCE	0.02	0	500 CE	0.07	0.08
1500 BCE	0.02	0.01	600 CE	0.04	0.09
1400 BCE	0.03	0.01	700 CE	0.04	0.11
1300 BCE	0.03	0.01	800 CE	0.04	0.07
1200 BCE	0.04	0.02	900 CE	0.05	0.07
1100 BCE	0.03	0.02	1000 CE	0.06	0.08
1000 BCE	0.03	0.03	1100 CE	0.07	0.09
900 BCE	0.04	0.03	1200 CE	0.08	0.09
800 BCE	0.05	0.02	1300 CE	0.09	0.11
700 BCE	0.07	0.02	1400 CE	0.11	0.12
600 BCE	0.07	0.03	1500 CE	0.13	0.10
500 BCE	0.08	0.04	1600 CE	0.18	0.12
400 BCE	0.09	0.05	1700 CE	0.35	0.15
300 BCE	0.09	0.06	1800 CE	0.50	0.12
200 BCE	0.10	0.07	1900 CE	5.00	1.00
100 BCE	0.11	0.08	2000 CE	250.00	12.50

I have opted for a 50:1 ratio between Western war-making capacity in 2000 CE and what it had been in 1900. This produces a Western war-making capacity in 1900 of just 5 points (as against 250 in 2000). This score is, obviously, no more than a guesstimate. A 100:1 ratio, producing a score for 1900 of 2.5 points, might be just as good a guess, although a 25:1 ratio, producing a score for 1900 of 10 points, strikes me as unlikely.

This margin of error is much higher than what I suggest for the social development index as a whole (chapter 7), but the enormous gap between the Western war-making score for 2000 CE and the scores for all earlier periods means that we can easily halve or double all pre-2000 scores without making any discernable difference to the

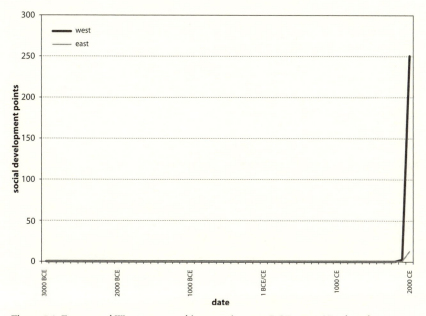

Figure 5.1. Eastern and Western war-making capacity, 3000 BCE–2000 CE, plotted on a linear-linear scale.

index. Table 5.1, figure 5.1, and figure 5.2 show Eastern and Western war-making scores since 4000 BCE using the numbers I have estimated. Figures 5.3 and 5.4 also show the scores if we reduce all pre-2000 CE estimates by 50 percent.

Using a logarithmic scale on the vertical axis makes the differences easier to see, and so figure 5.2 shows the scores I have calculated on log-linear axes and figure 5.4 represents the revised numbers (i.e., with reduced scores for all periods before 2000 CE) in the same way. The revised figures of course make the boom in destructive power in the twentieth century twice as big as in my estimates, but other than increasing the modern/premodern contrast, the main consequence of halving the pre-2000 CE scores is to make the East-West differences between 100 BCE and 200 CE too small to measure (as opposed to my estimates, representing the Roman Empire as having slightly greater war-making capacity than the Han Empire). The conclusion must be that any reasonable estimate of the ratio of war-making capacity in 2000 CE to that in 1900 CE—whether we set it at 50:1, as I have done, at 100:1, or at just 25:1—makes little difference to the larger social development index.

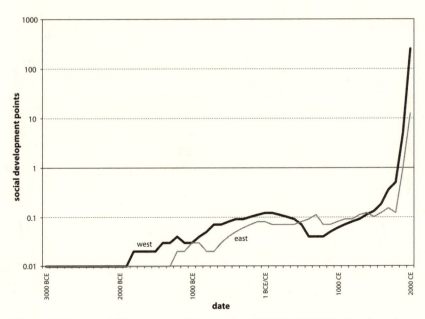

Figure 5.2. Eastern and Western war-making capacity, 3000 BCE–2000 CE, plotted on a log-linear scale.

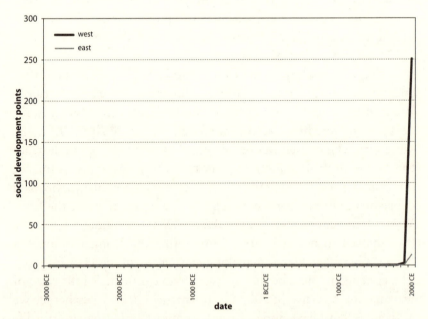

Figure 5.3. Eastern and Western war-making capacity, 3000 BCE–2000 CE, decreasing all scores before 2000 CE by 50 percent.

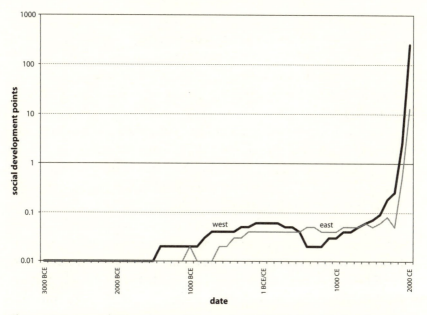

Figure 5.4. Eastern and Western war-making capacity, 3000 BCE–2000 CE, plotted on a log-linear scale and decreasing all scores before 2000 CE by 50 percent.

THE EUROPEAN MILITARY REVOLUTION, 1500–1800 CE

The leap in Western war-making capacity between 1800 and 1900 CE was nowhere near as great as that between 1900 and 2000, but it was nevertheless enormous. The ranges and accuracy of weapons, their speed of firing, the force of projectiles (magnified by the invention of explosive shells), the size of armies, the speed of transport, and the scale of logistics, often increased by an order of magnitude across the nineteenth century.[19] However, our assessments of pure technical power must always be tempered by the ways people responded to such power. The military analyst Stephen Biddle calculates that if one Napoleonic infantry battalion of one thousand men charged another around 1800, the defenders would be able to fire roughly two shots per attacking soldier; but if the same battalions repeated the exercise a century later, more than two hundred bullets would be fired at each soldier. Surprisingly, though, the proportion of armies killed in battles actually fell between 1815 and 1918, because tacticians adopted new fighting styles that minimized troops' exposure to direct fire.[20]

The French introduction of the *levée en masse* in the 1790s pushed army sizes up toward 500,000—about half the size of the biggest armies in 1900—but the principal weapon, the smooth bore musket, was far less effective than the rifles of 1900. Even well-trained Napoleonic infantry could get off only about four shots per minute. Muskets could shoot up to 400 m, but at ranges more than 50–75 m they were so inaccurate that individual fire was virtually useless; and even when fired at less than 75 m, only masses of volleying men had much chance of hitting their target. In one eighteenth-century exercise, fewer than half the musketeers firing at a target 30 m wide at a range of 60 m managed to hit it.[21]

Smoothbore cannons, particularly twelve pounders that could fire four to six rounds per minute and were effective at ranges up to 500 m, were starting to become the dominant arm on battlefields in 1800,[22] but they remained far less effective than the rifled cannons of 1900; and flat-trajectory explosive shells did not become common until the 1850s.

The best warships in 1800, like HMS *Victory* (launched in 1765), could manage 8–9 knots (15–17 km/h) with a good wind, but were much slower in bad weather. The *Victory* carried 104 cannons, totaling roughly 1 ton of solid shot, with a range of up to about 2 km.[23] The disparity between this and pre-dreadnought battleships with their steel armor, steam engines, explosive shells, and torpedoes is again glaring.

Once again reducing the complexity of military systems to a single score is a highly subjective exercise, but I suggest a ratio between Western war-making capacity in 1900 and in 1800 of roughly 10:1, producing a score for 1800 of 0.5 points. This guess could be just as wide of the mark as my guess for 1900 (or as a Napoleonic musket shot), and the true ratio could easily be 20:1. If I have overestimated war-making capacity relative to 2000 CE for both 1800 and 1900, instead of scores of 250 points for 2000, 5 points for 1900, and 0.5 points for 1800, we could conceivably get scores of 250 points for 2000, 2.5 points for 1900, and 0.13 points for 1800, producing the results we see in figures 5.5 (linear-linear) and 5.6 (log-linear). But even the now greatly reduced pre-1900 CE scores make only a minuscule difference to the social development index as a whole because the absolute numbers involved are so tiny.

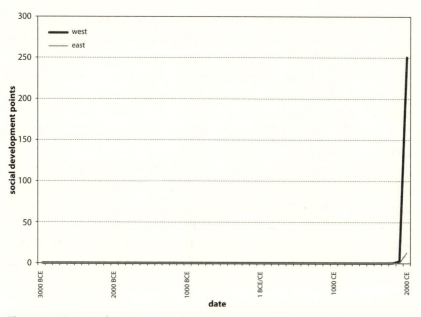

Figure 5.5. Eastern and Western war-making capacity, 3000 BCE–2000 CE, decreasing scores before 1900 CE.

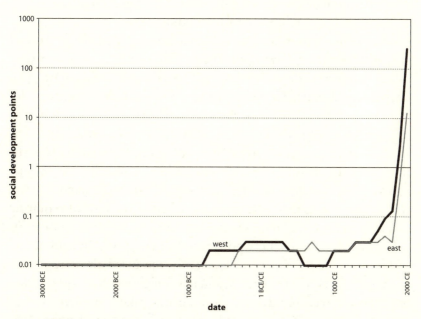

Figure 5.6. Eastern and Western war-making capacity, 3000 BCE–2000 CE, plotted on a log-linear scale and decreasing scores before 1900 CE.

Since the pioneering work of Michael Roberts and above all Geoffrey Parker, the period 1500–1800 has come to be known as the "European military revolution," characterized by enormous increases in the size, efficiency, firepower, and reach of armies and navies.[24] Compared to the changes between 1800 and 1900, those during the military revolution were actually quite small, but they nevertheless left the war-making capacity of medieval European societies far behind.

Improvements in firearms and organizational changes within societies to exploit these improvements account for much of the military revolution. Gunpowder weapons reached Europe in the 1320s, but a hundred years passed before they began to be important on battlefields on land or sea.[25] Even in 1500, musketeers' rate of fire was measured in minutes per round, not rounds per minute, and their guns were effective at only very short ranges. Particularly in England, some soldiers wondered whether longbows—which, in trained hands, could discharge ten arrows per minute and were accurate up to 200 m—might not still be superior weapons, and on the steppes, where cavalry were much more important, bows did continue to dominate the battlefield well into the seventeenth century.

Even early matchlock muskets could throw projectiles (lead musket balls) that were heavier than arrows, and therefore had greater penetrating power, but their main advantage was that they called for very little skill compared to what an archer needed to learn. Massed musketeers could, under the right circumstances, defeat bows and pikes, as they showed in the Italian Wars at Ravenna (1512), Marignano (1515), and Bicocca (1522). As early as 1490 Venice decided to replace its crossbows with guns, and by the 1560s the English fondness for longbows was looking decidedly anachronistic. By 1594 Dutch armies had introduced line tactics and volleys, greatly increasing their effectiveness (albeit at the cost of requiring much more training and supervision), and in the 1630s Gustavus Adolphus showed just how powerful the new approach could be.

Flintlock firing mechanisms sharply increased the rate of fire during the seventeenth century, and in the eighteenth century socket bayonets allowed musketeers to double as pikemen. Artillery advanced even faster. Cannons had already made medieval stone fortifications obsolete by the time of Charles VIII's invasion of Italy in

1494, but by the mid-seventeenth century intricate earthworks had restored the defensive advantage.

Organizational advances in the later eighteenth century—particularly the French invention of column attacks and divisional structures on land and British tactical innovations at sea—further improved the performance of armed forces, but the biggest changes were organizational. France, the strongest West European state, could muster 40,000–50,000 troops for war in 1500; 80,000 in 1600; 400,000 in 1700; and 600,000 in Napoleon's invasion of Russia in 1812. Fleets grew more slowly, with the British (the strongest), Spanish, and Russian all roughly doubling their numbers of ships of the line between 1700 and 1800, while the French fleet actually shrank after Louis XIV's plan to invade England collapsed in 1689. At the beginning of this period, Ottoman Turkish armies and fleets were the strongest in the West; by its end, the balance of military power had shifted decisively toward Western Europe.

Converting this complicated mass of information into single scores for Western war-making capacity once again involves very subjective guesstimates, but despite their revolutionary nature, the changes between 1500 and 1800 were clearly much smaller than those between 1800 and 1900 (let alone those between 1900 and 2000). I suggest that Western war-making capacity increased roughly 50 percent during the sixteenth century, 100 percent during the seventeenth, and another 50 percent in the eighteenth, for a total fourfold increase during the whole period of the military revolution (as opposed to my estimates of a tenfold increase during the nineteenth century and a twentyfold increase during the twentieth). Working backward from the figure of 0.5 points suggested for 1800, these estimates produce rough figures of 0.35 points for 1700, 0.18 points for 1600, and 0.13 points for 1500 (figure 5.7).

FROM CAESAR TO SULEIMAN, 1–1500 CE

Most general military histories agree that Western war-making capacity generally declined in the first half of this long period and then recovered in the second half.[26] Consensus is not complete, and in a series of studies, Bernard Bachrach has argued that post-Roman

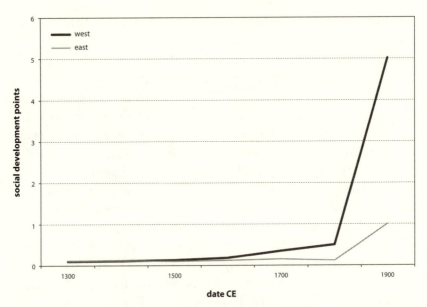

Figure 5.7. Eastern and Western war-making capacity, 1300–1900 CE.

Western European armies were larger, were more dominated by infantry, were more able to wage long-distance campaigns, and were used more for sieges than for battles than other historians assume.[27] However, this is very much a minority view, and I follow the mainstream opinion, that Western European military capacities began declining after 200 CE, falling faster after 400, languishing between 600 and 800, and then recovering slowly, with the recovery accelerating after 1300.[28] There is little sign of a post–Black Death military slump in the fourteenth century to compare with those in energy capture and city size.

Yet although there were important changes on the battlefield, such as the rise of heavy cavalry as bigger horses and stirrups became available and the increasing effectiveness of mounted bowmen in Muslim armies, the tactical continuities between 500 CE and 1300 CE (and indeed across the whole two millennia since 700 BCE, by which time iron weapons and cavalry were in general use) are even more striking.[29] The basics—iron weapons, metal armor, combined infantry and cavalry tactics, archery, siege machinery, oar- and wind-powered ships—changed rather little across this long period, and the real changes were logistical and organizational.

In the 30s BCE the Roman Republic had roughly 250,000 men under arms, organized into devastatingly effective legions, supported by the most extraordinary logistical system in the premodern world. They were led (much of the time) by outstandingly professional junior officers and NCOs, even if their senior officers—particularly under the Republic—sometimes left much to be desired.[30]

After the crises of the third century CE the army expanded, probably reaching around 500,000 men in the middle of the fourth century.[31] There is much debate about the quality of the late Roman army, with some historians suggesting that the real issue was that the nature of the mission changed. There was a shift toward defense in depth rather than frontier defense, and consequent changes in organization, with a growing distinction between garrison and field armies, with the latter using smaller units and more cavalry than the early imperial army, and with all forces relying more on immigrant troops.[32]

Yet while some older claims about the ineffectiveness of the garrison troops may have been overstated,[33] Roman military capacity probably did decline seriously (though not catastrophically) between the time of the Antonine Plague in the 160s CE and the battle of Adrianople in 378.

Between Adrianople and Khusrau II of Persia's invasion of the Byzantine Empire in 609 CE, the size and fighting power of Western armies fell much further, driven by a combination of declining population and crumbling administrative structures. By the seventh century armies had shrunk to a few tens of thousands of men, and the rapid Arab conquest of the Persian Empire and much of the Byzantine Empire owed more to the collapse of imperial structures than to any great military strength on the caliphs' side.[34]

Throughout the Western Middle Ages armed forces remained tiny, disorganized, and poorly supplied,[35] rarely reaching one-tenth the size of imperial Roman forces and never coming close to matching Roman effectiveness. Medieval European armies have been intensively studied,[36] but the less thoroughly researched Byzantine and particularly Muslim forces probably remained more powerful through most of the period circa 630–1500, especially after armies of Turkic mounted archers tens of thousands strong became common.[37]

Western European crusaders managed to take Jerusalem in 1099, and Byzantine armies regained some lost territory, but on the whole the advantage lay with the Turks in the tenth through fifteenth centuries. In 1527 the Turkish sultan Suleiman the Magnificent claimed to be able to muster 75,000 cavalry (mostly archers) and 28,000 infantry with guns, plus field artillery. Despite his failure to take Vienna in 1529, Turkish armies remained the most powerful in the West throughout the sixteenth century, and arguably some way into the seventeenth. Similarly, despite its famous defeat at Lepanto in 1571, the Turkish fleet remained a serious rival for Christian forces in the Mediterranean until well after 1600.[38]

Reducing all this history to scores for war-making capacity again involves abstracting from the specific missions each armed force faced, but some basic conclusions seem reasonable. The biggest Western armies in 1500 CE were still much smaller than those available in late Republican or early imperial Rome, and did not begin to match the Romans' technical sophistication; but the growing power of firearms (especially against fortifications, and especially in combination with large field armies of light cavalry, such as those of Ottoman Turkey) makes me suspect that the military power available to Suleiman had finally regained the level of that available to Caesar.

If the war-making score for the West in 1500 was 0.13 points, a score of 0.12 points seems reasonable to me for the year 1 CE. If the consensus is correct that Roman military capacity remained high until the fourth century then declined sharply, we might estimate scores of 0.1 points in 300 CE, tumbling to just 0.04 in 600, on the eve of the Arab conquests, reviving to 0.08 by 1200, and then climbing more quickly to 0.13 in 1500 (figure 5.8). (Historians who feel that the Roman score should be a little higher [say, 0.13 or 0.14 points] or a little lower [scores anywhere between 0.10 and 0.14 points seem perfectly plausible] should adjust the scores for 300–1200 CE accordingly.)

These numbers seem to me to be consistent with the qualitative assessments in the historical literature. They also, however, involve all kinds of abstractions and subjective judgments, which rival observers might choose not to accept. That said, figure 5.9 shows what is perhaps the most important point: all premodern scores for war-making capacity, including those for Caesar's and Suleiman's times, are so tiny when seen from the perspective of 2000 CE that no con-

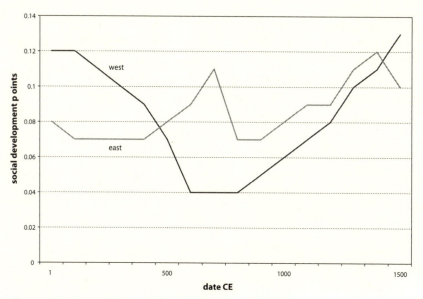

Figure 5.8. Eastern and Western war-making capacity, 1–1500 CE.

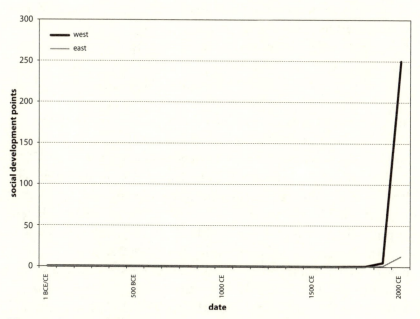

Figure 5.9. Eastern and Western war-making capacity, 1–2000 CE.

ceivable adjustment would make much difference to the social development index. And this is not just an artifact of the extraordinary level of military power in our own times; figure 5.10 shows that even judged from the standpoint of 1900 CE, the changes in Western military power between the first and eighth centuries CE are still too small to see. Only when we look back from the perspective of 1800 CE (figure 5.11) can we see serious differences in the earlier scores. Even if we were to double the scores for 600–800 CE, or to decide that Roman war-making capacity was surpassed only in 1600 rather than 1500 CE, it would make little difference.

EARLY WARFARE, 3000–1 BCE

The last three millennia BCE, taking us from the age of Narmer, the first Egyptian pharaoh, to that of Augustus, the first Roman emperor, saw a huge relative increase in war-making capacity.[39] Among the main battlefield advances in this long period we might list the replacement of stone by bronze weapons across the third millennium BCE, the rise of heavy infantry by 2500, the spread of horse-drawn chariots around 1600, the replacement of simple (self) by composite (reflex) bows probably around the same time, the replacement of bronze by iron weapons after 1100, the introduction of cavalry after about 900, the spread of the trireme after 700, the rise of phalanx tactics by 600 and their successive improvements, the introduction of torsion catapults and bigger ships (quadriremes, quinqueremes) after 400, the improvement of fortifications around 300, and the development of more flexible infantry tactics by 200.

We can compile a similar list of advances for organization. The first evidence for proper battlefield formations appears around 2500 BCE, the first known standing army around 2350, the establishment of professional charioteers around 1500, the rise of tax-based standing armies after 750 and of full-time fleets after 500, and Roman innovations in recruitment after 400 BCE. Force sizes show a similar upward path, from the 5,400 men that Sargon of Akkad boasted about circa 2350 BCE, through the roughly 30,000 infantry and 5,000 chariots that fought on each side at the battle of Kadesh in

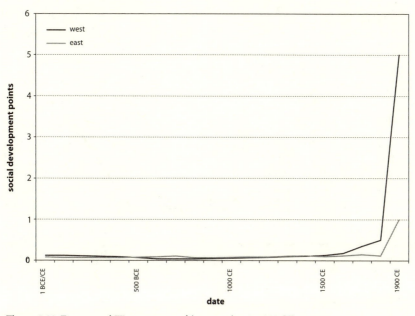

Figure 5.10. Eastern and Western war-making capacity, 1–1900 CE.

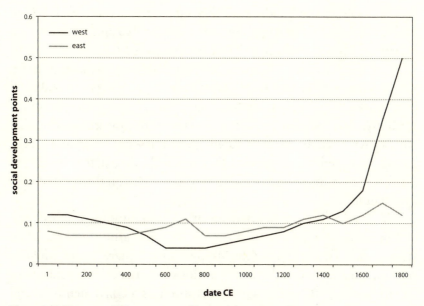

Figure 5.11. Eastern and Western war-making capacity, 1–1800 CE.

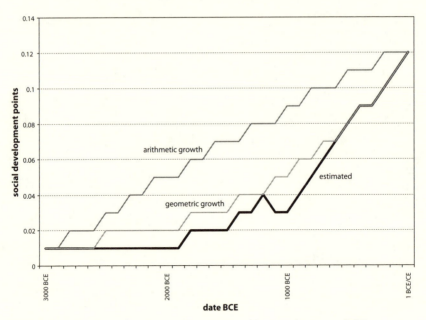

Figure 5.12. Three ways of estimating Western war-making capacity, 3000–1 BCE.

1274 and the 100,000 men who marched with Shalmaneser III of Assyria in 845, to the hundreds of thousands (the precise numbers are debated) raised by Persia to invade Greece in 480 and by Rome and Carthage to man their fleets in the 260s to 240s BCE.

Figure 5.12 shows three ways of representing war-making capacity in the period 3000–1 BCE numerically. By scoring pre-3000 BCE war making at zero I am not signaling support for the once-fashionable view that prestate societies were peaceful places; that theory has been decisively refuted.[40] The zero score is a purely technical issue, reflecting the fact that too little destructive force was available to communities making war to register on the social development index.

We could certainly start from other assumptions, for instance, setting scores at zero until the first standing army we hear of in twenty-fourth-century BCE Mesopotamia. There is no obvious reason to favor one of these assumptions over the others. I start with 0.01 points in 3000 BCE simply because it is a conveniently round number, but no other plausible assumption would make any discernible difference to the social development index.

The top line in figure 5.12 shows war-making capacity rising by simple arithmetic increments from 3000 to 1 BCE, the middle line shows war-making capacity rising by geometric steps (i.e., at a steady rate of increase of 8.65 percent per century), and the bottom line shows my estimates for the rate of change. (The arithmetic and geometric curves do not rise smoothly from 0.01 points in 3000 BCE to the 0.12 points calculated for 1 BCE; because the numbers involved are so tiny and the minimum step is 0.01 points, the lines inevitably move up in jerks.)

Arithmetic growth clearly does not correspond to reality. It would mean that by 2200 BCE the armies of Sharkalisharri of Akkad and Pepy II of Egypt (which had mostly bronze weapons but still included some stone-armed warriors, lacked armored infantry almost completely, fielded no chariots or cavalry, and had only very rudimentary fortifications),[41] scoring 0.04 points, were already as powerful as those of the Umayyad and Abbasid caliphates (which had iron weapons, reflex bows, cavalry and camel corps, and sophisticated qasrs).[42] It would also mean that by 1300 BCE the army of Ramses II was as strong (0.08 points) as that of Justinian in the sixth century CE. Neither of these conclusions is remotely plausible.

The geometric curve seems more believable, although it surely oversimplifies reality by glossing over the collapse of 1200–1000 BCE. The collapse of 2200–2000 BCE also had a serious impact on war-making capacity, but the scores are again so small in that period (just 0.01 points) that the decline cannot be registered on the graph unless we assume that in 2100 BCE Mesopotamian and Egyptian war making had reverted to prestate, prebronze levels, which does not seem likely.

My estimated growth rates diverge from the geometric simplification in positing a slower takeoff in the third millennium BCE, a decline (from 0.04 to 0.03 points) in the 1200–1000 BCE "dark age," followed by a faster increase in the early first millennium BCE. (The scores for 400 and 300 BCE on both the geometric and estimated curves are identical [at 0.07 points] not because there were no military developments—this century took war making from the hoplites and triremes of the Peloponnesian War to the combined-arms tactics and quinqueremes of Alexander and Carthage—but because of the rounding of very small numbers; the scores in 400 BCE are

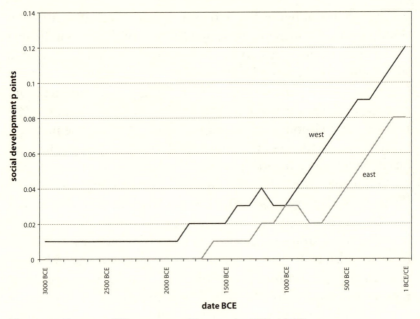

Figure 5.13. Eastern and Western war-making capacity, 3000–1 BCE.

just big enough to round up to 0.07, while those in 300 BCE are not quite big enough to round up to 0.08.)

The geometric and estimated curves both imply that war-making capacity in the thirteenth century BCE, when the kings of the International Age seemed well on the way to turning the east Mediterranean into a single large empire, was at roughly the same level (0.04 points) that it would fall back to in the seventh century CE, when the Byzantine and Sassanian Persian Empires disintegrated and the Arab conquerors took over their former territories. The estimated curve also implies that ancient war making regained the thirteenth-century BCE level around 900 BCE, when Assyrian kings such as Adad-Nirari II were also building up large empires. In *Why the West Rules—For Now*, I argue that these are all plausible conclusions.[43] Finally, my estimates also suggest that Roman war-making capacity between 200 BCE and 200 CE compared closely with that in the West between 1300 and 1500 CE—a suggestion that late medieval Europeans probably would have found believable.

Figure 5.13 shows my estimates for war-making capacity in the past three millennia BCE.

EASTERN WAR-MAKING CAPACITY

The East-West Military Balance in 2000 CE

The greatest military power in the East in 2000 CE was the People's Republic of China, but while it is easy enough to obtain approximate figures for its military strength,[44] it is much more difficult to decide how many social development points to award Eastern warmaking capacity in 2000 CE relative to the West's 250 points.

In 2000 the United States outspent China more than 20:1 at market exchange rates and more than 9:1 at purchasing power parity rates, and outnumbered it more than 25:1 in nuclear warheads, more than 10:1 in intercontinental ballistic missiles, 14:1 in nuclear-armed submarines, and 11:0 in aircraft carrier battle groups. In numbers of main battle tanks the two armies were roughly equal, but the quality of America's tanks was far higher than that of China's, and in every other arm—from trucks to helicopters—the United States had overwhelming superiority. In general technological capacity, the U.S. lead was even greater. Western military dominance was certainly not total, and analysts regularly expressed doubts as to whether American naval forces would dare to confront directly the masses of Chinese submarines and antiship missiles based in the Taiwan Strait; but China had little ability to project military power beyond its immediate surroundings, while the United States bestrode the rest of the world like a colossus.

In 2000 CE Western war-making capacity was clearly very much higher than the East's,[45] but just how much higher? I know of very few attempts to boil it down to a single score. The best-known numerical comparison is probably the Composite Index of National Capability (CINC), a scoring system widely used in international relations, which aims to describe what percentage of the world's hard power belongs to each nation.[46] Its scores go back to 1816, but can be used only to make synchronic comparisons between nations rather than to measure diachronic change in capacity.

The national capability that the CINC measures, however, is much broader than the war-making capacity I am examining here. The index gives each country a score based on its population size, urbanization, iron and steel production, energy consumption, military expenditure, and total military personnel. By 2000, according to the CINC, China (16 percent) had already overtaken the United States (14 percent), despite the massive military imbalance between the two powers.[47]

The war game designer James Dunnigan took a very different approach in his book *How to Make War*, assigning "combat power" scores to different nations. He gave separate scores for land and sea power, ranking the United States first in both categories. On land the United States scored 2,488 points, and China, which placed second, scored 827 points. On sea the United States scored 302 points, and China, which ranked fifth, scored 16 points (Britain ranked second, with 46 points; Russia third, with 45 points; and Japan fourth, with 26 points).[48]

If we follow the technique I use in the social development index of focusing only on the most developed region in East and West, Dunnigan's figures would give a West:East ratio for war-making capacity in 2000 CE of roughly 3:1 on land and 19:1 at sea. If we add together the land and sea scores we get 2,790 points for the United States and 843 points for China (a ratio of 3.3:1). If instead we weight land and sea power equally, converting the U.S. score in each category to 125 points to add up to the same 250-point system that I use here, China scores 48.17 points (41.55 on land, 6.62 at sea), producing a West:East ratio of a little over 5:1.

Dunnigan does not explain how he arrived at his scores, but a West:East war-making capacity ratio in the 3:1 to 5:1 range involves assuming diminishing returns to investment, given that the United States outspent China by somewhere between 9:1 and 21:1 in 2000 CE. It also weights mass over sophistication, given that U.S. dominance is much greater in complex, technology-intensive weapons such as ICBMs, antimissile systems, stealth bombers, precision-guided munitions, and aircraft carriers than in simple weapons such as assault rifles and grenades. How much of a lead the United States retains in electronic warfare remains to be seen, although the success of the Stuxnet and Flame cyberattacks in 2010 and 2012, respectively, suggests that America's advantage may be considerable.[49]

The difficulties the United States and its allies have had in defeating low-tech enemies in Iraq and Afghanistan suggest that Dunnigan's assumptions have merits, but there is also some evidence that these difficulties owe at least as much to strategic and doctrinal missteps as to inherent limitations on Western war-making capacity.[50] Other military analysts suggest that there are in fact increasing returns to investment,[51] and that the Revolution in Military Affairs, driven by improved information processing and accuracy of delivery systems, has already transformed war making as dramatically as (and much faster than) the early-modern European "military revolution." The extraordinary one-sidedness of the battles against Iraqi conventional forces in 1991 and 2003 suggests that this perspective also has merits.[52] The Revolution in Military Affairs seems to have transformed the ways conventional interstate wars are fought, dramatically increasing the West's lead in war-making capacity over the rest of the world, but it has had much less impact on occupying and pacifying defeated nations.[53]

I suggest a West:East war-making capacity ratio for 2000 CE of roughly 20:1, much higher than Dunnigan's range of 3:1 to 5:1. This would be by far the highest West:East war-making ratio in history, dwarfing even those of the nineteenth and twentieth centuries, but the vast technological gap that separated Eastern and Western military forces in 2000 CE seems to me to justify it.

If my estimate is reasonably accurate, Eastern war-making capacity in 2000 earned just 12.5 points on the index of social development, as compared to the West's 250 points. If Dunnigan's estimates are better, in 2000 the East earned somewhere between 48.17 (the "low estimate" in figure 5.14) and 75.54 points (the "high estimate").

The East's Modern Military Revolution, 1850–2000 CE

The arrival of modern Western war-making systems in the Pacific in the mid-nineteenth century was the most profound rupture in Eastern military history. Chinese armies had been using firearms longer than Western, but had failed to keep pace with Western advances in gunpowder weapons since the fifteenth century. Japan, by contrast, adopted firearms relatively late, but became a center of innovation in the sixteenth century. However, the unification of Japan and the abandonment of Hideyoshi's expansionist programs meant that Jap-

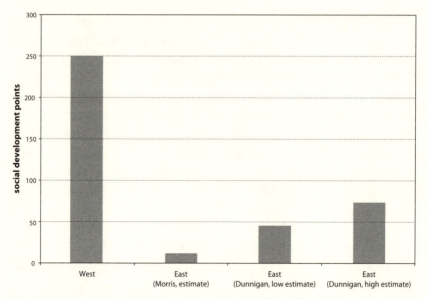

Figure 5.14. Alternative quantitative estimates of the East:West military balance, 2000 CE.

anese armies did little serious fighting between the early seventeenth century and the early nineteenth century, and Japanese firearms stagnated across this long period.[54]

China and Japan began emulating Western military practices after the arrival of naval expeditions on their shores in 1840 and 1853, respectively, but Japan adapted to the new challenges far more successfully.[55] The government introduced European-style conscription in 1873, reduced the samurai to impotence later in the decade, and then built up its army first on French and then on German lines and its navy on British lines. In 1880 it still lagged very far behind the Western powers, with just 71,000 men under arms (just one-sixth as many as Germany) and a naval tonnage of just 15,000 (one-fortieth as much as Britain), but by 1900 it had leapt ahead to 234,000 soldiers (almost half as many as Germany) and 187,000 tons (almost one-fifth as much as Britain).[56]

The quality of Japanese armed forces also improved sharply.[57] In 1894–95 they showed mastery of Western military thought, discipline, and organization (as well as hardware) in crushing Chinese forces; in 1900, Japanese troops played the main part in relieving the diplomatic quarter in Beijing during the Boxer Rebellion; in 1902,

Britain concluded that a naval alliance with Japan was the best way to preserve its voice in Pacific affairs; and in 1904–5 Japan won a shattering victory over Russia (even if the war almost drove the country into bankruptcy). Japanese war-making capacity remained much lower than that of any of the major European powers, but it had become a regional power, and probably the only non-Western power in the world that could stand up to European violence.[58]

Japan's spectacular successes in 1914–15 and 1941–42 were won while the Western powers were heavily distracted in Europe. Japan got most of what it wanted in the Treaty of Versailles (although its demand that the text include a clause insisting on racial equality was defeated), but when it did have to face serious resistance from the United States in 1942–45 (even though the United States made the Pacific a secondary front) the continuing gap between Eastern and Western war-making capacity was made painfully clear.[59]

Japan largely demilitarized in 1945 (although by the end of the twentieth century its navy was once again a significant regional force), but with the end of its civil wars in 1949 China revived as an East Asian power. It intervened to great effect (albeit at horrific cost) in Korea in 1950, won a small border conflict with India in 1962, and tested its first atomic bomb in 1964. Training and professionalism in the People's Liberation Army (PLA) suffered greatly in the 1960s during the Cultural Revolution, however, and while its forces on the northern frontier did manage to hold their own in skirmishes with the Soviet Union in 1969 (despite losing roughly eight hundred dead to the Soviets' one hundred), in the 1970s serious shortcomings in organization, doctrine, and equipment became clear. The PLA performed poorly in a limited war with Vietnam in 1979,[60] and Deng Xiaoping launched a military modernization program in the same year. Military budgets began growing significantly in the 1990s, quadrupling during that decade and again in the following one, with particular emphasis on strengthening the navy and developing asymmetric responses to the potentially overwhelming advantages of the American alliance.[61] By the 2020s Chinese military spending may catch up with that of the United States, but as of 2012, the East-West military gulf remains enormous.

Eastern war-making capacity trailed the West's throughout the twentieth century. Japanese forces won notable victories over Western troops in the early 1940s and Sino-Korean and Vietnamese armies also got the better of Europeans and Americans in the 1950s and 1960s, but in each case the Eastern powers were able to exploit the fact that from a Western perspective these conflicts were secondary theaters within larger struggles for the domination of Europe, first against Nazi Germany and then against the Soviet Union.[62] The East-West gap in war-making capacity narrowed between 1900 and 1940 but remained large, and then grew much wider still across the next sixty years.

Putting a single value on the East-West military ratio in 1900 is less difficult than in 2000. As noted above, in 1900 the German army outnumbered Japan's by more than 2:1 and the British navy outnumbered Japan's nearly 6:1, and in both cases the European forces also had major qualitative strengths. I estimate that the West:East ratio in 1900 was roughly 5:1, which, with Western war-making capacity pegged at 5.0 points, would mean that the East scored 1.0 point in 1900. Further implications of this would be that Eastern war-making capacity grew 12.5-fold during the twentieth century, while Western capacity grew fiftyfold, and that Eastern military power in 2000 was 2.5 times greater than the West's had been in 1900. If, however, we adopt Dunnigan's estimates, which imply that Eastern military capacity scored between 48.17 and 75.54 points in 2000, we would have to accept a correspondingly greater increase (fifty- to seventy-five-fold) in Eastern war-making across the twentieth century, which seems excessive.

Eastern War-Making Capacity in the Gunpowder Era, 1500–1850 CE

Thanks to a string of recent studies, the broad shape of war-making capacity in the East across China's two-thousand-year imperial history is reasonably clear.[63] Once again the main challenge is deciding on the precise scores to assign, but in the East the numbers involved (and hence the margins of plausible error) are for most of the period even smaller than those in the West.

Directly comparing Eastern and Western war-making capacity before 1900 CE is a very rough-and-ready business. The West was clearly much stronger by 1800, and probably already somewhat stronger by 1500, at the start of the Western military revolution. The Ming dynasty could muster large armies when it saw fit (particularly for the steppe campaigns of the first half of the fifteenth century), but failed to exploit gunpowder technology as effectively as Europeans.

Western guns were already recognized as superior to Eastern in the sixteenth century. The Ming government may have had access to a few Western cannons as early as the 1520s, but if so, they remained curiosities until the 1540s. By then Japanese armorers were producing very effective copies, although these too remained rather scarce. Even the celebrated Qi's Army that turned the tide in the mid-sixteenth-century pirate wars featured very few musketeers compared to contemporary European armies.[64] Their guns were often amateurishly made and tended to explode, which discouraged gunners from getting close enough to their weapons to aim them properly.[65] Qi's Army never numbered above ten thousand troops, and had more impact on naval warfare than on the vast Ming army. Qi's new naval arrangements were desperately needed; the Ming navy had declined spectacularly since the early fifteenth century,[66] and much desperate scrambling was required to create the force that co-operated with Korean ships to hold off Japan in the 1590s. The same was true of the land forces. The garrison of Beijing, for instance, shifted from clay cannonballs to lead only in 1564, moving on to iron (like the Europeans) in 1568, and only in the 1570s did Qi Jiguang introduce light cannons on carts protected by wicker barriers, like those the Hungarians had used against the Ottomans at Varna in 1444.[67]

Ming war-making capacity was certainly much weaker than that of the Habsburg Empire (let alone the Ottoman Empire) in the sixteenth century, and in some ways weaker than that of the tiny Dutch Republic too. I suggest a score of 0.12 for the East in 1600 CE (as compared to 0.18 for the West), at the time of Hideyoshi's wars in Korea, when Japanese military capacity equaled China's,[68] and just 0.1 in 1500 (as compared to 0.13 for the West). This would mean that Chinese war making rose to match the peak Roman levels only around 1600, even though firearms had by then been in use for three or four centuries.

Chinese war-making capacity rose across the seventeenth century, and by 1696 Kangxi could take 235 heavy cannon (weighing 4–5 tons each) and 104 light cannon (weighing 40–400 kg) on his campaign against the Zunghar nomads.[69] But European war-making capacity had increased much faster. I estimate that European capacity roughly doubled between 1600 and 1700, from 0.18 to 0.35 points; I would suggest that Eastern capacity increased by only 25 percent, from 0.12 to 0.15 points (meaning that Kangxi's military power was midway between that of the Roman emperor Augustus [0.12 points] and that of the Habsburg emperor Philip II [0.18 points]).

Between 1750 and 1800 Chinese and Japanese military capacities both decayed sharply.[70] The Qing dynasty commanded about 850,000 soldiers in 1800, a quarter of a million of whom were supposedly elite Manchu bannermen.[71] Against that large number, though, we must set the fact that the quality, organization, and logistics of these forces had all collapsed since Kangxi's day. Emperor Qianlong took the honorific title the Old Man of the Ten Complete Military Victories in 1792, but in reality his forces suffered serious reverses in Burma, Vietnam, and Nepal.

By the time Lord Robert Jocelyn (quoted at the beginning of this chapter) saw Chinese armies and flotillas in action, in 1840, the gap between Western and Eastern weapons and organization was enormous.[72] In a famous comparison, the British officer Armine Mountain suggested that the Chinese forces looked like illustrations to Froissart's fourteenth-century chronicle of the Anglo-French Hundred Years' War, "exactly as if the subjects of his old prints had assumed life and substance and colour, and were moving and acting before me unconscious of the march of the world through centuries, and of all modern usage, invention, or improvement."[73]

I estimated that Western war-making capacity increased from 0.10 points in 1300 CE to 0.11 in 1400; if that estimate is reliable, and if Armine's judgment was reliable too, that would mean that between 1700 and 1840 Eastern war making declined from 0.15 to about 0.11 points. I suspect that Armine overstated the case by only a small amount, and that between 1700 and 1800, while European war-making capacity grew by almost 50 percent, from 0.35 to 0.5 points, Chinese capacity fell by 25 percent, from 0.15 points to just 0.12 points (and Japanese military effectiveness fell still lower).

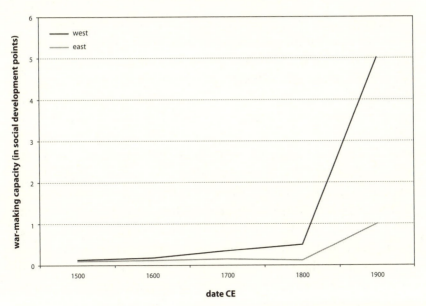

Figure 5.15. Eastern and Western war-making capacity in the age of military revolution, 1500–1900 CE.

This would mean that Qing armies in 1800 were no more effective than the Ming forces that had faced Hideyoshi shortly before 1600, but were at least somewhat more effective than the knights and archers who clashed at Crecy, Poitiers, and Agincourt. It would also mean that Eastern war-making capacity increased tenfold across the nineteenth century to produce the Japanese score in 1900 of 1.0 points (figure 5.15).

IMPERIAL CHINA AND THE NOMAD ANOMALY, 200 BCE–1500 CE

For much of China's two-thousand-year imperial history its war-making capacity was greater than that of any rival in the East (or even the world), but there were exceptions. The most interesting relate to what in *Why the West Rules—For Now* I called "the nomad anomaly."[74]

On the whole, scores on the four traits I use to measure social development show considerable redundancy, but there are unusual social formations that buck that trend. Steppe nomads are the most important: these groups generally scored very poorly on organization and information technology and fairly poorly on energy capture, but before the age of gunpowder only the most efficient agrarian empires could get the better of them on the battlefield.

In the East, agrarian empires clearly reached this level of efficiency between about 100 BCE and 100 CE, when Han armies regularly defeated the Xiongnu, and again in the seventh century CE, when Tang armies achieved even greater dominance over the Turks. It was only after 1700, however, with drastic improvements in gunpowder weapons, that Qing armies really mastered the steppes.[75] Before and between these periods of Chinese domination—around 200 BCE, 200–500 CE, and 800–1500 CE—steppe nomads could muster more military power than any agrarian state.[76]

Throughout this long period, the strongest steppe societies probably scored around 0.1 points (± 25–50 percent, I would guess) for war making on the social development index. The lowest scores (perhaps around 0.06 or 0.07 points) were in the first two centuries CE, when the Roman, Parthian, and Han Empires successfully disrupted the rise of major new pastoral empires anywhere on the steppes, and the highest (perhaps around 1.3 points, roughly twice as high as the Xiongnu) in the age of Genghis Khan.

This would imply that Genghis Khan's Mongol hordes could have overrun the Roman Empire and would have been a match even for the Ottomans around 1500. There is of course no way to know if this is true, but Tamerlane did humble the Ottomans in 1402 and considered his own Mongol hordes strong enough to overthrow the Ming in 1405. Another Mongol army did capture the Ming emperor on 1450 and could probably have sacked Beijing had it chosen to do so. For what it is worth, the assumptions behind the GMT "Great Battles of History" game system also give Genghis Khan's armies the tactical edge over Julius Caesar's.[77]

Famously, however, nomad rulers struggled when they tried to convert their war-making capacity into political power. Only those who came from "seminomad" backgrounds, such as the Xianbei in the sixth century CE, the Jurchens in the twelfth, and the Manchus in the seventeenth, succeeded, establishing themselves as ruling dynasties (the Sui-Tang, Jin, and Qing, respectively). Fully nomadic conquerors, such as the Mongols in the thirteenth and fourteenth centuries CE, seem to have found it too difficult to make the cultural adjustments necessary for ruling an agrarian empire. Consequently, I have assigned scores for Chinese rather than nomadic war-making capacity throughout the period 200 BCE–1800 CE.

The broad shape of Eastern military history across this period is reasonably clear, although assigning precise scores is again a subjective matter. I will begin in the fifteenth century CE and work back to 200 BCE.

In 1400 CE, on the eve of Zheng He's voyages and Yongle's invasions of the steppes, Ming military power was enormous. On paper, the emperors commanded a coastal fleet of 3,500 ships (1,750 warships, 1,350 patrol boats, and 400 armed transports) and an army of 1.2 million troops.[78] In reality, these forces were considerably smaller, but the biggest steppe invasion in 1414 did involve about half a million men.[79] Ming war-making capacity was certainly greater than of the contemporary Ottomans (to whom I assigned 0.11 points), but probably less than that of the Mongols at the height of their strength in the mid-thirteenth century; I therefore estimate an Eastern score in 1400 of 0.12 points.

By 1300, after their conquest of China, Mongol military power had probably declined somewhat from its peak in the mid-thirteenth century, but remained formidable by premodern standards. The Mongol Yuan dynasty even revived China's fleets after they had fallen into disrepair in the mid-thirteenth century,[80] and reportedly sent 4,500 ships with 150,000 soldiers against Japan in 1274.[81] I suggest a score of 0.11 points, slightly lower than the early Ming dynasty peak, but this can only be a guess; estimates of 0.1 or 0.12 points would be just as plausible.

The Song dynasty, despite its famously antimilitary credentials, rapidly developed its armies in the late tenth century, reportedly commanding 650,000 men at Taizong's death in 997 and nearly a million at Zhengtong's in 1022.[82] Wang Anshi's reforms, brought on by the eleventh-century fiscal crises, shifted the balance away from salaried professionals toward militias and reduced overall strengths, but the army remained strong. It mustered 320,000 troops and a similar number of porters in 1081,[83] supported by enormous centralized armories, and even in the 1120s and 1130s the dynasty could still field forces of 100,000–200,000.[84]

Southern Song rulers greatly strengthened their fleets for the twelfth-century wars with the Jurchens, introducing much bigger ships, including paddleboats that could overcome winds and tides, and new weapons, such as flaming arrows, rockets, and flamethrowers. Twelfth-century paddleboats could be 60–90 m long, with eight wheels and crews of 700–800. By the 1130s the biggest were more than 100 m long, and by 1200 some were armored with iron plates.[85]

Song military capacity between 1000 and 1200 was clearly much greater than anything in the fragmented West, where the Byzantine Empire had probably the strongest forces in 1000 and the Seljuk Turks in 1100 and 1200. I assigned 0.06 points to the Byzantines in 1000 and 0.07 and 0.08 to the Seljuks in 1100 and 1200. I tentatively suggest scoring Eastern capacity at 0.08 in 1000 and 0.09 in 1100–1200. That would mean that even at its height, Song war-making capacity did not equal imperial Rome's.

Under the Tang dynasty, however, war-making capacity came much closer Rome's. The sources for the early eighth century suggest that the Tang had about half a million men under arms, in a highly centralized system with good discipline and long-service professional troops.[86]

Tang military power rested on the fusion of steppe heavy cavalry with mass infantry developed by the states of Northern Wei and Northern Zhou and the successor Sui dynasty in the sixth century.[87] This began with the Xianbei conquest of much of northern China in the early fifth century and accelerated with Emperor Xiaowen's reforms in the late fifth century, but even in the 530s, 100,000 men still counted as a huge army.[88]

Only in the late sixth century did the consolidation of northern China's states generate vastly greater military power. In 589 the Sui emperor Wendi could muster 518,000 troops in the Yangzi Valley for his conquest of southern China, supported by five-decker ships carrying up to 800 men and equipped with spiked booms for fixing and boarding enemy vessels (which sound strikingly like Rome's *corvus*-bearing quinqueremes developed in the late 260s BCE).

The Tang navy shrank steadily after the huge fleets built by the Sui for the unification of China in 589 and the disastrous wars against Koguryo in 612–14. That, however, was largely because there was no credible threat to the empire from the sea, and (at least until 755) China's internal peace required no major armed presence on its rivers. On the rare occasions that ships were needed, as when war broke out again with Korea in the 660s, the strong Tang state was able to build or requisition hundreds at short notice, and could mount large campaigns.[89]

The civil wars that followed An Lushan's revolt in 755–63 hugely weakened the Tang Empire. In November 763 a Tibetan force was able to sack Chang'an, and for the next two centuries Chinese military energy was absorbed in recurring civil wars and partially successful efforts to fend off Tibetan raids. When central authority collapsed, provinces maintained their own armies, but not even the biggest (e.g., Pinglu) rose above 100,000 men. What troops there were tended to be poorly equipped, supplied, and led.[90]

Before the early fifth-century Xianbei unification of northern China, armies had been relatively large, but were much less powerful than those of Tang times. In 279 CE, for instance, the state of Jin mustered 200,000 troops and supporting fleets to invade southern China down the Yangzi Valley. The campaign was strikingly like the one in which Sui Wendi accomplished the same goal in the same region in 589, but the forces involved were only 40 percent of the size of Wendi's, and organizationally had more in common with the campaigns of the Han dynasty than with those of the Sui.

Across the next two hundred years cavalry armies came to dominate China. Grave goods, figurines, and tomb reliefs provide plenty of information about weapons, showing that stirrups came into common use for cavalry in the fourth century. Combined with evidence from grave goods for increasing use of shock weapons and the spread of horse armor, this suggests that tactics went through major changes.[91]

While there were clearly significant developments in war-making capacity between 200 and 600 CE, it is not easy to assign scores to this Period of Disunion. Eastern military forces never sank to anything like the level of weakness found in the West in the seventh through ninth centuries, and state infrastructures survived. Even in the fourth century armies of 50,000–100,000 men remained common, and although siege trains virtually disappeared from northern Chinese armies, southern China's fortifications remained strong.[92] Military capacity rose faster after 400 CE than before; working backward from the score of 0.09 points I assigned to the Sui forces in 600, I therefore propose scores of 0.08 points in 500 and 0.07 points for the whole period 200–400.

This flat score masks important changes, but unless we push the score for 600 higher, we are forced either to assume (as I do) that the changes between 200 and 400 were not large enough to register on the index or else to propose that the score fell below 0.07 points at some moment after 200 CE then climbed quickly. A score of 0.06 points would be equivalent to that for the West in the early sixth century CE or around 1000 CE, but my impression from the literature I have consulted is that Eastern war-making capacity remained above those levels throughout the Period of Disunion.[93]

War-making capacity under the Western Han dynasty (206 BCE–9 CE) was higher still. The great wars of the third century BCE had generated mass infantry armies that regularly ran into the hundreds of thousands on each side, using sophisticated siege craft and logistics and developing a body of profound military theory.[94]

In 200 BCE navies were weak because control of the seas and rivers was rarely decisive; so too were cavalry forces, and many troops still used bronze rather than iron weapons. Over the next two centuries, however, iron arms steadily replaced bronze, and cavalry grew in importance as the main arena for conflict shifted from wars between Chinese armies to wars against Xiongnu nomads.

The size of Western Han armies fluctuated, declining after 200 BCE as emperors disarmed their client kings but spiking up again for great wars, such as the army of 140,000 infantry and 70,000 cavalry that Wudi sent against the Xiongnu in 97 BCE. Overall, though, the trend was downward, and in 31 CE the Eastern Han dynasty (ruled 25–220 CE) abolished universal military service and set about demilitarizing the core of the empire in earnest.[95] By the 50s CE the Han Empire was shifting toward large garrison forces on the frontiers (often of allied cavalry under only the loosest imperial control) and a small standing army of about 40,000 men at the empire's core.

Han armies seem never to have reached the level of effectiveness of the Roman Empire's. I suggest scores of 0.08 points (as compared to a Roman peak of 0.12 points) in 100 BCE and 1 BCE/CE, then a

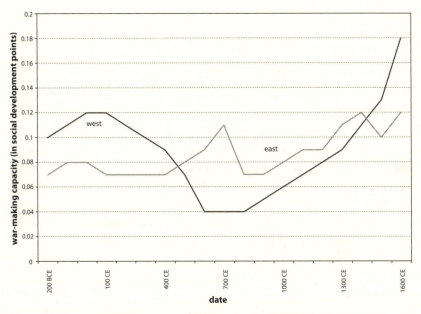

Figure 5.16. Eastern and Western war-making capacity, 200 BCE–1600 CE.

slight decline to 0.07 points in 100 and 200 CE. As with most of the estimates in this section, there is a strong element of subjectivity, and Western Han scores could certainly be raised to 0.1 points without straining the limits of the evidence too much. However, unless we assume that the Han military actually was a match for the Roman, there is no way to change the Eastern war-making score enough to have a serious impact on the social development index.

The shape of the curves for Western and Eastern war-making capacity between 200 BCE and 1500 CE (figure 5.16) suggests that it was probably impossible for any state (including even the strongest steppe confederations) to push their military effectiveness up very far above the 0.1–0.12 range before the gunpowder revolution took off. Despite all the difficulties of making sweeping comparisons across huge swathes of time and space,[96] iron-armed imperial Roman, early Tang, and early Ming war-making techniques do seem to have reached roughly the same level. No amount of reorganizing command and control and tightening up logistics could advance much beyond this.

EARLY CHINA, 1600–200 BCE

As in analyses of early Western war making, the very small scores possible on the index produce a rather schematic effect (see figure 5.13).

Archaeologists have found plenty of evidence for violence in Chinese prehistory, but only in the early second millennium BCE do we see regular use of metal weapons and signs of military organization that we can reasonably think of as state-style warfare.[97] Following the same principles that I applied to early Western war making, I therefore assign the first score of 0.01 points in 1600 BCE, which coincides roughly with the episodes conventionally associated with the arrival of the Shang. Eastern war-making was at roughly the same level in the mid-second millennium BCE as that in the Western core in the third millennium BCE, waged with bronze-armed and usually unarmored militias of just a few thousand men, no cavalry or chariots, no purpose-built warships, and fairly simple fortifications.

The time lag between Eastern and Western war-making capacity shrank sharply during the later second millennium BCE. The spread of chariot warfare from Central Asia to both regions (reaching the West around 1800 BCE and the East around 1200 BCE) probably had a lot to do with this. Late Shang warfare seems to have been conducted on a much larger scale than that of Early Shang times.[98] According to the indications in the oracle bones, Shang expeditionary forces were normally around three thousand strong, but on at least one occasion King Wuding and Lady Fushao assembled ten thousand men.[99] By 1200 BCE these armies were using chariots, but they seem to have limited them primarily to transporting officers. I suggest that war-making capacity had risen sufficiently to lift the score to 0.02 points by 1200 BCE. I estimate that the Western score rose to 0.02 points in 1800 BCE, suggesting that the gap between Eastern and Western military power had narrowed to about six hundred years.

In the West the pace of military change accelerated after 1500 BCE, as chariot corps became the central arm in the kingdoms around the east Mediterranean and increasingly professional forces developed under highly centralized leadership. I suggested that the score for war-making capacity increased to 0.03 points in 1400 BCE, then to 0.04 points in 1300. The East, it seems, went through a similar period of accelerating increases in military capacity in the late second millennium BCE. By 1000 BCE the Zhou were using chariots en masse, much as Western armies had been doing since 1500 BCE,[100] and according to the *Shi ji* (admittedly, compiled almost a millennium later), in 1045 BCE King Wu of Zhou led 45,000 infantry, 6,000 allies, and 300 chariots in the war that overthrew the Shang.[101] Even if the actual numbers were only half as large, this force would have been quite respectable by the standards of Western war making in 1500 BCE (although it would not have impressed the Western kings of the thirteenth century BCE). I therefore suggest a score of 0.03 points for Eastern war making in 1000 BCE.

Zhou armies seem to have grown during the tenth century BCE, and carried royal power far beyond the Wei and Yellow River Valleys. After King Zhao's disastrous defeat on the Han River in 957 BCE, however, the state began to unravel. Assigning scores to such poorly known institutions is a rather arbitrary exercise, but I assume that Zhou military capacity did not increase enough between 1000 and 900 BCE to raise the score above 0.03 points, but that the chaos into which the state descended after about 850 did lower the score back to 0.02 points.

Military capacity increased rapidly and steadily in the mid- and late first millennium BCE. The most important changes were organizational, with a shift away from aristocrats raising levies and leading them in their own chariots to rulers taxing and conscripting free peasants in mass infantry armies. In the seventh century, ten thousand men was still considered a sizeable force. By the late sixth century, however, a major effort might raise fifty thousand troops, and a century later, the greatest armies were twice as big.[102]

By the fifth century BCE, Chinese scholars were ranking states by the number of chariots they could field, with a thousand chariots (probably 50 percent more than Duke Wen used in the great battle at Chengdu in 632 BCE) counting as small and ten thousand as large.[103] Across the fourth and third centuries, however, army sizes exploded. The numbers provided by our sources (which reach 600,000) are often suspect, but the state of Qin could certainly field a few hundred thousand troops at a time by 250 BCE.[104] Iron weapons did not become the norm until after 200 BCE, but the fourth and third centuries BCE also saw chariots being replaced by cavalry and great advances in siege warfare, including the straddling of much of northern China with long mud-brick walls designed to keep steppe raiders out.[105]

In figure 5.13 I represent the Eastern score for war making as increasing steadily between 700 and 100 BCE, from 0.02 to 0.08 points. This is certainly an oversimplification, and the rate of increase probably accelerated after 400 BCE, but given the tiny number of points involved, this seemed less arbitrary than inserting plateaus and periods of faster change.

WAR-MAKING CAPACITY: DISCUSSION

Like social organization, war-making capacity has been a function of energy capture, with quite small changes at the margin of energy capture regularly producing wild swings in war-making capacity (figures 5.17, 5.18).

In East and West alike, after a long period when war-making capacity grew too slowly to be measurable on the index, it then spiked up sharply, rising from 0.01 to 0.08 points in the space of roughly a millennium (between 1800 and 500 BCE in the West and between 1200 and 100 BCE in the East). In both regions, war-making capacity then seems to have pressed against what we might call a military hard ceiling, between 0.08 and 0.12 points, for nearly two thousand years (figure 5.19).

Within this 0.08–0.12 band, Eastern and Western war-making capacity followed somewhat different paths. In the East, we see a series of crests (100 BCE–100 CE, 700 CE, 1400 CE) separated by collapses (200–400 CE and 800–900 CE), with each crest peaking higher than the earlier ones (at 0.08 points between 100 BCE and 100 CE, 0.11 points in 700 CE, and 0.12 points in 1400 CE, returning to that level in 1600 CE after a slight decline around 1500).

Premodern Western war-making capacity has a more dramatic history, rising fairly steadily from 500 BCE until 100 BCE (as noted

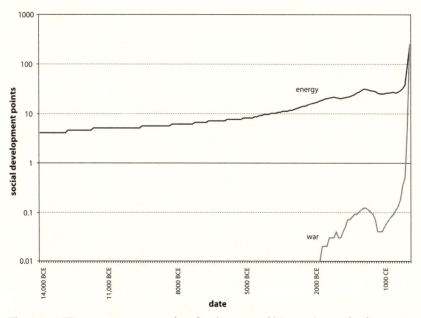

Figure 5.17. Western energy capture plotted against war-making capacity on a log-linear scale, 14,000 BCE–2000 CE, measured in social development points.

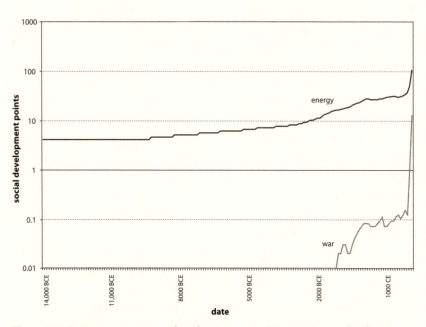

Figure 5.18. Eastern energy capture plotted against war-making capacity on a log-linear scale, 14,000 BCE–2000 CE, measured in social development points.

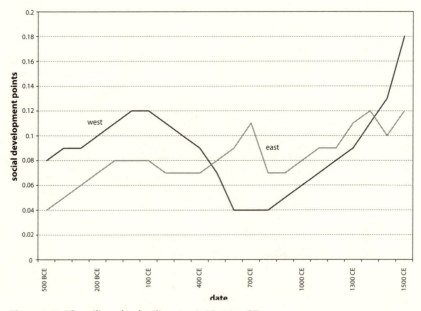

Figure 5.19. The military hard ceiling, 500 BCE–1600 CE.

earlier, the fourth-century BCE flat period of the graph is just a product of rounding the very tiny scores) to a very high level of 0.12 points, then collapsing spectacularly to 0.04 points by 600 CE, before rising steadily from 800 CE onward, breaking through the 0.12 points ceiling around the 1440s CE—just the moment when gunners from Ottoman Turkey to Burgundy, France, and England began experimenting with new designs and new tactics.

Figure 5.19 illustrates well the argument made by theorists of the early-modern European Military Revolution: guns were a necessary but not a sufficient condition for Europe's military takeoff. It was guns that made it possible for fifteenth-century European armies to outperform imperial Rome's in significant ways, but it took transformations in tactics, logistics, and command and control to realize the potential of the new weapons.

As Kenneth Chase argues,[106] these transformations began in Europe—and particularly Western Europe—rather than in China, India, Iran, or Turkey, because (a) Europe's distance from the steppes made it difficult to maintain large cavalry armies, which meant that its battlefields contained a lot of slow-moving infantry, against which slow-firing guns could be effective; (b) Europe had a lot of

Table 5.2
Factors driving the military revolution, ca. 1400–1700 CE

	Infantry	*Cities*	*Fragmentation*
Christendom	X	X	X
Islam	x		x
East		x	

Key: X = very important; x = somewhat important; blank = unimportant.

walled cities, against which cannons were effective; and (c) Europe's political fragmentation meant that there were a lot of wars going on, rewarding innovation.

Table 5.2 crudely sums up the regional differences, separating the Eurasian lucky latitudes into just three regions, of Christendom, the Muslim world, and the East. In the Muslim world (defined loosely as reaching from the Balkans to India) infantry often had a significant battlefield role, but steppe cavalry generally remained dominant. Sieges rarely decided wars, and while India was sometimes politically fragmented and the Ottomans fought some long wars against Persia, Egypt, and other neighbors, political divisions were less violent than in Europe.[107] In the East, by contrast, fortified cities were major targets, but other than the great war in Korea in 1592–98, interstate wars were rare, and the major conflicts were fought between Chinese border forces and steppe cavalry.[108] The incentives for military innovation were much stronger in late-medieval and early-modern Europe than anywhere else in Eurasia, and so Western Europeans were the first people to unlock the potential of musketry and artillery, and to organize their societies for more modern kinds of war.

That said, no amount of efficient organization could take early-modern war making as high even as 1.0 points on the social development index. Only the industrial revolution and the application of the natural sciences to transport, supply, and firepower could do that. Comparing figures 5.17 and 5.18 with figures 4.2 and 4.3 shows that the industrial revolution has had far more impact on war making than on city sizes.

CHAPTER 6

||||||||||||||||||||||||||||||||||||||||||||||||||

INFORMATION TECHNOLOGY

CATEGORIZING INFORMATION TECHNOLOGY

With only trivial exceptions, humans differ from all other animals in being able to evolve culturally by accumulating information, ideas, and best practices over time. Proto-humans may have had something resembling modern speech as far back as *Homo ergaster*, 1.8 million years ago, and Heidelberg Man—the shared ancestor of Neanderthals and modern humans—had hyoid bones that could produce speech sounds and inner ears that could probably have distinguished the sounds of conversational speech.[1] However, the evolution of modern *Homo sapiens* in the past 150,000 years represents a revolution in this regard.

For tens of thousands of years, the transmission and storage of information depended entirely on speech and memory. The first unmistakable evidence for communication through material symbols goes back nearly a hundred thousand years, in the form of engraved fragments of ocher from Klasies River Cave 1 in South Africa.[2] However, symbols of this kind remained not only rare but also very simple until about fifty thousand years ago, when they suddenly (by prehistoric standards, at least) become common wherever humans are found. Archaeologists often refer to this as "the big bang of human consciousness."[3]

The first evidence for symbols that unambiguously represent numbers and speech appears a little over five thousand years ago in Southwest Asia,[4] and since then these technologies have spread all over the world. Almost by definition, we are relatively well informed about the history of information technology since the origins of writing and numbers because every document that survives from the past is by its nature a piece of evidence for the sophistication and spread of such technology. Consequently, we can trace in some detail the rise of systems for storing and communicating information, the relative ease of accessing data, and the sophistication of the various technologies.[5]

The ability to store and transmit information is central to mastering the intellectual environment, and as such is a fundamental part of the concept of social development. However, despite the archaeological visibility of physical traces of writing and counting, it can be very difficult to measure the extent of use of different technologies. Historians of Europe have made some valiant efforts to count how many people could read and write and at what levels of competence in the past two to three thousand years.[6] Numeracy has received less attention than literacy, despite its obvious importance, though again there have been some valuable studies.[7]

Since the 1980s there has been a reaction against quantification among scholars of literacy, with many Europeanists concluding that since there are many kinds of literacy, there is no point in trying to count how many people could read and write.[8] But while the first observation—that there are multiple kinds of literacy (and, for that matter, of numeracy)—is undoubtedly true, the second— that counting how many people could read and write is pointless— does not follow from it. So long as we are explicit about what is meant by literacy and numeracy,[9] and recognize that other historians, asking other questions, may prefer to define the terms in other ways, quantification remains a necessary approach. As with the broader turn against quantification in the humanities and many of the social sciences, it is largely a matter of what questions we are trying to answer.

To use information technology as a trait in the social development index we need to calculate separate scores for (a) the sophistication of the technologies available in East and West at specific points in time and (b) the extent of their use; and then we need to multiply the two numbers together to produce a series of scores for Eastern and Western information technology through history.

As in the case of war-making capacity, the greatest difficulty is not the scarcity of evidence for premodern times but the dramatic leap in technological sophistication during the twentieth century, which makes it difficult to compare the information technology of 2000 CE with that of earlier periods. In *Why the West Rules—For Now*,[10] I observed that Moore's Law, which states that the cost-effectiveness of information storage and retrieval has been doubling every eighteen months since 1950, might be taken to imply that the Western information technology score in 2000 CE should be well over a billion times higher than that for 1950 CE. The Western score of 250 points in 2000 CE would in fact fall to the lowest measurable score, of 0.01 points, before we even get back to 1970.

Many of us remember the reel-to-reel tape machines and mainframe computers of the 1970s, machines that seem positively archaic next to the iPods and iPads of our own enlightened times; yet it is ridiculous to suggest that information technology in the era of the first moon landing was too primitive to be measurable. Calculating information technology scores requires weighting different kinds of systems and recognizing that shifts between them are not linear or straightforward. Writing has not replaced speech; nor has the telephone or tweeting replaced face-to-face communication. New forms of information technology may eventually completely replace those that evolved over the past few hundred thousand years, but this has not happened yet, and in calculating historical scores for information technology we will have to recognize the complicated, overlapping patterns.

The evidence for how many people could read, write, and count, at which levels of skill, and using which technologies is fragmentary and open to competing interpretations; and the need to make allowance for the partialness of changes through time adds a further level of subjectivity to the calculations. Scores for information technology are therefore even more open to debate than those for the other three traits.

CALCULATING INFORMATION TECHNOLOGY SCORES

The difficulties of categorizing information technology call for a two-stage approach to scoring.

1. Skills. Following common practice among historians, I divide the populations being studied into three skill levels—full, medium, and basic—describing their ability in using the information technology available in their age. Again following standard practice, I define each category in a way that sets the bar low. "Basic" skills involve being able to read and write a name or record simple numbers; "medium" means being able to read or write a simple sentence or use basic problems in addition, subtraction, multiplication, and division; and "full" means being able to read or write more connected prose or use more advanced mathematical techniques.

Some anthropologists and historians have suggested that definitions of this kind are Eurocentric, and that there are cultural traditions in which language and mathematics work in entirely different ways.[11] However, although the question deserves more study, at present there seems to be little empirical support for these claims.[12] The division into basic, medium, and full literacy levels, for instance, was independently developed by the Chinese Communist Party in its 1950 literacy drive, which defined full literacy as the ability to recognize 1,000+ characters, semiliteracy as the ability to recognize 500–1,000 characters, and basic literacy as the ability to recognize 300–500 characters.[13]

Drawing on the available scholarship (using experts' quantitative estimates when they are available, and extrapolating from the qualitative discussions when they are not), I divide the adult male population at different periods across these three categories of full, medium, and basic. I assign 0.5 information technology points (ITP) for each 1 percent of the adult male population that falls into the full-skills category, 0.25 ITP for each 1 percent of the adult male population that falls into the medium-skills category, and 0.15 ITP for each 1 percent of the adult male population that falls into the basic-skills category.

These numbers are, and can only be, arbitrary estimates of the difference between each level of mastery of information technology.

They may be quite reasonable for some times and places but are surely very wide of the mark in others. However, consistency in scoring seems more important than spurious and highly subjective attempts at greater accuracy. Adding together the scores yields a single "male ITP" result for each period. If the numbers I have suggested for the high-, medium-, and low-skill categories seem unreasonable, critics can of course experiment with other numbers and find out how much they need to be changed in order to make a serious difference to the social development index.

The evidence for female literacy and numeracy is generally even poorer than that for male literacy and numeracy, though we can be sure that in most or all times and places before the twentieth century, fewer (usually far fewer) women could read, write, and perform mathematical calculations than men, and usually at lower levels.

There are simply no reliable statistics for male/female differences in premodern times, which means that I am once again reduced to guesswork, constrained only by general impressions drawn from the historical sources. However, making explicit guesses should be more constructive than leaving assumptions implicit, so I hazard a series of estimates for others to challenge if they see fit. I then apply the estimated gender multiplier for each period to the male ITP score to produce a female ITP score; adding the two scores together yields a single score in ITP for East or West at a specific point in time.

In the Western core in 2000 CE, I place 100 percent of males in the full-skills category as defined here, generating a male ITP score of 50 (i.e., 100 percent × 0.5), and female skills score 100 percent of the male rate, generating a female ITP score of 50 (i.e., the male 50 points × 100 percent).[14] The West's score in ITP for 2000 CE is therefore 100.

Professional literacy and numeracy providers in the Western core conventionally set much higher standards for basic, medium, or full skills than historians use, and would consequently disagree not only with my assertion that 100 percent of males have full skills but also with the claim that female numeracy skills match male.[15] However, while setting the bars for basic, medium, and full literacy and numeracy at very high levels is completely appropriate for those seeking to raise standards within complex twenty-first-century societies, it would be unhelpful for long-term cross-cultural comparisons, because it would reduce all pre-1900 scores to zero.

2. *Speed and reach of technologies.* The second stage in calculating scores is to establish another multiplier to reflect the changing speed and reach of technologies for storing and communicating information. I divide tools for handling information into three broad categories: electronic (in widespread use in East and West alike in 2000 CE), electrical (in widespread use in the West but not in the East in 1900 CE), and pre-electrical (in use in the West for perhaps eleven thousand years and in the East for perhaps nine thousand years).

I assign multiplier values of 2.5 for the most advanced forms of electronic media, in use in the West in 2000 CE. In the East in 2000 CE similar media were in use, but were less widely available. Telephones (both landline and mobile) and televisions were roughly equally common in West and East, but computers and Internet hosts were more common in the West (62.3 computers per 100 people in the United States as compared to 38.5 computers/100 people in Hong Kong and 34.9 computers/100 people in Japan; 375.1 Internet hosts/100 people in the United States as compared to 97.3 Internet hosts/100 people in Taiwan and 72.7 Internet hosts/100 people in Japan).[16] Since the Western multiplier in 2000 CE is set at 2.5, I use a multiplier of 1.89 for the Eastern core. The West's score for information technology on the social development index in 2000 CE is 250 points (i.e., 100 ITP × 2.5); the East's is 189 (i.e., 100 ITP × 1.89).

The electronic multiplier of 2.5 for the Western core in 2000 CE is fixed by the fact that the maximum score possible for a trait is 250 points, but the values for electrical and pre-electrical media are much harder to calculate. I am not aware of previous attempts to calculate the overall increase in the capacity of information technology across the twentieth century, but drawing on the expert literature,[17] my guess is that the electronic media available in 2000 CE represented something like a fiftyfold increase in capacity over the electrical media available in the West in 1900 CE. This would mean that the multiplier for the Western core in 1900 was 0.05.

The nineteenth century also saw extraordinary improvements in information technology,[18] though they were clearly not on such a scale as those of the twentieth century. I suggest that the electrical media available in the West in 1900 CE in turn represented something like a fivefold increase in capacity over the pre-electrical media available in 1800 CE, leading to a multiplier of 0.01 for 1800. I treat this as a base level for all pre-electrical information technology systems going back to the first documented experiments with visual notations, around 9000 BCE in the West and 6250 BCE in the East.

Others may disagree with the numbers I propose, and of course there were many variations within my crude category of pre-electrical information technology. Historians may particularly notice that I have not made a categorical distinction between print and preprint media, even though the impact of printing presses on European elite culture in the fifteenth century and Eastern elite culture since the seventh century is well known.[19]

I made this decision because the main contribution of printing was to generate more and cheaper materials, rather than to transform information storage and retrieval the way that the telegraph and the Internet would do in the nineteenth and twentieth centuries, and these purely quantitative changes are already factored into the index. However, even if other scholars disagree with this assumption, the numbers involved in information technology scores before 1900 CE are so tiny that—even more than in the case of war-making capacity—it would take enormous revisions of these multipliers to have much impact on the final social development scores.

For similar reasons, I have not distinguished between forms of notation, treating alphabetic, syllabic, ideographic, and other styles of writing simply as variants on pre-electrical systems. This oversimplifies reality,[20] but because (a) judgments on the relative efficiency of writing systems descend too easily into culture-bound value judgments and (b) the tiny scores at all points before 1700 CE mean that no plausible adjustment would have a serious impact, I decided simply to treat all versions of pre-electrical information technology systems as identical and to concentrate on measuring the extent of their use.

Finally, I have not made a separate category for pre-electrical calculating devices like the abacus, first attested in Mesopotamia around 2500 BCE, or the Inca quipu, which, in a simple form, may

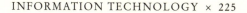

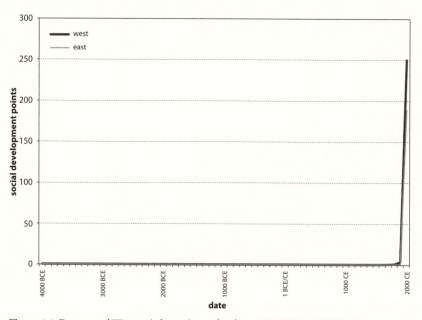

Figure 6.1. Eastern and Western information technology, 4000 BCE–2000 CE, shown on a linear-linear scale.

be roughly equally old.[21] This is for the same reason that I did not make a distinction with the printing press; pre-electrical calculators speeded up counting and improved its accuracy, but did not transform the process as computers have done.

Figure 6.1 shows the scores I have calculated, on a linear-linear scale: the Western score in 1900 CE is just about visible, but no earlier scores can be seen at this scale. Figure 6.2 shows the same data on a log-linear scale. Changing the Western multiplier for 1500–1800 CE to 0.02 to reflect a greater impact from the printing press and changing the Eastern multiplier for 1400–1900 CE to 0.02 to reflect the great expansion of printing in that period make no visible changes to a linear-linear representation (figure 6.3) and very little change on a log-linear scale (figure 6.4).

This method of calculation rests on one further key assumption: that the adoption of visible symbols for recording concepts is crucially important. Humans were talking and counting for tens of thousands of years before they started writing or using numeri-

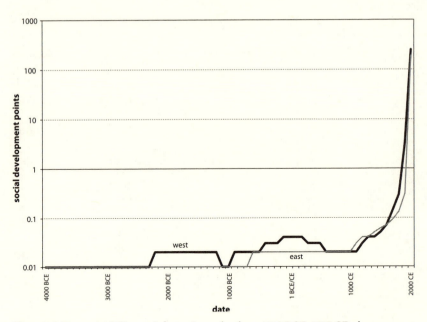

Figure 6.2. Eastern and Western information technology, 4000 BCE–2000 CE, shown on a log-linear scale.

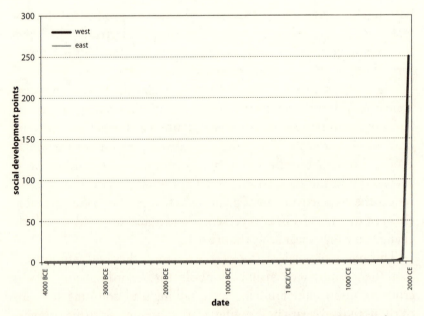

Figure 6.3. Eastern and Western information technology, 4000 BCE–2000 CE, scores doubled for printing in the East for 1400–1900 CE and in the West for 1500–1800 CE.

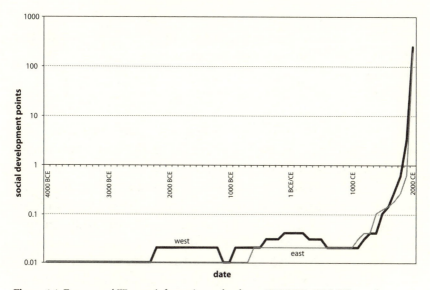

Figure 6.4. Eastern and Western information technology, 4000 BCE–2000 CE, on a log-linear scale, scores doubled for printing in the East for 1400–1900 CE and in the West for 1500–1800 CE.

cal notations, and they preserved and communicated enormous amounts of information in their traditions, rituals, and art. By definition, however, all purely oral systems of information technology automatically score zero on the social development index.

I have three reasons for proceeding in this way. First, a biological consideration: Human brains are the same everywhere, and despite the claims mentioned earlier for extreme variations between cultures, no convincing evidence has yet appeared for major differences in the abilities of people in different oral cultures to process and store information in their heads or to communicate it in speech. If this is correct, for comparative purposes preliterate information technology systems effectively zero out. Only with the development of more sophisticated techniques of literacy and numeracy do measurable differences start to emerge.

Second, a practical consideration: Even if the assumption described in the previous paragraph is in fact false, I know of no way to measure and compare the information technology systems of different nonliterate cultures in the past. If Eastern oral cultures processed, stored, and/or communicated information better than Western oral cultures in the era before the first evidence for systems of notation in either region (around 9300 BCE in the West and 7000 BCE in the East), or vice versa, there is no way that we will ever know about it.

Third, an empirical consideration: The revolutionary consequences of using visible symbols to record verbal and mathematical concepts are well established.[22] Critics, who often label those who stress the efficiency of visual recording "evolutionists," have pointed out plenty of reasons to exercise caution about extreme claims and to be flexible in interpreting the impact of writing;[23] but after half a century of arguments, it still seems clear that whether the shift from purely oral to various combinations of oral and written information technology empowered the individual, created hierarchy, or did both at once, it also marked a major step in increasing human abilities to store, access, and transmit information. In the West, where the evidence has received particularly detailed study, the earliest notations were probably for accounting, with verbal forms emerging gradually from them.[24] In the East the evidence is less clear,[25] but the same pattern may apply there too.

I present my full calculations in tables 6.1 and 6.2 and in figures 6.1 and 6.2.

ESTIMATES OF WESTERN INFORMATION TECHNOLOGY

The nature of the evidence changes significantly as we move back through time, but a very rough picture can nevertheless be put together. Between the mid-1960s and mid-1980s, historians did pioneering work on European literacy rates between 1600 and 1900 CE,[26] discussing different levels of male and female literacy across time. A smaller amount of work of this kind was also done on the United States.[27]

Since the mid-1980s this kind of statistical approach has been criticized, and historians have steadily abandoned quantification in favor of the cultural histories of the book and communities of read-

Table 6.1
Western information technology scores

Dates	Full (@ 0.5 pts)	Medium (@ 0.25 pts)	Basic (@ 0.15 pts)	Male points	Female (% M)	Literacy points	Multiplier	Total points
2000 CE	100 (50)	0	0	50	100% = 50	100	× 2.5	250
1900	40 (20)	50 (12.5)	7 (1.05)	33.6	90% = 30.2	63.8	× 0.05	3.19
1800	20 (10)	25 (6.25)	20 (3)	19.3	50% = 9.65	28.95	× 0.01	0.29
1700	10 (5)	15 (3.75)	25 (3.75)	12.5	10% = 1.25	13.75	× 0.01	0.14
1600	5 (2.5)	10 (2.5)	10 (1.5)	6.5	2% = 0.13	6.63	× 0.01	0.071
1500	4 (2)	8 (2)	6 (0.9)	4.9	2% = 0.10	5.0	× 0.01	0.05
1400	3 (1.5)	6 (1.5)	4 (0.6)	3.6	1% = 0.04	3.64	× 0.01	0.04
1300	3 (1.5)	6 (1.5)	4 (0.6)	3.6	1% = 0.04	3.64	× 0.01	0.04
1200	3 (1.5)	6 (1.5)	4 (0.6)	3.6	1% = 0.04	3.64	× 0.01	0.04
1100	2 (1)	4 (1)	2 (0.3)	2.3	1% = 0.02	2.32	× 0.01	0.02
1000	2 (1)	4 (1)	2 (0.3)	2.3	1% = 0.02	2.32	× 0.01	0.02
600–900	2 (1)	2 (0.5)	1 (0.15)	1.65	1% = 0.02	1.67	× 0.01	0.02
300–500	3 (1.5)	4 (1)	3 (0.45)	2.95	1% = 0.03	2.98	× 0.01	0.03
100 BCE–200 CE	4 (2)	6 (1.5)	5 (0.75)	4.25	1% = 0.04	4.29	× 0.01	0.04
500–200 BCE	2 (1)	3 (0.75)	2 (0.3)	2.05	1% = 0.02	2.07	× 0.01	0.02
900–600 BCE	2 (1)	2 (0.5)	1 (0.15)	1.65	1% = 0.02	1.67	× 0.01	0.02
1100–1000 BCE	2 (1)	1 (0.25)	1 (0.15)	1.4	1% = 0.01	1.41	× 0.01	0.01
2200–1200 BCE	2 (1)	2 (0.5)	1 (0.15)	1.65	1% = 0.02	1.67	× 0.01	0.02
2700–2300 BCE	2 (1)	1 (0.25)	1 (0.15)	1.4	1% = 0.01	1.41	× 0.01	0.01
3300–2800 BCE	0	1 (0.25)	2 (0.3)	0.55	1% = 0.01	0.56	× 0.01	0.01
6000–3400 BCE	0	0	1 (0.15)	0.15	1% = 0	0.15	× 0.01	0.01
9000–6100 BCE	0	0	0	0	0	0	× 0.01	0
9300–9000 BCE	0	0	1 (0.15)	0.15	1% = 0	0.15	× 0.01	0

Categories (percentages)

Table 6.2
Eastern information technology scores

Dates	Full (@ 0.5 pts)	Medium (@ 0.25 pts)	Basic (@ 0.15 pts)	Male points	Female (% M)	Literacy points	Multiplier	Total points
					Categories (percentages)			
3000	100 (50)	0	0	50	100% = 50	100	× 1.89	189.00
1900	15(7.5)	60 (15)	10 (1.5)	24	25% = 6	30	× 0.01	0.30
1800	5 (2.5)	35 (8.75)	10 (1.5)	12.75	5% = 0.64	13.39	× 0.01	0.13
1700	5 (2.5)	20 (5)	10 (1.5)	9	2% = 0.18	9.18	× 0.01	0.09
1600	4 (2)	15 (3.75)	10 (1.5)	7.25	2% = 0.15	7.4	× 0.01	0.07
1500	3 (1.5)	10 (2.5)	10 (1.5)	5.5	2% = 0.11	5.61	× 0.01	0.06
1400	3 (1.5)	10 (2.5)	10 (1.5)	5.5	2% = 0.11	5.61	× 0.01	0.06
1300	3 (1.5)	5 (1.25)	5 (0.75)	3.5	1% = 0.04	3.51	× 0.01	0.04
1200	3 (1.5)	5 (1.25)	5 (0.75)	3.5	1% = 0.04	3.51	× 0.01	0.04
1100	2 (1)	2 (0.5)	3 (0.45)	1.95	1% = 0.02	1.97	× 0.01	0.02
600 BCE–1000 CE	2 (1)	2 (0.5)	2 (0.3)	1.8	1% = 0.02	1.82	× 0.01	0.02
1000–700 BCE	2 (1)	1 (0.25)	1 (0.15)	1.4	1% = 0.01	1.14	× 0.01	0.01
1300–1100 BCE	1 (0.5)	1 (0.25)	1 (0.15)	0.9	1% = 0.01	0.91	× 0.01	0.01
7000–1400 BCE	0	0	1 (0.15)	1.15	1% = 0	0.15	× 0.01	0

ers.[28] The methodological problems involved in reconstructing early-modern literacy rates are certainly severe,[29] but the shift in research seems to be driven more by the broader historiographical trend away from quantification than by convincing evidence that the results of the 1960s to 1980s were seriously flawed.

The general picture that emerges from the specialist studies is one of local variations in literacy rates combined with a broad trend across Europe and North America from 1600 CE onward toward increasing literacy at all levels plus a declining gap between male and female literacy.[30] On my index, the numbers proposed by Cipolla, Stone, and others translate to scores roughly doubling each century between 1600 and 1800 CE, rising (in social development points) from 0.07 points in 1600 to 0.29 in 1800, then shooting up to 3.19 points in 1900.

Before 1600 CE the evidence is less good. Medievalists have studied the European sources for literacy intensively,[31] but numeracy has been relatively neglected.[32] In the Muslim core, the opposite situation applies; very little has been written on literacy,[33] but science and mathematics have received more attention.[34] There have been fewer studies focusing specifically on medieval Islamic education and the extent of literacy and numeracy among the broader Muslim population.[35]

There seems to be some agreement that male literacy and numeracy were rising slowly in Western Europe from the time of what historians sometimes call the "twelfth-century renaissance,"[36] and that levels were very low indeed before 1100 CE. Numbers of literate and numerate women probably began rising steadily only after 1500.

Scholars of Islamic education are rarely willing to hazard any quantitative estimates at all, but it would seem that while the top Muslim scholars were more numerate and at least as literate as those in Christendom before 1100, literacy was restricted to very narrow circles. We might characterize medieval Islamic literacy as a scribal and priestly phenomenon, while literacy in Christian Europe was becoming characteristic of a broader craftsman stratum (even if the writing being read was often biblical). The Muslim world saw nothing like Europe's sixteenth-century boom in male reading of holy texts or its expansion of female literacy.

Probably fewer than 10 percent of Western men could read even at the basic level in 1100, and an even smaller number (perhaps 2 percent?) could be said to be fully literate. The numbers for women are particularly elusive, but seem to have been so tiny—perhaps one literate woman for every hundred literate men—that they make almost no difference to the scores. I estimate a social development score of just 0.02 points for the West around 1100 CE, rising by slow increments to 0.05 in 1500, and then increasing more rapidly.

Literacy and numeracy seem to have been wider and deeper phenomena in classical antiquity than in the Middle Ages,[37] particularly in democratic Athens (508–322 BCE) and Italy between about 200 BCE and 200 CE. William Harris has provided particularly solid quantitative estimates, which I generally follow.[38]

Much recent scholarship on ancient Greco-Roman literacy, like that among medievalists and anthropologists, emphasizes that literacy was a more complicated phenomenon than can be captured by a single score,[39] but Harris's work already took the variety of forms of literacy into account in calculating rates.

Other recent work has suggested that in addition to oversimplifying the complexity of literacy, Harris's figures perhaps also understate the levels of popular accomplishment in information technology in classical Athens and the early Roman Empire, where archaeological finds have revealed surprising levels of literacy among ordinary soldiers on the Roman frontiers in Britain and Libya.[40]

Bearing these criticisms in mind, I estimate that the social development score for information technology in the Western core peaked around 0.04 points between 100 BCE and 200 CE. After 200 CE it declined;[41] I estimate scores of 0.03 points for 300–500 CE, then, for lack of any clearer evidence and because the numbers involved are so small, a fairly static level of 0.02 until the revival after 1100 CE.

Looking back before 100 BCE, I suggest that between 400 and 200 BCE information technology scored 0.03 points in the core areas around the shores of the Aegean and the eastern Mediterranean, rising from 0.02 points in the earlier first millennium BCE. With such tiny scores, precision and nuance both become impossible; I treat information technology as basically flat between 2200 BCE (the rise of the bureaucratic states of Akkad and Ur III) and 500 BCE (the beginning of the spread of democratic states in Greece), representing a combination of what historians often call "scribal literacy" and "craft literacy" (and, I would add, numeracy).

By scribal/craft literacy I mean that a tiny educated elite (perhaps 1 percent of the male population) had full mastery of a literary canon, a slightly larger (perhaps 2 percent of the male population) bureaucratic elite had mastery of recording techniques, and another small (1–2 percent?) group of artisans could read or write their own names and perform the calculations they needed in their professions. This scribal/craft information technology scores 0.02 social development points, apart from an interruption during the period of collapse between 1200 and 1000 BCE, when evidence for writing of all kinds contracts sharply. In Greece writing probably went out of use altogether, and around the eastern Mediterranean as a whole very few documents survive. During this "dark age" I assign scores of 0.01 points.

The first convincing evidence of scribal numeracy and literacy appears around 3300 BCE in southern Mesopotamia,[42] and I begin assigning scores of 0.01 points at that date. Information technology increased in sophistication and extent of use across the next thousand years, but given that 0.01 points is the smallest increment available on the social development index, figure 6.2 represents the curve as flat until it jumps around 2250 BCE. There are hints of symbolic activity that some scholars choose to call writing or mathematics going back as far as 9000 BCE,[43] but these traces are so scarce that I treat them as scoring zero.

ESTIMATES OF EASTERN
INFORMATION TECHNOLOGY

There has been much less quantitative analysis of Eastern literacy and numeracy in the languages accessible to me than of Western levels, and this is reflected in the flat scores in figure 6.2 and the brevity of table 6.2. The scores I assign to the East necessarily oversimplify a more complicated pattern, full of ebbs and flows like those represented in the Western scores.

In 2000 CE, I follow the UN HDI in treating Eastern literacy rates in the Japanese core as roughly similar to those in the Western core,[44] but as I explained in the "Calculating Information Technology Scores" section I use a multiplier of 1.89, rather than the West's 2.5, to reflect the narrower availability of electronic media in Japan than in the United States in 2000.

In 1900, strenuous efforts by the Japanese government had begun raising literacy rates. While standards were low compared to the Western core, they were far higher than in premodern cultures, and perhaps 85 percent of boys and 25 percent of girls had at least some skills.[45] There is room for some debate over the levels attained, but because Japanese information technology remained largely pre-electrical even in 1900, the East-West gap in social development points was at this stage enormous.

I calculate that the Eastern score (30 ITP × a multiplier of just 0.01, reflecting the pre-electrical stage) was just 0.3 points, as compared to 3.19 points in the West. Chinese literacy and numeracy levels were even lower than Japanese levels around 1900, thanks to the educated elite's ambivalence toward mass education.[46] Chinese levels had been very high by premodern standards, and probably at least 50 percent of boys reached the basic standard in 1900 CE, but steps toward mass education remained hesitant. Only after the communist takeover in 1949 did mass education really take off.[47]

Before 1900, Qing China had seen a steady expansion of basic education and craft literacy. Around 1700 CE perhaps just 5 percent of men could be said to read reasonably fluently and 35 percent of boys learned a few characters, but by 1800 as many as half of the boys in northern China were learning a few characters.[48]

Female literacy and numeracy were much more restricted. Western literacy and numeracy rates were higher than Eastern rates in the eighteenth and nineteenth centuries (particularly for women), but the numbers were still small enough that the actual differences in social development points (by my calculations, 0.14 for the West in 1700, doubling to 0.29 in 1800, as compared to 0.09 for the East in 1700, rising by about half to 0.13 in 1800) were relatively small.

In Ming dynasty times the scores seem to have been lower, although they were probably higher than in the West before it began its information boom after 1600 CE. There may not have been great differences between elites of education at each end of Eurasia, but China seems to have had a significantly bigger group of people (overwhelmingly men) with medium literacy and numeracy levels.[49] Actual numbers are necessarily impressionistic (I calculate 0.06 points in 1500 CE and 0.07 in 1600 CE, as against 0.05 and 0.07 in the West), but because the scores are so low before the seventeenth century, the margin of error would need to be very large to have a serious impact on the social development index. Levels in Japan were probably quite close to those in China.[50]

Moving back into earlier periods of course involves even more imprecision. Elite education improved drastically in Tang and Song times, and the boom in books and financial record keeping in the tenth through twelfth centuries suggests to me that the use of information technology was roughly comparable with that in the West under the Roman Empire (i.e., a score of 0.04 points).[51] Scores of 0.03 or 0.05 look equally plausible, but scores as low as 0.02 (comparable to that I assigned to the West between 600 and 900 CE) or as high as 0.06 (comparable to the sixteenth-century West) seem unlikely. I suggest that scores rose rapidly from about 0.02 points in 1000 CE to 0.06 in 1400.

In the absence of any good reason to do otherwise, I have simply hypothesized a flat score of 0.02 points for the long period between 600 BCE and 1000 CE. Literacy and numeracy rates certainly fluctuated across these sixteen centuries. The qualitative evidence suggests that both probably rose between 600 BCE and 100 CE, fell between 100 and 400 CE, and rose again after 400 CE.[52] Increasing amounts of writing are being recovered from the Han Empire, particularly in the arid northwest and wet south, where conditions allow the survival of bamboo strips. However, at present it looks as if Chinese literacy and numeracy remained below Roman levels. It also seems likely that the post-Han decline in information technology was less severe than the West's post-Roman decline. Historically important as they must have been, the Chinese variations around the score of 0.02 points are probably too small to register on the index of social development.

The earliest evidence for symbolic notations in China comes from Jiahu around 6250 BCE, and there is enough evidence to suggest some continuity in practices across the next five thousand

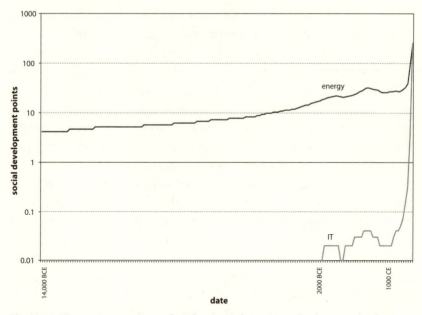

Figure 6.5. Western energy capture plotted against information technology on a log-linear scale, 14,000 BCE–2000 CE, measured in social development points.

years.[53] It is only around 1300 BCE, however, that Chinese use of writing and mathematical notation seems comparable to that seen in Mesopotamia around 3000 BCE, earning 0.01 points. Across the next thousand years, the evidence suggests a fairly constant process of expansion of the use of symbolic systems, from oracle bones through inscriptions on bronze vessels to extensive painting in ink on bamboo strips and silk. However, the scores are so tiny that the improvements register on the social development index only as a jump from 0.01 to 0.02 points, which I place around 600 BCE.

INFORMATION TECHNOLOGY: DISCUSSION

Figures 6.5 and 6.6 show very clearly that in East and West alike, information technology has been extraordinarily sensitive to the broader changes of the past few centuries.

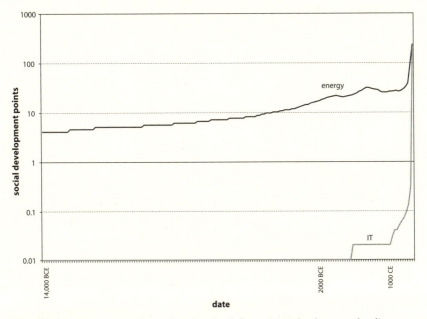

Figure 6.6. Eastern energy capture plotted against information technology on a log-linear scale, 14,000 BCE–2000 CE, measured in social development points.

Information technology and energy capture have been involved in a feedback loop. The original late-eighteenth-century British industrial revolution would have been impossible without certain levels of literacy and numeracy,[54] and the late-nineteenth-century "second industrial revolution," bringing chemistry more fully into the factory, depended even more heavily on information technology. In our own times, the links between the productivity explosions of the late twentieth and early twenty-first centuries and the underlying takeoff of entirely new forms of information technology are extremely strong.

The recent information explosion means that all information technology scores before 1700 CE are necessarily extremely small. Information technology is the most difficult of the four traits to measure, but because the premodern scores have been so low, it seems unlikely that the margins of error make any noticeable difference to the overall social development scores.

CHAPTER 7

||||||||||||||||||||||||||||||||||||||||||||

DISCUSSION: THE LIMITS AND POTENTIAL OF MEASURING DEVELOPMENT

IN THIS BOOK I HAVE PRESENTED THE EVIDENCE AND methods behind an analytical tool, the social development index. It therefore seems sensible to close not with a set of conclusions but with a more open-ended discussion of what this tool can, and cannot, do.

I start with two sections discussing possible problems with the index. First, I offer a few comments on margins of error and falsification. One of the greatest drawbacks of the neo-evolutionist indices was that because they were not really built to answer specific questions, it was very difficult for their designers to say exactly how they could be falsified. Error terms depend on the questions being asked, and in the case of the why-the-West-rules question, we can be reasonably precise about how much error can be tolerated before we have to conclude that the index is misleading.

In the next section I turn to the issue of displaying the data. There is no such thing as a neutral way to display statistical information; each format tends to emphasize one or more dimensions of the index over others. I have systematically opted for what seemed to me to be the simplest formats, favoring linear-linear graphs whenever possible, but other formats also have merits.

I then return to the issues considered in chapter 1, asking how the index described here might contribute to a unified evolutionary theory of history. I am optimistic that such a theory is possible, and that a social development index can be an important part of it. Finally, I ask whether such a theory really can make the past a guide to the future, as Spencer claimed more than a hundred fifty years ago.

MARGINS OF ERROR AND FALSIFICATION

Almost every detail discussed in chapters 3–6 can be challenged. The evidence is almost always open to multiple interpretations. There is more than one way to define energy capture, city size/organization, war-making capacity, and information technology. I could have calculated the scores in other ways. Long chains of argument and inference are involved at every stage of generating a social development index.

As a result, another inquirer could have come up with a different set of social development scores. In fact, it is highly unlikely that any other inquirer would have come up with exactly the same set of scores as I have done. For that matter, if I were to start the exercise of calculating social development scores all over again, I would myself probably come up with different numbers.

Consequently, there is little to be gained from asking whether the index is right. No index can ever be "right," whether we mean that in the strong sense that every one of the 530 numbers in tables 7.1 and 7.2 perfectly corresponds to reality, or in the weak sense that all experts would agree on them. The scores I have calculated are bound to be wrong; the only useful question to ask is *how* wrong they are. Are they so wrong that the basic shape of history depicted in figure 2.6 is misleading, in which case the whole of *Why the West Rules—For Now* is fatally flawed? Or are the errors in fact fairly trivial?

The only way to know for sure will be for other archaeologists and historians to work through the evidence I set out in chapters 3–6 and to test my arguments. Here, though, I can at least be fairly precise about just how wrong the scores in the index can afford to be, and what would constitute falsification of my claims. If the scores I have calculated are typically within 10 percent of the numbers other analysts calculate, the basic shape of the pattern I am trying to explain will remain much the same. If my numbers are typically 15

Table 7.1

Western social development scores, trait by trait, 14,000 BCE–2000 CE

	Energy capture	Organization	War-making capacity	Information technology	Total
14,000 BCE	4.36	0.00	0.00	0.00	4.36
13,000 BCE	4.36	0.00	0.00	0.00	4.36
12,000 BCE	4.90	0.00	0.00	0.00	4.90
11,000 BCE	5.45	0.00	0.00	0.00	5.45
10,000 BCE	5.45	0.00	0.00	0.00	5.45
9000 BCE	5.99	0.00	0.00	0.00	5.99
8000 BCE	6.54	0.00	0.00	0.00	6.54
7000 BCE	7.08	0.01	0.00	0.00	7.09
6000 BCE	7.63	0.03	0.00	0.00	7.66
5000 BCE	8.72	0.04	0.00	0.00	8.76
4000 BCE	10.90	0.05	0.00	0.00	10.95
3500 BCE	11.99	0.09	0.00	0.00	12.98
3000 BCE	13.08	0.42	0.01	0.01	13.52
2500 BCE	15.26	0.47	0.01	0.01	16.29
2250 BCE	17.44	0.33	0.01	0.01	17.79
2000 BCE	18.52	0.56	0.01	0.02	19.11
1750 BCE	20.65	0.61	0.02	0.02	21.30
1500 BCE	22.34	0.70	0.03	0.02	23.09
1400 BCE	22.88	0.75	0.03	0.02	23.68
1300 BCE	23.43	0.75	0.03	0.02	24.23
1200 BCE	22.88	0.75	0.04	0.02	23.69
1100 BCE	22.34	0.47	0.03	0.01	22.85
1000 BCE	21.79	0.47	0.03	0.01	22.30
900 BCE	22.34	0.47	0.04	0.02	22.87
800 BCE	22.88	0.70	0.05	0.02	23.65
700 BCE	23.43	0.94	0.07	0.02	24.45
600 BCE	23.97	1.17	0.07	0.02	25.23
500 BCE	25.06	1.40	0.08	0.03	26.56
400 BCE	26.15	1.40	0.09	0.03	27.67
300 BCE	28.33	1.40	0.09	0.03	29.85
200 BCE	29.42	2.81	0.10	0.03	32.36
100 BCE	31.06	3.75	0.11	0.04	35.50
1 BCE/CE	33.78	9.36	0.12	0.04	43.30
100 CE	33.78	9.36	0.12	0.04	43.30

Table 7.1 (*continued*)

	Energy capture	Organiza- tion	War- making capacity	Information technology	Total
200 CE	32.69	9.36	0.11	0.04	42.20
300 CE	31.60	7.49	0.10	0.03	39.22
400 CE	31.06	7.49	0.09	0.03	38.67
500 CE	30.51	4.23	0.07	0.03	34.84
600 CE	28.33	1.41	0.04	0.02	29.80
700 CE	27.24	1.17	0.04	0.02	28.47
800 CE	27.24	1.64	0.04	0.02	28.94
900 CE	27.24	1.64	0.05	0.02	28.95
1000 CE	28.33	1.87	0.06	0.02	30.28
1100 CE	28.33	2.34	0.07	0.02	30.76
1200 CE	28.88	2.34	0.08	0.03	31.33
1300 CE	29.42	3.75	0.09	0.04	33.31
1400 CE	28.33	1.17	0.11	0.04	29.65
1500 CE	29.42	3.75	0.13	0.05	33.35
1600 CE	31.06	3.75	0.18	0.07	35.60
1700 CE	34.87	5.62	0.35	0.14	40.98
1800 CE	41.41	8.43	0.50	0.29	50.63
1900 CE	100.25	61.80	5.00	3.19	170.24
2000 CE	250.00	156.37	250.00	250.00	906.37

percent wide of the mark, that may—depending on the details— change the shape of the development curves enough to falsify my argument. If they are wrong by 20 percent or more, that would defi- nitely falsify my argument.

According to the index, shown on a log-linear scale in figure 7.1, Western social development pulled ahead of the East's after 14,000 BCE. The East slowly caught up, especially after 2000 BCE, and through most of the first millennium BCE the West's lead was nar- row. Around 100 BCE the West pulled further ahead again, but in 541 CE the Eastern line for the first time rose above the Western. The Eastern score then stayed ahead until 1773. Western develop- ment has been higher than Eastern for 92.5 percent of the time since the end of the Ice Age.

Table 7.2
Eastern social development scores, trait by trait, 14,000 BCE–2000 CE

	Energy capture	Organization	War-making capacity	Information technology	Total
14,000 BCE	4.36	0.00	0.00	0.00	4.36
13,000 BCE	4.36	0.00	0.00	0.00	4.36
12,000 BCE	4.36	0.00	0.00	0.00	4.36
11,000 BCE	4.36	0.00	0.00	0.00	4.36
10,000 BCE	4.36	0.00	0.00	0.00	4.36
9000 BCE	4.90	0.00	0.00	0.00	4.90
8000 BCE	5.45	0.00	0.00	0.00	5.45
7000 BCE	5.99	0.00	0.00	0.00	5.99
6000 BCE	6.54	0.00	0.00	0.00	6.54
5000 BCE	7.08	0.00	0.00	0.00	7.08
4000 BCE	7.63	0.00	0.00	0.00	7.63
3500 BCE	8.17	0.02	0.00	0.00	8.19
3000 BCE	8.72	0.05	0.00	0.00	8.77
2500 BCE	10.35	0.09	0.00	0.00	10.44
2250 BCE	11.44	0.13	0.00	0.00	11.57
2000 BCE	11.99	0.10	0.00	0.00	12.09
1750 BCE	14.17	0.22	0.00	0.00	14.39
1500 BCE	16.35	0.33	0.01	0.00	16.69
1400 BCE	16.89	0.33	0.01	0.00	17.23
1300 BCE	17.44	0.33	0.01	0.01	17.79
1200 BCE	17.44	0.47	0.02	0.01	17.94
1100 BCE	17.98	0.47	0.02	0.01	18.48
1000 BCE	18.52	0.33	0.03	0.01	18.89
900 BCE	19.07	0.37	0.03	0.01	19.48
800 BCE	19.61	0.42	0.02	0.01	20.06
700 BCE	20.16	0.51	0.02	0.01	20.70
600 BCE	21.79	0.61	0.03	0.02	22.45
500 BCE	22.88	0.75	0.04	0.02	23.69
400 BCE	23.97	0.94	0.05	0.02	24.98
300 BCE	24.52	1.17	0.06	0.02	26.87
200 BCE	26.15	2.81	0.07	0.02	29.05
100 BCE	27.79	3.45	0.08	0.02	31.64
1 BCE/CE	29.42	4.68	0.08	0.02	34.20
100 CE	29.42	3.93	0.08	0.02	33.44
200 CE	28.33	1.12	0.07	0.02	29.54

Table 7.2 (*continued*)

	Energy capture	Organization	War-making capacity	Information technology	Total
300 CE	28.33	1.31	0.07	0.02	29.73
400 CE	28.33	1.87	0.07	0.02	29.99
500 CE	28.33	1.87	0.08	0.02	30.30
600 CE	29.42	5.63	0.09	0.02	35.16
700 CE	29.42	9.36	0.11	0.02	38.91
800 CE	30.51	9.36	0.07	0.02	39.96
900 CE	31.06	7.00	0.07	0.02	38.69
1000 CE	32.15	9.36	0.08	0.02	41.61
1100 CE	32.69	9.36	0.09	0.02	42.17
1200 CE	33.23	9.36	0.09	0.03	42.71
1300 CE	32.69	7.50	0.11	0.04	40.34
1400 CE	31.06	4.68	0.12	0.05	35.91
1500 CE	32.69	6.35	0.10	0.06	39.20
1600 CE	33.78	6.55	0.12	0.07	40.52
1700 CE	35.96	6.09	0.15	0.09	45.29
1800 CE	39.23	10.30	0.12	0.13	49.78
1900 CE	53.40	16.39	1.00	0.30	71.09
2000 CE	113.33	250.00	12.50	189.00	564.83

Figure 7.2 shows on a log-linear scale shows what the Eastern and Western trends would look like if I have consistently underestimated Western development scores by 10 percent and overestimated Eastern scores by the same amount (i.e., the graph increases all the Western scores I have calculated by 10 percent, and reduces all the Eastern scores by 10 percent), and figure 7.3 shows the outcome if I have made the opposite error, underestimating Eastern development scores by 10 percent and overestimating Western scores by the same amount.

The first point to note is how much figures 7.2 and 7.3 strain credibility. Figure 7.2, raising Western and lowering Eastern scores by 10 percent, requires us to accept that in 1400 CE, as Zheng He was preparing to set sail on the Indian Ocean, the West was more

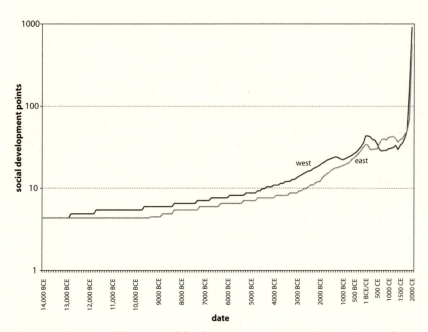

Figure 7.1. Eastern and Western social development scores, 14,000 BCE–2000 CE, on a log-linear scale.

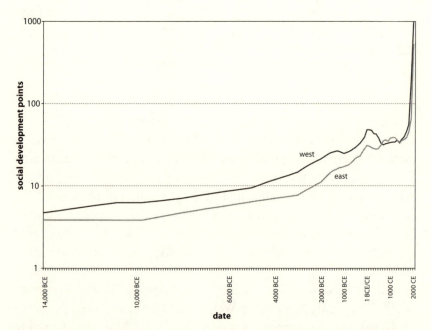

Figure 7.2. Eastern and Western social development scores, 14,000 BCE–2000 CE, on a log-linear scale, increasing all Western scores 10 percent and decreasing all Eastern scores 10 percent.

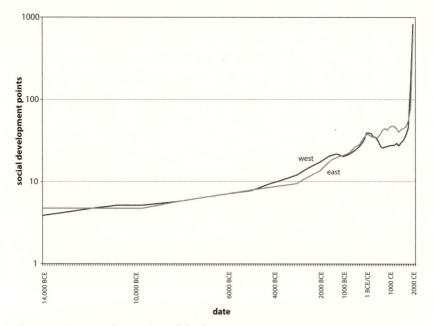

Figure 7.3. Eastern and Western social development scores, 14,000 BCE–2000 CE, on a log-linear scale, decreasing all Western scores 10 percent and increasing all Eastern scores 10 percent.

developed than the East; it also means that when Hannibal led his elephants to attack Rome in 218 BCE, Western development was already higher than the East's would be in Zheng's time. And as if these conclusions were not peculiar enough, it also tells us that the West was more developed when Julius Caesar was murdered in 44 BCE than the East would be when China's emperor Qianlong rejected Lord Macartney's trade embassy in 1793 CE. None of these conclusions fits well with the mass of historical evidence available.

Figure 7.3, which increases Eastern scores by 10 percent and decreases Western scores by the same amount, is even more peculiar. The development score it gives to the West in 700 CE, for instance, when Arab caliphs in Damascus ruled an empire stretching from Portugal to Pakistan, is lower than that for the East in the age of Confucius, which seems highly unlikely; and it would make the Western score in 1800 CE, when the industrial revolution was already under way and the British and French Empires straddled vast reaches of the globe, lower than the Eastern scores under the Song dynasty in 1000–1200 CE, which seems even less believable.

Yet even if historians could swallow such odd conclusions, the shapes of history as represented in figures 7.2 and 7.3 are still not different enough from those in figure 7.1 to change the basic pattern that needs explaining. Short-term accident theories remain inadequate because even in figure 7.3, the West's score is still higher for most of the period since the end of the Ice Age (although "most" now means 56 percent rather than 92.5 percent). Long-term lock-in theories also remain inadequate because even in figure 7.2 the East does take the lead for seven centuries. The pattern produced by the scores that I have calculated—of a Western lead for most of the past fifteen thousand years, interrupted for twelve hundred years by an "Eastern Age"—remains intact.[1]

To change the fundamental patterns in need of explanation, my estimates would have to be 20 percent wide of the mark. Figure 7.4 shows how history would look if I have consistently underestimated Western development scores by 20 percent and overestimated Eastern scores by the same amount; figure 7.5 shows the outcome if I have underestimated Eastern development scores by 20 percent and overestimated Western scores by the same amount.

This time the patterns are very different. In figure 7.4 the Western score is always higher than the Eastern, making long-term lock-in theories seem very plausible and also invalidating the claim that I make throughout *Why the West Rules—For Now* that social development changes the meaning of geography. Figure 7.5, by contrast, effectively reverses the conclusions of my actual index, having the East lead 90 percent of the time since the Ice Age.

If either figure 7.4 or figure 7.5 is correct, everything in *Why the West Rules—For Now* is wrong. We can be confident, though, that they are not correct. Figure 7.4, raising Western scores and reducing Eastern scores by 20 percent, tells us that imperial Rome's development in 1 BCE/CE was only 5 points behind industrial Japan's in 1900 CE, which cannot be true. Figure 7.5, on the other hand, raising Eastern scores and reducing Western scores by 20 percent, means that Eastern development was higher in pre-Shang times than Western would be under the Persian Empire; that the West caught up with the East only in 1828 CE, on the eve of the Opium War; and that Western rule has already ended (as of 2003, in fact). None of this seems credible.

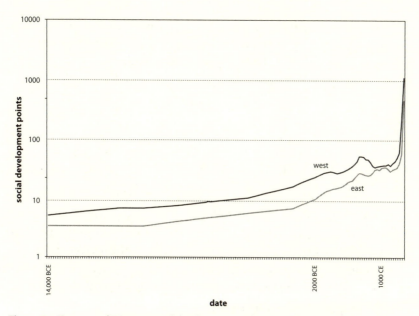

Figure 7.4. Eastern and Western social development scores, 14,000 BCE–2000 CE, on a log-linear scale, increasing all Western scores 20 percent and decreasing all Eastern scores 20 percent.

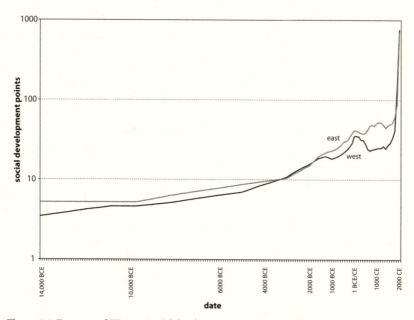

Figure 7.5. Eastern and Western social development scores, 14,000 BCE–2000 CE, on a log-linear scale, decreasing all Western scores 20 percent and increasing all Eastern scores 20 percent.

Hence my conclusions that (a) the margin of error in my estimates is probably less than 10 percent and definitely less than 20 percent and (b) even if the margin of error does rise to 10 percent, the basic historical patterns I am trying to explain still hold good.

THE VISUAL DISPLAY OF THE INDEX

It is one thing to calculate development scores; it is another altogether to display the results. Every conceivable visual arrangement inevitably privileges one aspect of the information over another.[2] Consequently, another possible objection to the index and the interpretation of it I made in *Why the West Rules—For Now* might be that the graphical decisions I made may be obscuring other, equally valid, interpretations of the record.

One issue has already been drawn to my attention by Isaac Opper, a graduate student in Stanford's economics department.[3] As I explained in chapter 2, I calculated the index scores by giving out 250 points for the maximum value (in 2000 CE) on each trait, dividing that by 250 to establish what performance was necessary to earn 1 point, and then setting 0.01 points as the minimum score worth recording on the index. The consequence of this is that the scores fall all the way to zero for social organization (dropping to that level in 8000 BCE in the West and 4000 BCE in the East), war making (3500 BCE in the West and 1750 BCE in the East), and information technology (3500 BCE in the West and 1400 BCE in the East), but not for energy capture. This is because people could not survive unless they absorbed a minimum of about 4,000 kcal (scoring 4.36 points) of energy per day.

As a result, energy capture accounted for more than 90 percent of the total social development score in East and West alike until 100 BCE (table 7.3); and even after that date, energy capture continued to be responsible for more than 75 percent of the scores for another two thousand years, until organization, war making, and information technology scores all exploded in the twentieth century.

Table 7.3

Percentage of total social development scores accounted for
by energy capture

Date	West	East	Date	West	East
14,000–4000 BCE	100*	100	100 BCE	87	87
			1 BCE/CE	78	86
3500 BCE	92	100*	100 CE	78	88
3000 BCE	97	99	200 CE	78	96
2500 BCE	94	99	300 CE	81	95
2250 BCE	98	99	400 CE	80	94
2000 BCE	97	99	500 CE	88	93
1750 BCE	97	98	600 CE	95	84
1500 BCE	97	98	700 CE	96	76
1400 BCE	97	98	800 CE	94	76
1300 BCE	97	98	900 CE	94	80
1200 BCE	97	97	1000 CE	94	77
1100 BCE	98	97	1100 CE	92	78
1000 BCE	98	98	1200 CE	92	78
900 BCE	98	98	1300 CE	88	81
800 BCE	97	98	1400 CE	96	86
700 BCE	96	97	1500 CE	88	83
600 BCE	95	97	1600 CE	87	83
500 BCE	94	97	1700 CE	85	79
400 BCE	95	96	1800 CE	82	79
300 BCE	95	91	1900 CE	59	75
200 BCE	91	90	2000 CE	28	20

*Organization scores begin registering in 8000 BCE in the West and 3500 BCE in the East, but until 3500 BCE in the West and 3000 BCE in the East they remain so small that they contribute less than 0.5 percent of the total development score, meaning that they disappear as a rounding error.

I discussed the way that the energy scores swamp the other three traits in *Why the West Rules—For Now*, but decided that arbitrary weightings or bump ups for the other traits would create more problems than they solved. Not everyone agrees, but Isaac Opper has pointed out that there is a much easier way to bring the other three traits into focus.[4]

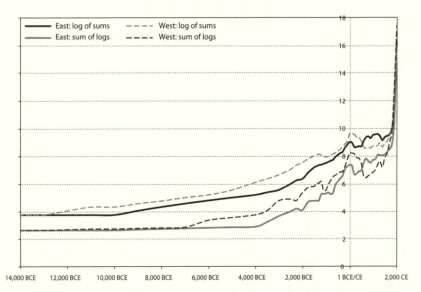

Figure 7.6. The social development scores seen on a log-linear scale. The upper two lines show the log of the sum of the four traits for West and East (i.e., adding together the scores on the four traits and then calculating the logarithm of the sum); the lower two lines show the sum of the logs of the four traits for West and East (i.e., calculating the logarithms of the scores on the four traits and then adding the four logarithms together). The sum of the logs, while less intuitively obvious, is more sensitive to small premodern changes in organization, war making, and information technology. Graph prepared by Isaac Opper.

The simplest way to bring out the variations in premodern social development scores is by representing the data on a log-linear graph. I did this at several points in *Why the West Rules—For Now*,[5] adding up the scores on the four traits and then calculating the logarithm of the sum. This has its uses, but if we instead calculate the separate logarithms of the four traits and then add up the logs to produce a single score, we end up with a graph that is no longer dominated by the high energy capture scores. The two upper lines in figure 7.6 show the log of the sum of the traits for West and East, while the two lower lines show the sum of the logs of the traits. As can be seen, summing the logs of the traits produces curves that are more sensitive to even quite small pre-twentieth-century CE changes in organization, war making, and information technology.

The collapse of Old Kingdom Egypt and the Akkadian Empire in the Western core after 2200 BCE, the destruction of Taosi in the

East around 2000 BCE, and the fall of the Western Zhou state in China in 771 BCE—all of which were swamped by the continuities in the energy capture scores when represented in other formats—can now be seen quite clearly. Furthermore, the post-Roman break-down in the West, which has been minimized by so many scholars since the 1960s, now looms even larger.

The lower lines in figure 7.6 also change the shape of the slopes in the left-hand part of the graph. Rather than being driven exclusively by changes in energy capture (above all, the coming of agriculture), this version's greater sensitivity to the other traits lowers the date at which the West pulled ahead of the East from circa 12,500 BCE (the end of the Ice Age) to about 7000 BCE, when the first settlements with populations of one thousand people (Beidha, Basta, Çatal-höyük) appeared. The tempo of Western development now seems to accelerate around 3500 BCE, with the rise of the first states, and accelerates again around 300 BCE, with the Roman Empire's unifi-cation of much of the Mediterranean Sea within a single political framework marking another threshold. In between these dates, though, the collapses of 2200 and 1200 BCE now stand out clearly as sharp interruptions of the trend line, in each case followed by a rapid convergence back to the norm.

The shape of the Eastern curve in ancient times also changes in interesting ways. Once again, the coming of agriculture has less im-pact, and the tempo does not really accelerate until after 4000 BCE, when Xipo grows to about a thousand residents. The Eastern line then rises smoothly (with interruptions around 2000, 1600, and 800 BCE that were all much milder than the West's great collapses around 2200 and 1200 BCE) until about 600 BCE, when the tempo of change picks up until about 100 CE. Further comparative re-search should be able to show whether the smoothness of the East-ern curve relative to the Western represents historical reality or is just a function of our more detailed knowledge of Western archaeol-ogy and ancient history.

Summing the logs of the traits rather than calculating the log of the sum of the traits has rather less impact on the shape of the curves in the two thousand years CE, because by this point the scores for organization, war making, and information technology are big enough to show up using either method. However, summing the logs of the traits does accentuate the scale of the departures from the overall trend lines.

One of my aims in *Why the West Rules—For Now* was to provide additional support for the argument that Chinese development did not stagnate under the Ming and Qing dynasties. The lower Eastern line in figure 7.6 makes this even clearer, with the scores between 1400 and 1800 CE closely tracking the longer post-Han trend.

Summing the logs of the traits also serves to make the explosion in Western development between 1400 and 1800 CE even clearer, emphasizing the point that modern Western domination was not predicated on a prior "decline of the East": Eastern societies performed well between 1400 and 1800 CE, but Western ones performed even better. Premodern globalization was driving Western social development up just as fast as Mediterraneanization drove up Roman social development in the last three centuries BCE.[6]

The lower Western line in figure 7.6 highlights two arguments I made in *Why the West Rules—For Now*. The first was that early modern European growth really did have a lot in common with Roman Republican growth, and that seventeenth- and eighteenth-century Europeans were quite right to speak of a "battle of ancients and moderns" as their social development regained the levels it had attained nearly two millennia earlier; and the second was that despite the impressive performance of early-modern Europe, truly revolutionary changes came only after 1800 CE, as Northwest Europeans unlocked and applied the energy trapped in fossil fuels.[7] Summing the logs of the traits provides a more sensitive visual representation of social development than logging the sum of the traits, but energy capture remains the foundation of human history.

CULTURE AND SOCIAL DEVELOPMENT

I have suggested that one of the major contributions of the social development index is that it forces analysts to be explicit. Those who, like me, think that an index is a valuable tool for describing patterns that need to be explained are forced to spell out in detail their evidence and methods. Those who disagree, or who think the index has been designed or applied incorrectly, are able to see exactly how the index works and to criticize the arguments in detail.[8] Neither side of the debate is forced to resort to the kind of vague denunciations that became so popular in the neo-evolutionism arguments of the 1980s and 1990s.

In *Why the West Rules—For Now* I focused on just two regions of the world, but the social development index could of course be expanded into a genuinely global tool. This, I like to think, could make a contribution to some of the longest-running debates in the social sciences, such as the relative importance of material and cultural forces in shaping history.

I came down strongly on the materialist side in *Why the West Rules—For Now*, arguing that the striking similarities between Eastern and Western social development over the past sixteen thousand years showed that the cultural peculiarities of the two regions did not make much difference. Consistently, I concluded, each age got the thought it needed (or perhaps the thought it deserved). At best, though, this remains a hypothesis, and a properly global social development index would be an obvious way to test it further, treating different parts of the world as natural experiments on history.[9]

The most useful such comparison might be between the Old and New Worlds, since they experienced little meaningful contact between about 10,000 BCE and 1500 CE. The same is true of Eurasia and Australia, but the New World has another advantage that makes comparisons with Eurasia fruitful. Like the Old World and unlike Australia, the New World had a zone of lucky latitudes containing dense concentrations of domesticable plants and animals at the end of the Ice Age. Australia does have a Mediterranean climate zone in its southwest, but at the end of the Ice Age no local equivalents of wheat, barley, rice, corn, potatoes, sheep, goats, pigs, or cattle had evolved in them, making domestication and the indigenous development of complex societies much more difficult than in Eurasia.[10]

If culture really is a dependent variable, we might expect the New World's core areas to have expanded in similar ways to those in the Old World, generating an equivalent set of advantages of backward-

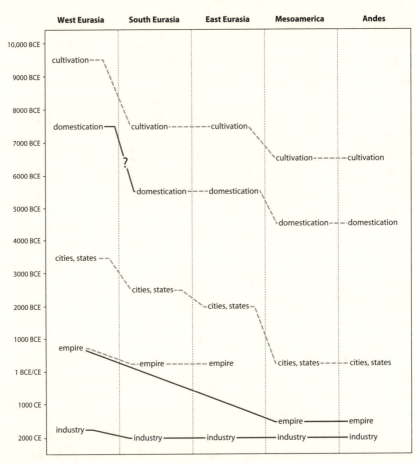

Figure 7.7. Broad stages of ancient cultural development in five regions of the world. Solid lines represent diffusion of innovations from one zone to another; broken lines do not.

ness, paradoxes of development, social collapses, and all the other phenomena I described in *Why the West Rules—For Now*.

Extending the social development index to the New World, I suspect, will show that that is precisely what did happen. Domestication came first in the New World's lucky latitudes, in Oaxaca and highland Peru. As social development rose in these regions and cities and states appeared, new cores (e.g., Yucatan, the Valley of Mexico) emerged alongside the original homelands of domestication. Figure 7.7, a simple chart showing some of the main cultural transitions in five regions of ancient complex society, reinforces the impression that the original agricultural cores in the Old and New

Worlds moved largely independently through the same stages of development, on roughly the same timetable.

The lag between the beginning of cultivation (i.e., human intervention in the life cycle of plants that produces selective pressures leading to plants with unnaturally large seeds) and the beginning of domestication (i.e., human intervention that genetically modifies plants and animals so much that they turn into new species that can survive only with continued human intervention) was typically about two millennia in the Old World. In the New World it typically took four millennia, probably because the New World crops were less adaptable than those in the Old World. Turning teosinte into corn, for example, requires far more genetic changes than turning wild wheat, barley, or rice into their domesticated forms.

However, this was partly evened out by a shorter lag between domestication and the rise of cities and states in the New World (about three millennia) than in the Old (three to four millennia). In the Old World, it took another one and a half to three millennia for states such as Old Kingdom Egypt or Shang China to turn into true empires, ruling areas of two million-plus square kilometers and populations in the multiple tens of millions. In the New World, the conquistadors arrived about one and a half millennia after the rise of the first true states such as the Moche culture and Teotihuacán, cutting off the Native American experiment; but by that point Inca and Aztec conquests had produced organizations of roughly the same scale as the earliest Old World empires. Had they been left alone for another millennium, these might well have developed along the same lines as Old World imperial states.

My impression, as an outsider looking at the New World's archaeological record, is that a social development index produced by an expert in this material would show that the Americas systematically lagged behind Eurasia, in a pattern that fits very nicely with the arguments in *Why the West Rules—For Now*. In energy capture, some New World crops outperformed those in the Old World, but the absence of draft animals in the Americas must have severely reduced the energy available per capita. The absence of such useful animals probably does a lot to explain the limited use of the wheel in New World transport, although in Eurasia wheelbarrows pushed by humans were apparently independently invented in the fifth century BCE in Greece and the first century BCE in China.[11]

In information technology, systems of recording words and numbers came into use along with the first cities and states in both the Old and New Worlds, but when compared with Egyptian or Mesopotamian practices around 1500 BCE or Chinese practices around 500 BCE, Mesoamerican and Andean uses of these technologies around 1500 CE seem very limited.[12]

In war-making capacity, some techniques introduced around the time of the first states in the Old World (such as fortifications) appear at equivalent points in the New World, but over the subsequent fifteen hundred years did not spread as rapidly in the Americas as in Eurasia. Other techniques (such as bronze weapons and armor), however, never got established in the Americas at all; and, because all wild equids that might have evolved into domesticated horses disappeared from the Americas after the arrival of humans, New World armies of course never developed chariots or cavalry.

The fate of the bow and arrow in the Old and New Worlds is even more interesting. Bows were invented in Africa more than sixty thousand years ago and then spread all across the Old World.[13] By the first millennium BCE powerful compound bows were in use in all of the Old World's complex societies and crossbows had been invented in China. So far as we can tell, however, the first settlers of the Americas did not import the bow, and there is no sign that anyone reinvented it until arrowheads appear in Alaska and Canada on sites of the Arctic Small Tool Tradition around 2300 BCE. These weapons then spread very slowly across North America, not reaching Mesoamerica until about 1100 CE, and never attaining the sophistication of Old World bows.[14]

By contrast, city size seems to have increased faster in some parts of the New World than in the Old. By 500 CE, Teotihuacán had probably 100,000–200,000 residents, making it much bigger than any Eurasian site had been less than one millennium after the first cities appeared in a region. The first Old World site to reach the lower end of the likely range for Teotihuacán was Nineveh, around 700 BCE; the upper end was matched only in the third century BCE, by Alexandria.

The explanation for these Old/New World differences may already be in hand. In his book *Guns, Germs, and Steel*, Jared Diamond points out that Eurasia has enjoyed three major geographical advantages over the Americas, which may do much to account for Eurasia's lead in what I would call social development.[15]

First, Diamond observes, Eurasia had a richer natural resource basis than America at the end of the Ice Age, which made it easier for people in Southwest and East Asia to domesticate plants and animals than for people in Mesoamerica or the Andes;[16] second, most of the New World's potentially domesticable large (i.e., weighing more than 100 pounds) mammals were wiped out in the megafauna extinctions that followed fairly swiftly after the initial human colonization of the continent;[17] and third, even the layout of the continents worked against Native Americans. Eurasia runs basically east-west, so that ideas, institutions, and practices originating in Southwest Asia could spread thousands of miles to Europe or China within the kind of unified ecological zone that geographers call a "biome."[18] The Americas, by contrast, run basically north-south, meaning that ideas, institutions, and practices bubbling to the surface in Mesoamerica or the Andes could circulate only among a small group of people (relative to the Old World) before having to be carried across very different biomes.[19] Consequently, New World ideas, institutions, and practices took longer to appear and much longer to spread.[20]

Given the small number of continents, it is difficult to test Diamond's claims, although one recent study of linguistic diversity does offer at least limited support.[21] New World societies certainly had unique features, and their combination of precocious (relative to Old World societies) urbanization and slow adoption of new war-making methods and information technology cries out for explanation. Extension of the social development index on a global scale may make it easier to see whether Diamond's geographical framework can account for the New/Old World differences or whether we need to grant a major role to cultural factors.

SOCIAL DEVELOPMENT AND UNILINEAR EVOLUTION

"There is little doubt that one of the most vexing issues in cultural evolutionary theory is that of unilinear versus multilinear evolution," Robert Carneiro concluded toward the end of his survey of the field.[22]

Like many such issues, though, much of the vexation has stemmed from lack of clarity over what the question means and implicit assumptions about the appropriate level of abstraction.[23] To some scholars, asking whether social evolution is unilinear seems to mean asking whether there is just one path to modernity (and, by extension, asking whether there is more than one kind of modernity); to others, it seems to mean asking more generally whether societies can develop in multiple directions (and, by extension, asking whether there are so many multiple paths that speaking of development at all is a mistake).

The social development index suggests that the answer to the first version of the question—whether there is just one path to modernity—is an unequivocal yes. The index reveals not only a very clear progression from foragers to farmers to factory workers and beyond but also a series of hard ceilings limiting how far development could go under each broad form of organization. No foraging society has developed much beyond six or seven points on the index; no agricultural village society much beyond ten to twelve points; and no agrarian empire beyond the low forties. No society has leapt from foraging or agricultural villages directly to industrialism without going through the stage of agrarian empires—unless it comes under the influence of another society that has already gone through these stages; and no society has evolved from pastoral nomadism to industrialism without first being conqued by an agrarian empire.

Anthropologists, historians, and sociologists have argued endlessly over what modernity means,[24] but all the societies they customarily treat as "modern" have got there through one of the two paths described in the last paragraph. In every case, modernity has consisted of an explosion in energy capture, provided by an industrial revolution tapping into the power of fossil fuels, followed by the application of energy to new walks of life. The debates over whether modernity is multiple or singular largely come down to disagreements over the most useful level for generalizations about these societies.

If we take the unilinear versus multilinear question in the second sense—as asking whether societies can develop in multiple directions—the answer depends heavily on our chronological perspective and where we set the endpoint of our investigation. If we start by looking at the world a thousand years ago, we would unequivocally conclude that the answer is yes: societies very clearly were developing in multiple directions, ranging from Kalahari hunters through Turkic nomads and Mississippian farmers to Song dynasty China.

However, culture—which has played an enormous role in arguments in favor of multilinear evolution—has a rather limited role in explaining this diversity. Within a given biome, societies tended to develop in broadly similar ways. Farming took hold in the lucky latitudes, and spread outward from there. Pastoralists settled the steppes, developing through foot, cart, and mounted stages. Hunting and gathering dominated environments that could not support farming or herding.

Once again, the level of abstraction at which we work also shapes what we see. Lifestyles in (for example) Chinese, Indian, Arabic, Christian, and Toltec states certainly differed in all kinds of ways, and scholars are perfectly free to choose to emphasize these differences over their similarities. However, the social development index forces us to recognize that the similarities within biomes were real and important. The major factor producing multilinear evolution was geography, not culture.

That said, if we look at the world in the twenty-first century, we might instead conclude that the answer to the question is no: societies have not developed in multiple directions. For millennia, geography pushed development down different paths in different biomes, but as social development increased in the world's lucky latitudes, the most developed societies expanded spatially. By 200 BCE, traders from Eurasia's agrarian empires were moving goods from one end of the Old World to the other. By 600 CE, we have concrete evidence of individuals going the whole way from Europe to China. By 1400 CE, Eurasians had ships that could reliably cross any ocean, and by 1900 CE, Europeans and their colonists overseas had tied almost the whole world into a single economy. Globalization has been going on for centuries, and once one society had crossed the threshold to fossil fuels it became inevitable that the whole world would rapidly become modern.[25]

Whether we answer yes or no to the question of whether societies can develop in multiple directions, then, depends entirely on the chronological scale we work at. Prehistoric archaeologists and premodern historians can comfortably say yes, but any perspective that includes the twenty-first century forces us to say no.

The social development index, I believe, points toward qualified unilinearity. On the one hand, there was only one path to modernity; on the other, it was available only to people living in certain places. But on the third hand, once enough people had gone far enough down that path, everyone else was dragged down it too.

THE DIRECTION OF SOCIAL EVOLUTION

Biological evolution is often described as a directionless process. In a vivid image, the naturalist Stephen Jay Gould once suggested that if we could somehow replay the tape of life, it is highly unlikely that it would again lead to us. "The divine tape player holds a million scenarios," he argued, "each perfectly sensible. Little quirks at the outset, occurring for no particular reason, unleash cascades of consequences that make a particular future seem inevitable in retrospect. But the slightest early nudge contacts a different groove, and history veers into another plausible channel.... And so, for ourselves, I think we can only exclaim, O brave—and improbable—new world, that has such people in it!"[26]

Insofar as evolution is the right framework for thinking about human societies, we should follow Gould in seeing continuities between biology and culture, concluding, perhaps, that nothing made the pattern of rising social development across the past fifteen thousand years inevitable. The numbers on the index started climbing because global warming after 12,700 BCE made rising development a successful adaptation. Change the environmental context and you change the fitness landscape; what flourished in one setting, such as groups with high levels of development, might not have flourished in another.

The implication of this argument would seem to be that there is no more direction to social evolution than to biological evolution, and that a social development index, whatever its descriptive value for making sense of the past, has no predictive power. But that might be throwing the baby out with the bathwater. There are in fact very obvious and very strong patterns in the history of life, and plenty of biologists have concluded that the evolution of animals as intelligent as humans—and probably looking something quite like humans—was so likely that we can call it inevitable.[27]

Gould himself was willing to concede that despite what he saw as the essential randomness of life's lottery, a "rightward skewing of complexity" has been going on fairly steadily throughout the history of life.[28] The history of societies has been punctuated by just as many crashes as the history of species, yet it too has, over the past fifteen thousand years, seen equally steady rightward skewing. The obvious implication of all this history is that—other things being equal, and over the long run—we might expect continuing increases in social development scores.

In *Why the West Rules—For Now*,[29] I suggested that this is indeed the case, and argued that we can get some sense of what might happen if we project the social development index's trends forward across the twenty-first century. My projection was very crude, simply assuming that social development scores in East and West will continue to increase in the twenty-first century at the same rate as in the twentieth century. If they do this, the Eastern score will catch up with the Western score in 2103, at which point both regions will have reached about five thousand points on the index (figure 7.8).

This argument has attracted broader attention than any other part of the book.[30] It is highly unlikely that the twenty-first century will actually follow the course of this simplistic linear projection, but the value of making the projection lies less in whether it comes true (virtually no predictions do) than in making us ask how much we need to change our assumptions to produce a radically different outcome.

Projecting the twentieth century's index trend lines forward across the next century suggests that the "rise of the East" in the past fifty years is not a temporary hiccup in the story of Western dominance.[31] It is the outcome of a medium-term historical trend, driven by changes in the meaning of geography (above all, the effective shrinking of the Pacific Ocean) that go back more than a century. Western governments may be able to manage the shift in wealth and power toward the East, and the most sophisticated Western policy

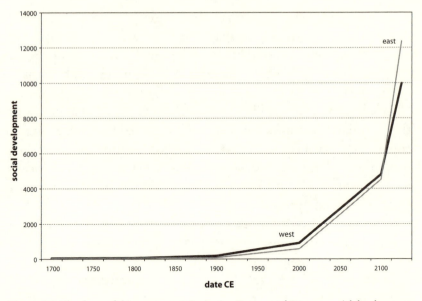

Figure 7.8. The shape of things to come? Projecting Eastern and Western social development scores into the twenty-first century CE.

forecasters are concentrating on precisely this.[32] Blocking or reversing the rise of the East, however, will call for as-yet-unidentified developments that will make geography once again change its meanings dramatically and start working to the West's renewed advantage.

The most significant implication of projecting twentieth-century trends forward, though, is that social development will reach five thousand points in the next hundred years. Between 14,000 BCE and 2000 CE, development rose by nine hundred points. This took humanity from Paleolithic cave paintings to the Internet. According to the assumptions behind figure 7.8, though, between 2000 and 2100 CE development will rise by a further four thousand points; and if anything, this may be an underestimate. All the signs in the dozen years since the new century began suggest that development is increasing exponentially, not just as a linear extension of what the last century saw.

Once again, the important question to ask is not whether the specific predictions I discussed in *Why the West Rules—For Now* will come true but what will need to happen to make reality depart so far from the assumptions my predictions rested on that social development ends up nowhere near five thousand points in 2100 CE. Judging from the shape of the social development curves across the past fifteen thousand years, the most plausible answer seems to be a new social collapse.

The five-thousand-point scenario assumes that humanity has permanently escaped Malthusian constraints, but there is an obvious alternative interpretation of post–Ice Age history: that industrialization merely pushed these constraints outward. It did so dramatically, increasing the world's population by an order of magnitude and lifting billions out of poverty; but all the same, this reading of the index would suggest, industrial societies will face built-in hard ceilings, just like the hard ceilings that constrained the growth of agrarian societies.

The Roman and Song agrarian empires faltered and failed when their social development rose above forty points, and perhaps modern societies will encounter a new hard ceiling somewhere between one thousand and five thousand points. And if development stagnates in a world of ten billion people, unpredictable climate change, nuclear proliferation, and rapid, unevenly distributed advances in robotic, cyber-, and nano-warfare, the consequences could be even more catastrophic than when development stagnated in the agrarian age.

The index implies that the next fifty years will be the most important in history.[33] If the energy bonanza of the nineteenth and twentieth centuries turns out to have been a one-time deal, the twenty-first century promises to be the worst of times for everyone; if, on the other hand, the industrial revolution turns out to have been merely the first stage of a longer energy revolution, the coming century will surely transform humanity out of all recognition. By the 2060s, we will probably have found out which way the world is going.

A social development index is not, of course, going to solve any of these problems, but it might be a valuable tool for identifying some of them. "If superior creatures from space ever visit earth," Richard Dawkins speculates at the start of his classic work *The Selfish Gene*, "the first question they will ask, in order to assess the level of our civilization, is: 'Have they discovered evolution yet?'"[34] And when this happens, I suspect that they will be asking about social as well as biological evolution.

NOTES

CHAPTER 1

1. David Gress, *From Plato to NATO: The Idea of the West and Its Opponents* (New York: Free Press, 1998) discusses the history of these arguments.

2. Victor Davis Hanson, *Carnage and Culture: Landmark Battles in the Rise of Western Power* (New York: Anchor, 2001), and Roger Osborne, *Civilization: A New History of the Western World* (New York: Pegasus, 2008), are widely read recent examples of arguments for Greco-Roman roots, while Ricardo Duchesne, *The Uniqueness of Western Civilization* (Leiden: Brill, 2011) has championed Indo-European roots and Francis Fukuyama, *The Origins of Political Order: From Prehuman Times to the French Revolution* (New York: Farrar, Straus and Giroux, 2011) has argued for medieval ones.

3. Eric Jones, *The European Miracle: Environments, Economies and Geopolitics in the History of Europe and Asia*, 3rd ed. (Cambridge, UK: Cambridge University Press, 2003) is probably the most influential example.

4. For example, David Landes, *The Wealth and Poverty of Nations* (New York: Norton, 1998).

5. Oded Galor and Omer Moav, "Natural Selection and the Origin of Economic Growth," *Quarterly Journal of Economics* 117 (2002): 1133–91; Gregory Clark, "Genetically Capitalist? The Malthusian Era and the Formation of Modern Preferences," http://www.econ.ucdavis.edu/faculty/gclark/papers/capitalism%20genes.pdf.

6. Gregory Cochran and Henry Harpending, *The Ten Thousand Year Explosion: How Civilization Accelerated Evolution* (New York: Basic Books, 2009), and their website http://westhunt.wordpress.com/.

7. For example, Andre Gunder Frank, *ReOrient: Global Economy in the Asian Age* (Berkeley: University of California Press, 1998); John Hobson, *The Eastern Origins of Western Civilisation* (Cambridge, UK: Cambridge University Press, 2004).

8. State structures: Bin Wong, *China Transformed* (Ithaca, NY: Cornell University Press, 1997) and Jean-Laurent Rosenthal and Bin Wong, *Before and Beyond*

Divergence: The Politics of Economic Change in China and Europe (Princeton: Princeton University Press, 2011); natural endowments: Kenneth Pomeranz, *The Great Divergence: China, Europe, and the Making of the Modern World Economy* (Princeton: Princeton University Press, 2000); physical and political geography: Jared Diamond, *Guns, Germs, and Steel: The Fates of Human Societies* (New York: Norton, 1997); intellectual trends: Jack Goldstone, *Why Europe? The Rise of the West in World History, 1500–1850* (New York: McGraw-Hill, 2009).

9. Updated annually and available at http://hdr.undp.org/en/.

10. Robert W. Fogel and Stanley Engerman, *Time on the Cross: The Economics of American Negro Slavery*, 2 vols. (Boston: Little, Brown, 1974).

11. Ian Morris, *Why the West Rules—For Now: The Patterns of History, and What They Reveal about the Future* (New York: Farrar, Straus and Giroux, 2010); http://www.ianmorris.org.

12. Peter Turchin, *Historical Dynamics: Why States Rise and Fall* (Princeton: Princeton University Press, 2003), 1.

13. See, among many others, Debraj Ray, *Development Economics* (Princeton: Princeton University Press, 1998); Yujiro Hayami, *Development Economics: From the Poverty to the Wealth of Nations* (Oxford: Oxford University Press, 2001).

14. Kenneth Pomeranz, "How Big Should Historians Think? A Review Essay on *Why the West Rules—For Now* by Ian Morris," *Cliodynamics* 2 (2011): 307–9; Michael Mann, *The Sources of Social Power I: A History of Power from the Beginning to AD 1760* (Cambridge, UK: Cambridge University Press, 1986).

15. The formulation of John Gerring, *Social Science Methodology* (Cambridge, UK: Cambridge University Press, 2001), 80.

16. As formulated in Morris, *Why the West Rules*, 144.

17. I have been particularly influenced by Marvin Harris, *The Rise of Anthropological Theory* (New York: Crowell 1968), Adam Kuper, *Anthropology and Anthropologists*, 2nd ed. (London: Routledge Kegan Paul, 1983), Stephen Sanderson, *Social Evolutionism: A Critical History* (Oxford: Blackwell, 1990), and Bruce Trigger, *Sociocultural Evolution* (Oxford: Blackwell, 1998) and *A History of A rchaeological Thought*, 2nd ed. (Cambridge, UK: Cambridge University Press, 2006).

18. Herbert Spencer, "Progress: Its Laws and Cause," *Westminster Review* 67 (1857): 445–85, with the fascinating account in Mark Francis, *Herbert Spencer and the Invention of Modern Life* (Ithaca, NY: Cornell University Press, 2007).

19. Spencer, "Progress," 465.

20. Herbert Spencer, *The Principles of Sociology*, 3 vols. (New York: Appleton, 1874–96).

21. Edward Tylor, *Primitive Culture: Researches into the Development of Mythology, Philosophy, Religion, Language, Art and Custom*, 2 vols. (London: John Murray, 1871); Lewis H. Morgan, *Ancient Society, or Researches in the Lines of Human Progress from Savagery through Barbarism to Civilisation* (1877; repr., Gloucester, MA: Peter Smith, 1974); Friedrich Engels, *The Origins of the Family, Private Property and the State, in the Light of the Researches of Lewis H. Morgan* (1884; repr., London: Lawrence & Wishart, 1972).

22.   Kristian Kristiansen, "Genes versus Agents: A Discussion of the Widening Theoretical Gap in Archaeology," *Archaeological Dialogues* 11 (2004): 77–132.

23.   For example, Arthur Radcliffe-Brown, *A Natural Science of Society* (1936; repr., Glencoe, IL: Free Press, 1957).

24.   Bruce Trigger, *Gordon Childe: Revolutions in Archaeology* (London: Thames & Hudson, 1980).

25.   V. Gordon Childe, *The Dawn of European Civilisation*, 1st ed. (London: Kegan Paul, 1925).

26.   V. Gordon Childe, *Man Makes Himself* (London: Watts & Co., 1936); *What Happened in History* (Harmondsworth, UK: Penguin, 1942); *Social Evolution* (London: Watts & Co., 1951).

27.   William Peace, "Vere Gordon Childe and American Anthropology," *Journal of Anthropological Research* 44 (1988): 417–33.

28.   Walt W. Rostow, *The Stages of Economic Growth: A Non-Communist Manifesto*, 1st ed. (Cambridge, UK: Cambridge University Press, 1960).

29.   Talcott Parsons, "Evolutionary Universals in Society," *American Sociological Review* 29 (1964): 339–57; *Societies: Evolutionary and Comparative Perspectives* (Englewood Cliffs, NJ: Prentice Hall, 1966); *The System of Modern Societies* (Englewood Cliffs, NJ: Prentice Hall, 1971).

30.   Parsons, "Evolutionary Universals," 340–41.

31.   For example, Anthony D. Smith, *The Concept of Social Change: A Critique of the Functionalist Theory of Social Change* (London: Routledge Kegan Paul, 1973), 135–45; Christopher Lloyd, *Explanation in Social History* (Oxford: Blackwell, 1986), 213.

32.   Leslie White, "Energy and the Evolution of Culture," *American Anthropologist* 45 (1943): 335–56; *The Science of Culture* (New York: Grove Press, 1949); *The Evolution of Culture* (New York: McGraw-Hill, 1959).

33.   White, "Energy," 338, emphasis original.

34.   White, *Science of Culture*, 390–91.

35.   White, "Energy," 343–44.

36.   Sebald Steinmetz, "Classification des types sociaux," *L'Année Sociologique* 3 (1898–99): 43–147.

37.   Hans J. Nieboer, *Slavery as an Industrial System* (The Hague: Nyhoff, 1910); Leonard Hobhouse et al., "The Material Culture and Social Institutions of the Simpler Peoples," *Sociological Review* 7 (1914): 203–31, 332–68, reprinted as a book under the same title by Chapman and Hall, London, 1930.

38.   Carleton Coon, *A Reader in General Anthropology* (New York: Holt, 1948), 612–13; Raoul Naroll, "A Preliminary Index of Social Development," *American Anthropologist* 58 (1956): 687–715.

39.   http://www.yale.edu/hraf/; Melvin Ember, "Evolution of the Human Relations Area Files," *Cross-Cultural Research* 31 (1997): 3–15; Carol Ember and Marvin Ember, *Cross-Cultural Research Methods* (Walnut Creek, CA: AltaMira, 2001).

40.   Charles Darwin, *Voyages of the* Adventure *and* Beagle, vol. 3 (London: Henry Colburn, 1839), chap. 10.

41. Robert Carneiro, "Scale Analysis as an Instrument for the Study of Cultural Evolution," *Southwestern Journal of Anthropology* 18 (1962): 149–69.

42. Ibid., 162.

43. Ibid., 160, emphasis original.

44. Robert Carneiro, "The Measurement of Cultural Development in the Ancient Near East and in Anglo-Saxon England," *Transactions of the New York Academy of Sciences Series 2* 31 (1969): 1013–23.

45. For example, Edgar Bowden, "A Dimensional Model of Multilinear Sociocultural Evolution," *American Anthropologist* 67 (1969): 864–70; Robert Carneiro, "Ascertaining, Testing, and Interpreting Sequences of Cultural Development," *Southwestern Journal of Anthropology* 24 (1968): 354–74, and "Scale Analysis, Evolutionary Sequences, and the Rating of Cultures," in Naroll and Cohen, *Handbook of Method in Cultural Anthropology*, 834–71; Edwin Erickson, "Other Cultural Dimensions: Selective Rotations of Sawyer and LeVine's Factor Analysis of the World Ethnographic Sample," *Behavior Science Notes* 7 (1972): 95–155; Linton Freeman and Robert Winch, "Societal Complexity: An Empirical Test of a Typology of Societies," *American Journal of Sociology* 62 (1957): 461–66; Charles McNett, "A Settlement Pattern Scale of Cultural Complexity," in Naroll and Cohen, *Handbook of Method*, 872–86, "A Cross-Cultural Method for Predicting Nonmaterial Traits in Archeology," *Behavior Science Notes* 5 (1970): 195–212, and "Factor Analysis of a Cross-Cultural Sample," *Behavior Science Notes* 8 (1973): 233–57; George Murdock and Caterina Provost, "Measurement of Cultural Complexity," *Ethnology* 12 (1973): 379–92; Raoul Naroll, "The Culture-Bearing Unit in Cross-Cultural Surveys," in Naroll and Cohen, *Handbook of Method*, 721–65; Jack Sawyer and Robert LeVine, "Cultural Dimensions: A Factor Analysis of the World Ethnographic Sample," *American Anthropologist* 68 (1966): 708–31; Terrence Tatje and Raoul Naroll, "Two Measures of Societal Complexity," in Naroll and Cohen, *Handbook of Method*, 766–833.

46. On burials, see Arthur Saxe, "Social Dimensions of Mortuary Practices" (PhD thesis, University of Michigan, 1970); Lewis Binford, "Mortuary Practices: Their Study and Their Potential," in James Brown, ed., *Approaches to the Social Dimensions of Mortuary Practices* (New York: Memoirs of the Society for American Archaeology 25, 1971), 6–29; Joseph Tainter, "Social Inference and Mortuary Practices: An Experiment in Numerical Classification," *World Archaeology* 7 (1975): 1–15 and "Mortuary Practices and the Study of Prehistoric Social Systems," *Advances in Archaeological Method and Theory* 1 (1978): 105–41. On settlement patterns, Kent Flannery, "The Cultural Evolution of Civilizations," *Annual Review of Ecology and Systematics* 3 (1972): 399–426; Gregory Johnson, *Local Exchange and Early State Development in Southwest Iran* (Ann Arbor, MI: Museum of Anthropology Occasional Papers 51, 1973); Henry Wright and Gregory Johnson, "Population, Exchange, an Early State Formation in Southwestern Iran," *American Anthropologist* 77 (1975): 267–89.

47. Robert Carneiro, *Evolutionism in Cultural Anthropology* (Boulder, CO: Westview, 2003), 167–68.

48. Elman Service, *Primitive Social Organization: An Evolutionary Perspective*, 1st ed. (New York: Random House, 1962); Morton Fried, *The Evolution of Political Society: An Essay in Political Anthropology* (New York: Random House, 1967).

49. Neo-institutional economics: Douglass North, *Structure and Change in Economic History* (New York: Norton, 1981), and Douglass North et al., *Violence and Social Orders: A Conceptual Framework for Interpreting Recorded Human History* (Cambridge, UK: Cambridge University Press, 2009), are among the classics. On the Soviet bloc, see Don Karl Rowney, ed., *Soviet Quantitative History* (Beverly Hills, CA: Sage, 1984).

50. Michael Rowlands, "A Question of Complexity," in Daniel Miller et al., eds., *Domination and Resistance* (London: Allen & Unwin, 1988), 29–40.

51. Carneiro, *Evolutionism*, 286.

52. Robert Dunnell, "Evolutionary Theory and Archaeology," *Advances in Archaeological Method and Theory* 9 (1980): 50.

53. Robert Boyd and Peter Richerson, *Culture and the Evolutionary Process* (Chicago: University of Chicago Press, 1985) and William Durham, *Coevolution: Genes, Culture, and Human Diversity* (Stanford: Stanford University Press, 1991) were particularly important in starting this development.

54. Diamond, *Guns, Germs, and Steel*.

55. For a few examples among many: in political science, Fukuyama, *Origins of Political Order* and Daron Acemoglu and James Robinson, *Why Nations Fail* (New York: Crown Books, 2012). In economics, Geerat Vermeij, *Nature: An Economic History* (Princeton: Princeton University Press, 2004) and *The Evolutionary World: How Adaptation Explains Everything from Seashells to Civilization* (New York: Thomas Dunne/St. Martin's, 2010). Philosophy of religion, David Sloan Wilson, *Darwin's Cathedral: Evolution, Religion, and the Nature of Society* (Chicago: University of Chicago Press, 2002), Daniel Dennett, *Breaking the Spell: Religion as a Natural Phenomenon* (New York: Simon & Schuster, 2006) and Richard Dawkins, *The God Delusion* (New York: Houghton Mifflin Harcourt, 2007). In psychology, Susan Blackmore, *The Meme Machine* (Oxford: Oxford University Press, 1999) and Steven Pinker, *The Blank Slate: The Modern Denial of Human Nature* (New York: Viking, 2002) and *The Better Angels of Our Nature: Why Violence Has Declined* (New York: Penguin, 2011). In archaeology, Stephen Shennan, *Genes, Memes and Human History: Darwinian Archaeology and Cultural Evolution* (London: Thames & Hudson, 2002). In anthropology, Peter Richerson and Robert Boyd, *Not by Genes Alone* (Chicago: University of Chicago Press, 2005). In history, David Christian, *Maps of Time: An Introduction to Big History* (Berkeley: University of California Press, 2004), Albert Crosby, *Ecological Imperialism*, 2nd ed. (Cambridge, UK: Cambridge University Press, 2003) and *Children of the Sun: A History of Humanity's Unappeasable Appetite for Energy* (New York: Norton, 2006), and Charles Mann, *1491: New Revelations of the Americas Before Columbus* (New York: Knopf, 2005) and *1493: Uncovering the New World Columbus Created* (New York: Knopf, 2011).

56.   Samuel Bowles and Herbert Gintis, *A Cooperative Species: Human Reciprocity and Its Evolution* (Princeton: Princeton University Press, 2011); Alex Mesoudi, *Cultural Evolution: How Darwinian Theory Can Explain Human Culture & Synthesize the Social Sciences* (Chicago: University of Chicago Press, 2011).

57.   Randall McGuire, "Breaking Down Cultural Complexity," *Advances in Archaeological Method and Theory* 6 (1983): 91–142.

58.   See Saxe, "Social Dimensions," Binford, "Mortuary Practices," and Tainter, "Social Inference" and "Mortuary Practices."

59.   See Ian Hodder, *Symbols in Action* (Cambridge, UK: Cambridge University Press, 1982), 163–70, Ellen Jane Pader, *Symbolism, Social Relations and the Interpretation of Mortuary Remains* (Oxford: British Archaeological Reports, 1982), Michael Parker Pearson, "Mortuary Practices, Society and Ideology," in Ian Hodder, ed., *Symbolic and Structural Archaeology* (Cambridge, UK: Cambridge University Press, 1982), 99–113, and Christopher Carr, "Mortuary Practices: Their Social, Philosophical-Religious, Circumstantial, and Physical Determinants," *Journal of Archaeological Method and Theory* 2 (1995): 105–200.

60.   Carneiro, "Scale Analysis, Evolutionary Sequences," 854–70.

61.   See Ernest Gellner, *Nations and Nationalism* (Oxford: Blackwell, 1983).

62.   Charles Tilly, *Big Structures, Large Processes, Huge Comparisons* (New York: Russell Sage Foundation, 1984), 46–50.

63.   Ian Morris, "Economic Growth in Ancient Greece," *Journal of Institutional and Theoretical Economics* 160 (2004): 709–42 and "The Greater Athenian State," in Morris and Scheidel, *Dynamics of Ancient Empires*, 99–177; Josiah Ober, *Democracy and Knowledge: Innovation and Learning in Classical Athens* (Princeton: Princeton University Press, 2008) and "Wealthy Hellas," *Transactions of the American Philological Association* 140 (2010): 241–86.

64.   Ian Morris, *Death-Ritual and Social Structure in Classical Antiquity* (Cambridge, UK: Cambridge University Press, 1992), 108–55.

65.   Tilly, *Big Structures*, 48; Anthony Giddens, *The Constitution of Society: Outline of the Theory of Structuration* (Stanford: Stanford University Press, 1984), xxxvi–xxxvii, 263–74.

66.   McGuire, "Breaking Down Cultural Complexity."

67.   For example, Per Bak et al., "Self-Organized Criticality," *Physical Review* 38 (1988); Murray Gell-Mann, *The Quark and the Jaguar* (New York: Freeman, 1994); John Holland, *Hidden Order: How Adaptation Builds Complexity* (Cambridge, MA: Perseus Books, 1995); Harold Morowitz, *The Emergence of Everything: How the World Became Complex* (New York: Oxford University Press, 2002).

68.   For example, John Miller and Scott Page, *Complex Adaptive Systems: An Introduction to Computational Models of Social Life* (Princeton: Princeton University Press, 2007); Scott Page, *Diversity and Complexity* (Princeton: Princeton University Press, 2010).

69.   Again, to give just a small selection from the vast literature, on anthropology, see Peter Richerson and Robert Boyd, "Complex Societies: The Evolutionary

Dynamics of a Crude Superorganism," *Human Nature* 10 (2000): 253–89. On archaeology, Alexander Bentley and Herbert Maschner, eds., *Complex Systems and Archaeology* (Salt Lake City: University of Utah Press, 2003) and Arthur Griffin, "Emergence of Fusion/Fission Cycling and Self-Organized Criticality from a Simulation Model of Early Complex Polities," *Journal of Archaeological Science* 38 (2011): 873–83. On management, Dennis Tafoya, *The Effective Organization: Practical Application of Complexity Theory and Organizational Design to Maximize Performance in the Face of Emerging Events* (London: Routledge, 2010) and Wanda Curlee and Robert Gordon, *Complexity Theory and Project Management* (New York: Wiley, 2010). On economics, Eric Beinhocker, *The Origin of Wealth: Evolution, Complexity, and the Radical Remaking of Economics* (Cambridge, MA: Harvard Business School, 2010). On history, Christian, *Maps of Time* and Turchin, *Historical Dynamics*. On international relations, Neil Harrison, ed., *Complexity in World Politics* (Albany: State University of New York Press, 2007) and Alexander Wendt, "Why a World State Is Inevitable," *European Journal of International Relations* 9 (2003): 491–542.

70.   Giddens, *Constitution*, 231–36.

71.   Quoted in Mesoudi, *Cultural Evolution*, 46.

72.   For example, Patrice Teltser, ed., *Evolutionary Archaeology* (Tucson: University of Arizona Press, 1995), Herbert Maschner, ed., *Darwinian Archaeologies* (New York: Academic Press, 1996), and Shennan, *Genes*.

73.   Robert Leonard, "Evolutionary Archaeology," in Ian Hodder, ed., *Archaeological Theory Today* (Oxford: Blackwell, 2001), 72.

74.   See, for example, Robert Dunnell, "What Is It That Actually Evolves?" in Teltser, *Evolutionary Archaeology*, 33–50.

75.   Michael Shanks and Christopher Tilley, *Archaeology and Social Theory* (Oxford: Polity, 1987), 164.

76.   McNett, "Settlement Pattern Scale."

77.   Colin Renfrew, "Monuments, Mobilization and Social Organization in Neolithic Wessex," in Colin Renfrew, ed., *The Explanation of Culture Change* (London: Duckworth, 1973), 539–58; Christopher Peebles and Susan Kus, "Some Archaeological Correlates of Ranked Societies," *American Antiquity* 42 (1977): 421–48.

78.   Hawaiian chiefdoms were a favorite example: Timothy Earle, "A Reappraisal of Redistribution," in Timothy Earle and J. Ericson, eds., *Exchange Systems in Prehistory* (New York: Academic Press, 1977), 213–29 and "Chiefdoms in Archaeological and Ethnohistorical Perspective," *Annual Review of Anthropology* 16 (1987): 279–308; R. H. Cordy, *A Theory of Prehistoric Social Change* (New York: Academic Press, 1981). Patrick Kirch, *How Chiefs Become Kings: Divine Kingship and the Rise of Archaic States in Ancient Hawai'i* (Berkeley: University of California Press, 2010), describes the current state of thinking on Hawaiian chiefdoms.

79.   Sawyer and LeVine, "Cultural Dimensions"; Erickson, "Other Cultural Dimensions"; McNett, "Factor Analysis."

80.   Gary Feinman and Jill Neitzel, "Too Many Types: An Overview of Sed-

entary Prestate Societies in the Americas," *Advances in Archaeological Method and Theory* 7 (1984): 77.

81. Robert Drennan, "Regional Demography in Chiefdoms," and Stedman Upham, "A Theoretical Consideration of Middle Range Societies," both in Robert Drennan and C. Uribe, eds., *Chiefdoms in the Americas* (Lanham, MD: University Press of America, 1987), 307–23, 345–67.

82. As, for instance, in Robert Chapman, *Archaeologies of Complexity* (London: Routledge, 2003), 41–59.

83. Elman Service, *Origins of the State and Civilization* (New York: Academic Press, 1975), 3–4.

84. Norman Yoffee, *Myths of the Archaic State* (Cambridge, UK: Cambridge University Press, 2005), 22–31.

85. Mann, *Sources of Social Power*, 17; Giddens, *Constitution*, 164; cf. Giddens, *A Contemporary Critique of Historical Materialism*, 2nd ed. (Stanford: Stanford University Press, 1995), 42–48.

86. Akhil Gupta and James Ferguson, "Culture, Power, Place," in Akhil Gupta and James Ferguson, eds., *Culture, Power, Place* (Durham, NC: Duke University Press, 1997), 4.

87. David Clarke, *Analytical Archaeology*, 2nd ed., revised by Robert Chapman (London: Methuen, 1978), 247.

88. Naroll, "Culture-Bearing Unit."

89. Michael Shanks and Christopher Tilley, *Re-Constructing Archaeology: Theory and Practice*, 2nd ed. (London: Routledge, 1992), 58.

90. Mark Granovetter, "Economic Action and Social Structure: The Problem of Embeddedness," *American Journal of Sociology* 91 (1985): 481–510.

91. Trigger, *Sociocultural Evolution*, and Carneiro, *Evolutionism*, mount particularly spirited defenses.

CHAPTER 2

1. The best discussion is still Geoffrey Elton and Robert Fogel, *Which Road to the Past?* (New Haven: Yale University Press, 1983).

2. http://hdr.undp.org/en/.

3. Mahbub ul Haq, *Reflections on Human Development* (New York: Oxford University Press, 1995).

4. http://hdr.undp.org/en/statistics/.

5. See David Hastings, "Filling the Gaps in the Human Development Index," United Nations Economic and Social Commission for Asia and the Pacific Working Paper WP/09/02, 2009, http://www.unescap.org/publications/detail.asp?id=1308; Mark McGillivray, "The Human Development Index: Yet Another Redundant

Composite Development Indicator?" *World Development* 19 (1991): 1461–68; Mark McGillivray and Howard White, "Measuring Development? The UNDP's Human Development Index," *Journal of International Development* 5 (2006): 183–92; Ambuj Sagara and Adil Najam, "The Human Development Index: A Critical Review," *Ecological Economics* 25 (1998): 249–64; T. N. Srinivasan, "Human Development: A New Paradigm or Reinvention of the Wheel?" *American Economic Review* 84 (1994): 238–43; Hendrik Wolff et al., "Classification, Detection and Consequences of Data Error: Evidence from the Human Development Index," *Economic Journal* 121: 843–70.

6.   I take my list from Gerring, *Social Science Methodology*, but other standard works on social science methods tend to use similar criteria. In his original social development index, Raoul Naroll ("Preliminary Index," 692) listed five of these six, omitting number 1.

7.   Diamond, *Guns, Germs, and Steel*, 93–175.

8.   Norman Davies, *Europe: A History* (New York: Oxford University Press, 1994), 25.

9.   Diamond, *Guns, Germs, and Steel*, remains the most lucid discussion of the consequences.

10.   Morris, *Why the West Rules*, 114–19.

11.   Shennan, *Genes*, 129–34.

12.   Pomeranz, *Great Divergence*, 3–10.

13.   Naroll, "Culture-Bearing Unit in Cross-Cultural Surveys," 721–65.

14.   Bradford de Long and Andrei Schleifer, "Princes and Merchants: European City Growth Before the Industrial Revolution," *Journal of Law and Economics* 36 (1993): 671–702, is a particularly fine example.

15.   Walter Scheidel, "Germs for Rome," in Catharine Edwards and Greg Woolf, eds., *Rome the Cosmopolis* (Cambridge, UK: Cambridge University Press, 2003), 158–76.

16.   See Richard Wrangham and Dale Petersen, *Demonic Males: Apes and the Origins of Human Violence* (New York: Mariner, 1996); Bowles and Gintis, *Cooperative Species*.

17.   Naroll, "Preliminary Index," 691.

18.   See the discussion in Philip Hoffman, review of Ian Morris, *Why the West Rules—For Now*, in *Journal of Economic History* 71 (2011): 545–47.

19.   *Habitus*: Pierre Bourdieu, *Outline of a Theory of Practice*, trans. Richard Nice from the 1972 French original (Cambridge, UK: Cambridge University Press, 1977). Structuration: Giddens, *Constitution*. Postmodern turns in demography and economics: Nancy Riley and James McCarthy, *Demography in the Age of Postmodernism* (Cambridge, UK: Cambridge University Press, 2003); Deirdre McCloskey, *Knowledge and Persuasion in Economics* (Cambridge, UK: Cambridge University Press, 1994).

20.   Ian Morris, "Gift and Commodity in Archaic Greece," *Man* 21 (1986): 1–17; *Burial and Ancient Society: The Rise of the Greek City-State* (Cambridge, UK:

Cambridge University Press, 1987); "The Early Polis as City and State," in John Rich and Andrew Wallace-Hadrill, eds., *City and Country in the Ancient World* (London: Routledge, 1991), 24–57.

21.   Service, *Primitive Social Organization*; Parsons, *Societies*; Fried, *Evolution of Political Society.*

22.   Ian Morris, "An Archaeology of Equalities? The Greek City-States," in Tom Charlton and Deborah Nichols, eds., *The Archaeology of City-States* (Washington, DC: Smithsonian Institution, 1997), 91–105; *Archaeology as Cultural History: Words and Things in Iron Age Greece* (Oxford: Blackwell, 2000).

23.   Morris, "Economic Growth in Ancient Greece"; "Archaeology, Standards of Living, and Greek Economic History," in Manning and Morris, *Ancient Economy: Evidence and Models*, 91–126; "The Growth of Greek Cities in the First Millennium BC," in Storey, *Urbanism in the Preindustrial World*, 27–51; "Early Iron Age Greece," in Scheidel et al., *Cambridge Economic History*, 211–41; "Greater Athenian State"; Michael Smith et al., "Archaeology as a Social Science." *Proceedings of the National Academy of Sciences* 109 (2012): 7617–21.

24.   Morris, *Why the West Rules*, 625–26, and chapter 7.

25.   Spencer, "Progress," 445–85.

26.   Carneiro, "Scale Analysis as an Instrument," 161–63; "Scale Analysis, Evolutionary Sequences," 854–70.

27.   McGuire, "Breaking Down Cultural Complexity."

28.   Morris, *Why the West Rules*, 40–41.

29.   Pomeranz, *Great Divergence*, 3–10.

CHAPTER 3

1.   White, "Energy," 335–56.

2.   Christian, *Maps of Time*, 505–11, has a good discussion of the historical implications of thermodynamics.

3.   There are, of course, important exceptions. Richard N. Adams, *Energy and Structure: A Theory of Social Power* (Austin: University of Texas Press, 1975), Crosby, *Children of the Sun*, and Vaclav Smil's *General Energetics* (Boulder, CO: Westview, 1991), *Energy in World History* (Boulder, CO: Westview, 1994), and *Energy in Nature and Society: General Energetics of Complex Systems* (Cambridge, MA: MIT Press, 2008) have been the most valuable for my own research.

4.   Earl Cook, "The Flow of Energy in an Industrial Society," *Scientific American* 225 (1971): 135–44.

5.   Thomas Malthus, *An Essay on the Principle of Population*, 1st ed. (London: P. Johnson, 1798), chap. 5.

6.   See, for example, A. Bogaard et al., "The Impact of Manuring on Nitrogen Isotope Ratios in Cereals," *Journal of Archaeological Science* 34 (2007): 335–43.

7. See Robert Fogel, *The Escape from Hunger and Premature Death, 1700–2100* (Cambridge, UK: Cambridge University Press, 2004).

8. Oded Galor, *Unified Growth Theory* (Princeton: Princeton University Press, 2011), offers a particularly sophisticated version of this theory.

9. Gregory Clark, *A Farewell to Alms: A Brief Economic History of the World* (Princeton: Princeton University Press, 2007), 1.

10. E. A. Wrigley, *Continuity, Chance and Change: The Character of the Industrial Revolution in England* (Cambridge, UK: Cambridge University Press, 1988).

11. http://www.livius.org/w/weights/weights4.html provides a convenient summary of ancient weights and measures.

12. Vaclav Smil, *Biomass Energies: Resources, Links, Constraints* (New York: Plenum, 1983); *Energy in World History*.

13. Food and Agriculture Organization, *Statistical Yearbook*, vol. 2, pt. 1 (Rome: Food and Agriculture Organization of the United Nations, 2006); United Nations, *2003 Energy Statistics Yearbook* (New York: United Nations, 2006).

14. See Paul Bairoch, "International Industrialization Levels from 1705 to 1980," *Journal of European Economic History* 11 (1982): 269–333; Nicholas Crafts, *British Economic Growth during the Industrial Revolution* (Oxford: Clarendon, 1985); Paolo Malanima, "The Path towards the Modern Economy: The Role of Energy," *Rivista di Politica Economica* (April–June 2010–11): 1–30, http://www.paolomalanima.it/default_file/Papers/ENERGY_AND_GROWTH.pdf.

15. For example, see E. P. Thompson, *The Making of the English Working Class* (London: Victor Gollancz, 1963), 207–488 on England between 1780 and 1832.

16. Smil, *General Energetics* and *Energy in World History*, 12, 119, fig. 5.15; Angus Maddison, *The World Economy: Historical Statistics* (Paris: OECD Publishing, 2003).

17. For example, Kenneth Hudson, *World Industrial Archaeology* (Cambridge, UK: Cambridge University Press, 1979); Stephen Mrozowski, *The Archaeology of Class in Urban America* (Cambridge, UK: Cambridge University Press, 2006); Paul Shackel, *An Archaeology of American Labor and Working Class Life* (Gainesville: University of Florida Press, 2009).

18. Robert Allen, "The Great Divergence in European Wages and Prices from the Middle Ages to the First World War," *Explorations in Economic History* 38 (2001): 411–48; "Pessimism Preserved: Real Wages in the British Industrial Revolution," Oxford University Department of Economics Working Paper 314, 2007, http://www.nuffield.ox.ac.uk/General/Members/allen.aspx; *The British Industrial Revolution in Global Perspective* (Cambridge, UK: Cambridge University Press, 2009).

19. See, for example, Christian, *Maps of Time*, table 13.1, identifying a 1,023 percent increase, which, corrected for population growth from Christian's table 11.1, yields a 402 percent increase in per capita industrial output across the nineteenth century.

20. Housing: James Deetz, *In Small Things Forgotten*, rev. ed. (New York:

Anchor, 1996); Christopher Dyer, *Standards of Living in the Later Middle Ages: Social Change in England c. 1200–1520*, rev. ed. (Cambridge, UK: Cambridge University Press, 1989), 109–210. Household goods: John Brewer and Roy Porter, eds., *Consumption and the World of Goods* (London: Routledge, 1993). Wages in northwestern Europe: Allen, "Great Divergence" and *British Industrial Revolution*. Expensive calories: S. Cavaciocchi, ed., *Alimentazione e nutrizione secc. XIII–XVIII* (Florence: Le Monnier, 1997); James Barrett et al., "'Dark Age Economics' Revisited: The English Fish Bone Evidence AD 600–1600," *Antiquity* 78 (2004): 618–36; Gundula Müldner and M. P. Richards, "Fast or Feast: Reconstructing Diet in Later Medieval England by Stable Isotope Analysis," *Journal of Archaeological Science* 32 (2005): 39–48 and "Stable Isotope Evidence for 1500 Years of Human Diet at the City of York, UK," *American Journal of Physical Anthropology* 133 (2007): 682–97; M. Salamon et al., "The Consilience of Historical and Isotopic Approaches in Reconstructing the Medieval Mediterranean Diet," *Journal of Archaeological Science* 35 (2008): 1667–72. Longer working hours: Jan de Vries, *The Industrious Revolution* (Cambridge, UK: Cambridge University Press, 2009).

21. Maddison, *World Economy*.

22. For instance, G. Federico, "The World Economy 0–2000 AD: A Review Article," *European Review of Economic History* 6 (2002): 111–20; Paolo Malanima and Elio Lo Cascio, "GDP in Pre-Modern Agrarian Economies (1–1820 AD): A Revision of the Estimates," *Rivista di storia economica* 25 (2009): 387–415.

23. M. Haines and Rick Steckel, *Childhood Mortality and Nutritional Status as Indicators of Standard of Living* (National Bureau of Economic Research Historical Paper 121, Cambridge, MA, 2000); Rick Steckel and Jerome Rose, eds., *The Backbone of History: Health and Nutrition in the Western Hemisphere* (Cambridge, UK: Cambridge University Press, 2002).

24. Nikola Koepke and Joerg Baten, "Agricultural Specialization and Height in Ancient and Medieval Europe," *Explorations in Economic History* 45 (2005): 127–46 and their website, http://www.uni-tuebingen.de/uni/wwl/twomillennia.html; Clark, *Farewell to Alms*, 55–62.

25. Allen, "Great Divergence."

26. Ur: Leonard Woolley and Max Mallowan, *Ur Excavations VII: The Old Babylonian Period* (London: Oxford University Press, 1976), with general discussion in Nicholas Postgate, *Early Mesopotamia* (London: Routledge, 1994). 'Ain Mallaha: François Valla et al., "Le natufien final et les nouvelles fouilles à Mallaha (Eynan), Israel 1996–1997," *Journal of the Israel Prehistoric Society* 28 (1999): 105–76, with general discussion in Ofer Bar-Yosef and François Valla, eds., *The Natufian Culture in the Levant* (Ann Arbor, MI: International Monographs in Prehistory, 1991).

27. Walter Scheidel, "Real Wages in Early Economies: Evidence for Living Standards from 1800 BCE to 1300 CE," *Journal of the Economic and Social History of the Orient* 53 (2010): 425–62 (Princeton/Stanford Working Papers in Classics no. 090904, http://www.princeton.edu/~pswpc/); Jan Luit van Zanden, "Wages and the

Standards of Living in Europe, 1500–1800," *European Review of Economic History* 3 (1999): 175–98.

28. R. van der Spek, "Commodity Prices in Babylon, 385–61 BC," 2008, www .iisg.nl/hpw/babylon.php.

29. Robert Loomis, *Wages, Welfare Costs and Inflation in Classical Athens* (Ann Arbor: University of Michigan Press, 1998).

30. See especially Hans-Joachim Drexhage, *Preise, Mieten/Pachten, Kosten und Löhne im römischen Ägypten* (St. Katharinen: Scripta Mercaturae Verlag, 1991) and Dominic Rathbone, "Monetisation, Not Price-Inflation, in Third-Century AD Egypt?" in C. E. King and D. G. Wigg, eds., *Coin Finds and Coin Use in the Roman World* (Berlin: Mann Verlag, 1996), 321–39; "Prices and Price Formation in Roman Egypt," in Jean Andreau et al., eds., *Prix et formation des prix dans les économies antiques* (Saint-Bertrand-des-Comminges: Musée Archéologique, 1997), 183–244; "The 'Muziris' Papyrus (SB XVIII 13167): Financing Roman Trade with India," in *Alexandrian Studies II in Honour of Mostafa el Abbadi, Bulletin de la société d'archéologie d'Alexandrie* 46 (2009): 39–50, all focusing on the uniquely abundant Egyptian data.

31. Elio Lo Cascio and Paolo Malanima, "Ancient and Pre-Modern Economies. GDP in the Roman Empire and Early Modern Europe" (paper, Quantifying Long-Run Economic Development conference, Venice, March 21–25, 2011), http:// www.paolomalanima.it/default_file/Papers/ANCIENT-PRE-MODERN-ECON OMIES.pdf, discuss these assumptions in detail.

32. Walter Scheidel and Steven Friesen, "The Size of the Economy and the Distribution of Income in the Roman Empire," *Journal of Roman Studies* 99 (2009): 63 (Princeton/Stanford Working Papers in Classics no. 010901, http://www.prince ton.edu/~pswpc/).

33. Keith Hopkins, "Taxes and Trade in the Roman Empire (200 BC–AD 200)," *Journal of Roman Studies* 70 (1980): 101–25; "Rome, Taxes, Rents and Trade," in Walter Scheidel and Sitta von Reden, eds., *The Ancient Economy* (Edinburgh: Edinburgh University Press, 2002), 190–230; "The Political Economy of the Roman Empire," in Morris and Scheidel, *Dynamics of Ancient Empires*, 178–204; R. W. Goldsmith, "An Estimate of the Size and Structure of the National Product of the Early Roman Empire," *Review of Income and Wealth* 30 (1984): 263–88; Angus Maddison, *Contours of the World Economy 1–2030 AD: Essays in Macroeconomic History* (New York: Oxford University Press, 2007).

34. Scheidel and Friesen, "Size of the Economy"; Maddison, *Contours*.

35. Scheidel, "Real Wages"; Cook, "Flow of Energy"; Hopkins, "Taxes and Trade"; Goldsmith, "Estimate"; Maddison, *Contours*; Scheidel and Friesen, "Size of the Economy."

36. Smil, *General Energetics* and *Energy in World History*.

37. A. H. V. Smith, "Provenance of Coals from Roman Sites in England and Wales," *Britannia* 28 (1997): 297–324.

38. Smil, *Energy in World History*, 119.

39. Morris, "Economic Growth," 709–42; "Archaeology, Standards of Living, and Greek Economic History," 91–126; "Early Iron Age Greece," 211–41.

40. M. Legouilloux, "L'alimentation carnée au Ier millenaire avant J.-C. en Grèce continentale et dans les Cyclades," *Pallas* 52 (2000): 69–95.

41. William Coulson and Sarah Vaughan, eds., *Palaeodiet in the Aegean* (Oxford: Oxbow, 2000); D. Kusan, "Rapport synthétique sur les recherches archéobotaniques dans le sanctuaire d'Héra de l'Île de Samos," *Pallas* 52 (2000): 99–108; Albert Prieto and Joseph Carter, *Living off the Chora: Food and Diet in Ancient Pantanello* (Austin, TX: Institute for Classical Archaeology, 2003); F. Megaloudi et al., "Plant Offerings from the Classical Necropolis of Limenas, Thasos, North Greece," *Antiquity* 81 (2007): 933–43; Anne Keenleyside et al., "Stable Isotopic Evidence in a Greek Colonial Population," *Journal of Archaeological Science* 36 (2009): 51–63; Efrossini Vika et al., "Aristophanes and Stable Isotopes: A Taste for Freshwater Fish in Classical Thebes (Greece)?" *Antiquity* 83 (2009): 1076–83; Ephraim Lytle, "Fish Lists in the Wilderness: The Social and Economic History of a Boiotian Price Decree," *Hesperia* 79 (2010): 253–303; Efrossini Vika, "Diachronic Dietary Reconstructions in Ancient Thebes, Greece: Results from Stable Isotope Analysis," *Journal of Archaeological Science* 38 (2011): 1157–63. Intersite variability in fish consumption: Efrossini Vika and Tatiana Theodoropoulou, "Reinvestigating Fish Consumption in Greek Antiquity: Results from $\delta^{13}C$ and $\delta^{15}C$ Analysis from Fish Bone Collagen," *Journal of Archaeological Science* 39 (2012): 1618–27.

42. Morris, "Economic Growth"; Geofrey Kron, "Anthropometry, Physical Anthropology, and the Reconstruction of Ancient Health, Nutrition, and Living Standards," *Historia* 54 (2005): 68–83.

43. Sub-Boreal to Sub-Atlantic: P. A. Mayewski et al., "Holocene Climate Variability," *Quaternary Research* 62 (2005): 243–55; B. van Geel et al., "Archaeological and Palynological Indications of an Abrupt Climate Change in the Netherlands, and Evidence for Climatological Teleconnections around 2630 BP," *Journal of Quaternary Science* 11 (1996): 451–60; F. M. Chambers et al., "Globally Synchronous Climate Change 2800 Years Ago: Proxy Data from Peat in South America," *Earth and Planetary Science Letters* 253 (2007): 439–44; "Peatland Archives of Late-Holocene Climate Change in Northern Europe," *PAGES News* 18 (2010): 4–6. Metastudy suggesting less change in the early first millennium BCE: Martin Finné et al., "Climate in the Eastern Mediterranean, and Adjacent Regions, during the Past 6000 Years," *Journal of Archaeological Science* 38 (2011): 3153–73. On the difficulties of reconciling different types of evidence for climatic and social change, see C. J. Caseldine and C. Turney, "The Bigger Picture: Towards Integrating Palaeoclimate and Environmental Data with a History of Societal Change," *Journal of Quaternary Science* 25 (2010): 88–93.

44. On population densities, see now Mogens Hansen, *The Shotgun Method: The Demography of the Ancient Greek City-States* (Columbia: University of Missouri Press, 2006) and "An Update on the Shotgun Method," *Greek, Roman, and Byzantine Studies* 48 (2008): 259–86.

45.   Stephen Hodkinson, "Animal Husbandry in the Greek Polis," in C. R. Whittaker ed., *Pastoral Economies in Classical Antiquity*, *Proceedings of the Cambridge Philological Society* 14, suppl. (1988): 35–73; John Cherry et al., *Landscape Archaeology as Long-Term History* (Los Angeles: Cotsen Institute, 1991); Michael Jameson et al., *A Greek Countryside: The Southern Argolid from Prehistory to the Present* (Stanford: Stanford University Press, 1994); Anthony Snodgrass, "Response: The Archaeological Aspect," in Ian Morris, ed., *Classical Greece: Ancient Histories and Modern Archaeologies* (Cambridge, UK: Cambridge University Press, 1994), 197–200; John Bintliff et al., eds., *Testing the Hinterland: The Work of the Boeotia Survey (1989–1991) in the Southern Approaches to the City of Thespiai* (Cambridge, UK: McDonald Institute, 2008).

46.   Eberhard Zangger et al., "The Pylos Regional Archaeological Project, Part II: Landscape Evolution and Site Preservation," *Hesperia* 66 (1997): 549–641; Warren Eastwood et al., "Holocene Climate Change in the Eastern Mediterranean Region," *Journal of Quaternary Science* 22 (2006): 327–41; Morteza Djamali et al., "A Late Holocene Pollen Record from Lake Almaiou in NW Iran," *Journal of Archaeological Science* 36 (2009): 1364–75.

47.   Wolfram Hoepfner and Ernst-Ludwig Schwandner, *Haus und Stadt im klassischen Griechenland*, 2nd ed. (Munich: Deutscher Kunstverlag, 1994), 150; Lisa Nevett, "A Real Estate 'Market' in Classical Greece? The Example of Town Housing," *Annual of the British School at Athens* 95 (2000): 329–44.

48.   Olynthus: David M. Robinson et al., *Excavations at Olynthus*, 14 vols. (Baltimore: Johns Hopkins University Press, 1929–52); Nicholas Cahill, *Household and City Organization at Olynthus* (New Haven: Yale University Press, 2002). Wharram Percy: Maurice Beresford and John Hurst, *Wharram Percy: Deserted Medieval Village* (New Haven: Yale University Press, 1991). Medieval and early modern Greece: Frederick Cooper, *Houses of the Morea: Vernacular Architecture of the Northwest Peloponnese (1205–1955)* (Athens: Melissa, 2002); Eleutherios Sigalos, *Housing in Medieval and Post-Medieval Greece* (Oxford: British Archaeological Reports International Series 1291, 2004); A. Vionis, "The Archaeology of Ottoman Villages in Central Greece: Ceramics, Housing and Everyday Life in Post-Medieval Boeotia," in A. Erkanal-Öktü et al., eds., *Studies in Honour of Itayat Erkanal* (Istanbul: Homer Kitabevi, 2006), 784–800; Johanna Vroom, "Early Modern Archaeology in Central Greece: The Contrasts of Artefact Rich and Sherdless Sites," *Journal of Mediterranean Archaeology* 11 (1998): 131–64.

49.   Hansen, *Shotgun Method* and "Update."

50.   Geofrey Kron, "The Use of Housing Evidence as a Possible Index of Social Equality and Prosperity in Classical Greece and Early Industrial England" (forthcoming). See also the works cited in note 41 above.

51.   Morris, "Early Iron Age Greece."

52.   Hopkins, "Rome, Taxes, Rents and Trade"; Alan Bowman, "Quantifying Egyptian Agriculture," and Roger Bagnall, "Response to Alan Bowman," both in Bowman and Wilson, *Quantifying the Roman Economy*, 177–204, 205–12.

53.   Animal bones: Anthony King, "Diet in the Roman World: A Regional

Inter-Site Comparison of the Mammal Bones," *Journal of Roman Archaeology* 12 (1999): 168–202; Mamoru Ikeguchi, "The Dynamics of Agricultural Locations in Roman Italy" (PhD dissertation, King's College London, 2007); Willem Jongman, "The Early Roman Empire: Consumption," in Scheidel et al., *Cambridge Economic History*, 592–618. Shipwrecks: A. J. Parker, *Ancient Shipwrecks of the Mediterranean and Roman Provinces* (Oxford: British Archaeological Reports, 1992); "Artifact Distributions and Wreck Locations: The Archaeology of Roman Commerce," in Robert Hohlfelder, ed., *The Maritime World of Ancient Rome* (Ann Arbor, MI: Memoirs of the American Academy in Rome supp. vol. 6, 2008), 177–96, to be read with Andrew Wilson, "Approaches to Quantifying Roman Trade" and Michael Fulford, "Approaches to Quantifying Roman Trade: Response," both in Bowman and Wilson, *Quantifying the Roman Economy*, 213–49 and 250–58. At the time of writing, in April 2012, the Oxford Roman Economy Project promises to present a new database of shipwrecks (http://oxrep.classics.ox.ac.uk/oxrepdb/). Lead pollution: François de Callataÿ, "The Graeco-Roman Economy in the Super-Long Run: Lead, Copper, and Shipwrecks," *Journal of Roman Archaeology* 18 (2005): 361–72; M. Kylander et al., "Refining the Preindustrial Atmospheric Pb-Isotope Evolution Curve in Europe Using an 8000 Year Old Peat Core from NW Spain," *Earth and Planetary Science Letters* 240 (2005): 467–85; V. Renson et al., "Roman Road Pollution Assessed by Elemental and Lead Isotope Geochemistry in Belgium," *Applied Geochemistry* 23 (2008): 3253–66; T. M. Mighall et al., "Ancient Copper and Lead Pollution Records from a Raised Bog Complex in Central Wales, UK," *Journal of Archaeological Science* 36 (2009): 1509–15. Tin pollution: Andrew Meharg et al., "First Comprehensive Peat Depositional Records for Tin, Lead and Copper Association with Antiquity of Europe's Largest Cassiterite Deposits," *Journal of Archaeological Science* 39 (2012): 717–27. Deforestation: William Harris, "Bois et déboisement dans la Méditerrannée antique," *Annales Histoires Sciences Sociales* 1 (2011): 105–40. Public inscriptions: Ramsay MacMullen, "The Epigraphic Habit in the Roman Empire," *American Journal of Philology* 103 (1982): 233–46; Willem Jongman, "Archaeology, Demography, and Roman Economic Growth," in Bowman and Wilson, *Quantifying the Roman Economy*, 115–26. Coins: Richard Duncan-Jones, *Money and Government in the Roman Empire* (Cambridge, UK: Cambridge University Press, 1994); Elio Lo Cascio, "Produzione monetaria, finanza pubblica ed economia nel principato," *Rivista storica italiana* 109 (1997): 650–77. Finds along the German frontier: E. Holstein, *Mitteleuropäische Eichenchronologie* (Mainz: von Zabern, 1980), 137; B. Schmidt and W. Gruhle, "Klimaextreme in römischen Zeit— ein Strukturanalyse dendrochronologische Daten," *Archäologisches Korrespondenzblatt* 33 (2003): 421–27. Julia Hoffmann-Salz, *Die wirtschaftlichen Auswirkungen der römischen Eroberung: vergleichende Untersuchungen der Provinzen Hispania Tarraconensis, Africa Proconsularis und Syria* (Stuttgart: Historia Einzelschrift 218, 2011) gives an overview of economic change in three provinces of the empire, with rich archaeological details.

54. Walter Scheidel, "In Search of Roman Economic Growth" and Andrew Wilson, "Indicators for Roman Economic Growth," both in *Journal of Roman Archaeology* 22 (2009): 46–61 and 63–78, debate some of these.

55.   http://ceipac.gh.ub.es/MOSTRA/u_expo.htm.

56.   Optimists: Jongman, "Early Roman Empire" and "Archaeology"; Kron, "Anthropometry". Pessimists: M. Giannecchini and J. Moggi-Cecchi, "Stature in Archaeological Samples form Central Italy: Methodological Issues and Diachronic Changes," *American Journal of Physical Anthropology* 135 (2008): 284–92; Walter Scheidel, "Roman Wellbeing and the Economic Consequences of the 'Antonine Plague,'" version 3.0 (Princeton/Stanford Working Papers in Classics no. 011001, http://www.princeton.edu/~pswpc/), to appear in print in Elio Lo Cascio, ed., *L'impatto della "peste antonina"*; "Physical Wellbeing in the Roman World," version 3.0 (Princeton/Stanford Working Papers in Classics no. 091001, http://www.princeton.edu/~pswpc/), to appear in print in Walter Scheidel, ed., *The Cambridge Companion to the Roman Economy* (Cambridge, UK: Cambridge University Press).

57.   I. M. Barton, *Roman Domestic Buildings* (Exeter: University of Exeter Press, 1996); Simon Ellis, *Roman Housing* (London: Duckworth, 2000); Robert Stephan, "House Size, Living Standards, and Economic Growth in the Roman World" (PhD dissertation, Stanford University, forthcoming); Kron, "Use of Housing Evidence."

58.   Richard Alston, *The City in Roman and Byzantine Egypt* (London: Routledge, 2001); Andrew Wallace-Hadrill, *Houses and Society in Pompeii and Herculaneum* (Princeton: Princeton University Press, 1994).

59.   Amphoras: John Paterson, "'Salvation from the Sea': Amphorae and Trade in the Roman World," *Journal of Roman Studies* 72 (1982): 146–57; D. P. S. Peacock and Dyfri Williams, *Amphorae and the Roman Economy* (London: Longman, 1986); André Tchernia, *Le vin de l'Italie romaine: essai de l'histoire économique d'après les amphores* (Paris: École française à Rome, 1986); C. Panella and A. Tchernia, "Produits agricoles transportés en amphores: l'huile et surtout le vin," in *L'Italie d'Auguste à Dioclétian* (Paris: École française à Rome, 1994), 145–65; Theodore Peña, *Roman Pottery in the Archaeological Record* (Cambridge, UK: Cambridge University Press, 2007). Iron tools: Sarah Harvey, "Iron Tools from a Roman Villa at Boscoreale, Italy," *American Journal of Archaeology* 114 (2010): 697–714.

60.   Peter Fibiger Bang, *The Roman Bazaar: A Comparative Study of Trade and Markets in a Tributary Empire* (Cambridge, UK: Cambridge University Press, 2009).

61.   Rathbone, "'Muziris' Papyrus"; P. J. Cherian et al., "The Muziris Heritage Project: Excavations at Pattanam—2007," *Journal of Indian Ocean Archaeology* 4 (2007): 1–10; Roberta Tomber, *Indo-Roman Trade* (London: Duckworth, 2008).

62.   Cook, "Flow of Energy."

63.   Maddison, *Contours*, 37; Scheidel and Friesen, "Size of the Economy"; Paolo Malanima, "Energy Consumption and Energy Crisis in the Roman World" (paper, American Academy in Rome, June 15–16, 2011); Lo Cascio and Malanima, "Ancient and Pre-Modern Economies."

64.   Vaclav Smil, *Why America Is Not a New Rome* (Cambridge, MA: MIT Press, 2010), 107–13.

65.   Smil, *Energy in World History*, table A1.4.

66. Lo Cascio and Malanima, "Ancient and Pre-Modern Economies"; Maddison, *Contours*; Scheidel and Friesen, "Size of the Economy".

67. Malanima, "Energy Consumption."

68. Malanima also suggests that my figure for 1900 CE (92,000 kcal/cap/day) is too high, instead proposing 41,500 kcal/cap/day. Here we have a classic unit definition problem. Malanima defines the Western core in 1900 as Sweden, Norway, the Netherlands, Germany, France, Spain, Portugal, and Italy, while I, for reasons I explain in the "Units of Analysis" section of chapter 2, define it as being the industrialized heartlands of Britain, the Low Countries, western Germany, northern France, and the northeastern United States. Malanima observes that for England alone the figure was 95,000 kcal/cap/day; for the larger Western industrial core, my estimate is 92,000 kcal/cap/day, in line with Cook's.

69. Malanima's figure for Roman consumption is 6,000–11,000 kcal/cap/day; for this calculation I have taken the midpoint of 8,500 kcal/cap/day.

70. Scheidel, "Real Wages"; Robert Allen, "How Prosperous Were the Romans? Evidence from Diocletian's Price Edict (AD 301)," in Bowman and Wilson, *Quantifying the Roman Economy*, 327–45; Scheidel and Friesen, "Size of the Economy," 10n29.

71. Michael McCormick, *Origins of the European Economy: Communications and Commerce, AD 300–900* (Cambridge, UK: Cambridge University Press, 2001); Bryan Ward-Perkins, *The Fall of Rome and the End of Civilization* (Oxford: Oxford University Press, 2005); Chris Wickham, *Framing the Early Middle Ages: Europe and the Mediterranean 400–800* (Oxford: Oxford University Press, 2005).

72. Wickham, *Framing*.

73. Morris, *Why the West Rules*, 292–308.

74. Walter Scheidel, "A Model of Demographic and Economic Change in Roman Egypt After the Antonine Plague," *Journal of Roman Archaeology* 15 (2002): 97–114; Scheidel, "Roman Wellbeing." Roger Bagnall, "Effects of Plague: Model and Evidence," *Journal of Roman Archaeology* 15 (2002): 114–20 offers a different view.

75. Michael McCormick et al., "Climate Change under the Roman Empire and Its Successors, 100 BC–800 AD: A First Synthesis Based on Multi-Proxy Natural Scientific and Historical Evidence," *Journal of Interdisciplinary History* 43 (2012): 169–220.

76. Jan Baeten et al., "Faecal Biomarkers and Archaeobotanical Analyses of Sediments from a Public Latrine Shed New Light on Ruralisation in Sagalassos, Turkey," *Journal of Archaeological Science* 39 (2012): 1143–59.

77. Roger Bagnall, *Egypt in Late Antiquity* (Berkeley: University of California Press, 1993); Andrew Watson, *Agricultural Innovation in the Early Islamic World* (Cambridge, UK: Cambridge University Press, 1982).

78. S. Mays and N. Beavan, "An Investigation of Diet in Early Anglo-Saxon England Using Carbon and Nitrogen Stable Isotope Analysis of Human Bone Collagen," *Journal of Archaeological Science* 39 (2012): 867–74.

79. See Bagnall, *Egypt in Late Antiquity*.

80. Peter Brown, *The World of Late Antiquity AD 150–750* (London: Thames & Hudson, 1971), 7.

81. Andrea Giardina, "The Transition to Late Antiquity," in Scheidel et al., *Cambridge Economic History*, 746.

82. Edward Luttwak, *The Grand Strategy of the Byzantine Empire* (Cambridge, MA: Harvard University Press, 2009), 1.

83. See particularly Ward-Perkins, *Fall of Rome*; Guy Halsall, *Barbarian Migrations and the Roman West, 367–568* (Cambridge, UK: Cambridge University Press, 2007); Willem Jongman, "Gibbon Was Right: The Decline and Fall of the Roman Economy," in Olivier Hekster et al., eds., *Crises and the Roman Empire* (Leiden: Brill, 2007), 183–99.

84. For example, see the British sites of Colchester (Christopher Hawkes and M. R. Hull, *Camulodunum I* [London: Reports of the Research Committee of the Society of Antiquaries 14, 1947]; Christopher Hawkes and P. J. Crummy, *Camulodunum II* [Colchester: Colchester Archaeological Report 11, 1995]; P. J. Crummy, *Aspects of Anglo-Saxon and Norman Colchester* [London: Council for British Archaeology Research Report 39 and Colchester: Colchester Archaeological Report 1, 1981], and *Excavations at Lion Walk, Balkerne Lane, and Middleborough, Colchester, Essex* [Colchester: Colchester Archaeological Report 3, 1984]); Wroxeter (R. White and Philip Barker, *Wroxeter: Life and Death of a Roman City* [London: Tempus, 1998]; Philip Barker, *The Baths Basilica, Wroxeter* [London: English Heritage, 1997]); St. Albans (D. Neal et al., *Excavations of the Iron Age, Roman, and Mediaeval Settlement at Gorhambury, St. Albans* [London: HBMC, 1990]), or London (W. F. Grimes, *The Excavation of Roman and Medieval London* [London 1968]); the Italian sites of Rome (Eva Margareta Steinby, ed., *Lexicon Topographicum Urbis Romae*, 6 vols. [Rome: Quasar, 1993–2000]; Roger Coates-Stephens, "Housing in Early Medieval Rome," *Papers of the British School at Rome* 64 [1996]: 239–59), Naples (Paul Arthur, *Naples, from Roman Town to City-State* [Rome: British School at Rome, 2002]), or San Giovanni di Ruoti (Joann Freed, "San Giovanni di Ruoti: Cultural Discontinuity Between the Early and Late Roman Empire in Southern Italy," in Caroline Malone and Simon Stoddart, eds., *Papers in Italian Archaeology* [Oxford: British Archaeological Reports International Series 246, 1985], 4:179–93, and the overall survey of Neil Christie, *From Constantine to Charlemagne: An Archaeology of Italy, AD 300–800* [London: Ashgate, 2006]); and the Egyptian sites of Coptos (Sharon Herbert and Andrea Berlin, "Excavations at Coptos (Qift) in Upper Egypt, 1987–1992," *Journal of Roman Archaeology* 53, suppl. [2003]) or Bakchias (G. Bitelli et al., *The Bologna and Lecce Universities Joint Archaeological Mission in Egypt: Ten Years of Excavation at Bakchias, 1993–2002* [Naples: Graus, 2003]).

85. Timothy Insoll, *The Archaeology of Islam* (Oxford: Blackwell, 1999); Marcus Milwright, *An Introduction to Islamic Archaeology* (Edinburgh: Edinburgh University Press, 2010).

86. Wickham, *Framing*.

87. Alan Harvey, *Economic Expansion in the Byzantine Empire 900–1200* (Cambridge, UK: Cambridge University Press, 1989); Angeliki Laiou, ed., *The Economic History of Byzantium: From the Seventh through the Fifteenth Century* (Washington, DC: Dumbarton Oaks, 2002); Branko Milanovic, "An Estimate of

Average Income and Inequality in Byzantium around the Year 1000," *Review of Income and Wealth* 52 (2006): 449–70.

88. Milanovic, "Estimate," 454.

89. Van Zanden, cited in Milanovic, "Estimate," 460; Gregory Clark, "The Condition of the Working Class in England, 1209–2004," *Journal of Political Economy* 113 (2005): 1308.

90. Milanovic, "Estimate," 450; Robert Lopez, "The Dollar of the Middle Ages," *Journal of Economic History* 11 (1951): 215.

91. Peter Lock and Guy Sanders, eds., *The Archaeology of Medieval Greece* (Oxford: Oxbow, 1996); Sigalos, *Housing*; John Bintliff and Hanna Stöger, eds., *Medieval and Post-Medieval Greece: The Corfu Papers* (Oxford: British Archaeological Reports International Series 2023, 2009); Lynne Schepartz et al., eds., *New Directions in the Skeletal Biology of Greece* (Princeton: American School of Classical Studies, 2009).

92. See, for example, James Graham-Campbell and Magdalena Valor, eds., *The Archaeology of Medieval Europe I: The Eighth to Twelfth Centuries* (Aarhus: Aarhus Universitetsforlag, 2006); Jane Grenville, *Medieval Housing* (London: Cassell, 1999); Tadhag O'Keefe, ed., *The Archaeology of Medieval Europe II: Twelfth to Sixteenth Centuries* (London: University College London, 2008); C. M. Woolgar et al., eds., *Food in Medieval England: Diet and Nutrition* (New York: Oxford University Press, 2009).

93. Laurie Reitsema et al., "Preliminary Evidence for Medieval Polish Diet from Carbon and Nitrogen Stable Isotopes," *Journal of Archaeological Science* 37 (2010): 1413–23.

94. Sevket Pamuk, "The Black Death and the Origins of the 'Great Divergence' across Europe, 1300–1600," *European Review of Economic History* 11 (2007): 289–317.

95. For example, Allen, "Great Divergence"; Clark, "Condition"; Paolo Malanima, "Wages, Productivity and Working Time in Italy 1300–1913," *Journal of European Economic History* 36 (2007): 127–74; "The Long Decline of a Leading Economy: GDP in Central and Northern Italy, 1300–1913," *European Review of Economic History* 15 (2010): 169–219; Pamuk, "Black Death."

96. Maddison, *World Economy*.

97. Luis Angeles, "GDP Per Capita or Real Wages? Making Sense of Conflicting Views on Pre-Industrial Europe," *Explorations in Economic History* 45 (2008): 147–63.

98. See the discussion in A. E. Aston and T. Philpin, eds., *The Brenner Debate* (Cambridge, UK: Cambridge University Press, 1985).

99. Sylvia Thrupp, "Medieval Industry 1000–1500," in Carlo Cipolla, ed., *The Fontana Economic History of Europe I: The Middle Ages* (Glasgow: Fontana, 1972), 221–73; Benjamin Kedar, *Merchants in Crisis: Genoese and Venetian Men of Affairs and the Fourteenth-Century Depression* (New Haven: Yale University Press, 1976); Maureen Mazzaoui, *The Italian Cotton Industry in the Later Middle Ages, 1100–1600* (Cambridge, UK: Cambridge University Press, 1981); Harry Miskimin, *The*

Economy of Early Renaissance Europe, 1300–1460 (Englewood Cliffs, NJ: Prentice Hall, 1969).

100. Edwin Hunt and James Murray, *A History of Business in Medieval Europe 1200–1550* (Cambridge, UK: Cambridge University Press, 1999), summarize this research.

101. E.g., B. H. Slicher van Bath, *The Agrarian History of Western Europe A.D. 500–1850* (London: Arnold, 1963); Gregory Clark, "Productivity Growth without Technical Change in European Agriculture before 1850," *Journal of Economic History* 47 (1987): 419–32; David Grigg, *The Transformation of Agriculture in the West* (Oxford: Blackwell, 1992).

102. Barrett et al., "Dark Age Economics" and "Interpreting the Expansion of Sea Fishing in Medieval Europe Using Stable Isotope Analysis of Archaeological Cod Bones," *Journal of Archaeological Science* 38 (2011): 1516–24; Cavaciocchi, *Alimentazione*; Müldner and Richards, "Fast or Feast" and "Stable Isotope Evidence"; Salamon et al., "Consilience of Historical and Isotopic Approaches," 1667–72.

103. Koepke and Baten, "Agricultural Specialization"; Carlo Cipolla, ed., *The Fontana Economic History of Europe II: The Sixteenth and Seventeenth Centuries* (Glasgow: Fontana, 1974).

104. There is a huge amount of evidence, much of it described in Fernand Braudel, *Civilization and Capitalism, 15th–18th Centuries I: The Structures of Everyday Life,* trans. Siân Reynolds (New York: Harper and Row, 1981); Carlo Cipolla, *Europe before the Industrial Revolution: European Society and Economy, 1000–1700,* 3rd ed. (London: Routledge, 1993); Dyer, *Standards of Living*; Christopher Dyer and Richard Jones, eds., *Deserted Villages Revisited* (Hertford: University of Hertfordshire Press, 2010); W. G. Hoskins, "The Rebuilding of Rural England, 1570–1640," *Past and Present* 4 (1953): 44–59; Matthew Johnson, *An Archaeology of Capitalism* (Oxford: Blackwell, 1996); Daniel Smail, *Goods and Debts in Mediterranean Europe* (Draft manuscript, 2010).

105. Production: Jan de Vries and Ad van der Woude, *The First Modern Economy: Success, Failure, and Perseverance in the Dutch Economy, 1500–1815* (Cambridge, UK: Cambridge University Press, 1997); John Blair and Nigel Ramsay, eds., *English Medieval Industries: Craftsmen, Techniques, Products* (London: Continuum, 2003); Elizabeth Smith and Michael Wolfe, eds., *Technology and Resource Use in Medieval Europe: Cathedrals, Mills, and Mines* (Aldershot, UK: Variorum, 1998). Longer hours: de Vries, *Industrious Revolution*. Fossil fuels: John Hatcher, *The History of the British Coal Industry I: Before 1700: Towards the Age of Coal* (Oxford: Oxford University Press, 1993); Paolo Malanima, "The Energy Basis for Early Modern Growth, 1650–1820," in M. Prak, ed., *Early Modern Capitalism: Economic and Social Change in Europe, 1400–1800* (London: Routledge, 2000); Richard Unger, "Energy Sources for the Dutch Golden Age: Peat, Wind, and Coal," *Research in Economic History* 9 (1984): 221–53.

106. M. Kleiber, *The Fire of Life: An Introduction to Animal Energetics* (New York: Wiley, 1961); T. H. Clutton-Brock, ed., *Primate Ecology* (New York: Academic Press, 1989).

107. R. Bailey, "The Behavioral Ecology of Efe Pygmy Men in the Ituru Forest, Zaire" (University of Michigan Museum of Anthropology Paper 86, Ann Arbor, 1991); P. Dwyer, "Etolo Hunting Performance and Energetics," *Human Ecology* 11 (1983): 145–74; Richard Lee, *The !Kung San: Men, Women, and Work in a Foraging Society* (Cambridge, UK: Cambridge University Press, 1979); G. Silberbauer, *Hunter and Habitat in the Central Kalahari Desert* (Cambridge, UK: Cambridge University Press, 1981); P. T. Katzmaryk et al., "Resting Metabolic Rate and Daily Energy Expenditure among Two Indigenous Siberian Groups," *American Journal of Human Biology* 6 (2005): 719–30; Llorenç Picornell Gelabert et al., "The Ethnoarchaeology of Firewood Management in the Fang Villages of Equatorial Guinea, Central Africa: Implications for the Interpretation of Wood Fuel Remains from Archaeological Sites," *Journal of Anthropological Archaeology* 30 (2011): 375–84.

108. Richard Klein, *The Human Career*, 3rd ed. (Chicago: University of Chicago Press, 2009), 262–71.

109. Ibid., table 4.10.

110. Richard Wrangham, *Catching Fire* (London: Profile, 2009).

111. N. Goren-Inbar et al., "Evidence of Hominin Control of Fire at Gesher Benot Ya'aqov, Israel," *Science* 204 (2004): 725–27; N. Alperson-Afil, "Continual Fire-Making by Hominins at Gesher Benot Ya'aqov, Israel," *Quaternary Science Reviews* 27 (2008): 1733–39.

112. John Gowlett, "The Early Settlement of Northern Europe: Fire History in the Context of Climate Change and the Social Brain," *Comptes Rendus de Palévolution* 5 (2006): 299–310; R. Preece et al., "Humans in the Hoxnian: Habitat, Context and Fire Use at Beeches Pit, West Stow, Suffolk, UK," *Journal of Quaternary Science* 21 (2006): 485–96; H. Thieme, "The Lower Paleolithic Art of Hunting," in Clive Gamble and M. Parr, eds., *The Hominid Individual in Context* (London: Routledge, 2005), 115–32.

113. H. Bocherens et al., "Paleoenvironmental and Paleodietary Implications of Isotopic Biogeochemistry of Last Interglacial Neanderthal and Mammoth Bones in Scladina Cane (Belgium)," *Journal of Archaeological Science* 26 (1999): 599–607; "New Isotopic Evidence for Dietary Habits of Neandertals from Belgium," *Journal of Human Evolution* 40 (2001): 497–505; Laura Niven, *The Palaeolithic Occupation of Vogelherd Cave: Implications for the Subsistence Behaviour of Late Neanderthals and Early Modern Humans* (Tübingen: Kerns, 2006); Michael Richards et al., "Neanderthal Diet at Vindija and Neanderthal Predation: The Evidence from Stable Isotopes," *Proceedings of the National Academy of Sciences* 97 (2000): 7663–66; "Isotopic Dietary Analysis of a Neanderthal and Associated Fauna from the Site of Jonzac (Charante-Maritime), France," *Journal of Human Evolution* 55 (2008): 179–85; Michael Richards and Ralf Schmitz, "Isotopic Evidence for the Diet of the Neanderthal Type Specimen," *Antiquity* 82 (2009): 553–59.

114. Anne Delagnes and William Rendu, "Shifts in Neanderthal Mobility, Technology and Subsistence Strategies in Western France," *Journal of Archaeological Science* 38 (2011): 1771–83.

115. W. Leonard and M. Robertson, "Comparative Primate Energetics and

Hominid Evolution," *American Journal of Physical Anthropology* 102 (1997): 265–81; Brent Sørenson and W. Leonard, "Neanderthal Energetics and Foraging Efficiency," *Journal of Human Evolution* 40 (2001): 483–95; Brent Sørenson, "Energy Use by Eem Neanderthals," *Journal of Archaeological Science* 36 (2009): 2201–5.

116. W. Leonard and M. Robertson, "Nutritional Requirements in Human Evolution: A Bioenergetics Approach," *American Journal of Human Biology* 4 (1992): 179–85.

117. Ralf Kittler et al., "Molecular Evolution of *Pediculus humanus* and the Origin of Clothing," *Current Biology* 13 (2003): 1414–17; Andrew Kitchen et al., "Genetic Analysis of Human Head and Clothing Lice Indicates an Early Origin of Clothing Use in Archaic Hominins" (paper, 79th annual meeting of the American Association of Physical Anthropologists, 2010), *Abstracts of AAPA Poster and Podium Sessions*, 154, http://physanth.org/annual-meeting/2010/79th-annual-meeting-2010/2010%20AAPA%20Abstracts.pdf.

118. Erik Trinkaus and Hong Shang, "Anatomical Evidence for the Antiquity of Human Footwear," *Journal of Archaeological Science* 35 (2008): 1928–33.

119. Klein, *Human Career*, 543–49.

120. Helen Wilkins, "Transformational Change in Proto-Buildings: A Quantitative Study of Thermal Behavior and Its Relationship with Social Functionality," *Journal of Archaeological Science* 36 (2009): 150–56.

121. D. Nadel, "The Organisation of Space in a Fisher-Hunter-Gatherers' Camp at Ohalo II, Israel," in M. Otte, ed., *Nature et culture* (Liège: Université de Liège, 1996), 373–88.

122. Bar-Yosef and Valla, *Natufian Culture in the Levant*, and Steven Mithen, *After the Ice: A Global Human History 20,000–5000 BC* (Cambridge, MA: Harvard University Press, 2003) offer good, if now somewhat dated, surveys.

123. Gordon Hillman et al., "New Evidence of Lateglacial Cereal Cultivation at Abu Hureyra on the Euphrates," *The Holocene* 11 (2001): 383–93.

124. See Mithen, *After the Ice*, 46–55; Graeme Barker, *The Agricultural Revolution in Prehistory: Why Did Foragers Become Farmers?* (Oxford: Oxford University Press, 2006), 117–31; Metin Eren, ed., *Hunter-Gatherer Behavior: Human Response during the Younger Dryas* (Walnut Creek, CA: Left Coast Press, 2012).

125. T. Watkins, "The Origins of the House and Home?" *World Archaeology* 21 (1990): 336–47; Peter Akkermans and Glenn Schwartz, *The Archaeology of Syria* (Cambridge, UK: Cambridge University Press, 2003), 49–57.

126. Dorian Fuller, "Contrasting Patterns in Crop Domestication and Domestication Rates," *Annals of Botany* (2007): 1–22; Susan Colledge et al., "Archaeobotanical Evidence for the Spread of Farming in the Eastern Mediterranean," *Current Anthropology* 45, suppl. (2004): S35–S58; Susan Colledge and James Connolly, eds., *The Origins and Spread of Domestic Plants in Southwest Asia and Europe* (Walnut Creek, CA: AltaMira, 2007).

127. Clark Larsen, "Biological Changes in Human Populations with Agriculture," *Annual Review of Anthropology* 24 (1995): 185–213; "The Agricultural Revolution as Environmental Catastrophe," *Quaternary International* 150 (2006): 12–20;

George Armelagos and Kristin Harper, "Genomics at the Origins of Agriculture," *Evolutionary Anthropology* 14 (2005): 68–77, 109–21.

128. See Barker, *Agricultural Revolution*; Fuller, "Contrasting Patterns"; Mark Nathan Cohen, ed., "Rethinking the Origins of Agriculture," *Current Anthropology* 50, suppl. (2009); Brian Boyd, *People and Animals in Levantine Prehistory, 10,000–8000 BC* (Cambridge, UK: Cambridge University Press, 2010).

129. Andrew Sherratt, *Economy and Society in Prehistoric Europe* (Edinburgh: Edinburgh University Press, 1997), 155–248.

130. Yosef Garfinkel et al., "The Domestication of Water: The Neolithic Well at Sha'ar Hagolan, Jordan Valley, Israel," *Antiquity* 80 (2006): 686–96; "Large-Scale Storage of Grain Surplus in the 6th Millennium BC: The Silos of Tel Tsaf," *Antiquity* 83 (2009): 309–25.

131. José Luis Araus et al., "Estimated Wheat Yields during the Emergence of Agriculture Based on the Carbon Isotope Discrimination of Grains: Evidence from a 10th Millennium BP Site on the Euphrates," *Journal of Archaeological Science* 28 (2001): 341–50; "Productivity in Prehistoric Agriculture," *Journal of Archaeological Science* 30 (2003): 681–89; Bogaard et al., "Impact of Manuring," 335–43.

132. Abu Hureyra: Andrew Moore et al., *Village on the Euphrates* (New York: Oxford University Press, 2000). Çatalhöyük: Ian Hodder, *The Leopard's Tale: Revealing the Mysteries of Çatalhöyük* (London: Thames & Hudson, 2006). Mesopotamia: Susan Pollock, *Ancient Mesopotamia* (Cambridge, UK: Cambridge University Press, 1999), 78–148; Michael Roaf, "'Ubaid Social Organization and Social Activities as Seen from Tell Madhhur," in Elizabeth Henrickson and Ingolf Thuesen, eds., *Upon This Foundation: The 'Ubaid Reconsidered* (Copenhagen: Museum Tusculanum, 1989), 91–146.

133. For the contested evidence from Jericho, see Ofer Bar-Yosef, "The Walls of Jericho: An Alternative Interpretation," *Current Anthropology* 27 (1986): 157–62; Thomas McClellan, "Early Fortifications: The Missing Walls of Jericho," *Baghdader Mitteilungen* 18 (2006): 593–610. Eridu: Fuad Safar et al., *Eridu* (Baghdad: State Organization of Antiquities and Heritage, 1981). Susa: M.-J. Stève and Hermann Gasche, *L'acropole de Suse* (Paris: Mémoires de la délégation archéologique française en Iran 46, 1971).

134. M. Littauer and Jan Crouwel, *Wheeled Vehicles and Ridden Animals in the Ancient Near East* (Leiden: Brill, 1981); Stuart Piggott, *The Earliest Wheeled Transport* (London: Thames & Hudson, 1983).

135. Charles Maisels, *The Emergence of Civilization: From Hunting and Gathering to Agriculture, Cities, and the State in the Near East* (London: Routledge, 1990); Hans Nissen, *The Early History of the Ancient Near East, 9000–2000 BC* (Chicago: University of Chicago Press, 1988); Pollock, *Ancient Mesopotamia*; Postgate, *Early Mesopotamia*; and Michael Roaf, *Cultural Atlas of Mesopotamia* (New York: Facts on File, 1990) provide excellent surveys of different parts of the period.

136. For example, Nathan MacDonald, *What Did the Ancient Israelites Eat?* (Grand Rapids, MI: Eerdmans, 2008); Carol Yokell, *Modeling Socioeconomic Evolu-*

tion and Continuity in Ancient Egypt: The Value and Limitations of Zooarchaeological Analyses (Oxford: Archeopress, 2004).

137. For example, Coulson and Vaughan, *Palaeodiet in the Aegean* and Sevi Triandaphyllou et al., "Isotopic Dietary Reconstruction of Humans from Middle Bronze Age Lerna, Argolid, Greece," *Journal of Archaeological Science* 35 (2008): 3028–34 for the Aegean.

138. Michael Jursa, "The Ancient Near East: Fiscal Regimes, Political Structures" (paper, Premodern Fiscal Regimes conference, Stanford University, May 27, 2010), table 1.

139. Postgate, *Early Mesopotamia*, 226–29.

140. Gary Feinman and Joyce Marcus, eds., *Archaic States* (Santa Fe, NM: School of American Research, 1998).

141. Eric Cline, *Sailing the Wine-Dark Sea: International Trade in the Aegean Late Bronze Age* (Oxford: British Archaeological Reports International Series 591, 1994); William Parkinson and Michael Galaty, eds., *Archaic State Interaction: The Eastern Mediterranean in the Bronze Age* (Santa Fe: School for American Research, 2010); George Bass, "Cape Gelidonya Shipwreck," and Cemal Pulak, "Uluburun Shipwreck," in Cline, *Oxford Handbook of the Bronze Age Aegean*, 797–803 and 862–76.

142. There are many surveys of Bronze Age Mediterranean archaeology, but the following have particularly good accounts and references to site reports—Egypt: Barry Kemp, *Ancient Egypt* (Cambridge, UK: Cambridge University Press, 1989); Mesopotamia: Postgate, *Early Mesopotamia*, 73–108, 191–240; Syria: Akkermans and Schwartz, *Archaeology of Syria*, 211–359; Aegean: Oliver Dickinson, *The Aegean Bronze Age* (Cambridge, UK: Cambridge University Press, 1994), 95–207; Elam: Daniel Potts, *The Archaeology of Elam* (Cambridge, UK: Cambridge University Press, 1999), 85–257.

143. John McEnroe, "A Typology of Minoan Neopalatial Houses," *American Journal of Archaeology* 86 (1982): 3–19.

144. Causes of the collapse: Nüzhet Dalfes et al., *Third Millennium BC Climate Change and Old World Collapse* (Berlin: Springer, 1997); Nadine Moeller, "The First Intermediate Period: A Time of Famine and Climate Change?" *Ägypten und Levante* 15 (2006): 153–67; Marc van de Mieroop, *A History of Ancient Egypt* (Oxford: Wiley-Blackwell, 2010), 86–96. Doubts over its reality: Lisa Cooper, *Early Urbanism on the Syrian Euphrates* (London: Routledge, 2006); Anne Porter, *Mobile Pastoralism and the Formation of Near Eastern Civilizations: Weaving Together Society* (Cambridge, UK: Cambridge University Press, 2012). Finné et al. ("Climate in the Eastern Mediterranean") suggest that the climatological data do point to arid conditions around 2200 BCE, but do not indicate the kind of rapid aridification that many of the climate-change theories propose.

145. Ugarit: O. Callot, *Une maison à Ugarit: études d'architecture domestique* (Paris: Editions recherché sur les civilisations, 1983) and *La tranchée "ville sud": études d'architecture domestique* (Paris: Editions recherché sur les civilisations, 1994); M. Yon, *La cité d'Ougarit sur le tell de Ras Shamra* (Paris: Editions recherché

sur les civilisations, 1997). Olynthus: Robinson et al., *Excavations at Olynthus*; Cahill, *Household and City*.

146. William Ward and Martha Joukowsky, eds., *The Crisis Years: The 12th Century BC* (Dubuque, IA: Kendall-Hunt, 1992); Robert Drews, *The End of the Bronze Age* (Princeton: Princeton University Press, 1993); Christopher Bachhuber and Gareth Roberts, eds., *Forces of Transformation: The End of the Bronze Age in the Mediterranean* (Oxford: Oxbow, 2009); Yasur-Landau Assaf, *The Philistines and Aegean Migration at the End of the Late Bronze Age* (Cambridge, UK: Cambridge University Press, 2010).

147. Akkermans and Schwartz, *Archaeology of Syria*, 360–77; Philip King and Lawrence Stager, *Life in Biblical Israel* (Louisville, KY: Westminster John Knox Press, 2001); Morris, "Early Iron Age Greece"; Sarah Murray, "Imports, Trade, and Society in Early Greece" (PhD dissertation, Stanford University, forthcoming).

148. Morris, "Early Iron Age Greece."

149. Lawrence Stager, "The Archaeology of the Family in Ancient Israel," *Bulletin of the American Schools of Oriental Research* 260 (1985): 1–35; Alexander Mazarakis Ainian, *From Rulers' Dwellings to Temples: Architecture, Religion, and Society in Early Iron Age Greece* (Jonsered, Sweden: Studies in Mediterranean Archaeology, 1997); Rosa Maria Albanese Procelli, *Sicani, Siculi, Elimi: Forme di identità, modi di contatto e processi di trasformazione* (Milan: Longanesi, 2003); Michel Py, *Les Gaulois du Midi: de la fin du l'âge du bronze à la conquête romaine* (Paris: Hachette, 1993).

150. Morris, "Early Iron Age Greece"; Legouilloux, "L'alimentation."

151. Anthony Snodgrass, "The Coming of the Iron Age in Greece: Europe's First Bronze/Iron Transition," in Marie-Louise Stig-Sørenson and Richard Thomas, eds., *The Bronze-Iron Transition in Europe* (Oxford: British Archaeological Reports International Series 483, 1989), 1:22–35.

152. First substantial cache of iron tools in Greece: Alexander Mazarakis Ainian, "Skala Oropou," *Praktika tis en Athinais Arkhaiologikis Etaireia* (1998): 132–44. Mediterranean pattern: Anthony Snodgrass, "Iron and Early Metallurgy in the Mediterranean," in Theodore Wertime and James Muhly, eds., *The Coming of the Age of Iron* (New Haven: Yale University Press, 1980), 335–74.

153. Near East: Peter Bedford, "The Persian Near East," in Scheidel et al., *Cambridge Economic History*, 302–29. West Mediterranean: Ramon Buxó, "Botanical and Archaeological Dimensions of the Colonial Encounter," in Michael Dietler and Caroline López-Ruiz, eds., *Colonial Encounters in Ancient Iberia* (Chicago: University of Chicago Press, 2009), 155–68; Carlos Gómez Bellard, *Ecohistoria del paisaje agrario: La agricultura fenicio-púnica en al Mediterráneo* (Valencia: University of Valencia Press, 2003); Michael Dietler, "The Iron Age in the Western Mediterranean," in Scheidel et al., *Cambridge Economic History*, 242–76; Jean-Paul Morel, "Early Rome and Italy," in Scheidel et al., *Cambridge Economic History*, 487–510; Morris, "Early Iron Age Greece"; Py, *Les Gaulois*.

154. Sherratt, *Economy and Society*.

155. Compare Sarah Morris, *Daidalos and the Origins of Greek Art* (Princeton: Princeton University Press, 1992) and Morris, "Early Iron Age Greece."

156. Walter Scheidel, "Demography," in Scheidel et al., *Cambridge Economic History*, 42.

157. Morris, *Why the West Rules*, 640–45.

158. Food and Agriculture Organization, *Statistical Yearbook*, table 4; United Nations, *2003 Energy Statistics*.

159. See Smil, *General Energetics* and *Energy in World History*; John L. Buck, *Chinese Farm Economy* (Chicago: University of Chicago Press, 1930) and *Land Utilization in China* (Shanghai: Nanjing University Press, 1937); Dwight Perkins, *Agricultural Development in China, 1368–1968* (Chicago: Aldine, 1969).

160. See the statistical tables in G. C. Allen, *A Short Economic History of Modern Japan, 1867–1937* (London: Allen & Unwin, 1946) and Thomas C. Smith, *Political Change and Industrial Development in Japan: Government Enterprise, 1868–1880* (Stanford: Stanford University Press, 1955).

161. Conrad Totman, *The Green Archipelago: Forestry in Preindustrial Japan* (Berkeley: University of California Press, 1989); *Early Modern Japan* (Berkeley: University of California Press, 1993), 223–79.

162. See Buck, *Chinese Farm Economy* and *Land Utilization* and Perkins, *Agricultural Development*, plus Philip Huang, *The Peasant Economy and Social Change in North China* (Stanford: Stanford University Press, 1985).

163. Discussed in Morris, *Why the West Rules*, 11–21.

164. Maddison, *World Economy*; Perkins, *Agricultural Development*; Mark Elvin, *The Pattern of the Chinese Past* (Stanford: Stanford University Press, 1973).

165. Harriet Zurndorfer, "Beyond Sinology," *Journal of the Economic and Social History of the Orient* 46 (2003): 355–71.

166. Pomeranz, *Great Divergence*, 39, 91–98; Sucheta Mazumdar, *Sugar and Society in China: Peasants, Technology, and the World Market* (Cambridge, MA: Harvard University Press, 1998).

167. Pessimists: Philip Huang, *The Peasant Family and Rural Development in the Lower Yangzi Region, 1350–1988* (Stanford: Stanford University Press, 1990); "Development or Involution in Eighteenth-Century Britain and China?" *Journal of Asian Studies* 61 (2002): 501–38. Wage data: Robert Allen, "Agricultural Productivity and Rural Incomes in England and the Yangzi Delta, c. 1620–c. 1820" (unpublished paper, 2006), http://www.nuffield.ox.ac.uk/General/Members/allen.aspx; Robert Allen et al., "Wages, Prices and Living Standards in China, 1738–1925: A Comparison with Europe, Japan and India," *Economic History Review* 64, supplement (2011): 8–38, http://www.nuffield.ox.ac.uk/General/Members/allen.aspx.

168. Robert Hartwell, "A Revolution in the Chinese Iron and Coal Industries during the Northern Sung, 960–1126 AD," *Journal of Asian Studies* 21 (1962): 155; see also Hartwell, "Markets, Technology, and the Structure of Enterprise in the Development of the 11th-Century Chinese Iron and Steel Industry," *Journal of Economic History* 26 (1966): 29–58; "A Cycle of Economic Change in Imperial

China: Coal and Iron in Northeast China, 750–1350," *Journal of Economic and Social History of the Orient* 10 (1967): 102–59.

169. Peter Golas, *Science and Civilisation in China V: Chemistry and Chemical Technology. Part 13: Mining* (Cambridge, UK: Cambridge University Press, 1999), 170n475.

170. Donald Wagner, *Science and Civilisation in China V: Chemistry and Chemical Technology. Part 11: Ferrous Metallurgy* (Cambridge, UK: Cambridge University Press, 2008), 279–80.

171. Cited from Dieter Kuhn, *The Age of Confucian Rule: The Song Transformation of China* (Cambridge, MA: Harvard University Press, 2009), 307–8n36.

172. Golas, *Science and Civilisation*, 376–83; Kuhn, *Age of Confucian Rule*, 231.

173. S. Hong et al., "A Reconstruction of Changes in Copper Production and Copper Emissions to the Atmosphere during the Past 7000 Years," *Science of the Total Environment* 188 (1996): 183–93.

174. Hartwell, "Revolution," 159–60.

175. Jang-Sik Park et al., "Transition in Cast Iron Technology of the Nomads of Mongolia," *Journal of Archaeological Science* 34 (2007): 1187–96; "A Technological Transition in Mongolia Evident in Microstructure, Chemical Composition, and Radiocarbon Age of Cast Iron Artifacts," *Journal of Archaeological Science* 35 (2008): 2465–70.

176. Elvin, *Pattern*; Kuhn, *Age of Confucian Rule*, 213–32.

177. http://news.bbc.co.uk/2/hi/asia-pacific/7156581.stm.

178. Kuhn, *Age of Confucian Rule*, 205; Klaas Ruitenbeek, *Carpentry and Building in Late Imperial China* (Leiden: Brill, 1993).

179. See note 155 above.

180. Perkins, *Agricultural Development*, 15.

181. See Jane Rowlandson, *Landowners and Tenants in Roman Egypt: The Social Relations of Agriculture in the Oxyrhynchite Nome* (Oxford: Clarendon, 1996), 247–52; Andrew Monson, *From the Ptolemies to the Romans: Political and Economic Change in Egypt* (Cambridge, UK: Cambridge University Press, 2012), 171–72.

182. Elvin, *Pattern*.

183. See Wong, *China Transformed*.

184. Maddison, *Contours*; Allen, "Agricultural Productivity"; Allen et al., "Wages, Prices, and Living Standards."

185. See Paul Smith and Richard von Glahn, eds., *The Song-Yuan-Ming Transition in Chinese History* (Cambridge, MA: Harvard University Press, 2003).

186. Frank, *ReOrient*; Rhoads Murphey, *The Outsiders: The Western Experience in India and China* (Ann Arbor: University of Michigan Press, 1977).

187. Samuel Adshead, *China in World History*, 3rd ed. (London: Longmans, 2000), 4–21 usefully highlights the similarities.

188. See particularly Walter Scheidel, ed., *Rome and China: Comparative Perspectives on Ancient World Empires* (New York: Oxford University Press, 2009) and Anna Razeto, "Imperial Structures and Urban Forms: A Comparative Study of Capital Cities in the Roman and Han Empires" (PhD thesis, University College

London, 2011). Fritz-Heiner Mutschler and Achim Mittag, eds., *Conceiving the Empire: China and Rome Compared* (New York: Oxford University Press, 2009) focuses more on comparing Roman and Han ideas of empire.

189. Sadao Nishijima, "The Economic and Social History of Former Han," and Patricia Ebrey, "The Economic and Social History of Later Han," both in Loewe, *Cambridge History of China*, 551–607 and 608–48.

190. Cho-yun Hsu, *Han Agriculture: The Formation of the Early Chinese Agrarian Economy (206 BC–AD 220)* (Seattle: University of Washington Press, 1980); Wang Zhiongshu, *Han Civilization*, trans. K. C. Chang (New Haven: Yale University Press, 1982).

191. Francesca Bray, *Science and Civilisation in China VI: Biology and Biological Technology. Part 6: Agriculture* (Cambridge, UK: Cambridge University Press, 1984).

192. Mark Lewis, *The Early Chinese Empires: Qin and Han* (Cambridge, MA: Harvard University Press, 2007), 103–15.

193. Francesca Bray, "The *Qimin yaoshu* (Essential Techniques for the Common People)" (unpublished paper, 2001, kindly provided to me by Professor Bray).

194. Hsu, *Han Agriculture*.

195. http://www.artsci.wustl.edu/~anthro/archy/projchina.html; http://english.peopledaily.com.cn/200602/22/eng20060222_244902.html.

196. Guo Qinghua, *The* Mingqi *Pottery Buildings of Han Dynasty China, 206 BC–AD 220* (Eastbourse, UK: Sussex University Press, 2010); Andrew Boyd, *Chinese Architecture and Town Planning: 1500 BC–AD 1911* (Chicago: University of Chicago Press, 1962); Robert Thorp, "Origins of Chinese Architectural Style: The Earliest Plans and Building Types," *Archives of Asian Art* 36 (1983): 22–39; Razeto, "Imperial Structures."

197. Donald Wagner, *Iron and Steel in Ancient China* (Leiden: Brill, 1993); Jang-Sik Park and Thilo Rehren, "Large-Scale 2nd to 3rd Century AD Bloomery Iron Smelting in Korea," *Journal of Archaeological Science* 38 (2011): 1180–90.

198. Walter Scheidel, "The Monetary Systems of the Han and Roman Empires," in Scheidel, *Rome and China*, 137–207.

199. Ying-shih Yü, *Trade and Expansion in Han China: A Study in the Structure of Sino-Barbarian Economic Relations* (Berkeley: University of California Press, 1967); Liu Xinru, *Ancient India and Ancient China: Trade and Religious Exchanges, AD 1–600* (Delhi: Oxford University Press, 1988); *Silk and Religion: An Exploration of Material Life and the Thought of People, AD 600–1200* (Delhi: Oxford University Press, 1996).

200. Morris, *Why the West Rules*, 270–75.

201. Mark Lewis, *China between Empires: The Northern and Southern Dynasties* (Cambridge, MA: Harvard University Press, 2009); Albert Dien, *Six Dynasties Civilization* (New Haven: Yale University Press, 2007).

202. Lien-Sheng Yang, "Notes on the Economic History of the Chin Dynasty," *Harvard Journal of Asiatic Studies* 9 (1947): 107–85.

203. Bray, *Science and Civilisation in China VI; The Rice Economy: Technology*

and Development in Asian Societies (Oxford: Oxford University Press, 1986); "*Qimin yaoshu.*"

204. Denis Twitchett, "The Monasteries and China's Economy in Medieval Times," *Bulletin of the School of Oriental and African Studies* 19 (1957): 526–49; "Lands under State Cultivation during the T'ang Dynasty," *Journal of the Economic and Social History of the Orient* 2 (1959): 162–203, 335–36; *Land Tenure and the Social Order in T'ang and Sung China* (London: School of Oriental and African Studies, 1961); Victor Xiong, "The Land-Tenure System of Tang China: A Study of the Equal Field System and the Turfan Documents," *T'oung Pao* 85 (1999): 328–90.

205. See Shufen Liu, "Jiankang and the Commercial Empire of the Southern Dynasties," in Scott Pearce et al., eds., *Culture and Power in the Reconstitution of the Chinese Realm, 200–600* (Cambridge, MA: Harvard University Press, 2001).

206. Denis Twitchett, "The Fragment of the T'ang Ordinances of the Department of Waterways Discovered at Tun-huang," *Asia Major* 6 (1957): 23–79; "Some Remarks on Irrigation under the T'ang," *T'oung Pao* 48 (1961): 175–94; "The T'ang Market System," *Asia Major* 12 (1966): 202–48.

207. Denis Twitchett, "Merchant, Trade, and Government in Late T'ang," *Asia Major* 14 (1968): 63–95.

208. Samuel Adshead, *Tang China* (London: Longmans, 2004); Lewis, *China between Empires.*

209. Yang Hong, "Changes in Urban Architecture, Interior Design, and Lifestyles Between the Han and Tang Dynasties," in Wu Hung, ed., *Between Han and Tang: Visual and Material Culture* (Beijing: Wenwu, 2003); John Kieschnick, *The Impact of Buddhism on Chinese Material Culture* (Princeton: Princeton University Press, 2003); Patricia Karetzky, *Court Art of the Tang* (Lanham, MD: University Press of America, 1996).

210. Cf. Wrigley, *Continuity, Chance and Change.*

211. See, for instance, Longwangcan in Shaanxi province: Shaanxi Institute of Archaeology, "The Upper Paleolithic Longwangcan Site in Shaanxi," *Chinese Archaeology* 8 (2008): 32–36; Zhang Jia-Fu et al., "The Palaeolithic Site of Longwangcan in the Middle Yellow River Valley, China," *Journal of Archaeological Science* 38 (2011): 1537–50.

212. Zhang Yue et al., "Zooarchaeological Perspectives on the Chinese Early and Late Paleolithic from the Ma'anshan Site (Guizhou, Southern China)," *Journal of Archaeological Science* 37 (2010): 2066–77; Elisabetta Boaretto et al., "Radiocarbon Dating of Charcoal and Bone Collagen Associated with Early Pottery at Yuchanyan Cave, Hunan Province, China," *Proceedings of the National Academy of Sciences* 106 (2009): 9595–9600, doi:10.1073/pnas.0900539106.

213. Yaroslav Kuzmin, "Chronology of the Earliest Pottery in East Asia," *Antiquity* 80 (2006): 362–71.

214. Abu Hureyra: Hillman et al., "New Evidence"; Diaotonghuan Cave: Z. Zhijun, "The Middle Yangtze Region in China Is One Place Where Rice Was Domesticated: Phytolith Evidence from the Diaotonghuan Cave, Northern Jiangxi,"

Antiquity 77 (1998): 885–97. Shizitan: Li Liu et al., "Plant Exploitation of the Last Foragers at Shizitan in the Middle Yellow River Valley, China," *Journal of Archaeological Science* 38 (2011): 3524–32. Yuchanyan: Mary Prendergast et al., "Resource Intensification in the Late Upper Paleolithic: A View from Southern China," *Journal of Archaeological Science* 36 (2009): 1027–37.

215. Zhang et al., "Palaeolithic Site of Longwangcan."

216. Biancamaria Aranguren et al., "Grinding Flour in Upper Palaeolithic Europe (25,000 Years BP)," *Antiquity* 81 (2007): 845–55.

217. Li Liu et al., "A Functional Analysis of Grinding Stones from an Early Holocene Site at Donghulin, North China," *Journal of Archaeological Science* (forthcoming).

218. Tao Dawei et al., "Starch Grain Analysis for Groundstone Tools from Neolithic Baiyinchanghan Site: Implications for their Function in Northeast China," *Journal of Archaeological Science* 38 (2011): 3577–83; Pia Atahan et al., "Early Neolithic Diets at Baijian, Wei River Valley, China: Stable Carbon and Nitrogen Analysis of Human and Faunal Remains," *Journal of Archaeological Science* 38 (2011): 2811–17.

219. I have benefited particularly from the papers given at the unpublished conference "The Origins of Sedentism and Agriculture in Early China," organized by Li Liu at Stanford University, April 23–24, 2012.

220. Jiang Lepin and Li Liu, "New Evidence for the Origins of Sedentism and Rice Domestication in the Lower Yangzi River, China," *Antiquity* 80 (2006): 355–61.

221. Dorian Fuller et al., "Presumed Domestication? Evidence for Wild Rice Cultivation and Domestication in the Fifth Millennium BC of the Lower Yangtze Region," *Antiquity* 81 (2007): 316–31.

222. Li Liu et al., "The Earliest Rice Domestication in China," *Antiquity* 81, no. 313 (2007), http://www.antiquity.ac.uk/liu1/index.html; "Evidence for the Early Beginning (c. 9000 ca. BP) of Rice Domestication: A Response," *The Holocene* 17 (2007): 1059–68; Dorian Fuller and Ling Qin, "Immature Rice and Its Archaeobotanical Recognition," *Antiquity* 82, no. 316 (2008), http://www.antiquity.ac.uk/projgall/fuller316; Fuller et al., "Rice Archaeobotany Revisited," *Antiquity* 82, no. 315 (2008), http://www.antiquity.ac.uk/projgall/fuller315.

223. Liu Xinyi et al., "River Valleys and Foothills: Changing Archaeological Perceptions of North China's Earliest Farms," *Antiquity* 83 (2009): 82–95; Chi Zhang and Hsiao-chun Hung, "The Emergence of Agriculture in Southern China," *Antiquity* 84 (2010): 11–25.

224. Zhang Zhongpei, "The Yangshao Period: Prosperity and the Transformation of Prehistoric Society," in Chang and Xu, *Formation of Chinese Civilization*, 60–64.

225. Hu Yaowu et al., "Stable Isotopic Analysis of Human Bones from Jiahu Site, Henan, China," *Journal of Archaeological Science* 33 (2006): 1319–30; "Stable Isotopic Analysis of Humans from Xiaojingshan Site," *Journal of Archaeological Science* 35 (2008): 2960–65; Jing et al., "Meat-Acquisition Patterns," 351–66; T. Cuc-

chi et al., "Early Neolithic Pig Domestication at Jiahu, Henan Province, China," *Journal of Archaeological Science* 38 (2011): 11–22.

226. Li Liu, *The Chinese Neolithic* (Cambridge, UK: Cambridge University Press, 2004), 35–38.

227. Jiang and Liu, "New Evidence," 355–61; Liu, *Chinese Neolithic*, 39–46, 74–95; Christian Peterson and Gideon Shelach, "Jiangzhai: Social and Economic Organization of a Middle Neolithic Chinese Village," *Journal of Archaeological Science* 31 (2012): 265–301.

228. Rita Lanehart et al., "Dietary Adaptation during the Longshan Period in China: Stable Isotope Analysis at Liangchengzhen (Southeastern Shandong)," *Journal of Archaeological Science* 38 (2011): 2171–81.

229. Shao Wangping, "The Formation of Civilization: The Interaction Sphere of the Longshan Period," in Chang and Xu, *Formation of Chinese Civilization*, 90.

230. Cho-yun Hsu, *Ancient China in Transition: An Analysis of Social Mobility, 722–222 BC* (Stanford: Stanford University Press, 1965), 107–8.

231. Li Feng, "Feudalism and the Western Zhou," *Harvard Journal of Asiatic Studies* 63 (2003): 115–44.

232. Shao, "Formation," 91; Lothar von Falkenhausen, *Chinese Society in the Age of Confucius (1000–250 BC)* (Los Angeles: Cotsen Institute, 2006), 410–11n30.

233. Benjamin Roberts et al., "The Development of Metallurgy in Eurasia," *Antiquity* 83 (2009): 1012–22.

234. Li Liu and Chen Xingcan, *State Formation in Early China* (London: Duckworth, 2003).

235. Lu Liancheng and Yan Wenming, "Society during the Three Dynasties," in Chang and Xu, *Formation of Chinese Civilization*, 158–60.

236. Jessica Rawson, "Western Zhou Archaeology," in Loewe and Shaughnessy, *Cambridge History of Ancient China*, 352–449; von Falkenhausen, *Chinese Society*.

237. Jessica Rawson, "A Bronze-Casting Revolution in the Western Zhou and Its Influence on the Provincial Industries," in Robert Maddin, ed., *The Beginning of the Use of Metals and Alloys* (Cambridge, MA: MIT Press, 1988), 228–38; Li Xueqin, *Eastern Zhou and Qin Civilization* (New Haven: Yale University Press, 1985), 272–76; Lu Liancheng, "The Eastern Zhou and the Growth of Regionalism," in Chang and Xu, *Formation of Chinese Civilization*, 205–10.

238. Liu, *Chinese Neolithic*, 108–11; Shanxi Fieldwork Team, "Monumental Structure from Ceremonial Precinct at Taosi Walled-Town in 2003," *Chinese Archaeology* 5 (2005): 51–58.

239. Kwang-chih Chang, *Shang Civilization* (New Haven: Yale University, 1980); Robert Thorp, *China in the Early Bronze Age* (Philadelphia: University of Pennsylvania Press, 2006).

240. Lu and Yan, "Society," 183–87.

241. von Falkenhausen, *Chinese Society*; Li Feng, *Landscape and Power in Early*

China: The Crisis and Fall of the Western Zhou 1045–771 BC (Cambridge, UK: Cambridge University Press, 2006), with references.

242. Hsu, *Ancient China*, 108–9.

243. Mark Lewis, "Warring States Political History," in Loewe and Shaughnessy, *Cambridge History of Ancient China*, 604–5.

244. Hsu, *Ancient China*, 81–88; "The Spring and Autumn Period," in Loewe and Shaughnessy, *Cambridge History of Ancient China*, 578.

245. Steven Sage, *Ancient Sichuan and the Unification of China* (Albany: State University of New York Press, 1992); Joseph Needham, *Science and Civilisation in China IV Part 3: Civil Engineering and Nautics* (Cambridge, UK: Cambridge University Press, 1971), 288–96.

246. Li, *Eastern Zhou*, 284–94; Wagner, *Iron and Steel*; von Falkenhausen, *Chinese Society*, 409–10n29.

247. Lothar von Falkenhausen, "The Waning of the Bronze Age: Material Culture and Social Developments, 770–481 BC," in Loewe and Shaughnessy, *Cambridge History of Ancient China*, 539; Li Xiating et al., *Art of the Houma Foundry* (Princeton: Princeton University Press, 1996).

248. Hsu, *Ancient China*, 117–18; Li, *Eastern Zhou*, 372–77; Scheidel, "Monetary Systems."

249. Roberts et al., "Development"; Li Chungxiang et al., "Ancient DNA Analysis of Desiccated Wheat Grains from a Bronze Age Cemetery in Xinjiang, China," *Journal of Archaeological Science* 38 (2011): 115–19.

250. J. P. Mallory and Victor Mair, *The Tarim Mummies* (London: Thames & Hudson, 2008).

251. Morris, *Why the West Rules*, 143–50, 625–26.

CHAPTER 4

1. For example, Robert Carneiro, "On the Relationship between Size of Population and Complexity of Social Organization," *Southwestern Journal of Anthropology* 23 (1967): 234–41; Andrew Forge, "Normative Factors in the Settlement Size of Neolithic Cultivators (New Guinea)," in Peter Ucko et al., eds., *Man, Settlement and Urbanism* (London: Duckworth, 1972), 363–76; Roland Fletcher, *The Limits of Settlement Growth* (Cambridge, UK: Cambridge University Press, 1995); de Long and Schleifer, "Princes and Merchants," 671–702; Edward Glaeser, *The Triumph of the City* (New York: Penguin, 2011).

2. *The Economist Pocket World in Figures, 2004 Edition* (London: Profile, 2004), 20.

3. Fletcher, *Limits*.

4. Hansen, *Shotgun Method*; Nicholas Postgate, "How Many Sumerians Per

Hectare? Probing the Anatomy of an Early City," *Cambridge Archaeological Journal* 4 (1994): 47–65.

5. Tertius Chandler, *Four Thousand Years of Urban Growth: An Historical Census* (Lewiston, NY: St David's University Press, 1987); Tertius Chandler and Gerald Fox, *Three Thousand Years of Urban Growth* (New York: Academic Press, 1974). Chandler's 1987 estimates for 2000 BCE–1988 CE are also available online, at http://web.archive.org/web/20080211233018/http://www.etext.org/Politics/World.Systems/datasets/citypop/civilizations/citypops_2000BC-1988AD. Paul Bairoch's *Cities and Economic Development: From the Dawn of History to the Present* (Chicago: University of Chicago Press, 1988) is also valuable, but less systematic. George Modelski's website "Cities of the Ancient World" (https://faculty.washington.edu/modelski/WCITI2.html) covers Southwest Asia and Egypt only in the period down to 1200 BCE. The Wikipedia entry "Historical Urban Community Sizes" (http://en.wikipedia.org/wiki/Historical_urban_community_sizes) depends largely on data gathered from Chandler, Modelski, and Bairoch.

6. Chandler, *Four Thousand Years*, 461; Morris, "Growth of Greek Cities," 42–43.

7. Morris, *Why the West Rules*, 158.

8. *Economist Pocket World*, 20.

9. Christopher Bayly, *The Birth of the Modern World 1789–1914* (Oxford: Blackwell, 2004), 189, and many other sources.

10. Chandler, *Four Thousand Years*, 492.

11. Fernand Braudel, *Civilization and Capitalism, 15th–18th Centuries* I: *The Structures of Everyday Life*, trans. Siân Reynolds (New York: Harper and Row, 1981), 528.

12. Chandler, for instance (*Four Thousand Years*, 485), says 681,000.

13. Cipolla, *Europe before the Industrial Revolution*, 304; Braudel, *Civilization and Capitalism*, 548.

14. Chandler, *Four Thousand Years*, 483; Bairoch, *Cities and Economic Development*, 378; John Haldon, personal communication, October 2005; http://www.medievallogistics.bham.ac.uk/.

15. Haldon, personal communication, October 2005.

16. Eric Jones, *The European Miracle: Environments, Economies and Geopolitics in the History of Europe and Asia*, 3rd ed. (Cambridge, UK: Cambridge University Press, 2003), 178; Chandler, *Four Thousand Years*, 481; Bairoch, *Cities and Economic Development*, 378.

17. Chandler, *Four Thousand Years*, 478.

18. Frank, *ReOrient*, 12; Bairoch, *Cities and Economic Development*, 378; Haldon, personal communication, October 2005. Cairo: Janet Abu-Lughod, *Cairo: 1,001 Years of the City Victorious* (Princeton: Princeton University Press, 1971).

19. Black Death: Ole Benedictow, *The Black Death 1346–1353: The Complete History* (Rochester, NY: Boydell Press, 2004). Cairo: Chandler, *Four Thousand Years*, 476; Abu-Lughod, *Cairo*; Michael Dols, *The Black Death in the Middle East* (Princeton: Princeton University Press, 1974).

20. Based on Michael Brett, "Population and Conversion to Islam in Egypt in the Mediaeval Period," in U. Vermeulen and J. van Steenbergen, eds., *Egypt and Syria in the Fatimid, Ayyubid and Mamluk Eras* (Leuven: Peeters, 2005), 4:4, suggesting that Cairo's population peaked at 450,000 on the eve of the Black Death in the 1340s.

21. Albert Hourani, *A History of the Arab Peoples*, 2nd ed. (New York: Warner, 2003), 112; Chandler, *Four Thousand Years*, 473; Bairoch, *Cities and Economic Development*, 378; Haldon, personal communication, October 2005.

22. Haldon, personal communication, October 2005.

23. Wickham, *Framing*, 612.

24. Cordoba: Bairoch, *Cities and Economic Development*, 118; de Long and Schleifer, "Princes and Merchants," 678; Chandler, *Four Thousand Years*, 467. Constantinople: Haldon, personal communication, October 2005. Baghdad: Richard Hodges and David Whitehouse, *Mohamed, Charlemagne, and the Origins of Europe* (London: Duckworth, 1983).

25. Chandler, *Four Thousand Years*, 468; Ira Lapidus, *A History of Islamic Societies*, 2nd ed. (Cambridge, UK: Cambridge University Press, 2002), 56. Other large preindustrial cities: Fletcher, *Limits*.

26. Chandler, *Four Thousand Years*, 468; Haldon, personal communication, October 2005.

27. Haldon, personal communication, October 2005. Population decline at Constantinople: John Haldon, *Byzantium in the Seventh Century* (Cambridge, UK: Cambridge University Press, 1990), 114–17.

28. Haldon, personal communication, October 2005.

29. Constantinople: Averil Cameron, *The Mediterranean World in Late Antiquity AD 395–600* (London: Routledge, 1993), 13; Wickham, *Framing*, 29; Chandler, *Four Thousand Years*, 465. Grain supply: Cyril Mango, *Le développement urbain de Constantinople (IVe–VIIe siècles)* (Paris: de Boccard, 1985); A. Sirks, "The Size of the Grain Distributions in Imperial Rome and Constantinople," *Athenaeum* 79 (1991): 215–37. Rome: Wickham, *Framing*, 33. Urban village: Wickham, *Framing*, 653.

30. Hodges and Whitehouse, *Mohamed*, 48–52; Charles Krautheimer, *Three Christian Capitals: Topography and Politics. Rome, Constantinople, Milan* (Berkeley: University of California Press, 1983), 109, although see also 154n12.

31. Wickham, *Framing*, 33.

32. For example, Keith Hopkins, *Conquerors and Slaves* (Cambridge, UK: Cambridge University Press, 1978), 96–98; Neville Morley, *Metropolis and Hinterland: The City of Rome and the Italian Economy, 200 BC–AD 200* (Cambridge, UK: Cambridge University Press, 1996), 33–54.

33. Glenn Storey, "The Population of Ancient Rome," *Antiquity* 71 (1997): 966–78.

34. Pierre Salmon, *Population et dépopulation dans l'empire romain* (Brussels: Latomus, 1974), 11–22.

35. Walter Scheidel, "Progress and Problems in Roman Demography," in Wal-

ter Scheidel, ed., *Debating Roman Demography* (Leiden: Brill, 2001), 52–57; Lo Cascio, "Produzione monetaria," 650–77.

36. See discussion in Morley, *Metropolis and Hinterland*, 39.

37. Walter Scheidel, "Creating a Metropolis: A Comparative Demographic Perspective," in William Harris and Giovanni Ruffini, eds., *Ancient Alexandria between Egypt and Greece* (Leiden: Brill, 2004), 1–31; Morley, *Metropolis and Hinterland*, 39.

38. Diana Delia, "The Population of Roman Alexandria," *Transactions of the American Philological Association* 118 (1989): 275–92.

39. Scheidel, "Creating a Metropolis."

40. T. Boiy, *Late Achaemenid and Hellenistic Babylon* (Leuven: Orientalia Lovaniensia Analecta 126, 2004); Scheidel, "Creating a Metropolis."

41. My estimate, calculated from D. J. Wiseman, *Nebuchadnezzar and Babylon* (New York: Oxford University Press, 1985), A. R. George, "Babylon Revisited: Archaeology and Philology," *Antiquity* 67 (1993): 734–46, and Boiy, *Late Achaemenid and Hellenistic Babylon*.

42. Herodotus 1.178, 191; Aristotle, *Politics* 1276a30; Charles Gates, *Ancient Cities* (London: Routledge, 2003), 181.

43. My estimate, derived from sources in Marc van de Mieroop, *The Ancient Mesopotamian City* (Oxford: Oxford University Press, 1997), 97.

44. Jonah 3:3, 4:1; K. Åkerman, "The 'Aussenhaken Area' in the City of Assur during the Second Half of the Seventh Century BC: A Study of a Neo-Assyrian City Quarter and Its Demography," *State Archives of Assyria Bulletin* 13 (2001): 217–72.

45. Extrapolated from Chandler, *Four Thousand Years*, 460.

46. Kenneth Kitchen, *The Third Intermediate Period (1100–650 BC) in Egypt* (Warminster, UK: Aris & Philips, 1986).

47. Chandler, *Four Thousand Years*, 460.

48. Ibid., 460; for Tanis, calculations from plans in Jean Yoyotte et al., eds., *Tanis, l'or des pharaohs* (Paris: Galeries nationals du grand palais, 1987).

49. Chandler, *Four Thousand Years*, 460. On Babylon generally, see Joan Oates, *Babylon* (London: Thames & Hudson, 1979); I. L. Finkel and M. J. Seymour, eds., *Babylon* (Oxford: Oxford University Press, 2009), and a convenient online summary from the *International Standard Bible Encyclopedia* (http://bibleencyclopedia.com/babylon.htm). On New Kingdom Thebes, C. F. Nims, *Thebes of the Pharaohs: Pattern for Every City* (London: Elek Books, 1965); Kemp, *Ancient Egypt*, 201–2.

50. Oskar Reuther, *Die Innenstadt von Babylon (Merkes)* (Leipzig: Hinrichs, 1926).

51. Chandler, *Four Thousand Years*, 460.

52. Ibid., 460.

53. Ibid., 460; van de Mieroop, *Ancient Mesopotamian City*, 95.

54. Christian, *Maps of Time*, 295.

55. Marc van de Mieroop, *King Hammurabi of Babylon* (Oxford: Wiley-Blackwell, 2004).

56. Oates, *Babylon*, 76–82; van de Mieroop, *Hammurabi*, 93.

57. Chandler, *Four Thousand Years*, 460.

58. See Postgate, "How Many Sumerians."

59. Robert McC. Adams, *Heartland of Cities* (Chicago: University of Chicago Press, 1981).

60. Chandler, *Four Thousand Years*, 460.

61. Modelski, "Cities," table 2; Adams, *Heartland*, 85.

62. Adams, *Heartland*, 85; Nissen, *Early History*; Maisels, *Emergence*, 141.

63. Adams, *Heartland*.

64. David Oates et al., *Excavations at Tell Brak III: The Uruk and Ubaid Periods* (Cambridge, UK: McDonald Institute, forthcoming); http://www.mcdon ald.cam.ac.uk/projects/brak/index.htm.

65. Hodder, *Leopard's Tale*.

66. Ibid.; Maisels, *Emergence*.

67. Maisels, *Emergence*, 93–94.

68. *Economist Pocket World*, 20.

69. Bayly, *Modern World*, 189, and many other sources.

70. Chandler, *Four Thousand Years*, 492, suggests 1.5 million.

71. Ibid., 485.

72. Braudel, *Civilization and Capitalism*, 526, 540; William Rowe, *China's Last Empire: The Great Qing* (Cambridge, MA: Harvard University Press, 2009), 90–148.

73. Chandler, *Four Thousand Years*, 483.

74. For example, Frederick Mote, *Imperial China, 900–1800* (Berkeley: University of California Press, 1999), 763, proposing 1.3 million.

75. Chandler, *Four Thousand Years*, 481, suggests the very precise number of 706,000.

76. Frank, *ReOrient*, 109, proposes about one million for Nanjing.

77. Chandler, *Four Thousand Years*, 478.

78. Mote, *Imperial China*, 763; "The Transformation of Nanking, 1350–1400," in Skinner, *City in Late Imperial China*, 150; Bairoch, *Cities and Economic Development*, 356.

79. Chandler, *Four Thousand Years*, 476, says 487,000.

80. Mote, "Transformation," 132, 138, 145.

81. Bairoch, *Cities and Economic Development*, 355.

82. Elvin, *Pattern*, 177; Gilbert Rozman, *Urban Networks in Ch'ing China and Tokugawa Japan* (Princeton: Princeton University Press, 1973), 35; Kuhn, *Age of Confucian Rule*, 205; Christian, *Maps of Time*, 368; William Skinner, "Introduction: Urban Development in Imperial China," in Skinner, *City in Late Imperial China*, 30.

83. Kuhn, *Age of Confucian Rule*, 205–9.

84. Mote, *Imperial China*, 164–65; Skinner, "Introduction," 30; Kuhn, *Age of Confucian Rule*, 195.

85. Chandler, *Four Thousand Years*, 467; Bairoch, *Cities and Economic Development*, 352; compare Kuhn, *Age of Confucian Rule*, 191–205; Christian de Pee,

"Purchase on Power: Imperial Space and Commercial Space in Song-Dynasty Kaifeng, 960–1127," *Journal of the Economic and Social History of the Orient* 53 (2010): 149–84.

86. Kuhn, *Age of Confucian Rule*, 195.

87. Kuhn, *Age of Confucian Rule*, 205.

88. Charles Benn, *China's Golden Age: Everyday Life Under the Tang Dynasty* (New York: Oxford University Press, 2002); Kuhn, *Age of Confucian Rule*, 191; cf. Arthur Wright, *The Sui Dynasty* (New York: Knopf, 1978), 201.

89. Skinner, "Introduction," 30.

90. Mark Lewis, *China's Cosmopolitan Empire: The Tang Dynasty* (Cambridge, MA: Harvard University Press, 2009), 72.

91. Benn, *China's Golden Age*, 46; Rozman, *Urban Networks*.

92. Skinner, "Introduction," 30; Kuhn, *Age of Confucian Rule*, 191.

93. Skinner, "Introduction," 30; Kuhn, *Age of Confucian Rule*, 191.

94. Wright, *Sui Dynasty*, 84–90; Lewis, *China between Empires*, 252.

95. Chandler, *Four Thousand Years*, 465.

96. David Graff, *Medieval Chinese Warfare, 300–900* (London: Routledge, 2002), 98.

97. Dien, *Six Dynasties Civilization*.

98. Graff, *Medieval Chinese Warfare*, 35–51.

99. Chandler, *Four Thousand Years*, 463.

100. Hans Bielenstein, "Lo-yang in the Later Han Times," *Bulletin of the Museum of Far Eastern Antiquities* 48 (1976): 3–142; Mark Lewis, *The Construction of Space in Early China* (Albany: State University of New York Press, 2006); *Early Chinese Empires*, 75–101; Li, *Eastern Zhou*; Nancy Steinhardt, *Chinese Imperial City Planning* (Honolulu: University of Hawaii Press, 1990), 46–53; Wang, *Han Civilization*; Wu Hung, "The Art and Architecture of the Warring States Period," in Loewe and Shaughnessy, *Cambridge History of Ancient China*, 653–65.

101. Lewis, *Early Chinese Empires*, 89.

102. Wu, "Art and Architecture," 653–65.

103. *Shi ji* 69, p. 2257 = William Nienhauser, *The Grand Scribe's Records VII: Memoirs of Pre-Han China* (Bloomington: Indiana University Press, 1994), 106.

104. Bairoch, *Cities and Economic Development*, 44.

105. Rawson, "Western Zhou Archaeology," 393–97; Li, *Landscape and Power*, 40–49, 62–66; von Falkenhausen, *Chinese Society*, 31–38.

106. von Falkenhausen, *Chinese Society*, 34.

107. I elaborate on my views on dispersed settlements in Morris, "Early Polis as City and State," 29–30.

108. Chandler's estimate in *Four Thousand Years*, 460.

109. Ibid., 460.

110. Thorp, *China in the Early Bronze Age*, 125–71; Kwang-chih Chang, *Shang Civilization* (New Haven: Yale University Press, 1980); Li Liu and Xingcan Chen, *The Archaeology of China: From the Late Palaeolithic to the Early Bronze Age* (Cambridge, UK: Cambridge University Press, 2012).

111. Thorp, *China in the Early Bronze Age*, 64.

112. Ibid., 62–116; Liu and Chen, *State Formation*, 92–99; Liu and Chen, *Archaeology of China*.

113. Li Liu, "Urbanization in China: Erlitou and its Hinterland," in Storey, *Urbanism in the Preindustrial World*, 184.

114. Liu, *Chinese Neolithic*, 111; Liu and Chen, *Archaeology of China*, chap. 7.

115. Liu, *Chinese Neolithic*, 110; Shao, "Formation of Civilization," 91–92.

116. Liu, *Chinese Neolithic*, 240.

117. Reported in Liu and Chen, *Archaeology of China*, chap. 7.

118. My estimate; cf. Liu, *Chinese Neolithic*, 108–10.

119. Ibid., 86–88.

120. Ibid., 83.

121. Ibid., 79; Peterson and Shelach, "Jiangzhai," 275–77.

122. Morris, *Why the West Rules*, 183–84, 207–9.

123. Morris, "Growth of Greek Cities."

124. In the senses defined by Mann, *Sources of Social Power*.

125. *Economist Pocket World*, 20.

126. Morris, *Why the West Rules*, 190–95, 206–7.

127. Ibid., 386–99.

128. Ibid., 590–613.

CHAPTER 5

1. Quoted in Peter Ward Fay, *The Opium War, 1840–1842*, 2nd ed. (Chapel Hill: University of North Carolina Press, 1997), 222.

2. Quoted in Philip Short, *Mao: A Life* (New York: Owl Books, 1999), 368.

3. Peter Turchin, "A Theory for Formation of Large Empires," *Journal of Global History* 4 (2009): 191–217; "Warfare and the Evolution of Social Complexity: A Multilevel-Selection Approach," *Structure and Dynamics* 4, no. 3 (2011): 1–37; Ian Morris, *War! What Is It Good For?* (New York: Farrar, Straus and Giroux, forthcoming).

4. F. W. Lanchester, *Aircraft in Warfare: The Dawn of the Fourth Arm* (London: Constable, 1916), summarized in Lanchester, "Mathematics in Warfare," in James Newman, ed., *The World of Mathematics* (New York: Simon & Schuster, 1956), 4:2139–57.

5. For instance, James Taylor, *Lanchester Models of Warfare*, 2 vols. (Arlington, VA: Operations Research Society of America, 1983).

6. Trevor Nevitt Dupuy, *Numbers, Predictions and War: The Use of History to Evaluate Combat Factors and Predict the Outcomes of Battles*, rev. ed. (Fairfax, VA: Hero Books, 1985); *Understanding War: History and Theory of Combat* (New York: Paragon House, 1992); Stephen Biddle, *Military Power: Explaining Victory*

and Defeat in Modern Battle (Princeton: Princeton University Press, 2004); David Rowland, *The Stress of Battle: Quantifying Human Performance in Combat* (London: HMSO, 2006).

7.   For example, Daniel Willard, *Lanchester as a Force in History: An Analysis of Land Battles of the Years 1618–1905* (McLean, VA: Research Analysis Corporation, 1962), Janice Fain, "The Lanchester Equations and Historical Warfare: An Analysis of Sixty World War II Land Engagements," *History, Numbers, and War* 1 (1977): 34–52, and John Lepingwell, "The Laws of Combat? Lanchester Reexamined," *International Security* 12, no. 1 (1987): 89–134, all testing Lanchester in different ways, with discussions at http://www.dupuyinstitute.org/.

8.   See Peter Perla, *The Art of Wargaming: A Guide for Professionals and Hobbyists* (Annapolis, MD: U.S. Naval Institute Press, 1990); James Dunnigan, *The Wargames Handbook: How to Play and Design Commercial and Professional Wargames*, 3rd ed. (Lincoln, NE: iUniverse, 2000); and especially Philip Sabin, *Lost Battles: Reconstructing the Great Clashes of the Ancient World* (London: Continuum, 2007) and *Simulating War: Studying Conflict through Simulation Games* (London: Continuum, 2012).

9.   Richard Berg, *Chariots of Fire: Warfare in the Bronze Age, 2300–1200 BC* (Hanford, CA: GMT Games, 2010); Richard Berg and Mark Herman, *SPQR: The Art of War in the Roman Republic*, 3rd ed. (Hanford, CA: GMT Games, 2008); Stephen Welch, *Chandragupta: Great Battles of the Mauryan Empire, India, 319– 261 BC* (Hanford, CA: GMT Games, 2008); Richard Berg and Mark Herman, *Devil's Horsemen: The Mongol War Machine* (Hanford, CA: GMT Games, 2004).

10.   Robert Massie, *Dreadnought: Britain, Germany, and the Coming of the Great War* (New York: Ballantine Books, 1993).

11.   Andrei Sakharov, *Memoirs* (New York: Knopf, 1990), 215–25; David Miller, *The Cold War: A Military History* (London: Pimlico, 1998), appendix 8; Gerard De Groot, *The Bomb: A Life* (Cambridge, MA: Harvard University Press, 2005).

12.   Miller, *Cold War*, 75–76.

13.   See, for example, S. Glasstone and P. J. Dolan, *The Effects of Nuclear Weapons* (Washington, DC: U.S. Department of Defense, 1977); William Daugherty et al., "The Consequences of 'Limited' Nuclear Attacks on the United States," *International Security* 10, no. 4 (1986): 3–45; Barbara Levi et al., "Civilian Casualties from 'Limited' Nuclear Attacks on the USSR," *International Security* 12, no. 3 (1987–88): 168–89.

14.   International Institute for Strategic Studies: http://www.iiss.org. Ravi Rikhye et al., *Concise World Armies 2009* (Alexandria, VA: General Data LLC, 2010), available at http://www.globalsecurity.org, is another excellent, up-to-date electronic resource.

15.   Robert Norris and Hans Kristensen, "Global Nuclear Stockpiles, 1945– 2006," *Bulletin of the Atomic Scientists* 62, no. 4 (2006): 66.

16.   I draw here primarily on P. E. Cleator, *Weapons of War* (London: Robert Hale, 1967); Bruce Gundmundsson, *On Artillery* (Westport, CT: Praeger, 1993); Ian

Hogg, *The New Illustrated Encyclopedia of Firearms* (New York: Booksales, 1992); International Institute for Strategic Studies, *The Military Balance 2001* (London: Routledge, 2001); Bernard Ireland and Eric Grove, eds., *Jane's War at Sea 1897–1997* (London: HarperCollins, 1997); Paul Kennedy, *The Rise and Fall of the Great Powers* (New York: Vintage, 1987).

17. C. J. Chivers, *The Gun* (New York: Simon & Schuster, 2010).

18. Max Boot, *War Made New: Technology, Warfare, and the Course of History, 1500 to Today* (New York: Gotham Books, 2006).

19. The sources I have used most heavily are Jean-Paul Bertaud, *The Army of the French Revolution*, trans. R. R. Palmer (Bloomington: Indiana University Press, 1988); Jeremy Black, *War in the Early Modern World, 1450–1815* (London: Routledge, 1998) and *Warfare in the Eighteenth Century* (Washington, DC: Smithsonian, 2006); Robert Bruce et al., *Fighting Techniques of the Napoleonic Age, 1792–1815* (New York: Thomas Dunne Books, 2008); David Chandler, *The Campaigns of Napoleon* (New York: Scribner, 1966); Charles Esdaile, *Napoleon's Wars* (New York: Penguin, 2007); Richard Harding, *Seapower and Naval Warfare, 1660–1830* (London: Longman, 1999); Chris McNab, *Armies of the Napoleonic Wars* (London: Osprey, 1999); Geoffrey Parker, *The Military Revolution: Military Innovation and the Rise of the West, 1500–1800*, 2nd ed. (Cambridge, UK: Cambridge University Press, 1996); N. A. M. Rodger, ed., *A Naval History of Britain II: 1649–1815* (Cambridge, UK: Cambridge University Press, 2004); Clifford Rogers, ed., *The Military Revolution Debate: Readings on the Military Transformation of Early Modern Europe* (Boulder, CO: Westview, 1995); Gunther Rothenberg, *The Art of Warfare in the Age of Napoleon* (Bloomington: Indiana University Press, 1978) and *The Napoleonic Wars* (Washington, DC: Smithsonian, 2006); Quincy Wright, *A Study of War*, 2nd ed. (Chicago: University of Chicago Press, 1965), 232–33.

20. Biddle, *Military Power*, 29–30.

21. Kenneth Chase, *Firearms: A Global History to 1700* (Cambridge, UK: Cambridge University Press, 2003), 74.

22. For example, David Hollins, *Austrian Napoleonic Artillery, 1792–1815* (London: Osprey, 2003).

23. Chris Henry, *Napoleonic Naval Armaments, 1792–1815* (Oxford: Osprey, 2004).

24. Michael Roberts, *Essays in Swedish History* (London: Weidenfeld & Nicholson, 1967), 195–225, reprinting a lecture originally given in 1955; Parker, *Military Revolution*.

25. I draw here primarily on Black, *War in the Early Modern World* and *European Warfare, 1494–1660* (London: Longmans, 2002); Chase, *Firearms*; Christopher Duffy, *Siege Warfare: The Fortress in the Early Modern World, 1494–1660* (London: Routledge, 1996) and *Fire and Stone: The Science of Fortress Warfare, 1660–1860* (New York: Booksales, 2006); Jan Glete, *Warfare at Sea, 1500–1650* (London: Longmans, 2000); Christer Jörgensen et al., *Fighting Techniques of the Early Modern World, AD 1500–1763: Equipment, Combat Skills, and Tactics* (New York: Thomas Dunne Books, 2006); John Lynn, ed., *Tools of War: Instruments,*

Ideas, and Institutions of Warfare, 1445–1871 (Urbana: University of Illinois Press, 1989); *Giant of the Grand Siècle: The French Army, 1610–1714* (Cambridge, UK: Cambridge University Press, 1997); *The Wars of Louis XIV, 1667–1714* (New York: Longman, 1999); Brent Nosworthy, *The Anatomy of Victory: Battle Tactics, 1689– 1763* (New York: Hippocrene Books, 1990); Parker, *Military Revolution*; Keith Roberts, *Pike and Shot Tactics 1590–1660* (Oxford: Osprey, 2010); Rogers, *Military Revolution Debate*; Martin van Creveld, *Supplying War: Logistics from Wallenstein to Patton*, 2nd ed. (Cambridge, UK: Cambridge University Press, 2004).

26.　See, for example, Hans Delbrück, *History of the Art of War within the Framework of Political History*, trans. Walter Renfroe, 4 vols. (first published 1920; repr., Westport, CT: Greenwood, 1975–85); J. F. C. Fuller, *A Military History of the Western World*, 2 vols. (New York: Funk and Wagnall, 1957); Azar Gat, *War in Human Civilization* (New York: Oxford University Press, 2006); John Keegan, *A History of Warfare* (New York: Vintage, 1993).

27.　Bernard Bachrach, *Merovingian Military Organization, 451–781* (Minneapolis: University of Minnesota Press, 1972); *Early Carolingian Warfare: Prelude to Empire* (Philadelphia: University of Pennsylvania Press, 2001).

28.　See, for instance, J. F. Verbruggen, *The Art of War in Western Europe during the Middle Ages*, 2nd ed. (Woodbridge, UK: Boydell Press, 1997); "The Role of Cavalry in Medieval Warfare," *Journal of Medieval Military History* 3 (2004): 46–71; Philip Contamine, *War in the Middle Ages*, trans. Michael Jones (Oxford: Blackwell, 1984); John France, "The Composition and Raising of Charlemagne's Armies," *Journal of Medieval Military History* 1 (2002): 61–82; Guy Halsall, *Warfare and Society in the Barbarian West 450–900* (London: Routledge, 2003).

29.　Gat, *War in Human Civilization*.

30.　From an enormous literature, I have benefited particularly from Duncan Campbell, *Greek and Roman Siege Machinery 399 BC–AD 363* (Oxford: Osprey, 2003); J. B. Campbell, *The Roman Army: A Sourcebook* (London: Routledge, 1994); Paul Erdkamp, ed., *A Companion to the Roman Army* (Oxford: Wiley-Blackwell, 2007); Adrian Goldsworthy, *The Roman Army at War, 100 BC–AD 200* (Oxford: Oxford University Press, 1996) and *The Complete Roman Army* (London: Thames & Hudson, 2003); Jonathan Roth, *The Logistics of the Roman Army at War, 264 BC–AD 235* (Leiden: Brill, 1999).

31.　I follow A. D. Lee, *War in Late Antiquity* (Oxford: Blackwell, 2007), 74–79 on this controversial topic.

32.　Defense in depth: Edward Luttwak, *The Grand Strategy of the Roman Empire* (Baltimore: Johns Hopkins University Press, 1976). Generally, see Hugh Elton, *Warfare in the Roman Empire, AD 350–425* (Oxford: Oxford University Press, 1996); Lee, *War in Late Antiquity*; Ward-Perkins, *Fall of Rome*; Luttwak, *Grand Strategy of the Byzantine Empire*.

33.　Ramsay MacMullen, *Soldier and Civilian in the Later Roman Empire* (Cambridge, MA: Harvard University Press, 1963) is an excellent presentation of the older views of the weakness of the *limitanei*.

34.　Haldon, *Byzantium in the Seventh Century*; *Warfare, State and Society in* the Byzantine World, 565–1204 (London: University College London Press, 1999); Haldon, ed., Byzantine Warfare (Aldershot, UK: Ashgate 2007); The Byzantine Wars (London: History Press, 2008); Walter Kaegi, Byzantium and the Early Islamic Conquests (Cambridge, UK: Cambridge University Press, 1992); Heraclius: Emperor of Byzantium (Cambridge, UK: Cambridge University Press, 2003); Hugh Kennedy, The Armies of the Caliphs: Military and Society in the Early Islamic State (London: Routledge, 2001); Luttwak, Grand Strategy of the Byzantine Empire.

35. John Haldon, ed., General Issues in the Study of Medieval Logistics: Sources, Problems, Methodologies (Leiden: Brill, 2005); International Medieval Logistics Project, http://www.medievallogistics.bham.ac.uk.

36. See, among many other titles, Matthew Bennett et al., Fighting Techniques of the Medieval World, AD 500–1500: Equipment, Combat Skills, and Tactics (New York: Thomas Dunne Books, 2005); Jim Bradbury, ed., The Routledge Companion to Medieval Warfare (London: Routledge, 2007); Contamine, War in the Middle Ages; Maurice Keen, Medieval Warfare: A History (Oxford: Oxford University Press, 1999); Clifford Rogers, ed., The Oxford Encyclopedia of Medieval Warfare and Military Technology (Oxford: Oxford University Press, 2010); Verbruggen, Art of War.

37. On Byzantine forces, I recommend Haldon, Warfare, State and Society and Byzantine Wars; Ian Heath, Byzantine Armies 886–1118 (Oxford: Osprey, 1979) and Byzantine Armies AD 1118–1461 (Oxford: Osprey, 1995); Savvas Kyriakidis, Warfare in Late Byzantium, 1204–1453 (Leiden: Brill, 2011); Eric McGeer, Sowing the Dragon's Teeth: Byzantine Warfare in the Tenth Century (Washington, DC: Dumbarton Oaks, 2008); and David Nicolle, Romano-Byzantine Armies 4th–9th Centuries (Oxford: Osprey, 1992). On Seljuk armies, I have consulted Osman Aziz Basan, The Great Seljuqs: A History (London: Routledge, 2010); Pal Fodor, "Ottoman Warfare, 1300–1453," in Kate Fleet, ed., The Cambridge History of Turkey I: Byzantium to Turkey, 1071–1453 (Cambridge, UK: Cambridge University Press, 2009), 192–226; John Freely, Storm on Horseback: The Seljuk Warriors of Turkey (London: Tauris, 2008).

38. Black, War in the Early Modern World; Amber Books et al., Fighting Techniques of the Oriental World, AD 1200–1854: Equipment, Combat Skills, and Tactics (New York: Thomas Dunne Books, 2008); Fighting Techniques of Naval Warfare, 1190 BC–Present: Strategy, Weapons, Commanders, and Ships (New York: Thomas Dunne Books, 2009); Colin Imber, The Ottoman Empire (London: Palgrave, 2002), 252–318; Rhoads Murphey, Ottoman Warfare 1500–1700 (London: Routledge, 1999); Susan Rose, Medieval Naval Warfare, 1000–1500 (London: Routledge, 2002).

39. There are many general reviews of pre-Roman Western warfare (for Roman war, see note 30 above). Those I have found particularly helpful include Simon Anglim et al., Fighting Techniques of the Ancient World, 3000 BC–AD 500: Equipment, Combat Skills, and Tactics (New York: Thomas Dunne Books, 2003); Richard Beal, The Organization of the Hittite Military (Heidelberg: Carl Winter, 1992); John Darnell and Colleen Manassa, Tutankhamun's Armies: Battle and Conquest during Ancient Egypt's Late Eighteenth Dynasty (New York: Wiley, 2007);

Marie-Christine de Graeve, *The Ships of the Ancient Near East, c. 2000–500 BC* (Louvain: Department Orientalistiek, 1981); Philip de Souza, ed., *The Ancient World at War* (London: Thames and Hudson, 2008); Robert Drews, *The Coming of the Greeks* (Princeton: Princeton University Press, 1988) and *End of the Bronze Age*; Richard Gabriel, *The Great Armies of Antiquity* (New York: Praeger, 2002); William Hamblin, *Warfare in the Ancient Near East to 1600 BC* (London: Routledge, 2006); Victor Davis Hanson, *The Western Way of War: Infantry Battle in Classical Greece* (New York: Oxford University Press, 1989); A. W. Lawrence, "Ancient Egyptian Fortifications," *Journal of Egyptian Archaeology* 51 (1965): 69–71; Littauer and Crouwel, *Wheeled Vehicles*; R. Miller et al., "Experimental Approaches to Ancient Near Eastern Archery," *World Archaeology* 18 (1986): 178–95; Ellen Morris, *The Architecture of Imperialism: Military Bases and the Evolution of Foreign Policy in Egypt's New Kingdom* (Leiden: Brill, 2005); Graham Philip, *Metal Weapons of the Early and Middle Bronze Ages in Syria-Palestine* (Oxford: British Archaeological Reports, 1989); Kurt Raaflaub and Nathan Rosenstein, eds., *War and Society in the Ancient and Medieval Worlds* (Cambridge, MA: Center for Hellenic Studies, 1999); Philip Sabin et al., eds., *The Cambridge History of Greek and Roman Warfare*, 2 vols. (Cambridge, UK: Cambridge University Press, 2008); Ian Shaw, *Egyptian Warfare and Weapons* (Oxford: Shire Publications, 1991); Anthony Spalinger, *War in Ancient Egypt: The New Kingdom* (Oxford: Wiley-Blackwell, 2005); Hans van Wees, *Greek Warfare* (London: Duckworth, 2004); Shelley Wachsmann, *Seagoing Ships and Seamanship in the Bronze Age Levant* (College Station: Texas A&M University, 1998).

40. See especially Lawrence Keeley, *War Before Civilization* (New York: Oxford University Press, 1996) and Gat, *War in Human Civilization*.

41. Yigael Yadin, *The Art of Warfare in Biblical Lands*, 2 vols. (New York: McGraw-Hill, 1963); Hamblin, *Warfare in the Ancient Near East*.

42. Kennedy, *Armies of the Caliphs*.

43. Morris, *Why the West Rules*, 195–200, 233–37, 343–63.

44. For example, e.g., International Institute for Strategic Studies, *Military Balance 2001*, 346–51; Norris and Kristensen, "Global Nuclear Stockpiles."

45. See, for example, Robert Kaplan, "How We Would Fight China," *The Atlantic* 295, no. 5 (2005): 49–64.

46. See Joel Singer, *The Correlates of War: Testing Some Realpolitik Models* (New York: Free Press, 1980), http://correlatesofwar.org/.

47. http://correlatesofwar.org/COW2%20Data/Capabilities/NMC_v4_0.csv.

48. James Dunnigan, *How to Make War: A Comprehensive Guide to Modern Warfare in the 21st Century*, 4th ed. (New York: Quill, 2003), 624–44.

49. Assuming, of course, that the United States was behind both attacks: see http://www.nytimes.com/2011/01/16/world/middleeast/16stuxnet.html ?_r=1&pagewanted=all and http://www.dailymail.co.uk/sciencetech/article -2157834/Cyber-weapons-Stuxnet-Flame-share-source-code.html.

50. See, for example, Seth Jones, *In the Graveyard of Empires: America's War in Afghanistan* (New York: Norton, 2009); Richard North, *Ministry of Defeat: The*

British War in Iraq, 2003–2009 (London: Continuum, 2009); George Packer, *The Assassin's Gate: America in Iraq* (New York: Farrar, Straus and Giroux, 2005); Thomas Ricks, *Fiasco: The American Military Adventure in Iraq* (New York: Penguin, 2006) and *The Gamble: General Petraeus and the American Military Adventure in Iraq* (New York: Penguin, 2009).

51.　For example, Thomas Adams, *The Army after Next: The First Postindustrial Army* (Stanford: Stanford University Press, 2008); Boot, *War Made New*; P. W. Singer, *Wired for War: The Robotics Revolution and Conflict in the 21st Century* (New York: Penguin, 2009).

52.　Boot, *War Made New*, 318–418; Michael Gordon and Bernard Trainor, *Cobra II: The Inside Story of the Invasion and Occupation of Iraq* (New York: Vintage, 2006). Biddle, *Military Power*, 132–49, offers important qualifications.

53.　Cf. John Nagl, *Learning to Eat Soup with a Knife: Counterinsurgency Lessons from Malaya and Vietnam*, updated ed. (Chicago: University of Chicago Press, 2005).

54.　Chase, *Firearms*, 193–96.

55.　Jonathan Spence, *The Search for Modern China* (New York: Norton, 1990); Marius Jansen, *The Making of Modern Japan* (Cambridge, MA: Harvard University Press, 2000); James Huffman, *Japan in World History* (Oxford: Oxford University Press, 2010), 72–90.

56.　Kennedy, *Rise and Fall*, 203.

57.　Meirion Harries and Susie Harries, *Soldiers of the Sun: The Rise and Fall of the Imperial Japanese Army, 1868–1945* (London: Heinemann, 1991); David Evans and Mark Peattie, *Kaigun: Strategy, Tactics, and Technology in the Imperial Japanese Navy, 1887–1941* (Annapolis, MD: U.S. Naval Institute Press, 1997).

58.　R. M. Connaughton, *The War of the Rising Sun and Tumbling Bear: A Military History of the Russo-Japanese War, 1904–5* (London: Routledge, 1988); S. C. M. Paine, *The Sino-Japanese War of 1894–1895* (Cambridge, UK: Cambridge University Press, 2003).

59.　John Ellis, *The World War II Databook: The Essential Facts and Figures for All the Combatants* (New York: Aurum, 1993); John Ellis and Michael Cox, *The World War I Databook: The Essential Facts and Figures for All the Combatants* (New York: Aurum, 2001).

60.　Bruce Elleman, *Modern Chinese Warfare, 1795–1989* (London: Routledge, 2001), 235–97; David Graff and Robin Higham, eds., *A Military History of China* (Boulder, CO: Westview, 2002).

61.　James Bussert and Bruce Elleman, *People's Liberation Army Navy: Combat System Technology, 1949–2010* (Annapolis, MD: U.S. Naval Institute Press, 2011); Andrew Erickson et al., eds., *China, the United States, and 21st-Century Sea Power* (Annapolis, MD: U.S. Naval Institute Press, 2010); Bernard Cole, *The Great Wall at Sea: China's Navy in the Twenty-First Century*, 2nd ed., (Annapolis, MD: U.S. Naval Institute Press, 2010); Richard Fisher, *China's Military Modernization: Building for Regional and Global Reach* (Stanford: Stanford University Press, 2010).

62.　John Lewis Gaddis, *The Cold War: A New History* (New York: Penguin,

2005); Odd Arne Westad, *The Global Cold War* (Cambridge, UK: Cambridge University Press, 2005).

63. See Thomas Barfield, *The Perilous Frontier: Nomadic Empires and China, 221 BC–AD 1757* (Oxford: Blackwell, 1989); Nicola Di Cosmo, *Ancient China and Its Enemies* (Cambridge, UK: Cambridge University Press, 2002); Di Cosmo, ed., *Warfare in Inner Asian History* (Leiden: Brill, 2002); Nicola Di Cosmo et al., eds., *Military Culture in Imperial China* (Cambridge, MA: Harvard University Press, 2009); Elleman, *Modern Chinese Warfare*; Karl Friday, *Samurai, Warfare and the State in Early Medieval Japan* (London: Routledge, 2004); Graff, *Medieval Chinese Warfare*; Graff and Higham, *Military History of China*; Frank Kierman and John Fairbanks, eds., *Chinese Ways in Warfare* (Cambridge, MA: Harvard University Press, 1974); Mark Lewis, *Sanctioned Violence in Early China* (Albany: State University of New York Press, 1990); Peter Lorge, *War, Politics and Society in Early Modern China, 900–1795* (London: Routledge, 2005); *The Asian Military Revolution: From Gunpowder to the Bomb* (Cambridge, UK: Cambridge University Press, 2008); Peter Perdue, *China Marches West: The Qing Conquest of Central Eurasia* (Cambridge, MA: Harvard University Press, 2005); Kenneth Swope, "Crouching Tigers, Secret Weapons: Military Technology Employed during the Sino-Japanese-Korean War, 1592–1598," *Journal of Military History* 69 (2005): 11–42; *A Dragon's Head and a Serpent's Tail: Ming China and the First Great East Asian War, 1592–1598* (Norman: University of Oklahoma Press, 2009); Hans van de Ven, ed., *Warfare in Chinese History* (Leiden: Brill, 2000); Joanna Waley-Cohen, *The Culture of War in China: Empire and the Military under the Qing Dynasty* (London: I. B. Tauris, 2006).

64. Ray Huang, "Military Expenditures in Sixteenth-Century Ming China," *Oriens Extremus* 17 (1970): 39–62.

65. Kwan-wai So, *Japanese Piracy in Ming China during the Sixteenth Century* (East Lansing: Michigan State University Press, 1975), 15–36.

66. Jung-Pang Lo, "The Decline of the Early Ming Navy," *Oriens Extremus* 5 (1958): 149–68.

67. Generally, see Chase, *Firearms*.

68. Swope, "Crouching Tigers" and *Dragon's Head*.

69. Perdue, *China Marches West*, 184.

70. Lorge, *War, Politics and Society*, 158–74.

71. Elleman, *Modern Chinese Warfare*, 5.

72. Fay, *Opium War*; Elleman, *Modern Chinese Warfare*, 3–34.

73. Cited in Fay, *Opium War*, 222.

74. Morris, *Why the West Rules*, 624.

75. Perdue, *China Marches West*.

76. Barfield, *Perilous Frontier*; Di Cosmo *Ancient China* and *Warfare in Inner Asian History*; Di Cosmo et al., *Military Culture*; Timothy May, *The Mongol Art of War: Chinggis Khan and the Mongol Military System* (London: Pen & Sword, 2007).

77. Comparing Berg and Herman, *Devil's Horsemen* to Mark Herman and Richard Berg, *Caesar: Conquest of Gaul* (Hanford, CA: GMT Games, 2006).

78. Lo, "Decline," 150; Lorge, *War, Politics and Society*, 111.

79. Lorge, *War, Politics and Society*, 116.

80. Jung-Pang Lo, "The Emergence of China as a Sea Power in the Late Sung and Early Yuan Periods," *Far Eastern Quarterly* 14 (1955): 489–503.

81. Morris Rossabi, *Khubilai Khan: His Life and Times* (Berkeley: University of California Press, 1988), 99–103.

82. Mote, *Imperial China*, 114; Lorge, *War, Politics and Society*, 48.

83. Lorge, *War, Politics and Society*, 49.

84. Mote, *Imperial China*, 302; Lorge, *War, Politics and Society*, 51.

85. Jung-Pang Lo, "China's Paddle-Wheel Boats: The Mechanized Craft Used in the Opium War and Their Historical Background," *Qinghua Journal of Chinese Studies* 5 (1958): 189–211; "Decline of the Early Ming Navy," 149–68; "Maritime Commerce and Its Relation to the Sung Navy," *Journal of Economic and Social History of the Orient* 12 (1969): 57–101; Joseph Needham, *Science and Civilisation in China IV Part 3: Civil Engineering and Nautics* (Cambridge, UK: Cambridge University Press, 1971); Rossabi, *Khubilai Khan*, 79.

86. Denis Twitchett, "Tibet in Tang's Grand Strategy," in van de Ven, *Warfare in Chinese History*, 106–79; Graff, *Medieval Chinese Warfare*, 210.

87. Graff, *Medieval Chinese Warfare*, 97–159.

88. Ibid., 104.

89. Ibid., 199.

90. Ibid., 227–51.

91. Albert Dien, "The Stirrup and Its Effect on Chinese Military History," *Ars Orientalis* 16 (1986): 33–56; *Six Dynasties Civilization*, 331–39.

92. Dien, *Six Dynasties Civilization*, 15–45.

93. Particularly Graff, *Medieval Chinese Warfare*; Lewis, *China between Empires*.

94. Lewis, *Sanctioned Violence*.

95. Mark Lewis, "The Han Abolition of Universal Military Service," in van de Ven, *Warfare in Chinese History*, 33–76.

96. On which see Tilly, *Big Structures*.

97. Kwang-chih Chang, *The Archaeology of Ancient China*, 4th ed. (New Haven: Yale University Press, 1986); Ralph Sawyer, *Ancient Chinese Warfare* (New York: Basic Books, 2011); Liu and Chen, *Archaeology of China*.

98. David Keightley, "The Shang: China's First Historical Dynasty," in Loewe and Shaughnessy, eds., *Cambridge History of Ancient China*, 232–91.

99. Robin Yates, "Early China," in Raaflaub and Rosenstein, *War and Society*, 13.

100. On this controversial topic, I follow Edward Shaughnessy, "Historical Perspectives on the Introduction of the Chariot into China," *Harvard Journal of Asiatic Studies* 48 (1988): 189–237.

101. Edward Shaughnessy, "Western Zhou History," in Loewe and Shaughnessy, *Cambridge History of Ancient China*, 309; Yates, "Early China," 18.

102. Lewis, *Sanctioned Violence*, 60; "Warring States Political History," 625.

103. Yates, "Early China," 20.

104. Lewis, *Sanctioned Violence*, 60–61.

105. Wagner, *Iron and Steel*; Joseph Needham and Robin Yates, *Science and Civilisation in China V: Chemistry and Chemical Technology. Part 6: Military Technology: Missiles and Sieges* (Cambridge, UK: Cambridge University Press, 1994).

106. Chase, *Firearms*.

107. Stephen Dale, *The Muslim Empires of the Ottomans, Safavids, and Mughals* (Cambridge, UK: Cambridge University Press, 2010); Kaveh Farrokh, *Iran at War, 1500–1988* (Oxford: Osprey, 2011); Jane Hathaway, *The Arab Lands under Ottoman Rule, 1516–1800* (London: Longman, 2008); Iqtidar Alam Khan, *Gunpowder and Firearms: Warfare in Medieval India* (New Delhi: Oxford University Press, 2004); Douglas Streusand, *The First Gunpowder Empires: The Ottomans, Safavids, and Mughals* (Boulder, CO: Westview, 2010).

108. Barfield, *Perilous Frontier*; Lorge, *War, Politics and Society*; Swopes, *Dragon's Head*.

CHAPTER 6

1. Klein, *Human Career*, 410–12; Ignacio Martinez et al., "On the Origin of Language: The Atapuerca Evidence" (paper, American Association of Physical Anthropologists annual meeting, Portland, OR, April 14, 2012), abstract available at http://physanth.org/annual-meeting/2012/81st-annual-meeting-2012/aapa-meeting-program-2012.

2. Francesco D'Errico et al., "Technical, Elemental and Colorific Analysis of an Engraved Ochre Fragment from the MSA Levels of Klasies River Cave 1, South Africa," *Journal of Archaeological Science* 39 (2012): 942–52.

3. Richard Klein and Blake Edgar, *The Dawn of Human Culture* (New York: Wiley, 2002).

4. Denise Schmandt-Besserat, *Before Writing*, 2 vols. (Austin: University of Texas Press, 1992).

5. See Barry Powell, *Writing: Theory and History of the Technology of Civilization* (Oxford: Blackwell, 2009).

6. The literature is large. The 1960s saw several foundational studies of the scale and significance of reading, which remain worth consulting (e.g., Lawrence Stone, "The Educational Revolution in England, 1560–1640," *Past and Present* 28 [1964]: 41–80 and "Literacy and Education in England 1640–1900," *Past and Present* 42 [1969]: 69–139; Jack Goody and Ian Watt, "The Consequences of Literacy," *Comparative Studies in Society and History* 5 [1963]: 304–45; and Jack Goody, ed., *Literacy in Traditional Societies* [Cambridge, UK: Cambridge University Press, 1968]). As noted in the text, scholarship has moved in rather different directions since the 1980s, but important new work has continued to appear, particularly on

the earlier periods (e.g., William Harris, *Ancient Literacy* [Cambridge, MA: Harvard University Press, 1989]; Michael Clanchy, *From Memory to Written Record: England, 1066–1307*, 2nd ed. [Oxford: Blackwell, 1993]; Reviel Netz, "The Bibliosphere of Ancient Science (Outside of Alexandria)," *NTM Zeitschrift für Geschichte der Wissenschaften, Technik und Medizin* 19 [2011]: 239–69; *Space, Scale, Canon: Parameters of Ancient Literary Culture* [forthcoming]).

7.   For example, Derk Bodde, *Chinese Thought, Society, and Science: The Intellectual and Social Background of Science and Technology in Pre-Modern China* (Honolulu: University of Hawaii Press, 1991); Albert Crosby, *The Measure of Reality: Quantification and Western Society, 1250–1600* (Cambridge, UK: Cambridge University Press, 1994); Reviel Netz, "Counter-Culture: Towards a History of Greek Numeracy," *History of Science* 40 (2002): 321–52; Stephen Chrisomalis, "A Cognitive Typology for Numerical Notation," *Cambridge Archaeological Journal* 14 (2004): 37–52; "The Origins and Co-Evolution of Literacy and Numeracy," in David Olson and Nancy Torrance, eds., *The Cambridge Handbook of Literacy* (Cambridge, UK: Cambridge University Press, 2009), 59–74; *Numerical Notation: A Comparative History* (Cambridge, UK: Cambridge University Press, 2010).

8.   For example, Brian Street, *Literacy in Theory and Practice* (Cambridge, UK: Cambridge University Press, 1984); "Orality and Literacy as Ideological Constructions: Some Problems in Cross-Cultural Studies," *Culture and History* 2 (1987): 7–30; Roger Chartier, ed., *The Culture of Print* (Princeton: Princeton University Press, 1989); Rosalind Thomas, *Literacy and Orality in Ancient Greece* (Cambridge, UK: Cambridge University Press, 1992).

9.   On these issues, I follow Shirley Heath, "Literacy," in William Frawley, ed., *International Encyclopedia of Linguistics*, 2nd ed., 4 vols. (New York: Oxford University Press, 2003), 2:503–6 and Chrisomalis, "Origins and Co-Evolution."

10.   Morris, *Why the West Rules*, 636.

11.   For example, Daniel Everett, "Cultural Constraints on Grammar and Cognition in Pirahã: Another Look at the Design Features of Human Language," *Current Anthropology* 46 (2005): 621–46; *Language: The Cultural Tool* (New York: Pantheon, 2012).

12.   On numeracy, see Thomas Crump, *The Anthropology of Numbers* (Cambridge, UK: Cambridge University Press, 1990) and Michael Frank et al., "Number as a Cognitive Technology: Evidence from Pirahã Language and Cognition," *Cognition* 108 (2008): 819–24; on spoken language, see the debate between Andrew Nevins et al., "Pirahã Exceptionality: A Reassessment," *Language* 85 (2009): 355–404 and "Evidence and Argumentation: A Reply to Everett," *Language* 85 (2009): 671–81, and Daniel Everett, "Pirahã Culture and Grammar: A Response to Some Criticism," *Language* 85 (2009): 405–42.

13.   Marianne Bastid, *Educational Reform in Early Twentieth-Century China* (Ann Arbor: University of Michigan Press, 1988); Paul Bailey, *Reform the People: Changing Attitudes Towards Popular Education in Early Twentieth-Century China* (Vancouver: University of British Columbia Press, 1990); Vilma Seeberg, ed., *Lit-*

eracy in China: The Effect of the National Development Context on Literacy Levels, 1949–79 (Bochum: Brockmeyer, 1990).

14. United Nations Development Programme, *Human Development Report 2011: Sustainability and Equity: A Better Future for All* (New York: United Nations Development Programme, 2011), 158, table 9, http://hdr.undp.org/en/media/HDR_2011_EN_Complete.pdf.

15. Kathryn St. John, personal communication, June 2012.

16. *Economist Pocket World in Figures*, 88, 89, 91.

17. Particularly Alfred Balk, *The Rise of Radio, from Marconi through the Golden Age* (New York: McFarland & Co., 2005); Erik Barnouw, *Tube of Plenty: The Evolution of American Television*, 2nd ed. (New York: Oxford University Press, 1990); Asa Briggs and Peter Burke, *A Social History of the Media: From Gutenberg to the Internet* (Oxford: Blackwell, 2002); Claude Fischer, *America Calling: A Social History of the Telephone to 1940* (Berkeley: University of California Press, 1994); Jeremy Norman, ed., *From Gutenberg to the Internet: A Sourcebook on the History of Information Technology* (Novato, CA: Historyofscience.com, 2005); Paul Starr, *The Creation of the Media: Political Origins of Mass Communication* (New York: Basic Books, 2005).

18. Briggs and Burke, *Social History of the Media*; Stephen Kern, *The Culture of Time and Space 1880–1918*, 2nd ed. (Cambridge, MA: Harvard University Press, 2003); Norman, *Gutenberg to the Internet*; Tom Standage, *The Victorian Internet: The Remarkable Story of the Telegraph and the Nineteenth Century's On-Line Pioneers* (New York: Walker & Co., 2007).

19. For example, Elizabeth Eisenstein, *The Printing Press as an Agent of Change* (Cambridge, UK: Cambridge University Press, 1979); T. H. Barrett, *The Woman Who Discovered Printing* (New Haven: Yale University Press, 2008); Cynthia Brokaw and Kai-wing Chow, eds., *Printing and Book Culture in Late Imperial China* (Berkeley: University of California Press, 2005); Kai-wing Chow, *Publishing, Culture, and Power in Early Modern China* (Stanford, CA: Stanford University Press, 2004); Joseph McDermott, *A Social History of the Chinese Book: Books and Literati Culture in Late Imperial China* (Hong Kong: Hong Kong University Press, 2006); David McKitterick, "The Beginning of Printing," in Christopher Allmand, ed., *The New Cambridge Medieval History* (Cambridge, UK: Cambridge University Press, 1998), 7:287–98.

20. Compare Powell, *Writing*.

21. Georges Ifrah, *The Universal History of Computing: From the Abacus to the Quantum Computer* (New York: Wiley, 2001); Paul Benyon-Davies, "Informatics and the Inca," *International Journal of Information Management* 27 (2007): 306–18.

22. See, for example, the classic studies of Goody and Watt, "Consequences"; Goody, *Literacy in Traditional Societies*; Goody, "Mémoire et apprentissage dans les sociétés avec et sans écriture," *L'Homme* 17 (1977): 42–49; *The Domestication of the Savage Mind* (Cambridge, UK: Cambridge University Press, 1977); *The Logic of Writing and the Organization of Society* (Cambridge, UK: Cambridge University Press, 1987); Walter Ong, *Orality and Literacy* (London, 1982).

23. For example, R. Pattison, *On Literacy: The Politics of the Word from Homer to the Age of Rock* (Oxford: Oxford University Press, 1982); Harvey Graff, *The Legacies of Literacy* (Bloomington: Indiana University Press, 1987); Ruth Finnegan, *Literacy and Orality* (Oxford: Oxford University Press, 1988); John Halverson, "Goody and the Implosion of the Literacy Thesis," *Man n.s.* 27 (1992): 301–17.

24. Schmandt-Besserat, *Before Writing.*

25. Paola Demattè, "The Origins of Chinese Writing: The Neolithic Evidence," *Cambridge Archaeological Journal* 20 (2010): 211–28.

26. Particularly Carlo Cipolla, *Literacy and Development in the West* (Harmondsworth, UK: Penguin, 1969); David Cressy, *Literacy and the Social Order: Reading and Writing in Tudor and Stuart England* (Cambridge, UK: Cambridge University Press, 1980); François Furet and Jacques Ozouf, *Reading and Writing: Literacy in France from Calvin to Jules Ferry* (Cambridge, UK: Cambridge University Press, 1982); R. A. Houston, "Literacy and Society in the West, 1500–1850," *Social History* 8 (1983): 269–93; *Literacy in Early Modern Europe: Culture and Education, 1500–1800* (London: Longman, 1988); M. J. Maynes, *Schooling for the People: Comparative Local Studies of Schooling History in France and Germany, 1750–1850* (London: Holmes and Meier, 1984); M. Sanderson, "Literacy and Social Mobility in the Industrial Revolution in England," *Past and Present* 56 (1972): 75–104; Roger Schofield, "The Measurement of Literacy in Pre-Industrial England," in Goody, *Literacy in Traditional Societies,* 311–25; "Dimensions of Illiteracy, 1750–1850," *Explorations in Economic History* 10 (1973): 437–54; W. B. Stephens, "Illiteracy in Devon during the Industrial Revolution, 1754–1844," *Journal of Educational Administration and History* 8 (1976): 1–5; Stone, "Educational Revolution" and "Literacy and Education."

27. K. A. Lockridge, *Literacy in Colonial New England: An Inquiry into the Social Context of Literacy in the Early Modern West* (New York: Norton, 1974); Lee Soltow and E. Stevens, *The Rise of Literacy and the Common School in the United States: A Socioeconomic Analysis to 1870* (Chicago: University of Chicago Press, 1981).

28. Keith Thomas, "The Meaning of Literacy in Early Modern England," in G. Baumann, ed., *The Written Word* (Oxford: Oxford University Press, 1986), 97–131, was perhaps the most influential critique. Carl Kaestle, "The History of Literacy and the History of Readers," *Review of Research in Education* 12 (1985): 11–53, provides a good overview of the issues.

29. See Cressy, *Literacy and the Social Order;* W. Gilmore, "Elementary Literacy on the Eve of the Industrial Revolution: Trends in Rural New England, 1760–1830," *Proceedings of the American Antiquarian Society* 92 (1982): 87–178; T. Hamerow, *The Birth of a New Europe* (Chapel Hill: University of North Carolina Press, 1983); Lockridge, *Literacy in Colonial New England;* Schofield, "Measurement of Literacy."

30. W. B. Stephens, "Illiteracy and Schooling in the Provincial Towns, 1640–1870," in D. Reader, ed., *Urban Education in the Nineteenth Century* (London: Taylor and Francis, 1977).

31.   For example, Franz-Josef Arlinghaus et al., eds., *Transforming the Medieval World: Uses of Pragmatic Literacy in the Middle Ages* (Turnhout: Brepols, 2006); Richard Britnell, *Pragmatic Literacy, East and West, 1200–1330* (Oxford: Boydell, 1997); Clanchy, *From Memory to Written Record*; Armando Petrucci, *"Scriptores in urbibus": alfabetismo e cultura scritta nell'Italia altomediovale* (Bologna: Mulino, 1992); Huw Pryce, *Literacy in Medieval Celtic Societies* (Oxford: Oxford University Press, 2006); Schofield, "Measurement of Literacy."

32.   Crosby, *Measure of Reality* and David Landes, *Revolution in Time: Clocks and the Making of the Modern World* (Cambridge, MA: Harvard University Press, 1983) are important exceptions.

33.   George Atiyeh, ed., *The Book in the Islamic World: The Written Word and Communication in the Middle East* (Edinburgh: Edinburgh University Press, 2005) is a partial exception, although most of the essays focus on modern times.

34.   See Ahmed Dallal, *Islam, Science, and the Challenge of History* (New Haven: Yale University Press, 2010); Donald Hill, *Islamic Science and Engineering* (Edinburgh: Edinburgh University Press, 1994); Muzaffar Iqbal, *The Making of Islamic Science*, 2nd ed. (Kuala Lumpur: Islamic Book Trust, 2009); Ehsan Masood, *Science and Islam: A History* (London: Icon, 2009); George Saliba, *Islamic Science and the Making of the European Renaissance* (Cambridge, MA: MIT Press, 2007); Howard Turner, *Science in Medieval Islam* (Austin: University of Texas Press, 1997), and the enormous bibliography in Mohamed Abattouy, *L'histoire des sciences arabes classiques: une bibliographie selective critique* (Casablanca: Fondation du Roi Abdul-Aziz, 2007).

35.   Jonathan Berkey, *The Transmission of Knowledge in Medieval Cairo* (Princeton: Princeton University Press, 1992) and George Makdisi, *The Rise of Colleges: Institutions of Learning in Islam and the West* (Edinburgh: Edinburgh University Press, 1981) are partial exceptions.

36.   Charles Haskins, *The Renaissance of the Twelfth Century* (1927; repr., Cambridge, MA: Harvard University Press, 1971); R. N. Swanson, *The Twelfth-Century Renaissance* (Manchester, UK: Manchester University Press, 1999).

37.   Mary Beard et al., "Literacy in the Roman World," *Journal of Roman Archaeology* 3, suppl. (1991); Alan Bowman and Gregory Woolf, eds., *Literacy and Power in the Ancient World* (Cambridge, UK: Cambridge University Press, 1997); Harris, *Ancient Literacy*; Netz, "Counter-Culture," "Bibliosphere," and *Space, Scale, Canon.*

38.   Harris, *Ancient Literacy.*

39.   For example, Thomas, *Literacy and Orality in Ancient Greece*; William Johnson and Holt Parker, eds., *Ancient Literacies: The Culture of Reading in Greece and Rome* (New York: Oxford University Press, 2009).

40.   Anna Missiou, *Literacy and Democracy in Fifth-Century Athens* (Cambridge, UK: Cambridge University Press, 2010), and Ober, *Democracy and Knowledge*, on Athenian learning and innovation. Literacy among ordinary Roman soldiers: Alan Bowman, *Life and Letters on the Roman Frontier* (London: British Museum, 1998); John Adams, "The Poets of Bu Njem: Language, Culture and the Centurionate," *Journal of Roman Studies* 89 (1999): 109–34.

41.   See, for instance, Nicholas Everett, *Literacy in Lombard Italy, c. 568–774* (Cambridge, UK: Cambridge University Press, 2010).

42.   Schmandt-Besserat, *Before Writing.*

43.   Akkermans and Schwartz, *Archaeology of Syria,* 88.

44.   United Nations Development Programme, *Human Development Report 2011.*

45.   I base these estimates largely on Benjamin Duke, *The History of Modern Japanese Education: Constructing the National School System, 1872–1890* (New Brunswick, NJ: Rutgers University Press, 2009).

46.   Bastid, *Educational Reform*; Bailey, *Reform the People.*

47.   Seeberg, *Literacy in China.*

48.   I extrapolate these numbers from Evelyn Rawski, *Education and Popular Literacy in Ch'ing China* (Ann Arbor: University of Michigan Press, 1978), Charles Ridley, "Educational Theory and Practice in Late Imperial China: The Teaching of Writing as a Specific Case" (PhD thesis, Stanford University, 1973), and Thomas Lee, *Education in Traditional China: A History* (Leiden: Brill, 2000).

49.   See Catherine Jami, "Learning Mathematical Sciences during the Early and Mid-Ch'ing," in Benjamin Elman and Alexander Woodside, eds., *Education and Society in Late Imperial China, 1600–1900* (Berkeley: University of California Press, 1994), 223–56; Timothy Brook, *The Confusions of Pleasure: Commerce and Culture in Ming China* (Berkeley: University of California Press, 1998), 56–65.

50.   Richard Rubinger, *Popular Literacy in Early Modern Japan* (Honolulu: University of Hawaii Press, 2007).

51.   See, for instance, Lee, *Education in Traditional China*; Bodde, *Chinese Thought*; Barrett, *Woman Who Discovered Printing*; Kuhn, *Age of Confucian Rule,* 120–37; Elvin, *Pattern,* 181–95.

52.   In general terms, see Mark Lewis, *Writing and Authority in Early China* (Albany: State University of New York Press, 1999); *Early Chinese Empires*; *China between Empires.*

53.   Demattè, "Origins."

54.   Compare Margaret Jacob, *Scientific Culture and the Making of the Industrial West* (New York: Oxford University Press, 1997); Joel Mokyr, *The Enlightened Economy: An Economic History of Britain, 1700–1850* (New Haven: Yale University Press, 2010).

CHAPTER 7

1.   Short-term accident theories: Morris, *Why the West Rules,* 18–21; long-term lock-in theories: ibid., 10–18.

2.   See, most famously, Edward Tufte, *The Visual Display of Quantitative Information* (New York: Graphics Press, 2001).

3.   Personal communication, November 23, 2010.

4. Morris, *Why the West Rules*, 151, 626; disagreements in Pomeranz, "How Big Should Historians Think?" 310–11.

5. Morris, *Why the West Rules*, 166, 558, 642, 644.

6. Ian Morris, "Mediterraneanization," *Mediterranean Historical Review* 18 (2003): 30–55.

7. Morris, *Why the West Rules*, 481–83, 489.

8. For example, Malanima, "Energy Consumption."

9. This approach is explained in detail in Jared Diamond and James Robinson, eds., *Natural Experiments of History* (Cambridge, MA: Harvard University Press, 2010).

10. Although perhaps not impossible: see Ian McNiven et al., "Dating Aboriginal Stone-Walled Fishtraps at Lake Condah, Southeast Australia," *Journal of Archaeological Science* 39 (2012): 268–86.

11. M. J. T. Lewis, "The Origins of the Wheelbarrow," *Technology and Culture* 35 (1994): 453–75; I thank Panagiotis Karras (personal communication, December 26, 2010) for this reference.

12. Elizabeth Boone and Gary Urton, eds., *Their Way of Writing: Scripts, Signs, and Pictographies in Pre-Columbia America* (Washington, DC: Dumbarton Oaks, 2011) provide a recent overview of New World writing. Some archaeologists (e.g., Joyce Marcus, *Mesoamerican Writing Systems: Propaganda, Myth, and History in Four Ancient Civilizations* [Princeton: Princeton University Press, 1992]) suggest that at least some forms of New World writing were not intended as information technology systems (in the sense of symbols used to store and communicate data to others), but the designers' and users' intentions are not at issue here. Whatever the aims of the scripts' makers, New World writing systems did function as information technology, albeit not as effectively as contemporary systems in the Old World.

13. Lucinda Blackwell et al., "Middle Stone Age Bone Tools from the Howiesons Poort Layers, Sibudu Cave, South Africa," *Journal of Archaeological Science* 35 (2008): 1566–80; Marlize Lombard, "Quartz-Tipped Arrows Older Than 60ka: Further Use-Trace Evidence from Sibudu, KwaZulu-Natal, South Africa," *Journal of Archaeological Science* 38 (2011): 1918–30.

14. Brian Fagan, *The First North Americans: An Archaeological Journey* (London: Thames & Hudson, 2012), 63; Ross Hassig, *War and Society in Ancient Mesoamerica* (Berkeley: University of California Press, 1992), 119.

15. Diamond, *Guns, Germs, and Steel*, 360–70.

16. Ibid., 93–156.

17. Ibid., 157–75. Diamond leans toward human agency in explaining these extinctions, but the evidence is very unclear (Donald Grayson and David Meltzer, "A Requiem for North American Overkill," *Journal of Archaeological Science* 30 [2003]: 585–93).

18. Robert Ricklefs, *The Economy of Nature*, 5th ed. (New York: Freeman, 2001).

19. Diamond, *Guns, Germs, and Steel*, 176–91.

20.   See also Peter Turchin et al., "East-West Orientation of Historical Empires and Modern Nations," *Journal of World Systems Research* 12 (2006): 218–29.

21.   David Laitin et al., "Geographic Axes and the Persistence of Cultural Diversity," *Proceedings of the National Academy of Sciences* 110 (2012): 10.1073/pnas. 1205338109.

22.   Carneiro, *Evolutionism*, 229.

23.   Sanderson, *Social Evolutionism*, 83–100, Trigger, *Sociocultural Evolution*, 162–85, and Carneiro, *Evolutionism*, 229–61, review much of the literature.

24.   The literature is large, but Arjun Appadurai, *Modernity at Large* (Minneapolis: University of Minnesota Press, 1996), Shmuel Eisenstadt, ed., *Multiple Modernities* (New York: Transaction Books, 1999), and Dilip Parameshwar Gaonkar, ed., *Alternative Modernities*, 2nd ed. (Durham, NC: Duke University Press, 2001) give a flavor of the discussions.

25.   The process is described in marvelous detail in Bayly, *Modern World*.

26.   Stephen Jay Gould, *Wonderful Life: The Burgess Shale and the Nature of History* (New York: Norton, 1989), 320–21.

27.   For example, Simon Conway Morris, *Life's Solution: Inevitable Humans in a Lonely Universe* (Cambridge, UK: Cambridge University Press, 2003).

28.   Stephen Jay Gould, "The Evolution of Life on Earth," *Scientific American* 271 (1994): 84–91.

29.   Morris, *Why the West Rules*, 170–71, 582–624.

30.   For example, Hugo Scott-Gall, "An Interview with . . . Prof. Ian Morris," *Goldman Sachs Fortnightly Thoughts* 23 (December 15, 2010): 5–7; Jane Smiley, "Who Cares What a Robot Thinks? You Will," *Washington Post*, January 30, 2011, http://www.washingtonpost.com/wp-dyn/content/article/2011/01/28/ AR2011012806988.html; Martin Wolf, "East and West Converge on a Problem,," *Financial Times*, January 11, 2011, http://www.ft.com/cms/s/0/4f590ec6-1dce-11e0 -badd-00144feab49a.html#axzz1AqLSQCea.

31.   As seems to be assumed in fascinating recent books by Niall Ferguson (*Civilization: The West and the Rest* [New York: Penguin, 2011]), George Friedman (*The Next Decade: Empire and Republic in a Changing World* [New York: Anchor, 2011]), and Robert Kagan (*The World America Made* [New York: Knopf, 2012]).

32.   For example, National Intelligence Council, *Global Trends 2030: Alternative Worlds* (Washington, DC: Government Printing Office, 2012).

33.   Morris, *War! What Is It Good For?*, chap. 7.

34.   Richard Dawkins, *The Selfish Gene* (Oxford: Oxford University Press, 1976), 1.

REFERENCES

Abattouy, Mohamed. 2007. *L'histoire des sciences arabes classiques: une bibliographie selective critique*. Casablanca: Fondation du Roi Abdul-Aziz.

Abu-Lughod, Janet. 1971. *Cairo: 1,001 Years of the City Victorious*. Princeton: Princeton University Press.

Acemoglu, Daron, and James Robinson. 2012. *Why Nations Fail*. New York: Crown Books.

Adams, John. 1999. "The Poets of Bu Njem: Language, Culture and the Centurionate." *Journal of Roman Studies* 89: 109–34.

Adams, Richard N. 1975. *Energy and Structure: A Theory of Social Power*. Austin: University of Texas Press.

Adams, Robert McC. 1981. *Heartland of Cities*. Chicago: University of Chicago Press.

———. 1996. *Paths of Fire: An Anthropologist's Inquiry into Western Technology*. Princeton: Princeton University Press.

———. 2001. "Complexity in Archaic States." *Journal of Anthropological Archaeology* 20: 345–60.

Adams, Thomas. 2008. *The Army after Next: The First Postindustrial Army*. Stanford: Stanford University Press.

Adshead, Samuel. 2000. *China in World History*. 3rd ed. London: Longmans.

———. 2004. *Tang China*. London: Longmans.

Åkerman, K. 2001. "The 'Aussenhaken Area' in the City of Assur during the Second Half of the Seventh Century BC: A Study of a Neo-Assyrian City Quarter and Its Demography." *State Archives of Assyria Bulletin* 13: 217–72.

Akkermans, Peter, and Glenn Schwartz. 2003. *The Archaeology of Syria*. Cambridge, UK: Cambridge University Press.

Albanese Procelli, Rosa Maria. 2003. *Sicani, Siculi, Elimi: Forme di identità, modi di contatto e processi di trasformazione*. Milan: Longanesi.

Allen, G. C. 1946. *A Short Economic History of Modern Japan, 1867–1937*. London: Allen & Unwin.

Allen, Robert. 2001. "The Great Divergence in European Wages and Prices from the Middle Ages to the First World War." *Explorations in Economic History* 38: 411–48.

———. 2006. "Agricultural Productivity and Rural Incomes in England and the Yangzi Delta, c. 1620–c. 1820." Unpublished paper. http://www.nuffield.ox .ac.uk/General/Members/allen.aspx.

———. 2007. "Pessimism Preserved: Real Wages in the British Industrial Revolution." Oxford University Department of Economics Working Paper 314. http://www.nuffield.ox.ac.uk/General/Members/allen.aspx.

———. 2009a. *The British Industrial Revolution in Global Perspective*. Cambridge, UK: Cambridge University Press.

———. 2009b. "How Prosperous Were the Romans? Evidence from Diocletian's Price Edict (AD 301)." In Bowman and Wilson, *Quantifying the Roman Economy*, 327–45.

Allen, Robert, et al. 2011. "Wages, Prices and Living Standards in China, 1738–1925: A Comparison with Europe, Japan and India." *Economic History Review* 64 (supplement): 8–38, http://www.nuffield.ox.ac.uk/General/Members/ allen.aspx.

Allen, Robert, Tommy Bengtsson, and Martin Dribe, eds. 2005. *Living Standards in the Past: New Perspectives on Well-Being in Asia and Europe*. Oxford: Oxford University Press.

Alperson-Afil, N. 2008. "Continual Fire-Making by Hominins at Gesher Benot Ya'aqov, Israel." *Quaternary Science Reviews* 27: 1733–39.

Alston, Richard. 2001. *The City in Roman and Byzantine Egypt*. London: Routledge.

Angeles, Luis. 2008. "GDP per Capita or Real Wages? Making Sense of Conflicting Views on Pre-Industrial Europe." *Explorations in Economic History* 45: 147–63.

Anglim, Simon, et al. 2003. *Fighting Techniques of the Ancient World, 3000 BC–AD 500: Equipment, Combat Skills, and Tactics*. New York: Thomas Dunne Books.

Appadurai, Arjun. 1996. *Modernity at Large*. Minneapolis: University of Minnesota Press.

Aranguren, Biancamaria, et al. 2007. "Grinding Flour in Upper Palaeolithic Europe (25,000 Years BP)." *Antiquity* 81: 845–55.

Araus, José Luis, et al. 2001. "Estimated Wheat Yields during the Emergence of Agriculture Based on the Carbon Isotope Discrimination of Grains: Evidence from a 10th Millennium BP Site on the Euphrates." *Journal of Archaeological Science* 28: 341–50.

———. 2003. "Productivity in Prehistoric Agriculture." *Journal of Archaeological Science* 30: 681–93.

Arlinghaus, Franz-Josef, et al., eds. 2006. *Transforming the Medieval World: Uses of Pragmatic Literacy in the Middle Ages*. Turnhout: Brepols.

Armelagos, George, and Kristin Harper. 2005. "Genomics at the Origins of Agriculture." *Evolutionary Anthropology* 14: 68–77, 109–21.

Arrighi, Giovanni. 2007. *Adam Smith in Beijing: Lineages of the Twenty-First Century*. London: Verso.

Arrighi, Giovanni, et al., eds. 2003. *The Resurgence of East Asia: 500, 150, and 50 Year Perspectives*. New York: Routledge.

Arthur, Paul. 2002. *Naples, from Roman Town to City-State*. Rome: British School at Rome.

Assaf, Yasur-Landau. 2010. *The Philistines and Aegean Migration at the End of the Late Bronze Age*. Cambridge, UK: Cambridge University Press.

Aston, A. E., and T. Philpin, eds. 1985. *The Brenner Debate*. Cambridge, UK: Cambridge University Press.

Atahan, Pia, et al. 2011. "Early Neolithic Diets at Baijian, Wei River Valley, China: Stable Carbon and Nitrogen Analysis of Human and Faunal Remains." *Journal of Archaeological Science* 38: 2811–17.

Atiyeh, George, ed. 2005. *The Book in the Islamic World: The Written Word and Communication in the Middle East*. Edinburgh: Edinburgh University Press.

Bachhuber, Christopher, and Gareth Roberts, eds. 2009. *Forces of Transformation: The End of the Bronze Age in the Mediterranean*. Oxford: Oxbow.

Bachrach, Bernard. 1972. *Merovingian Military Organization, 451–781*. Minneapolis: University of Minnesota Press.

———. 2001. *Early Carolingian Warfare: Prelude to Empire*. Philadelphia: University of Pennsylvania Press.

Baeten, Jan, et al. 2012. "Faecal Biomarkers and Archaeobotanical Analyses of Sediments from a Public Latrine Shed New Light on Ruralisation in Sagalassos, Turkey." *Journal of Archaeological Science* 39: 1143–59.

Bagnall, Roger. 1993. *Egypt in Late Antiquity*. Berkeley: University of California Press.

———. 2002. "Effects of Plague: Model and Evidence." *Journal of Roman Archaeology* 15: 114–20.

———. 2009. "Response to Alan Bowman." In Bowman and Wilson, *Quantifying the Roman Economy*, 205–12.

Bailey, Paul. 1990. *Reform the People: Changing Attitudes towards Popular Education in Early Twentieth-Century China*. Vancouver: University of British Columbia Press.

Bailey, R. 1991. "The Behavioral Ecology of Efe Pygmy Men in the Ituru Forest, Zaire." University of Michigan Museum of Anthropology Paper 86, Ann Arbor.

Bairoch, Paul. 1982. "International Industrialization Levels from 1705 to 1980." *Journal of European Economic History* 11: 269–333.

———. 1988. *Cities and Economic Development: From the Dawn of History to the Present*. Chicago: University of Chicago Press.

Bak, Per, et al. 1988. "Self-Organized Criticality." *Physical Review* 38: 364–74.

Balk, Alfred. 2005. *The Rise of Radio, from Marconi through the Golden Age*. New York: McFarland & Co.

Bang, Peter Fibiger. 2009. *The Roman Bazaar: A Comparative Study of Trade and Markets in a Tributary Empire*. Cambridge, UK: Cambridge University Press.

Barfield, Thomas. 1989. *The Perilous Frontier: Nomadic Empires and China, 221 BC–AD 1757*. Oxford: Blackwell.

Barker, Graeme. 2006. *The Agricultural Revolution in Prehistory: Why Did Foragers Become Farmers?* Oxford: Oxford University Press.

Barker, Philip. 1997. *The Baths Basilica, Wroxeter*. London: English Heritage.

Barnouw, Erik. 1990. *Tube of Plenty: The Evolution of American Television*. 2nd ed. New York: Oxford University Press.

Barrett, James, et al. 2004. "'Dark Age Economics' Revisited: The English Fish Bone Evidence AD 600–1600." *Antiquity* 78: 618–36.

———. 2011. "Interpreting the Expansion of Sea Fishing in Medieval Europe Using Stable Isotope Analysis of Archaeological Cod Bones." *Journal of Archaeological Science* 38: 1516–24.

Barrett, T. H. 2008. *The Woman Who Discovered Printing*. New Haven: Yale University Press.

Barton, I. M. 1996. *Roman Domestic Buildings*. Exeter: University of Exeter Press.

Bar-Yosef, Ofer. 1986. "The Walls of Jericho: An Alternative Interpretation." *Current Anthropology* 27: 157–62.

Bar-Yosef, Ofer, and François Valla, eds. 1991. *The Natufian Culture in the Levant*. Ann Arbor, MI: International Monographs in Prehistory.

Basan, Osman Aziz. 2010. *The Great Seljuqs: A History*. London: Routledge.

Bass, George. 2010. "Cape Gelidonya Shipwreck." In Cline, *Oxford Handbook of the Bronze Age Aegean*, 797–803.

Bastid, Marianne. 1988. *Educational Reform in Early Twentieth-Century China*. Ann Arbor: University of Michigan Press.

Bayly, Christopher. 2004. *The Birth of the Modern World 1789–1914*. Oxford: Blackwell.

Beal, Richard. 1992. *The Organization of the Hittite Military*. Heidelberg: Carl Winter.

Beard, Mary, et al. 1991. "Literacy in the Roman World." *Journal of Roman Archaeology* 3 (suppl.).

Bedford, Peter. 2007. "The Persian Near East." In Scheidel et al., *Cambridge Economic History*, 302–29.

Beinhocker, Eric. 2010. *The Origin of Wealth: Evolution, Complexity, and the Radical Remaking of Economics*. Cambridge, MA: Harvard Business School.

Bellwood, Peter. 2005. *First Farmers*. Oxford: Blackwell.

Benedictow, Ole. 2004. *The Black Death 1346–1353: The Complete History*. Rochester, NY: Boydell Press, 2004.

Bengtsson, Tommy, C. Campbell, and James Lee, eds. 2005. *Life Under Pressure: Mortality and Living Standards in Europe and Asia, 1500–1700*. Cambridge, UK: Cambridge University Press.

Benn, Charles. 2002. *China's Golden Age: Everyday Life under the Tang Dynasty*. New York: Oxford University Press.

Bennett, Matthew, et al. 2005. *Fighting Techniques of the Medieval World, AD 500–1500: Equipment, Combat Skills, and Tactics*. New York: Thomas Dunne Books.

Bentley, R. Alexander, and Herbert Maschner, eds. 2003. *Complex Systems and Archaeology*. Salt Lake City: University of Utah Press.

Benyon-Davies, Paul. 2007. "Informatics and the Inca." *International Journal of Information Management* 27: 306–18.

Beresford, Maurice, and John Hurst. 1991. *Wharram Percy: Deserted Medieval Village*. New Haven: Yale University Press.

Berg, Richard. 2010. *Chariots of Fire: Warfare in the Bronze Age, 2300–1200 BC*. Hanford, CA: GMT Games.

Berg, Richard, and Mark Herman. 1999. *Cataphract: The Reconquest of the Roman Empire*. Hanford, CA: GMT Games.

———. 2004. *Devil's Horsemen: The Mongol War Machine*. Hanford, CA: GMT Games.

———. 2008. *SPQR: The Art of War in the Roman Republic*. 3rd ed. Hanford, CA: GMT Games.

Berkey, Jonathan. 1992. *The Transmission of Knowledge in Medieval Cairo*. Princeton: Princeton University Press.

Bertaud, Jean-Paul. 1988. *The Army of the French Revolution*. Trans. R. R. Palmer. Bloomington: Indiana University Press.

Biddle, Stephen. 2004. *Military Power: Explaining Victory and Defeat in Modern Battle*. Princeton: Princeton University Press.

Bielenstein, Hans. 1976. "Lo-yang in the Later Han Times." *Bulletin of the Museum of Far Eastern Antiquities* 48: 3–142.

Binford, Lewis. 1971. "Mortuary Practices: Their Study and Their Potential." In James Brown, ed., *Approaches to the Social Dimensions of Mortuary Practices*: 6–29. New York: Memoirs of the Society for American Archaeology 25.

Bintliff, John, et al., eds. 2008. *Testing the Hinterland: The Work of the Boeotia Survey (1989–1991) in the Southern Approaches to the City of Thespiai*. Cambridge, UK: McDonald Institute.

Bintliff, John, and Hanna Stöger, eds. 2009. *Medieval and Post-Medieval Greece: The Corfu Papers*. Oxford: British Archaeological Reports International Series 2023.

Bitelli, G., et al. 2003. *The Bologna and Lecce Universities Joint Archaeological Mission in Egypt: Ten Years of Excavation at Bakchias, 1993–2002*. Naples: Graus.

Black, Jeremy. 1998. *War in the Early Modern World, 1450–1815*. London: Routledge.

———. 2002. *European Warfare, 1494–1660*. London: Longmans.

———. 2006. *Warfare in the Eighteenth Century*. Washington, DC: Smithsonian.

Blackmore, Susan. 1999. *The Meme Machine*. Oxford: Oxford University Press.

Blackwell, Lucinda, et al. 2008. "Middle Stone Age Bone Tools from the Howiesons Poort Layers, Sibudu Cave, South Africa." *Journal of Archaeological Science* 35: 1566–80.

Blair, John, and Nigel Ramsay, eds. 2003. *English Medieval Industries: Craftsmen, Techniques, Products*. London: Hambledon.

Blanton, Robert, et al. 1981. *Ancient Mesoamerica*. Cambridge, UK: Cambridge University Press.

Boaretto, Elisabetta, et al. 2009. "Radiocarbon Dating of Charcoal and Bone Collagen Associated with Early Pottery at Yuchanyan Cave, Hunan Province, China." *Proceedings of the National Academy of Sciences* 106: 9595–9600. doi:10.1073/pnas.0900539106.

Bocherens, H., et al. 1999. "Paleoenvironmental and Paleodietary Implications of Isotopic Biogeochemistry of Last Interglacial Neanderthal and Mammoth Bones in Scladina Cane (Belgium)." *Journal of Archaeological Science* 26: 599–607.

———. 2001. "New Isotopic Evidence for Dietary Habits of Neandertals from Belgium." *Journal of Human Evolution* 40: 497–505.

Bodde, Derk. 1991. *Chinese Thought, Society, and Science: The Intellectual and Social Background of Science and Technology in Pre-Modern China*. Honolulu: University of Hawaii Press.

Bogaard, A., et al. 2007. "The Impact of Manuring on Nitrogen Isotope Ratios in Cereals." *Journal of Archaeological Science* 34: 335–43.

Boiy, T. 2004. *Late Achaemenid and Hellenistic Babylon*. Leuven: Orientalia Lovaniensia Analecta 126.

Books, Amber, et al. 2008. *Fighting Techniques of the Oriental World, AD 1200–1854: Equipment, Combat Skills, and Tactics*. New York: Thomas Dunne Books.

———. 2009. *Fighting Techniques of Naval Warfare, 1190 BC–Present: Strategy, Weapons, Commanders, and Ships*. New York: Thomas Dunne Books.

Boone, Elizabeth, and Gary Urton, eds. 2011. *Their Way of Writing: Scripts, Signs, and Pictographies in Pre-Columbia America*. Washington, DC: Dumbarton Oaks.

Boot, Max. 2006. *War Made New: Technology, Warfare, and the Course of History, 1500 to Today*. New York: Gotham Books.

Boserup, Ester. 1965. *The Conditions of Agricultural Growth*. Chicago: Aldine.

———. 1981. *Population and Technological Change*. Chicago: University of Chicago Press.

Bourdieu, Pierre. 1977. *Outline of a Theory of Practice*. Trans. Richard Nice. Cambridge, UK: Cambridge University Press.

Bowden, Edgar. 1969. "A Dimensional Model of Multilinear Sociocultural Evolution." *American Anthropologist* 67: 864–70.

Bowles, Samuel, and Herbert Gintis. 2011. *A Cooperative Species: Human Reciprocity and Its Evolution*. Princeton: Princeton University Press.

Bowman, Alan. 1998. *Life and Letters on the Roman Frontier*. London: British Museum.

———. 2009. "Quantifying Egyptian Agriculture." In Bowman and Wilson, *Quantifying the Roman Economy*, 177–204.

Bowman, Alan, and Andrew Wilson, eds. 2009. *Quantifying the Roman Economy*. Oxford: Oxford University Press.

Bowman, Alan, and Gregory Woolf, eds. 1997. *Literacy and Power in the Ancient World*. Cambridge, UK: Cambridge University Press.

Boyd, Andrew. 1962. *Chinese Architecture and Town Planning: 1500 BC–AD 1911*. Chicago: University of Chicago Press.

Boyd, Brian. 2010. *People and Animals in Levantine Prehistory, 10,000–8000 BC*. Cambridge, UK: Cambridge University Press.

Boyd, Robert, and Peter Richerson. 1985. *Culture and the Evolutionary Process*. Chicago: University of Chicago Press.

Bradbury, Jim, ed. 2007. *The Routledge Companion to Medieval Warfare*. London: Routledge.

Braudel, Fernand. 1981. *Civilization and Capitalism, 15th–18th Centuries I: The Structures of Everyday Life*. Trans. Siân Reynolds. New York: Harper and Row.

Bray, Francesca. 1984. *Science and Civilisation in China VI: Biology and Biological Technology. Part 6: Agriculture*. Cambridge, UK: Cambridge University Press.

———. 1986. *The Rice Economy: Technology and Development in Asian Societies*. Oxford: Oxford University Press.

———. 2001. "The *Qimin yaoshu* (Essential Techniques for the Common People)." Unpublished paper.

Brett, Michael. 2005. "Population and Conversion to Islam in Egypt in the Mediaeval Period." In U. Vermeulen and J. van Steenbergen, eds., *Egypt and Syria in the Fatimid, Ayyubid and Mamluk Eras*: 4:1–32. Leuven: Peeters.

Brewer, John. 1988. *The Sinews of Power: War, Money and the English State, 1688–1783*. Cambridge, MA: Harvard University Press.

Brewer, John, and Roy Porter, eds. 1993. *Consumption and the World of Goods*. London: Routledge.

Briggs, Asa, and Peter Burke. 2002. *A Social History of the Media: From Gutenberg to the Internet*. Oxford: Blackwell.

Britnell, Richard. 1997. *Pragmatic Literacy, East and West, 1200–1330*. Oxford: Boydell.

Brokaw, Cynthia, and Kai-wing Chow, eds. 2005. *Printing and Book Culture in Late Imperial China*. Berkeley: University of California Press.

Brook, Timothy. 1998. *The Confusions of Pleasure: Commerce and Culture in Ming China*. Berkeley: University of California Press.

Brown, Peter. 1971. *The World of Late Antiquity AD 150–750*. London: Thames & Hudson.

Bruce, Robert, et al. 2008. *Fighting Techniques of the Napoleonic Age, 1792–1815*. New York: Thomas Dunne Books.

Brunk, Gregory. 2002. "Why Do Societies Collapse? A Theory Based on Self-Organized Criticality." *Journal of Theoretical Politics* 14: 195–230.

Buck, John L. 1930. *Chinese Farm Economy*. Chicago: University of Chicago Press.

———. 1937. *Land Utilization in China*. Shanghai: Nanjing University Press.

Bussert, James, and Bruce Elleman. 2011. *People's Liberation Army Navy: Combat System Technology, 1949–2010*. Annapolis, MD: U.S. Naval Institute Press.

Buxó, Ramon. 2009. "Botanical and Archaeological Dimensions of the Colonial Encounter." In Michael Dietler and Caroline López-Ruiz, eds., *Colonial Encounters in Ancient Iberia*: 155–68. Chicago: University of Chicago Press.

Cahill, Nicholas. 2002. *Household and City Organization at Olynthus*. New Haven: Yale University Press.

Callot, O. 1983. *Une maison à Ugarit: études d'architecture domestique*. Paris: Editions recherché sur les civilisations.

———. 1994. *La tranchée "ville sud": études d'architecture domestique*. Paris: Editions recherché sur les civilisations.

Cameron, Averil. 1993. *The Mediterranean World in Late Antiquity AD 395–600*. London: Routledge.

Campbell, Duncan. 2003. *Greek and Roman Siege Machinery 399 BC–AD 363*. Oxford: Osprey.

Campbell, J. Brian. 1994. *The Roman Army: A Sourcebook*. London: Routledge.

Carneiro, Robert. 1962. "Scale Analysis as an Instrument for the Study of Cultural Evolution." *Southwestern Journal of Anthropology* 18: 149–69.

———. 1967. "On the Relationship between Size of Population and Complexity of Social Organization." *Southwestern Journal of Anthropology* 23: 234–41.

———. 1968. "Ascertaining, Testing, and Interpreting Sequences of Cultural Development." *Southwestern Journal of Anthropology* 24: 354–74.

———. 1969. "The Measurement of Cultural Development in the Ancient Near East and in Anglo-Saxon England." *Transactions of the New York Academy of Sciences Series 2* 31: 1013–23.

———. 1970. "Scale Analysis, Evolutionary Sequences, and the Rating of Cultures." In Naroll and Cohen, *Handbook of Method in Cultural Anthropology*, 834–71.

———. 2003. *Evolutionism in Cultural Anthropology*. Boulder, CO: Westview.

Carr, Christopher. 1995. "Mortuary Practices: Their Social, Philosophical-Religious, Circumstantial, and Physical Determinants." *Journal of Archaeological Method and Theory* 2: 105–200.

Caseldine, C. J., and C. Turney. 2010. "The Bigger Picture: Towards Integrating Palaeoclimate and Environmental Data with a History of Societal Change." *Journal of Quaternary Science* 25: 88–93.

Cavaciocchi, S., ed. 1997. *Alimentazione e nutrizione secc. XIII–XVIII*. Florence: Le Monnier.

Chambers, F. M., et al. 2007. "Globally Synchronous Climate Change 2800 Years Ago: Proxy Data from Peat in South America." *Earth and Planetary Science Letters* 253: 439–44.

———. 2010. "Peatland Archives of Late-Holocene Climate Change in Northern Europe." *PAGES News* 18: 4–6.

Chandler, David. 1966. *The Campaigns of Napoleon*. New York: Scribner.

Chandler, Tertius. 1987. *Four Thousand Years of Urban Growth: An Historical Census*. Lewiston, NY: St. David's University Press.

Chandler, Tertius, and Gerald Fox. 1974. *Three Thousand Years of Urban Growth*. New York: Academic Press.

Chang, Kwang-chih. 1980. *Shang Civilization*. New Haven: Yale University Press.

———. 1986. *The Archaeology of Ancient China*. 4th ed. New Haven: Yale University Press.

Chang, Kwang-chih, and Xu Pingfang, eds. 2005. *The Formation of Chinese Civilization: An Archaeological Perspective*. New Haven: Yale University Press.

Chapman, Robert. 2003. *Archaeologies of Complexity*. London: Routledge.

Chartier, Roger, ed. 1989. *The Culture of Print*. Princeton: Princeton University Press.

Chase, Kenneth. 2003. *Firearms: A Global History to 1700*. Cambridge, UK: Cambridge University Press.

Chayanov, A. V. 1986. *The Theory of Peasant Economy*. Madison: University of Wisconsin Press.

Cherian, P. J., et al. 2007. "The Muziris Heritage Project: Excavations at Pattanam—2007." *Journal of Indian Ocean Archaeology* 4: 1–10.

Cherry, John, et al. 1991. *Landscape Archaeology as Long-Term History*. Los Angeles: Cotsen Institute.

Chi, Zhang, and Hsiao-chun Hung. 2010. "The Emergence of Agriculture in Southern China." *Antiquity* 84: 11–25.

Childe, V. Gordon. 1925. *The Dawn of European Civilisation*. 1st ed. London: Kegan Paul.

———. 1936. *Man Makes Himself*. London: Watts & Co.

———. 1942. *What Happened in History*. Harmondsworth, UK: Penguin.

———. 1951. *Social Evolution*. London: Watts & Co.

Chivers, C. J. 2010. *The Gun*. New York: Simon & Schuster.

Chow, Kai-wing. 2004. *Publishing, Culture, and Power in Early Modern China*. Stanford: Stanford University Press.

Chrisomalis, Stephen. 2004. "A Cognitive Typology for Numerical Notation." *Cambridge Archaeological Journal* 14: 37–52.

———. 2009. "The Origins and Co-evolution of Literacy and Numeracy." In David Olson and Nancy Torrance, eds., *The Cambridge Handbook of Literacy*: 59–74. Cambridge, UK: Cambridge University Press.

———. 2010. *Numerical Notation: A Comparative History*. Cambridge, UK: Cambridge University Press.

Christian, David. 2004. *Maps of Time: An Introduction to Big History*. Berkeley: University of California Press.

Christie, Neil. 2006. *From Constantine to Charlemagne: An Archaeology of Italy, AD 300–800*. London: Ashgate.

Cipolla, Carlo. 1969. *Literacy and Development in the West*. Harmondsworth, UK: Penguin.

———, ed. 1974. *The Fontana Economic History of Europe II: The Sixteenth and Seventeenth Centuries.* Glasgow: Fontana.

———. 1993. *Europe before the Industrial Revolution: European Society and Economy, 1000–1700.* 3rd ed. London: Routledge.

Clanchy, Michael. 1993. *From Memory to Written Record: England, 1066–1307.* 2nd ed. Oxford: Blackwell.

Clark, Colin, and Margaret Haswell. 1970. *The Economics of Subsistence Agriculture.* London: Macmillan.

Clark, Gregory. 1987. "Productivity Growth without Technical Change in European Agriculture before 1850." *Journal of Economic History* 47: 419–32.

———. 2005. "The Condition of the Working Class in England, 1209–2004." *Journal of Political Economy* 113: 1307–40.

———. 2007a. *A Farewell to Alms: A Brief Economic History of the World.* Princeton: Princeton University Press.

———. 2007b. "Genetically Capitalist? The Malthusian Era and the Formation of Modern Preferences." http://www.econ.ucdavis.edu/faculty/gclark/papers/capitalism%20genes.pdf.

Clarke, David. 1978. *Analytical Archaeology.* 2nd ed., revised by Robert Chapman. London: Methuen.

Cleator, P. E. 1967. *Weapons of War.* London: Robert Hale.

Cline, Eric. 1994. *Sailing the Wine-Dark Sea: International Trade in the Aegean Late Bronze Age.* Oxford: British Archaeological Reports International Series 591.

———, ed. 2010. *The Oxford Handbook of the Bronze Age Aegean.* Oxford: Oxford University Press.

Clutton-Brock, T. H., ed. 1989. *Primate Ecology.* New York: Academic Press.

Coates-Stephens, Roger. 1996. "Housing in Early Medieval Rome." *Papers of the British School at Rome* 64: 239–59.

Cochrane, Gregory, and Henry Harpending. 2009. *The Ten Thousand Year Explosion: How Civilization Accelerated Evolution.* New York: Basic Books.

Cohen, Mark Nathan, ed. 2009. "Rethinking the Origins of Agriculture." *Current Anthropology* 50 (suppl.).

Cole, Bernard. 2010. *The Great Wall at Sea: China's Navy in the Twenty-First Century.* 2nd ed. Annapolis, MD: U.S. Naval Institute Press.

Colledge, Susan, and James Connolly, eds. 2007. *The Origins and Spread of Domestic Plants in Southwest Asia and Europe.* Walnut Creek, CA: AltaMira.

Colledge, Susan, et al. 2004. "Archaeobotanical Evidence for the Spread of Farming in the Eastern Mediterranean." *Current Anthropology* 45 (suppl.): S35–S58.

Connaughton, R. M. 1988. *The War of the Rising Sun and Tumbling Bear: A Military History of the Russo-Japanese War, 1904–5.* London: Routledge.

Contamine, Philip. 1984. *War in the Middle Ages.* Trans. Michael Jones. Oxford: Blackwell.

Conway Morris, Simon. 2003. *Life's Solution: Inevitable Humans in a Lonely Universe*. Cambridge, UK: Cambridge University Press.

Cook, Earl. 1971. "The Flow of Energy in an Industrial Society." *Scientific American* 225: 135–44.

Coon, Carleton. 1948. *A Reader in General Anthropology*. New York: Holt.

Cooper, Frederick. 2002. *Houses of the Morea: Vernacular Architecture of the Northwest Peloponnese (1205–1955)*. Athens: Melissa.

Cooper, Lisa. 2006. *Early Urbanism on the Syrian Euphrates*. London: Routledge.

Cordy, R. H. 1981. *A Theory of Prehistoric Social Change*. New York: Academic Press.

Coulson, William, and Sarah Vaughan, eds. 2000. *Palaeodiet in the Aegean*. Oxford: Oxbow.

Crafts, Nicholas. 1985. *British Economic Growth during the Industrial Revolution*. Oxford: Clarendon.

Cressy, David. 1980. *Literacy and the Social Order: Reading and Writing in Tudor and Stuart England*. Cambridge, UK: Cambridge University Press.

Crosby, Albert. 1994. *The Measure of Reality: Quantification and Western Society, 1250–1600*. Cambridge, UK: Cambridge University Press.

———. 2003. *Ecological Imperialism*. 2nd ed. Cambridge, UK: Cambridge University Press.

———. 2006. *Children of the Sun: A History of Humanity's Unappeasable Appetite for Energy*. New York: Norton.

Crummy, P. J. 1981. *Aspects of Anglo-Saxon and Norman Colchester*. London: Council for British Archaeology Research Report 39; Colchester: Colchester Archaeological Report 1.

———. 1984. *Excavations at Lion Walk, Balkerne Lane, and Middleborough, Colchester, Essex*. Colchester: Colchester Archaeological Report 3.

Crump, Thomas. 1990. *The Anthropology of Numbers*. Cambridge, UK: Cambridge University Press.

Cucchi, T., et al. 2011. "Early Neolithic Pig Domestication at Jiahu, Henan Province, China." *Journal of Archaeological Science* 38: 11–22.

Curlee, Wanda, and Robert Gordon. 2010. *Complexity Theory and Project Management*. New York: Wiley.

Dale, Stephen. 2010. *The Muslim Empires of the Ottomans, Safavids, and Mughals*. Cambridge, UK: Cambridge University Press.

Dalfes, Nüzhet, et al. 1997. *Third Millennium BC Climate Change and Old World Collapse*. Berlin: Springer.

Dallal, Ahmed. 2010. *Islam, Science, and the Challenge of History*. New Haven: Yale University Press.

Darnell, John, and Colleen Manassa. 2007. *Tutankhamun's Armies: Battle and Conquest during Ancient Egypt's Late Eighteenth Dynasty*. New York: Wiley.

Darnton, Robert. 1982. "What Is the History of Books?" *Daedalus* 111: 65–83.

Darwin, Charles. 1839. *Voyages of the* Adventure *and* Beagle. Vol. 3. London: Henry Colburn.

Daugherty, William, et al. 1986. "The Consequences of 'Limited' Nuclear Attacks on the United States." *International Security* 10 (4): 3–45.

Davies, Norman. 1994. *Europe: A History*. New York: Oxford University Press.

Dawkins, Richard. 1976. *The Selfish Gene*. Oxford: Oxford University Press.

———. 2007. *The God Delusion*. New York: Houghton Mifflin Harcourt.

de Callataÿ, François. 2005. "The Graeco-Roman Economy in the Super-Long Run: Lead, Copper, and Shipwrecks." *Journal of Roman Archaeology* 18: 361–72.

Decker, Ethan, et al. 2007. "Global Patterns of City Size Distributions and their Fundamental Drivers." *PLoS ONE* 9. www.plosone.org.

Deetz, James. 1996. *In Small Things Forgotten*. Rev. ed. New York: Anchor.

de Graeve, Marie-Christine. 1981. *The Ships of the Ancient Near East, c. 2000–500 BC*. Louvain: Department Orientalistiek.

De Groot, Gerard. 2005. *The Bomb: A Life*. Cambridge, MA: Harvard University Press.

Delagnes, Anne, and William Rendu. 2011. "Shifts in Neanderthal Mobility, Technology and Subsistence Strategies in Western France." *Journal of Archaeological Science* 38: 1771–83.

Delbrück, Hans. 1920/1975–85. *History of the Art of War within the Framework of Political History*. 4 vols. Trans. Walter Renfroe. Westport, CT: Greenwood.

Delia, Diana. 1989. "The Population of Roman Alexandria." *Transactions of the American Philological Association* 118: 275–92.

de Long, Bradford, and Andrei Schleifer. 1993. "Princes and Merchants: European City Growth before the Industrial Revolution." *Journal of Law and Economics* 36: 671–702.

Demattè, Paola. 2010. "The Origins of Chinese Writing: The Neolithic Evidence." *Cambridge Archaeological Journal* 20: 211–28.

Dennett, Daniel. 2006. *Breaking the Spell: Religion as a Natural Phenomenon*. New York: Simon & Schuster.

de Pee, Christian. 2010. "Purchase on Power: Imperial Space and Commercial Space in Song-Dynasty Kaifeng, 960–1127." *Journal of the Economic and Social History of the Orient* 53: 149–84.

D'Errico, Francesco, et al. 2012. "Technical, Elemental and Colorific Analysis of an Engraved Ochre Fragment from the MSA Levels of Klasies River Cave 1, South Africa." *Journal of Archaeological Science* 39: 942–52.

de Souza, Philip, ed. 2008. *The Ancient World at War*. London: Thames and Hudson.

de Vleeschouwer, François. 2007. "Atmospheric Lead and Heavy Metal Pollution Records from a Belgian Peat Bog Spanning the Last 2 Millennia." *Science of the Total Environment* 377: 282–95.

de Vries, Jan. 2009. *The Industrious Revolution*. Cambridge, UK: Cambridge University Press.

de Vries, Jan, and Ad van der Woude. 1997. *The First Modern Economy: Success, Failure, and Perseverance in the Dutch Economy, 1500–1815*. Cambridge, UK: Cambridge University Press.

Diamond, Jared. 1997. *Guns, Germs, and Steel: The Fates of Human Societies*. New York: Norton.

Diamond, Jared, and James Robinson, eds. 2010. *Natural Experiments of History*. Cambridge, MA: Harvard University Press.

Dickinson, Oliver. 1994. *The Aegean Bronze Age*. Cambridge, UK: Cambridge University Press.

Di Cosmo, Nicola. 2002a. *Ancient China and Its Enemies*. Cambridge, UK: Cambridge University Press.

———, ed. 2002b. *Warfare in Inner Asian History*. Leiden: Brill.

Di Cosmo, Nicola, et al., eds. 2009a. *The Cambridge History of Inner Asia: The Chingissid Age*. Cambridge, UK: Cambridge University Press.

Di Cosmo, Nicola, et al., eds. 2009b. *Military Culture in Imperial China*. Cambridge, MA: Harvard University Press.

Dien, Albert. 1986. "The Stirrup and Its Effect on Chinese Military History." *Ars Orientalis* 16: 33–56.

———. 2007. *Six Dynasties Civilization*. New Haven: Yale University Press.

Dietler, Michael. 2007. "The Iron Age in the Western Mediterranean." In Scheidel et al., *Cambridge Economic History*, 242–76.

Djamali, Morteza, et al. 2009. "A Late Holocene Pollen Record from Lake Almaiou in NW Iran." *Journal of Archaeological Science* 36: 1364–75.

Dols, Michael. 1974. *The Black Death in the Middle East*. Princeton: Princeton University Press.

Dore, Ronald. 1965. *Education in Tokugawa Japan*. London: Routledge Kegan Paul.

Drennan, Robert. 1987. "Regional Demography in Chiefdoms." In Drennan and Uribe, *Chiefdoms in the Americas*, 307–23.

Drennan, Robert, and C. Uribe, eds. 1987. *Chiefdoms in the Americas*. Lanham, MD: University Press of America.

Drews, Robert. 1988. *The Coming of the Greeks*. Princeton: Princeton University Press.

———. 1992. *The End of the Bronze Age*. Princeton: Princeton University Press.

Drexhage, Hans-Joachim. 1991. *Preise, Mieten/Pachten, Kosten und Löhne im römischen Ägypten*. St. Katharinen: Scripta Mercaturae Verlag.

Duchesne, Ricardo. 2011. *The Uniqueness of Western Civilization*. Leiden: Brill.

Duffy, Christopher. 1996. *Siege Warfare: The Fortress in the Early Modern World, 1494–1660*. London: Routledge.

———. 2006. *Fire and Stone: The Science of Fortress Warfare, 1660–1860*. New York: Booksales.

Duke, Benjamin. 2009. *The History of Modern Japanese Education: Constructing the National School System, 1872–1890*. New Brunswick, NJ: Rutgers University Press.

Duncan-Jones, Richard. 1994. *Money and Government in the Roman Empire*. Cambridge, UK: Cambridge University Press.

Dunnell, Robert. 1980. "Evolutionary Theory and Archaeology." *Advances in Archaeological Method and Theory* 9: 35–99.

——. 1995. "What Is It That Actually Evolves?" In Teltser, *Evolutionary Archaeology*, 33–50.

Dunnigan, James. 2000. *The Wargames Handbook: How to Play and Design Commercial and Professional Wargames*. 3rd ed. Lincoln, NE: iUniverse.

——. 2003. *How to Make War: A Comprehensive Guide to Modern Warfare in the 21st Century*. 4th ed. New York: Quill.

Dupuy, Trevor Nevitt. 1985. *Numbers, Predictions and War: The Use of History to Evaluate Combat Factors and Predict the Outcomes of Battles*. Rev. ed. Fairfax, VA: Hero Books.

——. 1992. *Understanding War: History and Theory of Combat*. New York: Paragon House.

Durham, William. 1991. *Coevolution: Genes, Culture, and Human Diversity*. Stanford: Stanford University Press.

Dwyer, P. 1983. "Etolo Hunting Performance and Energetics." *Human Ecology* 11: 145–74.

Dyer, Christopher. 1989. *Standards of Living in the Later Middle Ages: Social Change in England c. 1200–1520*. Rev. ed. Cambridge, UK: Cambridge University Press.

Dyer, Christopher, and Richard Jones, eds. 2010. *Deserted Villages Revisited*. Hertford: University of Hertfordshire Press.

Earle, Timothy. 1977. "A Reappraisal of Redistribution." In Timothy Earle and J. Ericson, eds., *Exchange Systems in Prehistory*: 213–29. New York: Academic Press.

——. 1987. "Chiefdoms in Archaeological and Ethnohistorical Perspective." *Annual Review of Anthropology* 16: 279–308.

Eastwood, Warren, et al. 2006. "Holocene Climate Change in the Eastern Mediterranean Region." *Journal of Quaternary Science* 22: 327–41.

Ebrey, Patricia. 1986. "The Economic and Social History of Later Han." In Loewe, *Cambridge History of China*, 608–48.

Economist. 2004. *The Economist Pocket World in Figures, 2004 Edition*. London: Profile.

Eisenstadt, Shmuel, ed. 1999. *Multiple Modernities*. New York: Transaction Books.

Eisenstein, Elizabeth. 1979. *The Printing Press as an Agent of Change*. Cambridge, UK: Cambridge University Press.

Elleman, Bruce. 2005. *Modern Chinese Warfare, 1795–1989*. London: Routledge.

Ellis, John. 1993. *The World War II Databook: The Essential Facts and Figures for All the Combatants*. New York: Aurum.

Ellis, John, and Michael Cox. 2001. *The World War I Databook: The Essential Facts and Figures for All the Combatants*. New York: Aurum.

Ellis, Simon. 2000. *Roman Housing*. London: Duckworth.

Elton, Geoffrey, and Robert Fogel. 1983. *Which Road to the Past?* New Haven: Yale University Press.

Elton, Hugh. 1996. *Warfare in the Roman Empire, AD 350–425*. Oxford: Oxford University Press.

Elvin, Mark. 1973. *The Pattern of the Chinese Past*. Stanford: Stanford University Press.

Ember, Carol, and Melvin Ember. 2001. *Cross-Cultural Research Methods*. Walnut Creek, CA: AltaMira.

Ember, Melvin. 1997. "Evolution of the Human Relations Area Files." *Cross-Cultural Research* 31: 3–15.

Engels, Friedrich. 1884/1972. *The Origins of the Family, Private Property and the State, in the Light of the Researches of Lewis H. Morgan*. London: Lawrence & Wishart.

Epstein, Joshua. 1985. *The Calculus of Conventional War: Dynamic Analysis without Lanchester Theory*. Washington, DC: Brookings Institution.

Erdkamp, Paul, ed. 2007. *A Companion to the Roman Army*. Oxford: Wiley-Blackwell.

Eren, Metin, ed. 2012. *Hunter-Gatherer Behavior: Human Response during the Younger Dryas*. Walnut Creek, CA: Left Coast Press.

Erickson, Andrew, et al., eds. 2010. *China, the United States, and 21st-Century Sea Power*. Annapolis, MD: U.S. Naval Institute Press.

Erickson, Edwin. 1972. "Other Cultural Dimensions: Selective Rotations of Sawyer and LeVine's Factor Analysis of the World Ethnographic Sample." *Behavior Science Notes* 7: 95–155.

Esdaile, Charles. 2007. *Napoleon's Wars*. New York: Penguin.

Evans, David, and Mark Peattie. 1997. *Kaigun: Strategy, Tactics, and Technology in the Imperial Japanese Navy, 1887–1941*. Annapolis, MD: U.S. Naval Institute Press.

Everett, Daniel. 2005. "Cultural Constraints on Grammar and Cognition in Pirahã: Another Look at the Design Features of Human Language." *Current Anthropology* 46: 621–46.

———. 2009. "Pirahã Culture and Grammar: A Response to Some Criticism." *Language* 85: 405–42.

———. 2012. *Language: The Cultural Tool*. New York: Pantheon.

Everett, Nicholas. 2010. *Literacy in Lombard Italy, c. 568–774*. Cambridge, UK: Cambridge University Press.

Fagan, Brian. 2012. *The First North Americans: An Archaeological Journey*. London: Thames & Hudson.

Fain, Janice. 1977. "The Lanchester Equations and Historical Warfare: An Analysis of Sixty World War II Land Engagements." *History, Numbers, and War* 1: 34–52.

Farrokh, Kaveh. 2011. *Iran at War, 1500–1988*. Oxford: Osprey.

Fay, Peter Ward. 1997. *The Opium War, 1840–1842*. 2nd ed. Chapel Hill: University of North Carolina Press.

Federico, G. 2002. "The World Economy 0–2000 AD: A Review Article." *European Review of Economic History* 6: 111–20.

Feinman, Gary, and Joyce Marcus, eds. 1998. *Archaic States*. Santa Fe, NM: School of American Research.

Feinman, Gary, and Jill Neitzel. 1984. "Too Many Types: An Overview of Sedentary Prestate Societies in the Americas." *Advances in Archaeological Method and Theory* 7: 39–102.

Ferguson, Niall. 2004. *Colossus: The Price of America's Empire*. New York: Penguin.

———. 2007. *The War of the World: Twentieth-Century Conflict and the Descent of the West*. New York: Penguin.

———. 2011. *Civilization: The West and the Rest*. New York: Penguin.

Finkel, I. L., and M. J. Seymour, eds. 2009. *Babylon*. Oxford: Oxford University Press.

Finné, Martin, et al. 2011. "Climate in the Eastern Mediterranean, and Adjacent Regions, during the Past 6000 Years." *Journal of Archaeological Science* 38: 3153–73.

Finnegan, Ruth. 1988. *Literacy and Orality*. Oxford: Oxford University Press.

Fischer, Claude. 1994. *America Calling: A Social History of the Telephone to 1940*. Berkeley: University of California Press.

Fisher, Richard. 2010. *China's Military Modernization: Building for Regional and Global Reach*. Stanford: Stanford University Press.

Flannery, Kent. 1972. "The Cultural Evolution of Civilizations." *Annual Review of Ecology and Systematics* 3: 399–426.

Fletcher, Roland. 1995. *The Limits of Settlement Growth*. Cambridge, UK: Cambridge University Press.

Fodor, Pal. 2009. "Ottoman Warfare, 1300–1453." In Kate Fleet, ed., *The Cambridge History of Turkey I: Byzantium to Turkey, 1071–1453*: 192–226. Cambridge, UK: Cambridge University Press.

Fogel, Robert. 2004. *The Escape from Hunger and Premature Death, 1700–2100*. Cambridge, UK: Cambridge University Press.

Fogel, Robert, and Stanley Engerman. 1974. *Time on the Cross: The Economics of American Negro Slavery*. 2 vols. Boston: Little, Brown.

Food and Agriculture Organization. 2006. *Statistical Yearbook*. Vol. 2, pt. 1. Rome: Food and Agriculture Organization of the United Nations.

Forbes, Hamish. 1976. "'We Have a Little of Everything': The Ecological Basis of Some Agricultural Practices in Methana, Trizinia." In M. Dimen and Ernestine Friedl, eds., *Regional Variation in Modern Greece and Cyprus*: 236–50. New York: New York Academy of Sciences.

———. 1982. "Strategies and Soils: Technology, Production, and Environment in the Peninsula of Methana, Greece." PhD dissertation, University of Pennsylvania.

Forge, Andrew. 1972. "Normative Factors in the Settlement Size of Neolithic Cultivators (New Guinea)." In Peter Ucko et al., eds., *Man, Settlement and Urbanism*: 363–76. London: Duckworth.

France, John. 2002. "The Composition and Raising of Charlemagne's Armies." *Journal of Medieval Military History* 1: 61–82.

Francis, Mark. 2007. *Herbert Spencer and the Invention of Modern Life*. Ithaca, NY: Cornell University Press,

Francovich, Riccardo, and Richard Hodges. 2003. *From Villa to Village: The Transformation of the Roman Countryside in Italy, c. 400–1000*. London: Duckworth.

Frank, Andre Gunder. 1998. *ReOrient: Global Economy in the Asian Age*. Berkeley: University of California Press.

Frank, Michael, et al. 2008. "Number as a Cognitive Technology: Evidence from Pirahã Language and Cognition." *Cognition* 108: 819–24.

Freed, Joann. 1985. "San Giovanni di Ruoti: Cultural Discontinuity between the Early and Late Roman Empire in Southern Italy." In Caroline Malone and Simon Stoddart, eds., *Papers in Italian Archaeology*: 4:179–93. Oxford: British Archaeological Reports International Series 246.

Freely, John. 2008. *Storm on Horseback: The Seljuk Warriors of Turkey*. London: Tauris.

Freeman, Linton, and Robert Winch. 1957. "Societal Complexity: An Empirical Test of a Typology of Societies." *American Journal of Sociology* 62: 461–66.

Friday, Karl. 2004. *Samurai, Warfare and the State in Early Medieval Japan*. London: Routledge.

Fried, Morton. 1967. *The Evolution of Political Society: An Essay in Political Anthropology*. New York: Random House.

Friedman, George. 2011. *The Next Decade: Empire and Republic in a Changing World*. New York: Anchor.

Fukuyama, Francis. 2011. *The Origins of Political Order: From Prehuman Times to the French Revolution*. New York: Farrar, Straus and Giroux.

Fulford, Michael. 2009. "Approaches to Quantifying Roman Trade: Response." In Bowman and Wilson, *Quantifying the Roman Economy*, 250–58.

Fuller, Dorian. 2007. "Contrasting Patterns in Crop Domestication and Domestication Rates." *Annals of Botany* 2007: 1–22.

Fuller, Dorian, et al. 2007. "Presumed Domestication? Evidence for Wild Rice Cultivation and Domestication in the Fifth Millennium BC of the Lower Yangtze Region." *Antiquity* 81: 316–31.

———. 2008. "Rice Archaeobotany Revisited." *Antiquity* 82 (315). http://www.antiquity.ac.uk/projgall/fuller315.

Fuller, Dorian, and Ling Qin. 2008. "Immature Rice and Its Archaeobotanical Recognition." *Antiquity* 82 (316). http://www.antiquity.ac.uk/projgall/fuller316.

Fuller, J. F. C. 1957. *A Military History of the Western World*. 2 vols. New York: Funk and Wagnall.

Furet, François, and Jacques Ozouf. 1982. *Reading and Writing: Literacy in France from Calvin to Jules Ferry*. Cambridge, UK: Cambridge University Press.

Gabriel, Richard. 2002. *The Great Armies of Antiquity*. New York: Praeger.

Gaddis, John Lewis. 2005. *The Cold War: A New History*. New York: Penguin.

Galor, Oded. 2011. *Unified Growth Theory*. Princeton: Princeton University Press.

Galor, Oded, and Omer Moav. 2002. "Natural Selection and the Origin of Economic Growth." *Quarterly Journal of Economics* 117: 1133–91.

Gaonkar, Dilip Parameshwar, ed. 2001. *Alternative Modernities*. 2nd ed. Durham, NC: Duke University Press.

Garfinkel, Yosef, et al. 2006. "The Domestication of Water: The Neolithic Well at Sha'ar Hagolan, Jordan Valley, Israel." *Antiquity* 80: 686–96.

———. 2009. "Large-Scale Storage of Grain Surplus in the 6th Millennium BC: The Silos of Tel Tsaf." *Antiquity* 83: 309–25.

Gat, Azar. 2006. *War in Human Civilization*. New York: Oxford University Press.

Gates, Charles. 2003. *Ancient Cities*. London: Routledge.

Gell-Mann, Murray. 1994. *The Quark and the Jaguar*. New York: Freeman.

Gellner, Ernest. 1983. *Nations and Nationalism*. Oxford: Blackwell.

George, A. R. 1993. "Babylon Revisited: Archaeology and Philology." *Antiquity* 67: 734–46.

Gerring, John. 2001. *Social Science Methodology*. Cambridge, UK: Cambridge University Press.

Giannecchini, M., and J. Moggi-Cecchi. 2008. "Stature in Archaeological Samples form Central Italy: Methodological Issues and Diachronic Changes." *American Journal of Physical Anthropology* 135: 284–92.

Giardina, Andrea. 2007. "The Transition to Late Antiquity." In Scheidel et al., *Cambridge Economic History*, 743–68.

Giddens, Anthony. 1984. *The Constitution of Society: Outline of the Theory of Structuration*. Stanford: Stanford University Press.

———. 1981/1995. *A Contemporary Critique of Historical Materialism*. 2nd ed. Stanford: Stanford University Press.

Gilmore, W. 1982. "Elementary Literacy on the Eve of the Industrial Revolution: Trends in Rural New England, 1760–1830." *Proceedings of the American Antiquarian Society* 92: 87–178.

Glaeser, Edward. 2011. *The Triumph of the City*. New York: Penguin.

Glasstone, S., and P. J. Dolan. 1977. *The Effects of Nuclear Weapons*. Washington, DC: U.S. Department of Defense.

Glete, Jan. 2000. *Warfare at Sea, 1500–1650*. London: Longmans.

Golas, Peter. 1999. *Science and Civilisation in China V: Chemistry and Chemical Technology. Part 13: Mining*. Cambridge, UK: Cambridge University Press.

Goldsmith, R. W. 1984. "An Estimate of the Size and Structure of the National Product of the Early Roman Empire." *Review of Income and Wealth* 30: 263–88.

Goldstone, Jack. 2009. *Why Europe? The Rise of the West in World History, 1500–1850*. New York: McGraw-Hill.

Goldsworthy, Adrian. 1996. *The Roman Army at War, 100 BC–AD 200*. Oxford: Oxford University Press.

———. 2003. *The Complete Roman Army*. London: Thames & Hudson.

Gómez Bellard, Carlos, ed. 2003. *Ecohistoria del paisaje agrario: La agricultura fenicio-púnica en al Mediterráneo*. Valencia: University of Valencia Press.

Goody, Jack, ed. 1968. *Literacy in Traditional Societies*. Cambridge, UK: Cambridge University Press.

———. 1977a. *The Domestication of the Savage Mind*. Cambridge, UK: Cambridge University Press.

———. 1977b. "Mémoire et apprentissage dans les sociétés avec et sans écriture." *L'Homme* 17: 42–49.

———. 1987. *The Logic of Writing and the Organization of Society*. Cambridge, UK: Cambridge University Press.

———. 1996. *The East in the West*. Cambridge, UK: Cambridge University Press.

———. 2004. *Capitalism and Modernity: The Great Debate*. Oxford: Polity.

———. 2007. *The Theft of History*. Cambridge, UK: Cambridge University Press.

———. 2009. *The Eurasian Miracle*. Oxford: Polity.

Goody, Jack, and Ian Watt. 1963. "The Consequences of Literacy." *Comparative Studies in Society and History* 5: 304–45.

Gordon, Michael, and Bernard Trainor. 2006. *Cobra II: The Inside Story of the Invasion and Occupation of Iraq*. New York: Vintage.

Goren-Inbar, N., et al. 2004. "Evidence of Hominin Control of Fire at Gesher Benot Ya'aqov, Israel." *Science* 204: 725–27.

Goudsblom, Johan, Eric Jones, and Stephen Mennell. 1996. *The Course of Human History: Economic Growth, Social Progress, and Civilization*. New York: M.E. Sharpe.

Gould, Stephen Jay. 1989. *Wonderful Life: The Burgess Shale and the Nature of History*. New York: Norton.

———. 1994. "The Evolution of Life on Earth." *Scientific American* 271: 84–91.

Gowlett, John. 2006. "The Early Settlement of Northern Europe: Fire History in the Context of Climate Change and the Social Brain." *Comptes Rendus de Palévolution* 5: 299–310.

Graff, David. 2002. *Medieval Chinese Warfare, 300–900*. London: Routledge.

Graff, David, and Robin Higham, eds. 2002. *A Military History of China*. Boulder, CO: Westview.

Graff, Harvey. 1987. *The Legacies of Literacy*. Bloomington: Indiana University Press.

Graham, Robin, et al. 2007. "Nutritious Subsistence Food Systems." *Advances in Agronomy* 92: 1–74.

Graham-Campbell, James, and Magdalena Valor, eds. 2006. *The Archaeology of Medieval Europe I: The Eighth to Twelfth Centuries*. Aarhus: Aarhus Universitetsforlag.

Granovetter, Mark. 1985. "Economic Action and Social Structure: The Problem of Embeddedness." *American Journal of Sociology* 91: 481–510.

Grayson, Donald, and David Meltzer. 2003. "A Requiem for North American Overkill." *Journal of Archaeological Science* 30: 585–93.

Grenville, Jane. 1999. *Medieval Housing*. London: Cassell.

Gress, David. 1998. *From Plato to NATO: The Idea of the West and Its Opponents*. New York: Free Press.

Griffin, Arthur. 2011. "Emergence of Fusion/Fission Cycling and Self-Organized Criticality from a Simulation Model of Early Complex Polities." *Journal of Archaeological Science* 38: 873–83.

Grigg, David. 1992. *The Transformation of Agriculture in the West*. Oxford: Blackwell.

Grimes, W. F. 1968. *The Excavation of Roman and Medieval London*. New York: Praeger.

Gundmundsson, Bruce. 1993. *On Artillery*. Westport, CT: Praeger.

Guo, Qinghua. 2010. *The* Mingqi *Pottery Buildings of Han Dynasty China, 206 BC–AD 220*. Eastbourse, UK: Sussex University Press.

Gupta, Akhil, and James Ferguson. 1997. "Culture, Power, Place." In Akhil Gupta and James Ferguson, eds., *Culture, Power, Place*: 1–29. Durham, NC: Duke University Press.

Haines, M., and Rick Steckel. 2000. *Childhood Mortality and Nutritional Status as Indicators of Standard of Living*. National Bureau of Economic Research Historical Paper 121, Cambridge, MA.

Haldon, John. 1990. *Byzantium in the Seventh Century*. Cambridge, UK: Cambridge University Press.

——. 1999. *Warfare, State and Society in the Byzantine World, 565–1204*. London: University College London Press.

——, ed. 2005. *General Issues in the Study of Medieval Logistics: Sources, Problems, Methodologies*. Leiden: Brill.

——, ed. 2007. *Byzantine Warfare*. Aldershot, UK: Ashgate.

——. 2008. *The Byzantine Wars*. London: History Press.

Halper, Stefan. 2010. *The Beijing Consensus: How China's Authoritarian Model Will Dominate the Twenty-First Century*. New York: Basic Books.

Halsall, Guy. 2003. *Warfare and Society in the Barbarian West 450–900*. London: Routledge.

——. 2007. *Barbarian Migrations and the Roman West, 367–568*. Cambridge, UK: Cambridge University Press.

Halverson, John. 1992. "Goody and the Implosion of the Literacy Thesis." *Man* n.s. 27: 301–17.

Hamblin, William. 2006. *Warfare in the Ancient Near East to 1600 BC*. London: Routledge.

Hamerow, T. 1983. *The Birth of a New Europe*. Chapel Hill: University of North Carolina Press.

Hansen, Mogens. 2006. *The Shotgun Method: The Demography of the Ancient Greek City-States*. Columbia: University of Missouri Press.

——. 2008. "An Update on the Shotgun Method." *Greek, Roman, and Byzantine Studies* 48: 259–86.

Hanson, Victor Davis. 1989. *The Western Way of War: Infantry Battle in Classical Greece*. New York: Oxford University Press.

——. 2001. *Carnage and Culture: Landmark Battles in the Rise of Western Power*. New York: Anchor.

Harding, Richard. 1999. *Seapower and Naval Warfare, 1660–1830*. London: Longman.

Harries, Meirion, and Susie Harries. 1991. *Soldiers of the Sun: The Rise and Fall of the Imperial Japanese Army, 1868–1945*. London: Heinemann.

Harris, Marvin. 1968. *The Rise of Anthropological Theory*. New York: Crowell.

Harris, William. 1989. *Ancient Literacy*. Cambridge, MA: Harvard University Press.

———. 2011. "Bois et déboisment dans la Méditerrannée antique." *Annales Histoires Sciences Sociales* 1: 105–40.

Harrison, Neil, ed. 2007. *Complexity in World Politics*. Albany: State University of New York Press.

Hartwell, Robert. 1962. "A Revolution in the Chinese Iron and Coal Industries during the Northern Sung, 960–1126 AD." *Journal of Asian Studies* 21: 153–62.

———. 1966. "Markets, Technology, and the Structure of Enterprise in the Development of the 11th-Century Chinese Iron and Steel Industry." *Journal of Economic History* 26: 29–58.

———. 1967. "A Cycle of Economic Change in Imperial China: Coal and Iron in Northeast China, 750–1350." *Journal of Economic and Social History of the Orient* 10: 102–59.

Harvey, Alan. 1989. *Economic Expansion in the Byzantine Empire 900–1200*. Cambridge, UK: Cambridge University Press.

Harvey, Sarah. 2010. "Iron Tools from a Roman Villa at Boscoreale, Italy." *American Journal of Archaeology* 114: 697–714.

Haskins, Charles. 1927/1971. *The Renaissance of the Twelfth Century*. Cambridge, MA: Harvard University Press.

Hassig, Ross. 1992. *War and Society in Ancient Mesoamerica*. Berkeley: University of California Press.

Hastings, David. 2009. "Filling the Gaps in the Human Development Index." United Nations Economic and Social Commission for Asia and the Pacific Working Paper WP/09/02. http://www.unescap.org/publications/detail.asp?id=1308.

Hatcher, John. 1993. *The History of the British Coal Industry I: Before 1700: Towards the Age of Coal*. Oxford: Oxford University Press.

Hathaway, Jane. 2008. *The Arab Lands under Ottoman Rule, 1516–1800*. London: Longmans.

Hawkes, Christopher, and P. J. Crummy. 1995. *Camulodunum II*. Colchester: Colchester Archaeological Report 11.

Hawkes, Christopher, and M. R. Hull. 1947. *Camulodunum I*. London: Reports of the Research Committee of the Society of Antiquaries 14.

Hayami, Yujiro. 2001. *Development Economics: From the Poverty to the Wealth of Nations*. Oxford: Oxford University Press.

Heath, Ian. 1979. *Byzantine Armies 886–1118*. Oxford: Osprey.

———. 1995. *Byzantine Armies AD 1118–1461*. Oxford: Osprey.

Heath, Shirley. 2003. "Literacy." In William Frawley, ed., *International Encyclopedia of Linguistics*, 2nd ed., 4 vols.: 2:503–6. New York: Oxford University Press.

Henry, Chris. 2004. *Napoleonic Naval Armaments, 1792–1815*. Oxford: Osprey.

Herbert, Sharon, and Andrea Berlin. 2003. "Excavations at Coptos (Qift) in Upper Egypt, 1987–1992." *Journal of Roman Archaeology* 53 (suppl.).

Herman, Mark, and Richard Berg. 2006. *Caesar: Conquest of Gaul*. Hanford, CA: GMT Games.

Hill, Donald. 1994. *Islamic Science and Engineering*. Edinburgh: Edinburgh University Press.

Hillman, Gordon, et al. 2001. "New Evidence of Lateglacial Cereal Cultivation at Abu Hureyra on the Euphrates." *The Holocene* 11: 383–93.

Hobhouse, Leonard, et al. 1914. "The Material Culture and Social Institutions of the Simpler Peoples." *Sociological Review* 7: 203–31, 332–68.

Hobson, John. 2004. *The Eastern Origins of Western Civilisation*. Cambridge, UK: Cambridge University Press.

Hodder, Ian. 1982. *Symbols in Action*. Cambridge, UK: Cambridge University Press.

——. 2006. *The Leopard's Tale: Revealing the Mysteries of Çatalhöyük*. London: Thames & Hudson.

Hodges, Richard, and David Whitehouse. 1983. *Mohamed, Charlemagne, and the Origins of Europe*. London: Duckworth.

Hodkinson, Stephen. 1988. "Animal Husbandry in the Greek Polis." In C. R. Whittaker ed., *Pastoral Economies in Classical Antiquity. Proceedings of the Cambridge Philological Society* 14 (suppl.): 35–73.

Hoepfner, Wolfram, and Ernst-Ludwig Schwandner. 1994. *Haus und Stadt im klassischen Griechenland*. 2nd ed. Munich: Deutscher Kunstverlag.

Hoffman, Philip. 2011. Review of Morris 2010. *Journal of Economic History* 71: 545–47.

Hoffmann-Salz, Julia. 2011. *Die wirtschaftlichen Auswirkungen der römischen Eroberung: vergleichende Untersuchungen der Provinzen Hispania Tarraconensis, Africa Proconsularis und Syria*. Stuttgart: Historia Einzelschrift 218.

Hogg, Ian. 1992. *The New Illustrated Encyclopedia of Firearms*. New York: Booksales.

Holland, John. 1995. *Hidden Order: How Adaptation Builds Complexity*. Cambridge, MA: Perseus Books.

Hollins, David. 2003. *Austrian Napoleonic Artillery, 1792–1815*. London: Osprey.

Holstein, E. 1980. *Mitteleuropäische Eichenchronologie*. Mainz: von Zabern.

Hong, S., et al. 1996. "A Reconstruction of Changes in Copper Production and Copper Emissions to the Atmosphere during the Past 7000 Years." *Science of the Total Environment* 188: 183–93.

Hopkins, Keith. 1978. *Conquerors and Slaves*. Cambridge, UK: Cambridge University Press.

——. 1980. "Taxes and Trade in the Roman Empire (200 BC–AD 200)." *Journal of Roman Studies* 70: 101–25.

——. 1983a. "Introduction." In Peter Garnsey, Keith Hopkins, and C. R. Whittaker, eds., *Trade in the Ancient Economy*: ix–xxv. Cambridge, UK: Cambridge University Press.

——. 1983b. "Models, Ships and Staples." In Peter Garnsey and C. R. Whittaker, eds., *Trade and Famine in Classical Antiquity*: 84–109. Cambridge, UK: Cambridge University Press.

——. 2002. "Rome, Taxes, Rents and Trade." In Walter Scheidel and Sitta von Reden, eds., *The Ancient Economy*: 190–230. Edinburgh: Edinburgh University Press.

——. 2009. "The Political Economy of the Roman Empire." In Morris and Scheidel, *Dynamics of Ancient Empires*, 178–204.

Hoskins, W. G. 1953. "The Rebuilding of Rural England, 1570–1640." *Past and Present* 4: 44–59.

Hourani, Albert. *A History of the Arab Peoples*. 2nd ed. New York: Warner, 2003.

Houston, R. A. 1983. "Literacy and Society in the West, 1500–1850." *Social History* 8: 269–93.

——. 1988. *Literacy in Early Modern Europe: Culture and Education, 1500–1800*. London: Longman.

Hsu, Cho-yun. 1965. *Ancient China in Transition: An Analysis of Social Mobility, 722–222 BC*. Stanford: Stanford University Press.

——. 1980. *Han Agriculture: The Formation of the Early Chinese Agrarian Economy (206 BC–AD 220)*. Seattle: University of Washington Press.

——. 1999. "The Spring and Autumn Period." In Loewe and Shaughnessy, *Cambridge History of Ancient China*, 545–86.

Hu, Yaowu, et al. 2006. "Stable Isotopic Analysis of Human Bones from Jiahu Site, Henan, China." *Journal of Archaeological Science* 33: 1319–30.

——. 2008. "Stable Isotopic Analysis of Humans from Xiaojingshan Site." *Journal of Archaeological Science* 35: 2960–65.

Huang, Philip. 1985. *The Peasant Economy and Social Change in North China*. Stanford: Stanford University Press.

——. 1990. *The Peasant Family and Rural Development in the Lower Yangzi Region, 1350–1988*. Stanford: Stanford University Press.

——. 2002. "Development or Involution in Eighteenth-Century Britain and China?" *Journal of Asian Studies* 61: 501–38.

Huang, Ray. 1970. "Military Expenditures in Sixteenth-Century Ming China." *Oriens Extremus* 17: 39–62.

Hudson, Kenneth. 1979. *World Industrial Archaeology*. Cambridge, UK: Cambridge University Press.

Huffman, James. 2010. *Japan in World History*. Oxford: Oxford University Press.

Hunt, Edwin, and James Murray. 1999. *A History of Business in Medieval Europe 1200–1550*. Cambridge, UK: Cambridge University Press.

Ifrah, Georges. 2001. *The Universal History of Computing: From the Abacus to the Quantum Computer*. New York: Wiley.

Ikeguchi, Mamoru. 2007. "The Dynamics of Agricultural Locations in Roman Italy." PhD dissertation, King's College London.

Imber, Colin. 2002. *The Ottoman Empire*. London: Palgrave.

Insoll, Timothy. 1999. *The Archaeology of Islam*. Oxford: Blackwell.

International Institute for Strategic Studies. 2001. *The Military Balance 2001*. London: Routledge.

———. 2009. *The Military Balance 2009*. London: Routledge.

Iqbal, Muzaffar. 2009. *The Making of Islamic Science*. 2nd ed. Kuala Lumpur: Islamic Book Trust.

Ireland, Bernard, and Eric Grove, eds. 1997. *Jane's War at Sea 1897–1997*. London: HarperCollins.

Jacob, Margaret. 1997. *Scientific Culture and the Making of the Industrial West*. New York: Oxford University Press.

Jacques, Martin. 2009. *When China Rules the World: The Rise of the Middle Kingdom and the End of the Western World*. London: Allen Lane.

Jameson, Michael, et al. 1994. *A Greek Countryside: The Southern Argolid from Prehistory to the Present*. Stanford: Stanford University Press.

Jami, Catherine. 1994. "Learning Mathematical Sciences during the Early and Mid-Ch'ing." In Benjamin Elman and Alexander Woodside, eds., *Education and Society in Late Imperial China, 1600–1900*: 223–56. Berkeley: University of California Press.

Jansen, Marius. 2000. *The Making of Modern Japan*. Cambridge, MA: Harvard University Press.

Jiang, Lepin, and Li Liu. 2006. "New Evidence for the Origins of Sedentism and Rice Domestication in the Lower Yangzi River, China." *Antiquity* 80: 355–61.

Jing, Yuan, et al. 2008. "Meat-Acquisition Patterns in the Neolithic Yangzi River Valley, China." *Antiquity* 82: 351–66.

Johnson, Allen, and Timothy Earle. 2000. *The Evolution of Human Societies: From Foraging Group to Agriculture*. 2nd ed. Stanford: Stanford University Press.

Johnson, Gregory. 1973. *Local Exchange and Early State Development in Southwest Iran*. Ann Arbor, MI: Museum of Anthropology Occasional Papers 51.

Johnson, Matthew. 1996. *An Archaeology of Capitalism*. Oxford: Blackwell.

Johnson, William, and Holt Parker, eds. 2009. *Ancient Literacies: The Culture of Reading in Greece and Rome*. New York: Oxford University Press.

Jones, Eric. 2003. *The European Miracle: Environments, Economies and Geopolitics in the History of Europe and Asia*. 3rd ed. Cambridge, UK: Cambridge University Press.

Jones, Seth. 2009. *In the Graveyard of Empires: America's War in Afghanistan*. New York: Norton.

Jongman, Willem. 2007a. "The Early Roman Empire: Consumption." In Scheidel et al., *Cambridge Economic History*, 592–618.

———. 2007b. "Gibbon Was Right: The Decline and Fall of the Roman Economy." In Olivier Hekster et al., eds., *Crises and the Roman Empire*: 183–99. Leiden: Brill.

———. 2009. "Archaeology, Demography, and Roman Economic Growth." In Bowman and Wilson, *Quantifying the Roman Economy*, 115–26.

Jörgensen, Christer, et al. 2006. *Fighting Techniques of the Early Modern World, AD 1500–1763: Equipment, Combat Skills, and Tactics*. New York: Thomas Dunne Books.

Jursa, Michael. 2010. "The Ancient Near East: Fiscal Regimes, Political Structures." Paper presented at the Premodern Fiscal Regimes conference, Stanford University, May 27.

Kaegi, Walter. 1992. *Byzantium and the Early Islamic Conquests*. Cambridge, UK: Cambridge University Press.

——. 2003. *Heraclius: Emperor of Byzantium*. Cambridge, UK: Cambridge University Press.

Kaestle, Carl. 1985. "The History of Literacy and the History of Readers." *Review of Research in Education* 12: 11–53.

Kagan, Robert. 2012. *The World America Made*. New York: Knopf.

Kaplan, Robert. 2005. "How We Would Fight China." *The Atlantic* 295 (5): 49–64.

Karetzky, Patricia. 1996. *Court Art of the Tang*. Lanham, MD: University Press of America.

Katzmaryk, P. T., et al. 2005. "Resting Metabolic Rate and Daily Energy Expenditure among Two Indigenous Siberian Groups." *American Journal of Human Biology* 6: 719–30.

Kedar, Benjamin. 1976. *Merchants in Crisis: Genoese and Venetian Men of Affairs and the Fourteenth-Century Depression*. New Haven: Yale University Press.

Keegan, John. 1993. *A History of Warfare*. New York: Vintage.

Keeley, Lawrence. 1996. *War Before Civilization*. New York: Oxford University Press.

Keen, Maurice. 1999. *Medieval Warfare: A History*. Oxford: Oxford University Press.

Keenleyside, Anne, et al. 2009. "Stable Isotopic Evidence in a Greek Colonial Population." *Journal of Archaeological Science* 36: 51–63.

Keightley, David. 1999. "The Shang: China's First Historical Dynasty." In Loewe and Shaughnessy, *Cambridge History of Ancient China*, 232–91.

Kemp, Barry. 1989. *Ancient Egypt*. Cambridge, UK: Cambridge University Press.

Kennedy, Hugh. 2001. *The Armies of the Caliphs: Military and Society in the Early Islamic State*. London: Routledge.

Kennedy, Paul. 1987. *The Rise and Fall of the Great Powers*. New York: Vintage.

Kern, Stephen. 2003. *The Culture of Time and Space 1880–1918*. 2nd ed. Cambridge, MA: Harvard University Press.

Khan, Iqtidar Alam. 2004. *Gunpowder and Firearms: Warfare in Medieval India*. New Delhi: Oxford University Press.

Kierman, Frank, and John Fairbanks, eds. 1974. *Chinese Ways in Warfare*. Cambridge, MA: Harvard University Press.

Kieschnick, John. 2003. *The Impact of Buddhism on Chinese Material Culture*. Princeton: Princeton University Press.

King, Anthony. 1999. "Diet in the Roman World: A Regional Inter-Site Comparison of the Mammal Bones." *Journal of Roman Archaeology* 12: 168–202.

King, Philip, and Lawrence Stager. 2001. *Life in Biblical Israel*. Louisville, KY: Westminster John Knox.

Kirch, Patrick. 2010. *How Chiefs Become Kings: Divine Kingship and the Rise of Archaic States in Ancient Hawai'i*. Berkeley: University of California Press.

Kitchen, Andrew, et al. 2010. "Genetic Analysis of Human Head and Clothing Lice Indicates an Early Origin of Clothing Use in Archaic Hominins." Paper presented at the 79th annual meeting of the American Association of Physical Anthropologists. In *Abstracts of AAPA Poster and Podium Sessions*: 154. http://physanth.org/annual-meeting/2010/79th-annual-meeting-2010/2010%20AAPA%20Abstracts.pdf.

Kitchen, Kenneth. 1986. *The Third Intermediate Period (1100–650 BC) in Egypt*. Warminster, UK: Aris & Philips.

Kittler, Ralf, et al. 2003. "Molecular Evolution of *Pediculus humanus* and the Origin of Clothing." *Current Biology* 13: 1414–17.

Kleiber, M. 1961. *The Fire of Life: An Introduction to Animal Energetics*. New York: Wiley.

Klein, Richard. 2009. *The Human Career*. 3rd ed. Chicago: University of Chicago Press.

Klein, Richard, and Blake Edgar. 2002. *The Dawn of Human Culture*. New York: Wiley.

Koepke, Nikola, and Joerg Baten. 2005. "Agricultural Specialization and Height in Ancient and Medieval Europe." *Explorations in Economic History* 45: 127–46.

Kornicki, Peter. 2000. *The Book in Japan: A Cultural History from the Beginnings to the Nineteenth Century*. Honolulu: University of Hawaii Press.

Krautheimer, Charles. 1983. *Three Christian Capitals: Topography and Politics. Rome, Constantinople, Milan*. Berkeley: University of California Press.

Kristiansen, Kristian. 2004. "Genes versus Agents: A Discussion of the Widening Theoretical Gap in Archaeology." *Archaeological Dialogues* 11: 77–132.

Kron, Geofrey. 2005. "Anthropometry, Physical Anthropology, and the Reconstruction of Ancient Health, Nutrition, and Living Standards." *Historia* 54: 68–83.

———. Forthcoming. "The Use of Housing Evidence as a Possible Index of Social Equality and Prosperity in Classical Greece and Early Industrial England."

Kuhn, Dieter. 2009. *The Age of Confucian Rule: The Song Transformation of China*. Cambridge, MA: Harvard University Press.

Kuper, Adam. 1983. *Anthropology and Anthropologists*. 2nd ed. London: Routledge Kegan Paul.

Kusan, D. 2000. "Rapport synthétique sur les recherches archéobotaniques dans le sanctuaire d'Héra de l'Île de Samos." *Pallas* 52: 99–108.

Kuzmin, Yaroslav. 2006. "Chronology of the Earliest Pottery in East Asia." *Antiquity* 80: 362–71.

Kylander, M., et al. 2005. "Refining the Preindustrial Atmospheric Pb-Isotope Evolution Curve in Europe Using an 8000 Year Old Peat Core from NW Spain." *Earth and Planetary Science Letters* 240: 467–85.

Kyriakidis, Savvas. 2011. *Warfare in Late Byzantium, 1204–1453*. Leiden: Brill.

Laiou, Angeliki, ed. 2002. *The Economic History of Byzantium: From the Seventh through the Fifteenth Century*. Washington, DC: Dumbarton Oaks.

Laitin, David, et al. 2012. "Geographic Axes and the Persistence of Cultural Diversity." *Proceedings of the National Academy of Sciences* 110: 10.1073/pnas. 1205338109.

Lanchester, F. W. 1916. *Aircraft in Warfare: The Dawn of the Fourth Arm*. London: Constable.

———. 1956. "Mathematics in Warfare." In James Newman, ed., *The World of Mathematics*: 4:2139–57. New York: Simon & Schuster.

Landes, David. 1983. *Revolution in Time: Clocks and the Making of the Modern World*. Cambridge, MA: Harvard University Press.

———. 1998. *The Wealth and Poverty of Nations*. New York: Norton.

Lanehart, Rita, et al. 2011. "Dietary Adaptation during the Longshan Period in China: Stable Isotope Analysis at Liangchengzhen (Southeastern Shandong)." *Journal of Archaeological Science* 38: 2171–81.

Lapidus, Ira. *A History of Islamic Societies*. 2nd ed. Cambridge, UK: Cambridge University Press, 2002.

Larsen, Clark. 1995. "Biological Changes in Human Populations with Agriculture." *Annual Review of Anthropology* 24: 185–213.

———. 2006. "The Agricultural Revolution as Environmental Catastrophe." *Quaternary International* 150: 12–20.

Lawrence, A. W. 1965. "Ancient Egyptian Fortifications." *Journal of Egyptian Archaeology* 51: 69–71.

———. 1996. *Greek Architecture*. 5th ed., revised by R. A. Tomlinson. New Haven: Yale University Press.

Lee, A. D. 2007. *War in Late Antiquity*. Oxford: Blackwell.

Lee, Richard. 1979. *The !Kung San: Men, Women, and Work in a Foraging Society*. Cambridge, UK: Cambridge University Press.

Lee, Thomas. 1985. *Government Education and Examinations in Sung China*. New York: St. Martin's.

———. 2000. *Education in Traditional China: A History*. Leiden: Brill.

Legouilloux, M. 2000. "L'alimentation carnée au Ier millenaire avant J.-C. en Grèce continentale et dans les Cyclades." *Pallas* 52: 69–95.

Leonard, Robert. 2001. "Evolutionary Archaeology." In Ian Hodder, ed., *Archaeological Theory Today*: 65–97. Oxford: Blackwell.

Leonard, W., and M. Robertson. 1992. "Nutritional Requirements in Human Evolution: A Bioenergetics Approach." *American Journal of Human Biology* 4: 179–85.

———. 1997. "Comparative Primate Energetics and Hominid Evolution." *American Journal of Physical Anthropology* 102: 265–81.

Lepingwell, John. 1987. "The Laws of Combat? Lanchester Reexamined." *International Security* 12 (1): 89–134.

Le Roy Ladurie, Emmanuel. 1966. *Les paysans de Languedoc*. 2 vols. Paris: SEVPEN.

Levi, Barbara, et al. 1987–88. "Civilian Casualties from 'Limited' Nuclear Attacks on the USSR." *International Security* 12 (3): 168–89.

Lewis, Mark. 1990. *Sanctioned Violence in Early China.* Albany: State University of New York Press.

——. 1999a. "Warring States Political History." In Loewe and Shaughnessy, *Cambridge History of Ancient China,* 587–650.

——. 1999b. *Writing and Authority in Early China.* Albany: State University of New York Press.

——. 2000. "The Han Abolition of Universal Military Service." In van de Ven, *Warfare in Chinese History,* 33–76.

——. 2006. *The Construction of Space in Early China.* Albany: State University of New York Press.

——. 2007. *The Early Chinese Empires: Qin and Han.* Cambridge, MA: Harvard University Press.

——. 2009a. *China between Empires: The Northern and Southern Dynasties.* Cambridge, MA: Harvard University Press.

——. 2009b. *China's Cosmopolitan Empire: The Tang Dynasty.* Cambridge, MA: Harvard University Press.

Lewis, M. J. T. 1994. "The Origins of the Wheelbarrow." *Technology and Culture* 35: 453–75.

Li, Chungxiang, et al. 2011. "Ancient DNA Analysis of Desiccated Wheat Grains from a Bronze Age Cemetery in Xinjiang, China." *Journal of Archaeological Science* 38: 115–19.

Li, Feng. 2003. "Feudalism and the Western Zhou." *Harvard Journal of Asiatic Studies* 63: 115–44.

——. 2006. *Landscape and Power in Early China: The Crisis and Fall of the Western Zhou 1045–771 BC.* Cambridge, UK: Cambridge University Press.

Li, Xiating, et al. 1996. *Art of the Houma Foundry.* Princeton: Princeton University Press.

Li, Xueqin. 1985. *Eastern Zhou and Qin Civilization.* New Haven: Yale University Press.

Littauer, M., and Jan Crouwel. 1981. *Wheeled Vehicles and Ridden Animals in the Ancient Near East.* Leiden: Brill.

Liu, Li. 2004. *The Chinese Neolithic.* Cambridge, UK: Cambridge University Press.

——. 2006. "Urbanization in China: Erlitou and Its Hinterland." In Storey, *Urbanism in the Preindustrial World,* 161–89.

Liu, Li, and Xingcan Chen. 2003. *State Formation in Early China.* London: Duckworth.

——. 2012. *The Archaeology of China: From the Late Palaeolithic to the Early Bronze Age.* Cambridge, UK: Cambridge University Press.

Liu, Li, et al. 2007a. "The Earliest Rice Domestication in China." *Antiquity* 81 (313). http://www.antiquity.ac.uk/projgall/liu1/index.html.

———. 2007b. "Evidence for the Early Beginning (c. 9000 ca. BP) of Rice Domestication: A Response." *The Holocene* 17: 1059–68.

———. 2011. "Plant Exploitation of the Last Foragers at Shizitan in the Middle Yellow River Valley, China." *Journal of Archaeological Science* 38: 3524–32.

———. Forthcoming. "A Functional Analysis of Grinding Stones from an Early Holocene Site at Donghulin, North China." *Journal of Archaeological Science*.

Liu, Shufen. 2001. "Jiankang and the Commercial Empire of the Southern Dynasties." In Scott Pearce et al., eds., *Culture and Power in the Reconstitution of the Chinese Realm, 200–600*: 35–52. Cambridge, MA: Harvard University Press.

Liu, Xinru. 1988. *Ancient India and Ancient China: Trade and Religious Exchanges, AD 1–600*. Delhi: Oxford University Press.

———. 1996. *Silk and Religion: An Exploration of Material Life and the Thought of People, AD 600–1200*. Delhi: Oxford University Press.

Liu, Xinyi, et al. 2009. "River Valleys and Foothills: Changing Archaeological Perceptions of North China's Earliest Farms." *Antiquity* 83: 82–95.

Lloyd, Christopher. 1986. *Explanation in Social History*. Oxford: Blackwell.

Lo, Jung-Pang. 1955. "The Emergence of China as a Sea Power in the Late Sung and Early Yuan Periods." *Far Eastern Quarterly* 14: 489–503.

———. 1958a. "China's Paddle-Wheel Boats: The Mechanized Craft Used in the Opium War and Their Historical Background." *Qinghua Journal of Chinese Studies* 5: 189–211.

———. 1958b. "The Decline of the Early Ming Navy." *Oriens Extremus* 5: 149–68.

———. 1969. "Maritime Commerce and Its Relation to the Sung Navy." *Journal of Economic and Social History of the Orient* 12: 57–101.

Lo Cascio, Elio. 1997. "Produzione monetaria, finanza pubblica ed economia nel principato." *Rivista storica italiana* 109: 650–77.

Lo Cascio, Elio, and Paolo Malanima. 2011. "Ancient and Pre-Modern Economies. GDP in the Roman Empire and Early Modern Europe." Paper presented at the Quantifying Long-Run Economic Development conference, Venice, March 21–25, 2011. http://www.paolomalanima.it/default_file/Papers/ANCIENT-PRE-MODERN-ECONOMIES.pdf.

Lock, Peter, and Guy Sanders, eds. 1996. *The Archaeology of Medieval Greece*. Oxford: Oxbow.

Lockridge, K. A. 1974. *Literacy in Colonial New England: An Inquiry into the Social Context of Literacy in the Early Modern West*. New York: Norton.

Loewe, Michael. 1974. "The Campaigns of Han Wu-ti." In Kierman and Fairbanks, *Chinese Ways in Warfare*, 67–122.

———, ed. 1986. *The Cambridge History of China I: The Ch'in and Han Empires, 221 BC–AD 220*. Cambridge, UK: Cambridge University Press.

Loewe, Michael, and Edward Shaughnessy, eds. 1999. *The Cambridge History of Ancient China*. Cambridge, UK: Cambridge University Press.

Lombard, Marlize. 2011. "Quartz-Tipped Arrows Older Than 60ka: Further Use-Trace Evidence from Sibudu, KwaZulu-Natal, South Africa." *Journal of Archaeological Science* 38: 1918–30.

Loomis, Robert. 1998. *Wages, Welfare Costs and Inflation in Classical Athens*. Ann Arbor: University of Michigan Press.

Lopez, Robert. 1951. "The Dollar of the Middle Ages." *Journal of Economic History* 11: 209–34.

Lorge, Peter. 2005. *War, Politics and Society in Early Modern China, 900–1795*. London: Routledge.

———. 2008. *The Asian Military Revolution: From Gunpowder to the Bomb*. Cambridge, UK: Cambridge University Press.

Lu, Liancheng. 2005. "The Eastern Zhou and the Growth of Regionalism." In Chang and Xu, *Formation of Chinese Civilization*, 203–47.

Lu, Liancheng, and Yan Wenming. 2005. "Society during the Three Dynasties." In Chang and Xu, *Formation of Chinese Civilization*, 141–201.

Luttwak, Edward. 1976. *The Grand Strategy of the Roman Empire*. Baltimore: Johns Hopkins University Press.

———. 2009. *The Grand Strategy of the Byzantine Empire*. Cambridge, MA: Harvard University Press.

Lynn, John, ed. 1989. *Tools of War: Instruments, Ideas, and Institutions of Warfare, 1445–1871*. Urbana: University of Illinois Press.

———, ed. 1993. *Feeding Mars: Logistics in Western Warfare from the Middle Ages to the Present*. Boulder, CO: Westview.

———. 1997. *Giant of the Grand Siècle: The French Army, 1610–1714*. Cambridge, UK: Cambridge University Press.

———. 1999. *The Wars of Louis XIV, 1667–1714*. New York: Longman.

Lytle, Ephraim. 2010. "Fish Lists in the Wilderness: The Social and Economic History of a Boiotian Price Decree." *Hesperia* 79: 253–303.

MacDonald, Nathan. 2008. *What Did the Ancient Israelites Eat?* Grand Rapids, MI: Eerdmans.

MacMullen, Ramsay. 1963. *Soldier and Civilian in the Later Roman Empire*. Cambridge, MA: Harvard University Press.

———. 1982. "The Epigraphic Habit in the Roman Empire." *American Journal of Philology* 103: 233–46.

Maddison, Angus. 2003. *The World Economy: Historical Statistics*. Paris: OECD Publishing.

———. 2005. *Growth and Interaction in the World Economy: The Roots of Modernity*. Washington, DC: American Enterprise Institute Press.

———. 2007a. *Chinese Economic Performance in the Long Run 960–2030 AD*. Paris: OECD Publishing.

———. 2007b. *Contours of the World Economy 1–2030 AD: Essays in Macroeconomic History*. New York: Oxford University Press.

Maisels, Charles. 1990. *The Emergence of Civilization: From Hunting and Gathering to Agriculture, Cities, and the State in the Near East*. London: Routledge.

Makdisi, George. 1981. *The Rise of Colleges: Institutions of Learning in Islam and the West*. Edinburgh: Edinburgh University Press.

Malanima, Paolo. 2000. "The Energy Basis for Early Modern Growth, 1650–1820." In Maarten Prak, ed., *Early Modern Capitalism: Economic and Social Change in Europe, 1400–1800*: 49–66. London: Routledge.

———. 2007. "Wages, Productivity and Working Time in Italy 1300–1913." *Journal of European Economic History* 36: 127–74.

———. 2010. "The Long Decline of a Leading Economy: GDP in Central and Northern Italy, 1300–1913." *European Review of Economic History* 15: 169–219.

———. 2010–11. "The Path towards the Modern Economy: The Role of Energy." *Rivista di Politica Economica* (April–June): 1–30. http://www.paolomalanima.it/default_file/Papers/ENERGY_AND_GROWTH.pdf.

———. 2011. "Energy Consumption and Energy Crisis in the Roman World." Paper presented at the American Academy in Rome, June 15–16.

Malanima, Paolo, and Elio Lo Cascio. 2009. "GDP in Pre-Modern Agrarian Economies (1–1820 AD): A Revision of the Estimates." *Rivista di storia economica* 25: 387–415.

Mallory, J. P., and Victor Mair. 2008. *The Tarim Mummies*. London: Thames & Hudson.

Malthus, Thomas. 1798. *An Essay on the Principle of Population*. 1st ed. London: P. Johnson.

Mango, Cyril. 1985. *Le développement urbain de Constantinople (IVe–VIIe siècles)*. Paris: de Boccard.

Mann, Charles. 2005. *1491: New Revelations of the Americas Before Columbus*. New York: Knopf.

———. 2011. *1493: Uncovering the New World Columbus Created*. New York: Knopf.

Mann, Michael. 1986. *The Sources of Social Power I: A History of Power from the Beginning to AD 1760*. Cambridge, UK: Cambridge University Press.

Manning, J. G., and Ian Morris, eds. 2005. *The Ancient Economy: Evidence and Models*. Stanford: Stanford University Press.

Marcus, Joyce. 1992. *Mesoamerican Writing Systems: Propaganda, Myth, and History in Four Ancient Civilizations*. Princeton: Princeton University Press.

Martinez, Ignacio, et al. 2012. "On the Origin of Language: The Atapuerca Evidence." Paper presented at the American Association of Physical Anthropologists annual meeting, Portland, OR, April 14.

Maschner, Herbert, ed. 1996. *Darwinian Archaeologies*. New York: Academic Press.

Masood, Ehsan. 2009. *Science and Islam: A History*. London: Icon.

Massie, Robert. 1993. *Dreadnought: Britain, Germany, and the Coming of the Great War*. New York: Ballantine Books.

May, Timothy. *The Mongol Art of War: Chinggis Khan and the Mongol Military System*. London: Pen & Sword, 2007.

Mayewski, P. A., et al. 2005. "Holocene Climate Variability." *Quaternary Research* 62: 243–55.

Maynes, M. J. 1984. *Schooling for the People: Comparative Local Studies of Schooling History in France and Germany, 1750–1850*. London: Holmes and Meier.

Mays, S., and N. Beavan. 2012. "An Investigation of Diet in Early Anglo-Saxon England Using Carbon and Nitrogen Stable Isotope Analysis of Human Bone Collagen." *Journal of Archaeological Science* 39: 867–74.

Mazarakis Ainian, Alexander. 1997. *From Rulers' Dwellings to Temples: Architecture, Religion, and Society in Early Iron Age Greece*. Jonsered, Sweden: Studies in Mediterranean Archaeology.

———. 1998. "Skala Oropou." *Praktika tis en Athinais Arkhaiologikis Etaireia* 1998: 132–44.

Mazumdar, Sucheta. 1998. *Sugar and Society in China: Peasants, Technology, and the World Market*. Cambridge, MA: Harvard University Press.

Mazzaoui, Maureen. 1981. *The Italian Cotton Industry in the Later Middle Ages, 1100–1600*. Cambridge, UK: Cambridge University Press.

McClellan, Thomas. 2006. "Early Fortifications: The Missing Walls of Jericho." *Baghdader Mitteilungen* 18: 593–610.

McCloskey, Deirdre. 1994. *Knowledge and Persuasion in Economics*. Cambridge, UK: Cambridge University Press.

McCormick, Michael. 2001. *Origins of the European Economy: Communications and Commerce, AD 300–900*. Cambridge, UK: Cambridge University Press.

McCormick, Michael, et al. 2013. "Climate Change under the Roman Empire and Its Successors, 100 BC–800 AD: A First Synthesis Based on Multi-Proxy Natural Scientific and Historical Evidence." *Journal of Interdisciplinary History* 44.

McDermott, Joseph. 2006. *A Social History of the Chinese Book: Books and Literati Culture in Late Imperial China*. Hong Kong: Hong Kong University Press.

McEnroe, John. 1982. "A Typology of Minoan Neopalatial Houses." *American Journal of Archaeology* 86: 3–19.

McGeer, Eric. 2008. *Sowing the Dragon's Teeth: Byzantine Warfare in the Tenth Century*. Washington, DC: Dumbarton Oaks.

McGillivray, Mark. 1991. "The Human Development Index: Yet Another Redundant Composite Development Indicator?" *World Development* 19: 1461–68.

McGillivray, Mark, and Howard White. 2006. "Measuring Development? The UNDP's Human Development Index." *Journal of International Development* 5: 183–92.

McGuire, Randall. 1983. "Breaking Down Cultural Complexity." *Advances in Archaeological Method and Theory* 6: 91–142.

McKitterick, David. 1998. "The Beginning of Printing." In Christopher Allmand, ed., *The New Cambridge Medieval History*: 7:287–98. Cambridge, UK: Cambridge University Press.

McNab, Chris. 2009. *Armies of the Napoleonic Wars*. London: Osprey.

McNett, Charles. 1970a. "A Cross-Cultural Method for Predicting Nonmaterial Traits in Archeology." *Behavior Science Notes* 5: 195–212.

———. 1970b. "A Settlement Pattern Scale of Cultural Complexity." In Naroll and Cohen, *Handbook of Method in Cultural Anthropology*, 872–86.

———. 1973. "Factor Analysis of a Cross-Cultural Sample." *Behavior Science Notes* 8: 233–57.

McNiven, Ian, et al. 2012. "Dating Aboriginal Stone-Walled Fishtraps at Lake Condah, Southeast Australia." *Journal of Archaeological Science* 39: 268–86.

Megaloudi, F., et al. 2007. "Plant Offerings from the Classical Necropolis of Limenas, Thasos, North Greece." *Antiquity* 81: 933–43.

Meharg, Andrew, et al. 2012. "First Comprehensive Peat Depositional Records for Tin, Lead and Copper Association with Antiquity of Europe's Largest Cassiterite Deposits." *Journal of Archaeological Science* 39: 717–27.

Mesoudi, Alex. 2011. *Cultural Evolution: How Darwinian Theory Can Explain Human Culture & Synthesize the Social Sciences*. Chicago: University of Chicago Press.

Mighall, T. M., et al. 2009. "Ancient Copper and Lead Pollution Records from a Raised Bog Complex in Central Wales, UK." *Journal of Archaeological Science* 36: 1509–15.

Milanovic, Branko. 2006. "An Estimate of Average Income and Inequality in Byzantium around the Year 1000." *Review of Income and Wealth* 52: 449–70.

Milanovic, Branko, Peter Lindert, and Jeffrey Williamson. 2007. *Measuring Ancient Inequality*. National Bureau of Economic Research Working Paper 13550, Cambridge, MA.

Miller, David. 1998. *The Cold War: A Military History*. London: Pimlico.

Miller, John and Scott Page. 2007. *Complex Adaptive Systems: An Introduction to Computational Models of Social Life*. Princeton: Princeton University Press.

Miller, R., et al. 1986. "Experimental Approaches to Ancient Near Eastern Archery." *World Archaeology* 18: 178–95.

Milwright, Marcus. 2010. *An Introduction to Islamic Archaeology*. Edinburgh: Edinburgh University Press.

Miskimin, Harry. 1969. *The Economy of Early Renaissance Europe, 1300–1460*. Englewood Cliffs, NJ: Prentice Hall.

———. 1977. *The Economy of Later Renaissance Europe, 1460–1600*. Cambridge, UK: Cambridge University Press.

Missiou, Anna. 2010. *Literacy and Democracy in Fifth-Century Athens*. Cambridge, UK: Cambridge University Press.

Mitch, David. 1992. *The Rise of Popular Literacy in Victorian England*. Philadelphia: University of Pennsylvania Press.

Mithen, Steven. 2003. *After the Ice: A Global Human History 20,000–5000 BC*. Cambridge, MA: Harvard University Press.

Moeller, Nadine. 2006. "The First Intermediate Period: A Time of Famine and Climate Change?" *Ägypten und Levante* 15: 153–67.

Mokyr, Joel. 2010. *The Enlightened Economy: An Economic History of Britain, 1700–1850.* New Haven: Yale University Press.

Monson, Andrew. 2012. *From the Ptolemies to the Romans: Political and Economic Change in Egypt.* Cambridge, UK: Cambridge University Press.

Moore, Andrew, et al. 2000. *Village on the Euphrates.* New York: Oxford University Press.

Morel, Jean-Paul. 2007. "Early Rome and Italy." In Scheidel et al., *Cambridge Economic History,* 487–510.

Morgan, Lewis Henry. 1877/1974. *Ancient Society, or Researches in the Lines of Human Progress from Savagery through Barbarism to Civilisation.* Gloucester, MA: Peter Smith.

Morley, Neville. 1996. *Metropolis and Hinterland: The City of Rome and the Italian Economy, 200 BC–AD 200.* Cambridge, UK: Cambridge University Press.

Morowitz, Harold. 2002. *The Emergence of Everything: How the World Became Complex.* New York: Oxford University Press.

Morris, Ellen Fowler. 2005. *The Architecture of Imperialism: Military Bases and the Evolution of Foreign Policy in Egypt's New Kingdom.* Leiden: Brill.

Morris, Ian. 1986. "Gift and Commodity in Archaic Greece." *Man* 21: 1–17.

——. 1987. *Burial and Ancient Society: The Rise of the Greek City-State.* Cambridge, UK: Cambridge University Press.

——. 1991. "The Early Polis as City and State." In John Rich and Andrew Wallace-Hadrill, eds., *City and Country in the Ancient World*: 24–57. London: Routledge.

——. 1992. *Death-Ritual and Social Structure in Classical Antiquity.* Cambridge, UK: Cambridge University Press.

——. 1997. "An Archaeology of Equalities? The Greek City-States." In Tom Charlton and Deborah Nichols, eds., *The Archaeology of City-States*: 91–105. Washington, DC: Smithsonian Institution.

——. 2000. *Archaeology as Cultural History: Words and Things in Iron Age Greece.* Oxford: Blackwell.

——. 2003. "Mediterraneanization." *Mediterranean Historical Review* 18: 30–55.

——. 2004. "Economic Growth in Ancient Greece." *Journal of Institutional and Theoretical Economics* 160: 709–42.

——. 2005. "Archaeology, Standards of Living, and Greek Economic History." In Manning and Morris, *Ancient Economy*, 91–126.

——. 2006. "The Growth of Greek Cities in the First Millennium BC." In Storey, *Urbanism in the Preindustrial World*, 26–51.

——. 2007. "Early Iron Age Greece." In Scheidel et al., *Cambridge Economic History*, 211–41.

——. 2009. "The Greater Athenian State." In Morris and Scheidel, *Dynamics of Ancient Empires*, 99–177.

——. 2010. *Why the West Rules—For Now: The Patterns of History, and What They Reveal about the Future.* New York: Farrar, Straus and Giroux.

——. Forthcoming. *War! What Is It Good For?* New York: Farrar, Straus and Giroux.

Morris, Ian, et al. 2007. "Introduction." In Scheidel et al., *Cambridge Economic History*, 1–12.

Morris, Ian, and Walter Scheidel, eds. 2009. *The Dynamics of Ancient Empires: State Power from Assyria to Byzantium.* New York: Oxford University Press.

Morris, Sarah. 1992. *Daidalos and the Origins of Greek Art.* Princeton: Princeton University Press.

Mote, Frederick. 1977. "The Transformation of Nanking, 1350–1400." In Skinner, *City in Late Imperial China*, 101–54.

——. 1999. *Imperial China, 900–1800.* Berkeley: University of California Press.

Mrozowski, Stephen. 2006. *The Archaeology of Class in Urban America.* Cambridge, UK: Cambridge University Press.

Müldner, Gundula, and M. P. Richards. 2005. "Fast or Feast: Reconstructing Diet in Later Medieval England by Stable Isotope Analysis." *Journal of Archaeological Science* 32: 39–48.

——. 2007. "Stable Isotope Evidence for 1500 Years of Human Diet at the City of York, UK." *American Journal of Physical Anthropology* 133: 682–97.

Murdock, George, and Caterina Provost. 1973. "Measurement of Cultural Complexity." *Ethnology* 12: 379–92.

Murphey, Rhoads. 1977. *The Outsiders: The Western Experience in India and China.* Ann Arbor: University of Michigan Press.

——. 1999. *Ottoman Warfare 1500–1700.* London: Routledge.

Murray, Sarah. Forthcoming. "Imports, Trade, and Society in Early Greece." PhD dissertation, Stanford University.

Mutschler, Fritz-Heiner, and Achim Mittag, eds. 2009. *Conceiving the Empire: China and Rome Compared.* New York: Oxford University Press.

Nadel, D. 1996. "The Organisation of Space in a Fisher-Hunter-Gatherers' Camp at Ohalo II, Israel." In M. Otte, ed., *Nature et culture*: 373–88. Liège: Université de Liège.

Nagl, John. 2005. *Learning to Eat Soup with a Knife: Counterinsurgency Lessons from Malaya and Vietnam.* Updated ed. Chicago: University of Chicago Press.

Naroll, Raoul. 1956. "A Preliminary Index of Social Development." *American Anthropologist* 58: 687–715.

——. 1970. "The Culture-Bearing Unit in Cross-Cultural Surveys." In Naroll and Cohen, *Handbook of Method in Cultural Anthropology*, 721–65.

Naroll, Raoul, and Ronald Cohen, eds. 1970. *A Handbook of Method in Cultural Anthropology.* Garden City, NY: Natural History Press.

National Intelligence Council. 2012. *Global Trends 2030: Alternative Worlds.* Washington, DC: Government Printing Office.

Neal, D., et al. 1990. *Excavations of the Iron Age, Roman, and Mediaeval Settlement at Gorhambury, St. Albans.* London: HBMC.

Needham, Joseph. 1971. *Science and Civilisation in China IV Part 3: Civil Engineering and Nautics*. Cambridge, UK: Cambridge University Press.

Needham, Joseph, and Robin Yates. 1994. *Science and Civilisation in China V: Chemistry and Chemical Technology. Part 6: Military Technology: Missiles and Sieges*. Cambridge, UK: Cambridge University Press.

Netz, Reviel. 2002. "Counter-Culture: Towards a History of Greek Numeracy." *History of Science* 40: 321–52.

——. 2011. "The Bibliosphere of Ancient Science (Outside of Alexandria)." *NTM Zeitschrift für Geschichte der Wissenschaften, Technik und Medizin* 19: 239–69.

——. Forthcoming. *Space, Scale, Canon: Parameters of Ancient Literary Culture*.

Nevett, Lisa. 2000. "A Real Estate 'Market' in Classical Greece? The Example of Town Housing." *Annual of the British School at Athens* 95: 329–44.

Nevins, Andrew, et al. 2009a. "Evidence and Argumentation: A Reply to Everett." *Language* 85: 671–81.

——. 2009b. "Pirahã Exceptionality: A Reassessment." *Language* 85: 355–404.

Nicolle, David. 1992. *Romano-Byzantine Armies 4th–9th Centuries*. Oxford: Osprey.

——, ed. 2002. *A Companion to Medieval Arms and Armour*. Woodridge, UK: Boydell and Brewer.

Nieboer, Hans J. 1910. *Slavery as an Industrial System*. The Hague: Nyhoff.

Nienhauser, William. 1994. *The Grand Scribe's Records VII: Memoirs of Pre-Han China*. Bloomington: Indiana University Press.

Nims, C. F. 1965. *Thebes of the Pharaohs: Pattern for Every City*. London: Elek Books.

Nishijima, Sadao. 1986. "The Economic and Social History of Former Han." In Loewe, *Cambridge History of China*, 551–607.

Nissen, Hans. 1988. *The Early History of the Ancient Near East, 9000–2000 BC*. Chicago: University of Chicago Press.

Niven, Laura. 2006. *The Palaeolithic Occupation of Vogelherd Cave: Implications for the Subsistence Behaviour of Late Neanderthals and Early Modern Humans*. Tübingen: Kerns.

Norman, Jeremy, ed. 2005. *From Gutenberg to the Internet: A Sourcebook on the History of Information Technology*. Novato, CA: Historyofscience.com.

Norris, Robert, and Hans Kristensen. 2006. "Global Nuclear Stockpiles, 1945–2006." *Bulletin of the Atomic Scientists* 62 (4): 64–67.

North, Douglass. 1981. *Structure and Change in Economic History*. New York: Norton.

North, Douglass, et al. 2009. *Violence and Social Orders: A Conceptual Framework for Interpreting Recorded Human History*. Cambridge, UK: Cambridge University Press.

North, Richard. 2009. *Ministry of Defeat: The British War in Iraq, 2003–2009*. London: Continuum.

Nosworthy, Brent. 1990. *The Anatomy of Victory: Battle Tactics, 1689–1763*. New York: Hippocrene Books.

Oates, David, et al. Forthcoming. *Excavations at Tell Brak III: The Uruk and Ubaid Periods.* Cambridge, UK: McDonald Institute.

Oates, Joan. 1979. *Babylon.* London: Thames & Hudson.

Ober, Josiah. 2008. *Democracy and Knowledge: Innovation and Learning in Classical Athens.* Princeton: Princeton University Press.

———. 2010. "Wealthy Hellas." *Transactions of the American Philological Association* 140: 241–86.

O'Keefe, Tadhag, ed. 2008. *The Archaeology of Medieval Europe II: Twelfth to Sixteenth Centuries.* London: University College London.

Ong, Walter J. 1982. *Orality and Literacy.* London.

Osborne, Roger. 2008. *Civilization: A New History of the Western World.* New York: Pegasus.

Packer, George. 2005. *The Assassin's Gate: America in Iraq.* New York: Farrar, Straus and Giroux.

Pader, Ellen Jane. 1982. *Symbolism, Social Relations and the Interpretation of Mortuary Remains.* Oxford: British Archaeological Reports.

Page, Scott. 2010. *Diversity and Complexity.* Princeton: Princeton University Press.

Paine, S. C. M. 2003. *The Sino-Japanese War of 1894–1895.* Cambridge, UK: Cambridge University Press.

Pamuk, Sevket. 2007. "The Black Death and the Origins of the 'Great Divergence' across Europe, 1300–1600." *European Review of Economic History* 11: 289–317.

Panella, C., and A. Tchernia. 1994. "Produits agricoles transportés en amphores: l'huile et surtout le vin." In *L'Italie d'Auguste à Dioclétian*: 145–65. Rome: École française à Rome.

Park, Jang-Sik, et al. 2007. "Transition in Cast Iron Technology of the Nomads of Mongolia." *Journal of Archaeological Science* 34: 1187–96.

———. 2008. "A Technological Transition in Mongolia Evident in Microstructure, Chemical Composition, and Radiocarbon Age of Cast Iron Artifacts." *Journal of Archaeological Science* 35: 2465–70.

Park, Jang-Sik, and Thilo Rehren. 2011. "Large-Scale 2nd to 3rd Century AD Bloomery Iron Smelting in Korea." *Journal of Archaeological Science* 38: 1180–90.

Parker, A. J. 1992. *Ancient Shipwrecks of the Mediterranean and Roman Provinces.* Oxford: British Archaeological Reports.

———. 2008. "Artifact Distributions and Wreck Locations: The Archaeology of Roman Commerce." In Robert Hohlfelder, ed., *The Maritime World of Ancient Rome*: 6:177–96. Ann Arbor, MI: Memoirs of the American Academy in Rome.

Parker, Geoffrey. 1988/1996. *The Military Revolution: Military Innovation and the Rise of the West, 1500–1800.* 2nd ed. Cambridge, UK: Cambridge University Press.

———, ed. 2005. *The Cambridge History of Warfare.* Cambridge, UK: Cambridge University Press.

Parker Pearson, Michael. 1982. "Mortuary Practices, Society and Ideology." In Ian Hodder, ed., *Symbolic and Structural Archaeology*: 99–113. Cambridge, UK: Cambridge University Press.

Parkinson, William, and Michael Galaty, eds. 2010. *Archaic State Interaction: The Eastern Mediterranean in the Bronze Age*. Santa Fe: School for American Research.

Parsons, Talcott. 1964. "Evolutionary Universals in Society." *American Sociological Review* 29: 339–57.

———. 1966. *Societies: Evolutionary and Comparative Perspectives*. Englewood Cliffs, NJ: Prentice Hall.

———. 1971. *The System of Modern Societies*. Englewood Cliffs, NJ: Prentice Hall.

Paterson, John. 1982. "'Salvation from the Sea': Amphorae and Trade in the Roman World." *Journal of Roman Studies* 72: 146–57.

Pattison, R. 1982. *On Literacy: The Politics of the Word from Homer to the Age of Rock*. Oxford: Oxford University Press.

Peace, William. 1988. "Vere Gordon Childe and American Anthropology." *Journal of Anthropological Research* 44: 417–33.

Peacock, D. P. S., and Dyfri Williams. 1986. *Amphorae and the Roman Economy*. London: Longman.

Peebles, Christopher, and Susan Kus. 1977. "Some Archaeological Correlates of Ranked Societies." *American Antiquity* 42: 421–48.

Peña, Theodore. 2007. *Roman Pottery in the Archaeological Record*. Cambridge, UK: Cambridge University Press.

Perdue, Peter. 2005. *China Marches West: The Qing Conquest of Central Eurasia*. Cambridge, MA: Harvard University Press.

Peregrine, Peter, and Melvin Ember, eds. 2001–3. *Encyclopedia of Prehistory*. 9 vols. New York: Kluwer/Plenum.

Perkins, Dwight. 1969. *Agricultural Development in China, 1368–1968*. Chicago: Aldine.

Perla, Peter. 1990. *The Art of Wargaming: A Guide for Professionals and Hobbyists*. Annapolis, MD: U.S. Naval Institute Press.

Peterson, Christian, and Gideon Shelach. 2012. "Jiangzhai: Social and Economic Organization of a Middle Neolithic Chinese Village." *Journal of Archaeological Science* 31: 265–301.

Petrucci, Armando. 1992. *"Scriptores in urbibus": alfabetismo e cultura scritta nell'Italia altomediovale*. Bologna: Mulino.

Philip, Graham. 1989. *Metal Weapons of the Early and Middle Bronze Ages in Syria-Palestine*. Oxford: British Archaeological Reports.

Picornell Gelabert, Llorenç, et al. 2011. "The Ethnoarchaeology of Firewood Management in the Fang Villages of Equatorial Guinea, Central Africa: Implications for the Interpretation of Wood Fuel Remains from Archaeological Sites." *Journal of Anthropological Archaeology* 30: 375–84.

Piggott, Stuart. 1983. *The Earliest Wheeled Transport*. London: Thames & Hudson.

Pinker, Steven. 2002. *The Blank Slate: The Modern Denial of Human Nature*. New York: Viking.

———. 2011. *The Better Angels of Our Nature: Why Violence Has Declined*. New York: Penguin.

Pollard, Elizabeth. 2008. "Placing Greco-Roman History in World Historical Context." *Classical World* 102: 53–68.

Pollock, Susan. 1999. *Ancient Mesopotamia*. Cambridge, UK: Cambridge University Press.

Pomeranz, Kenneth. 2000. *The Great Divergence: China, Europe, and the Making of the Modern World Economy*. Princeton: Princeton University Press.

———. 2011. "How Big Should Historians Think? A Review Essay on *Why the West Rules—For Now* by Ian Morris." *Cliodynamics* 2: 304–29.

Porter, Anne. 2012. *Mobile Pastoralism and the Formation of Near Eastern Civilizations: Weaving Together Society*. Cambridge, UK: Cambridge University Press.

Postgate, Nicholas. 1994a. *Early Mesopotamia*. London: Routledge.

———. 1994b. "How Many Sumerians per Hectare? Probing the Anatomy of an Early City." *Cambridge Archaeological Journal* 4: 47–65.

Potts, Daniel T. 1999. *The Archaeology of Elam*. Cambridge, UK: Cambridge University Press.

Powell, Barry. 2009. *Writing: Theory and History of the Technology of Civilization*. Oxford: Blackwell.

Preece, R., et al. 2006. "Humans in the Hoxnian: Habitat, Context and Fire Use at Beeches Pit, West Stow, Suffolk, UK." *Journal of Quaternary Science* 21: 485–96.

Prendergast, Mary, et al. 2009. "Resource Intensification in the Late Upper Paleolithic: A View from Southern China." *Journal of Archaeological Science* 36: 1027–37.

Prieto, Albert, and Joseph Carter. 2003. *Living off the Chora: Food and Diet in Ancient Pantanello*. Austin, TX: Institute for Classical Archaeology.

Pryce, Huw, ed. 2006. *Literacy in Medieval Celtic Societies*. Oxford: Oxford University Press.

Pulak, Cemal. 2010. "Uluburun Shipwreck." In Cline, *Oxford Handbook of the Bronze Age Aegean*, 862–76.

Py, Michel. 1993. *Les Gaulois du Midi: de la fin du l'âge du bronze à la conquête romaine*. Paris: Hachette.

Raaflaub, Kurt, and Nathan Rosenstein, eds. 1999. *War and Society in the Ancient and Medieval Worlds*. Cambridge, MA: Center for Hellenic Studies.

Radcliffe-Brown, Arthur. 1936/1957. *A Natural Science of Society*. Glencoe, IL: Free Press.

Rathbone, Dominic. 1996. "Monetisation, Not Price-Inflation, in Third-Century AD Egypt?" In C. E. King and D. G. Wigg, eds., *Coin Finds and Coin Use in the Roman World*: 321–39. Berlin: Mann Verlag.

———. 1997. "Prices and Price Formation in Roman Egypt." In Jean Andreau et al., eds., *Prix et formation des prix dans les économies antiques*: 183–244. Saint-Bertrand-des-Comminges: Musée Archéologique.

———. 2006. "The 'Muziris' Papyrus (SB XVIII 13167): Financing Roman Trade with India." In *Alexandrian Studies II in Honour of Mostafa el Abbadi. Bulletin de la société d'archéologie d'Alexandrie* 46: 39–50.

——. 2009. "Earnings and Costs: Living Standards in the Roman Economy (I–III c. AD)." In Bowman and Wilson, *Quantifying the Roman Economy*, 299–326.

Rawski, Evelyn. 1978. *Education and Popular Literacy in Ch'ing China*. Ann Arbor: University of Michigan Press.

Rawson, Jessica. 1988. "A Bronze-Casting Revolution in the Western Zhou and Its Influence on the Provincial Industries." In Robert Maddin, ed., *The Beginning of the Use of Metals and Alloys*: 228–38. Cambridge, MA: MIT Press.

——. 1999. "Western Zhou Archaeology." In Loewe and Shaughnessy, *Cambridge History of Ancient China*, 352–449.

Ray, Debraj. 1998. *Development Economics*. Princeton: Princeton University Press.

Razeto, Anna. 2011. "Imperial Structures and Urban Forms: A Comparative Study of Capital Cities in the Roman and Han Empires." PhD thesis, University College London.

Reitsema, Laurie, et al. 2010. "Preliminary Evidence for Medieval Polish Diet from Carbon and Nitrogen Stable Isotopes." *Journal of Archaeological Science* 37: 1413–23.

Renfrew, Colin. 1973. "Monuments, Mobilization and Social Organization in Neolithic Wessex." In Colin Renfrew, ed., *The Explanation of Culture Change*: 539–58. London: Duckworth.

Renson, V., et al. 2008. "Roman Road Pollution Assessed by Elemental and Lead Isotope Geochemistry in Belgium." *Applied Geochemistry* 23: 3253–66.

Reuther, Oskar. 1926. *Die Innenstadt von Babylon (Merkes)*. Leipzig: Hinrichs.

Richards, Michael, et al. 2000. "Neanderthal Diet at Vindija and Neanderthal Predation: The Evidence from Stable Isotopes." *Proceedings of the National Academy of Sciences* 97: 7663–66.

——. 2008. "Isotopic Dietary Analysis of a Neanderthal and Associated Fauna from the Site of Jonzac (Charante-Maritime), France." *Journal of Human Evolution* 55: 179–85.

Richards, Michael, and Ralf Schmitz. 2009. "Isotopic Evidence for the Diet of the Neanderthal Type Specimen." *Antiquity* 82: 553–59.

Richerson, Peter, and Robert Boyd. 2000. "Complex Societies: The Evolutionary Dynamics of a Crude Superorganism." *Human Nature* 10: 253–89.

——. 2005. *Not by Genes Alone*. Chicago: University of Chicago Press.

Ricklefs, Robert. 2001. *The Economy of Nature*. 5th ed. New York: Freeman.

Ricks, Thomas. 2006. *Fiasco: The American Military Adventure in Iraq*. New York: Penguin.

——. 2009. *The Gamble: General Petraeus and the American Military Adventure in Iraq*. New York: Penguin.

Ridley, Charles. 1973. "Educational Theory and Practice in Late Imperial China: The Teaching of Writing as a Specific Case." PhD thesis, Stanford University.

Rikhye, Ravi, et al. 2010. *Concise World Armies 2009*. Alexandria, VA: General Data LLC. http://www.globalsecurity.org.

Riley, Nancy, and James McCarthy. 2003. *Demography in the Age of Postmodernism*. Cambridge, UK: Cambridge University Press.

Roaf, Michael. 1989. "'Ubaid Social Organization and Social Activities as Seen from Tell Madhhur." In Elizabeth Henrickson and Ingolf Thuesen, eds., *Upon This Foundation: The 'Ubaid Reconsidered*: 91–146. Copenhagen: Museum Tusculanum.

———. 1990. *Cultural Atlas of Mesopotamia*. New York: Facts on File.

Roberts, Benjamin, et al. 2009. "The Development of Metallurgy in Eurasia." *Antiquity* 83: 1012–22.

Roberts, Keith. 2010. *Pike and Shot Tactics 1590–1660*. Oxford: Osprey.

Roberts, Michael. 1967. *Essays in Swedish History*. London Weidenfeld & Nicholson.

Robinson, David M., et al. 1929–52. *Excavations at Olynthus*. 14 vols. Baltimore: Johns Hopkins University Press.

Rodger, N. A. M., ed. 2004. *A Naval History of Britain II: 1649–1815*. Cambridge, UK: Cambridge University Press.

Rogers, Clifford, ed. 1995. *The Military Revolution Debate: Readings on the Military Transformation of Early Modern Europe*. Boulder, CO: Westview.

———, ed. 2010. *The Oxford Encyclopedia of Medieval Warfare and Military Technology*. Oxford: Oxford University Press.

Rose, Susan. 2002. *Medieval Naval Warfare, 1000–1500*. London: Routledge.

Rosenthal, Jean-Laurent, and Bin Wong. 2011. *Before and Beyond Divergence: The Politics of Economic Change in China and Europe*. Princeton: Princeton University Press.

Rossabi, Morris. 1988. *Khubilai Khan: His Life and Times*. Berkeley: University of California Press.

Rostow, Walt. 1960. *The Stages of Economic Growth: A Non-Communist Manifesto*. 1st ed. Cambridge, UK: Cambridge University Press.

Roth, Jonathan. 1999. *The Logistics of the Roman Army at War, 264 BC–AD 235*. Leiden: Brill.

Rothenberg, Gunther. 1978. *The Art of Warfare in the Age of Napoleon*. Bloomington: Indiana University Press.

———. 2006. *The Napoleonic Wars*. Washington, DC: Smithsonian.

Rowe, William. 2009. *China's Last Empire: The Great Qing*. Cambridge, MA: Harvard University Press.

Rowland, David. 2006. *The Stress of Battle: Quantifying Human Performance in Combat*. London: HMSO.

Rowlands, Michael. 1988. "A Question of Complexity." In Daniel Miller et al., eds., *Domination and Resistance*: 29–40. London: Allen & Unwin.

Rowlandson, Jane. 1996. *Landowners and Tenants in Roman Egypt: The Social Relations of Agriculture in the Oxyrhynchite Nome*. Oxford: Clarendon.

Rowney, Don Karl, ed. 1984. *Soviet Quantitative History*. Beverly Hills, CA: Sage.

Rozman, Gilbert. 1973. *Urban Networks in Ch'ing China and Tokugawa Japan*. Princeton: Princeton University Press.

Rubinger, Richard. 2007. *Popular Literacy in Early Modern Japan*. Honolulu: University of Hawaii Press.

Ruitenbeek, Klaas. 1993. *Carpentry and Building in Late Imperial China*. Leiden: Brill.

Sabin, Philip. 2007. *Lost Battles: Reconstructing the Great Clashes of the Ancient World*. London: Continuum.

———. 2012. *Simulating War: Studying Conflict through Simulation Games*. London: Continuum.

Sabin, Philip, et al., eds. 2008. *The Cambridge History of Greek and Roman Warfare*. 2 vols. Cambridge, UK: Cambridge University Press.

Safar, Fuad, et al. 1981. *Eridu*. Baghdad: State Organization of Antiquities and Heritage.

Sagara, Ambuj, and Adil Najam. 1998. "The Human Development Index: A Critical Review." *Ecological Economics* 25: 249–64.

Sage, Steven. 1992. *Ancient Sichuan and the Unification of China*. Albany: State University of New York Press.

Sakharov, Andrei. 1990. *Memoirs*. New York: Knopf.

Salamon, M., et al. 2008. "The Consilience of Historical and Isotopic Approaches in Reconstructing the Medieval Mediterranean Diet." *Journal of Archaeological Science* 35: 1667–72.

Saliba, George. 2007. *Islamic Science and the Making of the European Renaissance*. Cambridge, MA: MIT Press.

Saller, Richard. 2005. "Framing the Debate over Growth in the Ancient Economy." In Manning and Morris, *Ancient Economy*, 223–38.

Salmon, Pierre. 1974. *Population et dépopulation dans l'empire romain*. Brussels: Latomus.

Sanderson, M. 1972. "Literacy and Social Mobility in the Industrial Revolution in England." *Past and Present* 56: 75–104.

Sanderson, Stephen. 1990. *Social Evolutionism: A Critical History*. Oxford: Blackwell.

Savage, Stephen. 1981. *The Theories of Talcott Parsons*. New York: St. Martin's.

Sawyer, Jack, and Robert LeVine. 1966. "Cultural Dimensions: A Factor Analysis of the World Ethnographic Sample." *American Anthropologist* 68: 708–31.

Sawyer, Ralph. 2011. *Ancient Chinese Warfare*. New York: Basic Books.

Saxe, Arthur. 1970. "Social Dimensions of Mortuary Practices." PhD thesis, University of Michigan.

Scheidel, Walter. 2001. "Progress and Problems in Roman Demography." In Walter Scheidel, ed., *Debating Roman Demography*: 1–81. Leiden: Brill.

———. 2002. "A Model of Demographic and Economic Change in Roman Egypt after the Antonine Plague." *Journal of Roman Archaeology* 15: 97–114.

———. 2003. "Germs for Rome." In Catharine Edwards and Greg Woolf, eds., *Rome the Cosmopolis*: 158–76. Cambridge, UK: Cambridge University Press.

———. 2004. "Creating a Metropolis: A Comparative Demographic Perspective."

In William Harris and Giovanni Ruffini, eds., *Ancient Alexandria between Egypt and Greece*: 1–31. Leiden: Brill.

———. 2007. "Demography." In Scheidel et al., *Cambridge Economic History*, 38–86.

———. 2009a. "In Search of Roman Economic Growth." *Journal of Roman Archaeology* 22: 46–70.

———. 2009b. "The Monetary Systems of the Han and Roman Empires." In Scheidel, *Rome and China*, 137–207.

———, ed. 2009c. *Rome and China: Comparative Perspectives on Ancient World Empires*. New York: Oxford University Press.

———. 2010a. "Physical Wellbeing in the Roman World." Version 3.0. Princeton/Stanford Working Papers in Classics no. 091001. http://www.princeton.edu/~pswpc/.

———. 2010b. "Real Wages in Early Economies: Evidence for Living Standards from 1800 BCE to 1300 CE." *Journal of the Economic and Social History of the Orient* 53: 425–62. Princeton/Stanford Working Papers in Classics no. 090904. http://www.princeton.edu/~pswpc/.

———. 2010c. "Roman Wellbeing and the Economic Consequences of the 'Antonine Plague.'" Version 3.0. Princeton/Stanford Working Papers in Classics no. 011001. http://www.princeton.edu/~pswpc/.

Scheidel, Walter, and Steven Friesen. 2009. "The Size of the Economy and the Distribution of Income in the Roman Empire." *Journal of Roman Studies* 99: 61–91. Princeton/Stanford Working Papers in Classics no. 010901. http://www.princeton.edu/~pswpc/.

Scheidel, Walter, Ian Morris, and Richard Saller, eds. 2007. *The Cambridge Economic History of the Greco-Roman World*. Cambridge, UK: Cambridge University Press.

Schepartz, Lynne, et al., eds. 2009. *New Directions in the Skeletal Biology of Greece*. Princeton: American School of Classical Studies.

Schmandt-Besserat, Denise. 1992. *Before Writing*. 2 vols. Austin: University of Texas Press.

Schmidt, B., and W. Gruhle. 2003. "Klimaextreme in römischen Zeit—ein Strukturanalyse dendrochronologische Daten." *Archäologisches Korrespondenzblatt* 33: 421–27.

Schofield, Roger. 1968. "The Measurement of Literacy in Pre-Industrial England." In Goody, *Literacy in Traditional Societies*, 311–25.

———. 1973. "Dimensions of Illiteracy, 1750–1850." *Explorations in Economic History* 10: 437–54.

Schudson, Michael. 1981. *Discovering the News: A Social History of American Newspapers*. New York: Basic Books.

Scott-Gall, Hugo. 2001. "An Interview with . . . Prof. Ian Morris." *Goldman Sachs Fortnightly Thoughts* 23 (December 15): 5–7.

Seeberg, Vilma, ed. 1990. *Literacy in China: The Effect of the National Development Context on Literacy Levels, 1949–79*. Bochum: Brockmeyer.

Service, Elman. 1962. *Primitive Social Organization: An Evolutionary Perspective.* 1st ed. New York: Random House.

———. 1975. *Origins of the State and Civilization.* New York: Academic Press.

Shaanxi Institute of Archaeology. 2008. "The Upper Paleolithic Longwangcan Site in Shaanxi." *Chinese Archaeology* 8: 32–36.

Shackel, Paul. 2009. *An Archaeology of American Labor and Working Class Life.* Gainesville: University of Florida Press.

Shanks, Michael, and Christopher Tilley. 1987. *Archaeology and Social Theory.* Oxford: Polity.

———. 1992. *Re-Constructing Archaeology: Theory and Practice.* 2nd ed. London: Routledge.

Shanxi Fieldwork Team. 2005. "Monumental Structure from Ceremonial Precinct at Taosi Walled-Town in 2003." *Chinese Archaeology* 5: 51–58.

Shao, Wangping. 2005. "The Formation of Civilization: The Interaction Sphere of the Longshan Period." In Chang and Xu, *Formation of Chinese Civilization,* 85–123.

Shaughnessy, Edward. 1988. "Historical Perspectives on the Introduction of the Chariot into China." *Harvard Journal of Asiatic Studies* 48: 189–237.

———. 1999. "Western Zhou History." In Loewe and Shaughnessy, *Cambridge History of Ancient China,* 292–351.

Shaw, Ian. 1991. *Egyptian Warfare and Weapons.* Oxford: Shire Publications.

Shennan, Stephen. 2002. *Genes, Memes and Human History: Darwinian Archaeology and Cultural Evolution.* London: Thames & Hudson.

Sherratt, Andrew. 1997. *Economy and Society in Prehistoric Europe.* Edinburgh: Edinburgh University Press.

Short, Philip. 1999. *Mao: A Life.* New York: Owl Books.

Sigalos, Eleutherios. 2004. *Housing in Medieval and Post-Medieval Greece.* Oxford: British Archaeological Reports International Series 1291.

Silberbauer, G. 1981. *Hunter and Habitat in the Central Kalahari Desert.* Cambridge, UK: Cambridge University Press.

Simmons, Ian. 1996. *Changing the Face of the Earth: Culture, Environment, History.* 2nd ed. Oxford: Blackwell.

Singer, Charles, et al. 1954–57. *A History of Technology.* 5 vols. Oxford: Oxford University Press.

Singer, Joel. 1980. *The Correlates of War: Testing Some Realpolitik Models.* New York: Free Press.

Singer, P. W. 2009. *Wired for War: The Robotics Revolution and Conflict in the 21st Century.* New York: Penguin.

Sirks, A. 1991. "The Size of the Grain Distributions in Imperial Rome and Constantinople." *Athenaeum* 79: 215–37.

Skinner, William, ed. 1977a. *The City in Late Imperial China.* Stanford: Stanford University Press.

———. 1977b. "Introduction: Urban Development in Imperial China." In Skinner, *City in Late Imperial China,* 3–31.

Slicher van Bath, B. H. 1963. *The Agrarian History of Western Europe A.D. 500–1850*. London: Arnold.

Smail, Daniel. 2010. *Goods and Debts in Mediterranean Europe*. Draft manuscript.

Smil, Vaclav. 1983. *Biomass Energies: Resources, Links, Constraints*. New York: Plenum.

———. 1991. *General Energetics*. Boulder, CO: Westview.

———. 1994. *Energy in World History*. Boulder, CO: Westview.

———. 2008. *Energy in Nature and Society: General Energetics of Complex Systems*. Cambridge, MA: MIT Press.

———. 2010. *Why America Is Not a New Rome*. Cambridge, MA: MIT Press.

Smiley, Jane. 2011. "Who Cares What a Robot Thinks? You Will." *Washington Post*, January 30. http://www.washingtonpost.com/wp-dyn/content/article/2011/01/28/AR2011012806988.html.

Smith, A. H. V. 1997. "Provenance of Coals from Roman Sites in England and Wales." *Britannia* 28: 297–324.

Smith, Adam T. 2003. *The Political Landscape*. Berkeley: University of California Press.

Smith, Anthony D. 1973. *The Concept of Social Change: A Critique of the Functionalist Theory of Social Change*. London: Routledge Kegan Paul.

Smith, Elizabeth, and Michael Wolfe, eds. 1998. *Technology and Resource Use in Medieval Europe: Cathedrals, Mills, and Mines*. Aldershot, UK: Variorum.

Smith, Michael, et al. 2012. "Archaeology as a Social Science." *Proceedings of the National Academy of Sciences* 109: 7617–21.

Smith, Paul, and Richard von Glahn, eds. 2003. *The Song-Yuan-Ming Transition in Chinese History*. Cambridge, MA: Harvard University Press.

Smith, Thomas C. 1955. *Political Change and Industrial Development in Japan: Government Enterprise, 1868–1880*. Stanford: Stanford University Press.

Snodgrass, Anthony. 1980. "Iron and Early Metallurgy in the Mediterranean." In Theodore Wertime and James Muhly, eds., *The Coming of the Age of Iron*: 335–74. New Haven: Yale University Press.

———. 1989. "The Coming of the Iron Age in Greece: Europe's First Bronze/Iron Transition." In Marie-Louise Stig-Sørenson and Richard Thomas, eds., *The Bronze-Iron Transition in Europe*: 1:22–35. Oxford: British Archaeological Reports International Series 483.

———. 1994. "Response: The Archaeological Aspect." In Ian Morris, ed., *Classical Greece: Ancient Histories and Modern Archaeologies*: 197–200. Cambridge, UK: Cambridge University Press.

So, Kwan-wai. 1975. *Japanese Piracy in Ming China during the Sixteenth Century*. East Lansing: Michigan State University Press.

Solow, Andrew. 2005. "Power Laws without Complexity." *Ecology Letters* 8: 361–63.

Soltow, Lee, and E. Stevens. 1981. *The Rise of Literacy and the Common School in the United States: A Socioeconomic Analysis to 1870*. Chicago: University of Chicago Press.

Sørenson, Brent. 2009. "Energy Use by Eem Neanderthals." *Journal of Archaeological Science* 36: 2201–5.

Sørenson, Brent, and W. Leonard. 1997. "Comparative Primate Energetics and Hominid Evolution." *American Journal of Physical Anthropology* 102: 265–81.

———. 2001. "Neanderthal Energetics and Foraging Efficiency." *Journal of Human Evolution* 40: 483–95.

Spalinger, Anthony. 2005. *War in Ancient Egypt: The New Kingdom*. Oxford: Wiley-Blackwell.

Spence, Jonathan. 1990. *The Search for Modern China*. New York: Norton.

Spencer, Herbert. 1857. "Progress: Its Laws and Cause." *Westminster Review* 67: 445–85.

———. 1874–96. *The Principles of Sociology*. 3 vols. New York: Appleton.

Srinivasan, T. N. 1994. "Human Development: A New Paradigm or Reinvention of the Wheel?" *American Economic Review* 84: 238–43.

Stager, Lawrence. 1985. "The Archaeology of the Family in Ancient Israel." *Bulletin of the American Schools of Oriental Research* 260: 1–35.

Standage, Tom. 2007. *The Victorian Internet: The Remarkable Story of the Telegraph and the Nineteenth Century's On-Line Pioneers*. New York: Walker & Co.

Starr, Paul. 2005. *The Creation of the Media: Political Origins of Mass Communication*. New York: Basic Books.

Steckel, Rick, and Jerome Rose, eds. 2002. *The Backbone of History: Health and Nutrition in the Western Hemisphere*. Cambridge, UK: Cambridge University Press.

Steinby, Eva Margareta, ed. 1993–2000. *Lexicon Topographicum Urbis Romae*. 6 vols. Rome: Quasar.

Steinhardt, Nancy. 1990. *Chinese Imperial City Planning*. Honolulu: University of Hawaii Press.

Steinmetz, Sebald. 1898–99. "Classification des types sociaux." *L'Année Sociologique* 3: 43–147.

Stephan, Robert. Forthcoming. "House Size, Living Standards, and Economic Growth in the Roman World." PhD dissertation, Stanford University.

Stephens, W. B. 1976. "Illiteracy in Devon during the Industrial Revolution, 1754–1844." *Journal of Educational Administration and History* 8: 1–5.

———. 1977. "Illiteracy and Schooling in the Provincial Towns, 1640–1870." In D. Reeder, ed., *Urban Education in the Nineteenth Century*: 27–40. London: Taylor and Francis.

Stève, M.-J., and Hermann Gasche. 1971. *L'acropole de Suse*. Paris: Mémoires de la délégation archéologique française en Iran 46.

Stone, Lawrence. 1964. "The Educational Revolution in England, 1560–1640." *Past and Present* 28: 41–80.

———. 1969. "Literacy and Education in England 1640–1900." *Past and Present* 42: 69–139.

Storey, Glenn. 1997. "The Population of Ancient Rome." *Antiquity* 71: 966–78.

——, ed. 2006. *Urbanism in the Preindustrial World: Cross-Cultural Approaches.* Tuscaloosa: University of Alabama Press.

Street, Brian. 1984. *Literacy in Theory and Practice.* Cambridge, UK: Cambridge University Press.

——. 1987. "Orality and Literacy as Ideological Constructions: Some Problems in Cross-Cultural Studies." *Culture and History* 2: 7–30.

Streusand, Douglas. 2010. *The First Gunpowder Empires: The Ottomans, Safavids, and Mughals.* Boulder, CO: Westview.

Swanson, R. N. 1999. *The Twelfth-Century Renaissance.* Manchester, UK: Manchester University Press.

Swope, Kenneth. 2005. "Crouching Tigers, Secret Weapons: Military Technology Employed during the Sino-Japanese-Korean War, 1592–1598." *Journal of Military History* 69: 11–42.

——. 2009. *A Dragon's Head and a Serpent's Tail: Ming China and the First Great East Asian War, 1592–1598.* Norman: University of Oklahoma Press.

Tafoya, Dennis. 2010. *The Effective Organization: Practical Application of Complexity Theory and Organizational Design to Maximize Performance in the Face of Emerging Events.* London: Routledge.

Tainter, Joseph. 1975. "Social Inference and Mortuary Practices: An Experiment in Numerical Classification." *World Archaeology* 7: 1–15.

——. 1978. "Mortuary Practices and the Study of Prehistoric Social Systems." *Advances in Archaeological Method and Theory* 1: 105–41.

——. 1988. *The Collapse of Complex Societies.* Cambridge, UK: Cambridge University Press.

Tao, Dawei, et al. 2011. "Starch Grain Analysis for Groundstone Tools from Neolithic Baiyinchanghan Site: Implications for Their Function in Northeast China." *Journal of Archaeological Science* 38: 3577–83.

Tatje, Terrence, and Raoul Naroll. 1970. "Two Measures of Societal Complexity." In Naroll and Cohen, *Handbook of Method in Cultural Anthropology*, 766–833.

Taylor, James. 1983. *Lanchester Models of Warfare.* 2 vols. Arlington, VA: Operations Research Society of America.

Tchernia, André. 1986. *Le vin de l'Italie romaine: essai de l'histoire économique d'après les amphores.* Paris: École française à Rome.

Teltser, Patrice, ed. 1995. *Evolutionary Archaeology.* Tucson: University of Arizona Press.

Temin, Peter. 2006. "Estimating GDP in the Early Roman Empire." In Elio Lo Cascio, ed., *Innovazione tecnica e progresso economico nel mondo romano*: 31–54. Bari: Edipuglia.

Thieme, H. 2005. "The Lower Paleolithic Art of Hunting." In Clive Gamble and M. Parr, eds., *The Hominid Individual in Context*: 115–32. London: Routledge.

Thomas, Keith. 1986. "The Meaning of Literacy in Early Modern England." In G. Baumann, ed., *The Written Word*: 97–131. Oxford: Oxford University Press.

Thomas, Rosalind. 1992. *Literacy and Orality in Ancient Greece*. Cambridge, UK: Cambridge University Press.

Thompson, E. P. 1963. *The Making of the English Working Class*. London: Victor Gollancz.

Thorp, Robert. 1983. "Origins of Chinese Architectural Style: The Earliest Plans and Building Types." *Archives of Asian Art* 36: 22–39.

———. 2006. *China in the Early Bronze Age*. Philadelphia: University of Pennsylvania Press.

Thrupp, Sylvia. 1972. "Medieval Industry 1000–1500." In Carlo Cipolla, ed., *The Fontana Economic History of Europe I: The Middle Ages*: 221–73. Glasgow: Fontana.

Tilly, Charles. 1984. *Big Structures, Large Processes, Huge Comparisons*. New York: Russell Sage Foundation.

Tomber, Roberta. 2008. *Indo-Roman Trade*. London: Duckworth.

Totman, Conrad. 1989. *The Green Archipelago: Forestry in Preindustrial Japan*. Berkeley: University of California Press.

———. 1993. *Early Modern Japan*. Berkeley: University of California Press.

———. 2000. *A History of Japan*. Oxford: Blackwell.

Triandaphyllou, Sevi, et al. 2008. "Isotopic Dietary Reconstruction of Humans from Middle Bronze Age Lerna, Argolid, Greece." *Journal of Archaeological Science* 35: 3028–34.

Trigger, Bruce. 1980. *Gordon Childe: Revolutions in Archaeology*. London: Thames & Hudson.

———. 1998. *Sociocultural Evolution*. Oxford: Blackwell.

———. 2003. *Understanding Early Civilizations*. Cambridge, UK: Cambridge University Press.

———. 2006. *A History of Archaeological Thought*. 2nd ed. Cambridge, UK: Cambridge University Press.

Trinkaus, Erik, and Hong Shang. 2008. "Anatomical Evidence for the Antiquity of Human Footwear." *Journal of Archaeological Science* 35: 1928–33.

Tufte, Edward. 2001. *The Visual Display of Quantitative Information*. New York: Graphics Press.

Turchin, Peter. 2003. *Historical Dynamics: Why States Rise and Fall*. Princeton: Princeton University Press.

———. 2006. *War and Peace and War: The Life Cycles of Imperial Nations*. New York: Pi Press.

———. 2009. "A Theory for Formation of Large Empires." *Journal of Global History* 4: 191–217.

———. 2011. "Warfare and the Evolution of Social Complexity: A Multilevel-Selection Approach." *Structure and Dynamics* 4 (3): 1–37.

Turchin, Peter, et al. 2006. "East-West Orientation of Historical Empires and Modern nations." *Journal of World Systems Research* 12: 218–29.

Turchin, Peter, and Sergey Nefedov. 2009. *Secular Cycles*. Princeton: Princeton University Press.

Turner, Howard. 1997. *Science in Medieval Islam*. Austin: University of Texas Press.

Twitchett, Denis. 1957a. "The Fragment of the T'ang Ordinances of the Department of Waterways Discovered at Tun-huang." *Asia Major* 6: 23–79.

———. 1957b. "The Monasteries and China's Economy in Medieval Times." *Bulletin of the School of Oriental and African Studies* 19: 526–49.

———. 1959. "Lands under State Cultivation during the T'ang Dynasty." *Journal of the Economic and Social History of the Orient* 2: 162–203, 335–36.

———. 1961a. *Land Tenure and the Social Order in T'ang and Sung China*. London: School of Oriental and African Studies.

———. 1961b. "Some Remarks on Irrigation under the T'ang." *T'oung Pao* 48: 175–94.

———. 1966. "The T'ang Market System." *Asia Major* 12: 202–48.

———. 1968. "Merchant, Trade, and Government in Late T'ang." *Asia Major* 14: 63–95.

———. 2000. "Tibet in Tang's Grand Strategy." In van de Ven, *Warfare in Chinese History*, 106–79.

Tylor, Edward. 1871. *Primitive Culture: Researches into the Development of Mythology, Philosophy, Religion, Language, Art and Custom*. 2 vols. London: John Murray.

ul Haq, Mahbub. 1995. *Reflections on Human Development*. New York: Oxford University Press.

Unger, Richard. 1984. "Energy Sources for the Dutch Golden Age: Peat, Wind, and Coal." *Research in Economic History* 9: 221–53.

United Nations. 2006. *2003 Energy Statistics Yearbook*. New York: United Nations.

United Nations Development Programme. 2011. *Human Development Report 2011: Sustainability and Equity: A Better Future for All*. New York: United Nations Development Programme.

Upham, Stedman. 1987. "A Theoretical Consideration of Middle Range Societies." In Drennan and Uribe, *Chiefdoms in the Americas*, 345–67.

Valla, François, et al. 1999. "Le natufien final et les nouvelles fouilles à Mallaha (Eynan), Israel 1996–1997." *Journal of the Israel Prehistoric Society* 28: 105–76.

van Creveld, Martin. 2004. *Supplying War: Logistics from Wallenstein to Patton*. 2nd ed. Cambridge, UK: Cambridge University Press.

van de Mieroop, Marc. 1997. *The Ancient Mesopotamian City*. Oxford: Oxford University Press.

———. 2004. *King Hammurabi of Babylon*. Oxford: Wiley-Blackwell.

———. 2010. *A History of Ancient Egypt*. Oxford: Wiley-Blackwell.

van der Spek, R. 2008. "Commodity Prices in Babylon, 385–61 BC." www.iisg.nl/hpw/babylon.php.

van de Ven, Hans, ed. 2000. *Warfare in Chinese History*. Leiden: Brill.

van Geel, B., et al. 1996. "Archaeological and Palynological Indications of an

Abrupt Climate Change in the Netherlands, and Evidence for Climatological Teleconnections around 2630 BP." *Journal of Quaternary Science* 11: 451–60.

van Wees, Hans. 2004. *Greek Warfare*. London: Duckworth.

van Zanden, Jan Luit. 1999. "Wages and the Standards of Living in Europe, 1500–1800." *European Review of Economic History* 3: 175–98.

Verbruggen, J. F. 1997. *The Art of War in Western Europe during the Middle Ages*. Amsterdam. 2nd ed. Woodbridge, UK: Boydell Press.

———. 2004. "The Role of Cavalry in Medieval Warfare." *Journal of Medieval Military History* 3: 46–71.

Vermeij, Geerat. 2004. *Nature: An Economic History*. Princeton: Princeton University Press.

———. 2010. *The Evolutionary World: How Adaptation Explains Everything from Seashells to Civilization*. New York: Tomas Dune/St. Martin's.

Vika, Efrossini. 2011. "Diachronic Dietary Reconstructions in Ancient Thebes, Greece: Results from Stable Isotope Analysis." *Journal of Archaeological Science* 38: 1157–63.

Vika, Efrossini, et al. 2009. "Aristophanes and Stable Isotopes: A Taste for Freshwater Fish in Classical Thebes (Greece)?" *Antiquity* 83: 1076–83.

Vika, Efrossini, and Tatiana Theodoropoulou. 2012. "Re-investigating Fish Consumption in Greek Antiquity: Results from $\delta^{13}C$ and $\delta^{15}C$ Analysis from Fish Bone Collagen." *Journal of Archaeological Science* 39: 1618–27.

Vionis, A. 2006. "The Archaeology of Ottoman Villages in Central Greece: Ceramics, Housing and Everyday Life in Post-Medieval Boeotia." In A. Erkanal-Öktü et al., eds., *Studies in Honour of Itayat Erkanal*: 784–800. Istanbul: Homer Kitabevi.

von Falkenhausen, Lothar. 1999. "The Waning of the Bronze Age: Material Culture and Social Developments, 770–481 BC." In Loewe and Shaughnessy, *Cambridge History of Ancient China*, 450–544.

———. 2006. *Chinese Society in the Age of Confucius (1000–250 BC)*. Los Angeles: Cotsen Institute.

Vroom, Johanna. 1998. "Early Modern Archaeology in Central Greece: The Contrasts of Artefact Rich and Sherdless Sites." *Journal of Mediterranean Archaeology* 11: 131–64.

Wachsmann, Shelley. 1998. *Seagoing Ships and Seamanship in the Bronze Age Levant*. College Station: Texas A&M University.

Wagner, Donald. 1993. *Iron and Steel in Ancient China*. Leiden: Brill.

———. 2008. *Science and Civilisation in China V: Chemistry and Chemical Technology. Part 11: Ferrous Metallurgy*. Cambridge, UK: Cambridge University Press.

Waley-Cohen, Joanna. 2006. *The Culture of War in China: Empire and the Military under the Qing Dynasty*. London: I. B. Tauris.

Wallace-Hadrill, Andrew. 1994. *Houses and Society in Pompeii and Herculaneum*. Princeton: Princeton University Press.

Wang, Zhiongshu. 1982. *Han Civilization*. Trans. K. C. Chang. New Haven: Yale University Press.

Ward, William, and Martha Joukowsky, eds. 1992. *The Crisis Years: The 12th Century BC*. Dubuque, IA: Kendall-Hunt.

Ward-Perkins, Bryan. 2005. *The Fall of Rome and the End of Civilization*. Oxford: Oxford University Press.

Watkins, T. 1990. "The Origins of the House and Home?" *World Archaeology* 21: 336–47.

Watson, Andrew. 1982. *Agricultural Innovation in the Early Islamic World*. Cambridge, UK: Cambridge University Press.

Welch, Stephen. 2008. *Chandragupta: Great Battles of the Mauryan Empire, India, 319–261 BC*. Hanford, CA: GMT Games.

Wendt, Alexander. 2003. "Why a World State Is Inevitable." *European Journal of International Relations* 9: 491–542.

Westad, Odd Arne. 2005. *The Global Cold War*. Cambridge, UK: Cambridge University Press.

White, Leslie. 1943. "Energy and the Evolution of Culture." *American Anthropologist* 45: 335–56.

———. 1949. *The Science of Culture*. New York: Grove Press.

———. 1959. *The Evolution of Culture*. New York: McGraw-Hill.

White, R., and Philip Barker. 1998. *Wroxeter: Life and Death of a Roman City*. London: Tempus.

Wickham, Christopher. 2005. *Framing the Early Middle Ages: Europe and the Mediterranean 400–800*. Oxford: Oxford University Press.

Wilkins, Helen. 2009. "Transformational Change in Proto-Buildings: A Quantitative Study of Thermal Behavior and Its Relationship with Social Functionality." *Journal of Archaeological Science* 36: 150–56.

Willard, Daniel. 1962. *Lanchester as a Force in History: An Analysis of Land Battles of the Years 1618–1905*. McLean, VA: Research Analysis Corporation.

Wilson, Andrew. 2009a. "Approaches to Quantifying Roman Trade." In Bowman and Wilson, *Quantifying the Roman Economy*, 213–49.

———. 2009b. "Indicators for Roman Economic Growth." *Journal of Roman Archaeology* 22: 46–61.

Wilson, David Sloan. 2002. *Darwin's Cathedral: Evolution, Religion, and the Nature of Society*. Chicago: University of Chicago Press.

Wiseman, D. J. 1985. *Nebuchadnezzar and Babylon*. New York: Oxford University Press.

Wolf, Martin. 2011. "East and West Converge on a Problem." *Financial Times*, January 11. http://www.ft.com/cms/s/0/4f590ec6-1dce-11e0-badd-00144feab49a.html#axzz1AqLSQCea.

Wolff, Hendrik, et al. 2011. "Classification, Detection and Consequences of Data Error: Evidence from the Human Development Index." *Economic Journal* 121: 843–70.

Wong, Bin. 1997. *China Transformed*. Ithaca, NY: Cornell University Press.

Woolgar, C. M., et al., eds. 2009. *Food in Medieval England: Diet and Nutrition.* New York: Oxford University Press.

Woolley, Leonard, and Max Mallowan. 1976. *Ur Excavations VII: The Old Babylonian Period.* London: Oxford University Press.

Wrangham, Richard. 2009. *Catching Fire.* London: Profile.

Wrangham, Richard, and Dale Petersen. 1996. *Demonic Males: Apes and the Origins of Human Violence.* New York: Mariner.

Wright, Arthur. 1978. *The Sui Dynasty.* New York: Knopf.

Wright, Henry, and Gregory Johnson. 1975. "Population, Exchange, an Early State Formation in Southwestern Iran." *American Anthropologist* 77: 267–89.

Wright, Quincy. 1965. *A Study of War.* 2nd ed. Chicago: University of Chicago Press.

Wrigley, E. A. 1988. *Continuity, Chance and Change: The Character of the Industrial Revolution in England.* Cambridge, UK: Cambridge University Press.

Wu, Hung. 1999. "The Art and Architecture of the Warring States Period." In Loewe and Shaughnessy, *Cambridge History of Ancient China,* 651–744.

Xiong, Victor. 1999. "The Land-Tenure System of Tang China: A Study of the Equal Field System and the Turfan Documents." *T'oung Pao* 85: 328–90.

Yadin, Yigael. 1963. *The Art of Warfare in Biblical Lands.* 2 vols. New York: McGraw-Hill.

Yang, Hong. 2003. "Changes in Urban Architecture, Interior Design, and Lifestyles between the Han and Tang Dynasties." In Wu Hung, ed., *Between Han and Tang: Visual and Material Culture.* Beijing: Wenwu.

Yang, Lien-Sheng. 1947. "Notes on the Economic History of the Chin Dynasty." *Harvard Journal of Asiatic Studies* 9: 107–85.

Yates, Robin. 1999. "Early China." In Raaflaub and Rosenstein 1999: 7–45.

Yoffee, Norman. 2005. *Myths of the Archaic State.* Cambridge, UK: Cambridge University Press.

Yokell, Carol. 2004. *Modeling Socioeconomic Evolution and Continuity in Ancient Egypt: The Value and Limitations of Zooarchaeological Analyses.* Oxford: Archeopress.

Yon, M. 1997. *La cité d'Ougarit sur le tell de Ras Shamra.* Paris: Editions recherché sur les civilisations.

Yoyotte, Jean, et al., eds. 1987. *Tanis, l'or des pharaohs.* Paris: Galeries nationals du grand palais.

Yü, Ying-shih. 1967. *Trade and Expansion in Han China: A Study in the Structure of Sino-Barbarian Economic Relations.* Berkeley: University of California Press.

Zangger, Eberhard, et al. 1997. "The Pylos Regional Archaeological Project, Part II: Landscape Evolution and Site Preservation." *Hesperia* 66: 549–641.

Zhang, Jia-Fu, et al. 2011. "The Palaeolithic Site of Longwangcan in the Middle Yellow River Valley, China." *Journal of Archaeological Science* 38: 1537–50.

Zhang, Yue, et al. 2010. "Zooarchaeological Perspectives on the Chinese Early and

Late Paleolithic from the Ma'anshan Site (Guizhou, Southern China)." *Journal of Archaeological Science* 37: 2066–77.

Zhang, Zhongpei. 2005. "The Yangshao Period: Prosperity and the Transformation of Prehistoric Society." In Chang and Xu, *Formation of Chinese Civilization*, 43–83.

Zhao, Dingxin. Forthcoming. *The Rise of the Confucian-Legalist State and Patterns of Chinese History*. Chicago: University of Chicago Press.

Zhijun, Z. 1998. "The Middle Yangtze Region in China Is One Place Where Rice Was Domesticated: Phytolith Evidence from the Diaotonghuan Cave, Northern Jiangxi." *Antiquity* 77: 885–97.

Zurndorfer, Harriet. 2003. "Beyond Sinology." *Journal of the Economic and Social History of the Orient* 46: 355–71.

INDEX

IIIIIIIIIIIIIIIIIIIIIIIIIIIIII